VYBORG 1944

The Last Soviet – Finnish Campaign on the Eastern Front

Bair Irincheev

Translated by Kevin Bridge

Helion & Company

Helion & Company Limited
Unit 8 Amherst Business Centre
Budbrooke Road
Warwick
CV34 5WE
England
Tel. 01926 499 619
Email: info@helion.co.uk
Website: www.helion.co.uk
Twitter: @helionbooks
Visit our blog http://blog.helion.co.uk/

Published by Helion & Company 2020
Designed and typeset by Mary Woolley, Battlefield Design (www.battlefield-design.co.uk)
Cover designed by Paul Hewitt, Battlefield Design (www.battlefield-design.co.uk)

Map term translation by Jamilya Magerramova and Kevin Bridge

ISBN 978-1-912390-27-4

British Library Cataloguing-in-Publication Data.
A catalogue record for this book is available from the British Library.

For details of other military history titles published by Helion & Company Limited contact the above address, or visit our website: http://www.helion.co.uk.

We always welcome receiving book proposals from prospective authors.

Contents

List of Illustrations

Photographic Section 2

Preface

Storming of the "VT Line" Beloostrov to Ihantala

The Vyborg–Petrozavodsk offensive operation became Stalin's fourth attack. This was how Soviet historiography dubbed the series of 10 strategic offensive operations in 1944. Fate played out in such a way that this operation was to become the final battle in the series of conflicts between East and West that had taken place in North-Western Russia over a 900 year period.

In the Soviet historiography, the narrative for the Vyborg Offensive Operation ends in the victory of 20 June 1944. The article in the *Encyclopaedia of the Great Patriotic War*, published in 1985, tells the story of the battle as follows:

> The Vyborg Operation in 1944, which was the offensive operation on the right flank of the Leningrad Front in conjunction with the Baltic Fleet and the Ladoga Naval Flotilla, took place between 10–20 June 1944; this operation formed part of the strategic Vyborg-Petrozavodsk Offensive Operation of 1944. The aim was to rout the Finnish troop alignment on the Karelian isthmus and to restore the state border with Finland at this location.

By 10 July 1944 the forces belonging to the right wing of the Leningrad Front (the General of this Army from 18 June 1944 was Marshal of the Soviet Union L.A. Govorov), comprised the 21st and 23rd Combined Arms Armies, and the 13th Air Army (in total around 260,000 men, 5.5 thousand guns and mortars, 881 rocket launchers, 628 tanks, and self-propelled guns, and more than 700 aircraft) occupied a line that ran from: Sestroretsk, Lembolovo, and Lake Ladoga (to the north of Verkhniye Nkulasi). They were opposed by the 3rd and 4th Finnish Army Corps, which from 15 June had been amalgamated into the "Karelian Isthmus" Operational Group (in total this comprised five infantry, and one tank division, one infantry and one cavalry brigade, as well as a number of separate units: 100,000 men, 960 guns and mortars, 110 tanks, and more than 200 aircraft).

The enemy had created a strong defence (to a depth of up to 120km) that consisted of three lines, Vyborg's defensive perimeters (both external and internal) that relied on natural barriers that proved difficult to access. The Soviet Command's intention was to launch the main attack in the direction of Vyborg using the forces of the 21st Army (under Lieutenant-General D.N. Gusev) together with an auxiliary attack on Valkjarvi using the forces of the 23rd Army (under Lieutenant-General A.I. Cherepanov).

On 10 June, the forces of the 21st Army supported by the Baltic Fleet (under Admiral V. Tributs) went on the offensive, they broke through the enemy's 1st line of defence and crossed the Sestra River. On 11 June the 23rd Army began its offensive. Having overcome stubborn enemy resistance the front line forces had by the end of the day on 17 June broken through the enemy's

2nd line of defence. Finnish command redeployed two infantry divisions and the 5th Army Corps to the Karelian Isthmus, and a German infantry division had been deployed to this same location. The Finnish also deployed a brigade of attack guns and a squadron of aircraft to the isthmus; the enemy however did not manage to halt the advance of Soviet forces. On 19 June formations serving with the 21st Army broke through the enemy's 3rd line of defence, the Vyborg defensive perimeters, and on 20 June they captured Vyborg.

At the same time, the 23rd Army supported by the Ladoga Naval Flotilla (under the command of Rear Admiral V.S. Cherokov) reached the enemy's defensive line that passed along the shores of the Vuoksi system of lakes.

The forces of the 21st Army subsequently broke through to a distance of 10–12km north-west of Vyborg, while the 23rd Army crossed the Vuoksi River and took a bridgehead on its northern bank. Some of the forces of the 59th Army that had been redeployed to the Karelian Isthmus from the area around Lake Chudskiy captured 15 islands in the Gulf of Finland in conjunction with the Baltic Fleet.

From 12 July Soviet forces began to defend the positions they had captured. As a result of the Vyborg operation Soviet forces routed a large alignment of Finnish forces, liberating part of the Leningrad Region, and ensuring the safety of the whole city of Leningrad. Favourable conditions were created for conducting the Svir-Petrazavodsk Operation in 1944. The 48 formations and units, which had distinguished themselves especially well in the battles during the course of this conflict, received honorary titles of "Vyborg" units. Some 27 combatants were awarded the title of Hero of the Soviet Union.

The artillery Commander of the Leningrad Front, the celebrated and decorated General Georgiy Fedotovich Odintsov, in his memoirs entitled: *Masters of Fire* also concludes the narrative of 20 June 1944 battle thus: "The Vyborg Operation continued for just 11 days. It was conceived and conducted in this way and demonstrated that the courage of Soviet Armed Forces had grown considerably. It also demonstrated the excellent combat skills of all the soldiers who took part, as well as the leadership talents of the military commanders who planned and executed the operation."

Lieutenant-General Boris Vladimirovich Bychevskiy, who was the Head of the Engineering Forces on the Leningrad Front, also wrote of the end of the Soviet offensive: "22 June 1944. In old notebooks from my military years I found the following entry for this day. "The third anniversary of the start of the war. Yesterday the Karelian Front began its offensive in the Svir-Petrazavodsk direction. Leningrad has grown tired of being a front line city."

In succeeding years just a few lines were written about the battles that had taken place on the Karelian Isthmus after 20 June 1944. There were it was true some "local battles," there were heroes who came out of them, and many of them were decorated posthumously.

The fight for Tali–Ihantala, which was passed over in Soviet historiography, became the largest in the history of the Karelian Isthmus over the entire decade of the existence of our region. The battle for the Vuoksi River was the bloodiest battle. The airborne assault operation and the sea battle in the Gulf of Finland was a battle for honour. The advance of Soviet forces in the area around Noskua (Gvardeyskoye) has become the most commonly forgotten battle. All these battles have fallen into oblivion for 70 years or more. The reason is that Soviet forces were not able to complete the combat missions that had been put before them in full. In the Soviet period it was acceptable to glorify victors, but failures were hushed up, or else played down.

The title of "Hero of the Soviet Union" was not awarded to 27 men, but at least 65 rank and file soldiers and commanders of the 21st, 23rd, and 59th Armies. The authors of the encyclopaedia articles about the Vyborg operation only counted those awarded by way of a decree dated 21 June

1944. There were several statutes issued for the award of the title of Hero of the Soviet Union for the Vyborg Operation, the last of them dated March 1945.

The Soviet period has run its course in Russian history. Now an opportunity has presented itself to tell the reader both impartially and objectively the story of the forgotten battles, as well as telling the story of the heroes of that summer of 1944. This was my primary aim for writing this book.

I have explored documents from the Central Archive of the Ministry of Defence of the Russian Federation, in addition to documents from the National Archive of Finland, together with publications in Russian, Finnish, English, Swedish and German, The memoirs of both Soviet and Finnish veterans were also examined. Moreover, I have made a number of battlefields visits simultaneous with the research for this book.

For reader convenience, all times provided in the descriptions of the battle are to be understood as Moscow time (this is also true of the quotes from Finnish archive documents). The orthography of the original documents is observed. The geographical names in the text are rendered as they were written as of 1944 in the original Finnish, the contemporary Russian names are provided in brackets. Having personally translated documents from Finnish, Swedish, English, and German, I am personally responsible for any errors, as well as interpretation of archival documents.

The reader may find lists of surnames, first names, and awards tedious … Ivan Ivanovich Ivanov in the battle for a farmstead … such and such a regiment … there were so many of them on the front lines of the Great Patriotic War. This is just information overload for almost anyone. For the Wife and Daughter of Ivan Ivanovich Ivanov, who never returned home however, it may be invaluable. One of the aims of my work is to tell the story of those who fought in our region. They should come back into our collective consciousness, at least through the pages of this book. All this information exists in the databases of the Ministry of Defence of the Russian Federation, but not all the parents and relatives of those who perished will make use of them.

I have been unable to gather all of the mosaic details to form a complete picture. Nevertheless, it is hoped that the reader is presented with a clear and complete understanding of the battles that occurred in our corner of the world during 1944. Furthermore, this volume was written to provide a greater appreciation for the land of the Karelian Isthmus, for which our ancestors paid such a high price. My sincere hope is that this modest contribution to the historiography will contribute to the collective memory of the Red Army commanders and soldiers who fought and died in the Great Patriotic War. I also hope that this narrative reminds the reader that a bad world is better than a good war.

Bair Irincheev
1 January 2020

1

Prelude

The Karelian Isthmus, as well as ancient Karelia, has seen a series of fierce battles over the years. Sweden and Velikiy Novgorod, then Sweden and the state of Muscovy, and after that Finland and Soviet Russia contested these lands on a number of occasions.

In the 20th century war has passed through the Karelian Isthmus leaving its scorch marks and bloodstains behind in four separate episodes. The first of these was during the Finnish Civil War in 1918. The second was during the Russo-Finnish War of 1939–40, when the Soviet Union expanded the border beyond Vyborg using military force. The third occasion was in the summer of 1941 when the Finnish Army regained the Karelian Isthmus, crossed the River Sestra, and stopped in front of the Principal line of the Karelian fortified sector. The battles of summer 1944 – Vyborg Offensive Operation – became the final battle to take place over this land, which has seen the blood of a good twenty generations spilled over it in abundance.

During the course of the offensive in 1941 the Finnish units reached the line of the old border on the Karelian Isthmus on 1 September. This event was widely reflected in the propaganda press by Finnish military correspondents. On 4 September, an offensive began for the line of the old border. This offensive was fraught with uprisings and protests in several Finnish regiments. Nevertheless the Finns reached the Principal line of the Karelian fortified sector and stopped in front of the powerful Leningrad defence belt.

In September 1941 German command approached Commander in Chief Mannerheim on two occasions for permission to continue the offensive. The Germans received a polite and diplomatic refusal on both occasions. The Finnish military, who had analysed the situation in the city of Leningrad, felt that Leningrad would fall in a matter of days and there was therefore no need to spill any more of their soldiers' blood. In the end the Finnish Army advanced from the 1944 border to the 1920 border at a high price. Over the course of July and August 1941 its losses reached approximately 25,000 killed. Finland lost around the same number over the course of 105 days during the previous war from 1939-40. Finnish plans concerning Leningrad in 1941-42 are worthy of separate research, in which the politics of the great powers, the ambitions of the military commanders, as well as the most complex and at the same time hopeless logistical operations, and the courage of rank and file soldiers and commanders are intertwined. This though is a story for another book.

On 9-10 September 1941 Soviet units launched a counterattack on the Finns in the area around Beloostrov. Our units were only able to hold back the Finns to a certain extent and were not able to beat them back from the *Millionaire* which had been captured in Beloostrov.

Following this, the environment on the front line on the Karelian Isthmus stabilised. The Finns continued to fire on the gun emplacements in Soviet pillboxes and gradually began to prepare themselves for winter. The usual rhythm of a positioning war established itself: both sides improved their positions, building fortifications, shelters, and lines of fencing. Snipers and propagandists began to operate on both sides.

Small skirmishes and pre-battle reconnaissance were constant although the intensiveness of the battles on the Karelian Isthmus could never be compared to the large-scale battles that were taking place to the south of Leningrad. In connection with this a humorous saying was doing the rounds on the Leningrad Front: "What three armies are not fighting in the Second World War? The Swedish, Turkish, and the 23rd Soviet."

During the battles for Leningrad, Leningrad Front units would advance onto the Karelian Isthmus for a rest, to accept reinforcements, and for combat training.

In the neighbouring Onezh Isthmus to the east of Lake Ladoga the Finnish Army continued the offensive and in the course of successful operations they captured Olonets, Medvezhegorsk, and Petrozavodsk. The Finns crossed the Svir River and captured the Svir hydroelectric power station. On the southern bank of the Svir the Finns created a wide bridgehead from Lake Onezh almost up to Lodeynoe Pole. On the occupied territories the Finnish leadership began to implement the policy of building a "Greater Finland."

Following the Battle of Stalingrad it had become clear to the Finnish upper leadership that the Soviet Union would come out of the war as the victor, while fascist Germany would be defeated. A curious probing of the possibilities for peace began–by way of mediation on the part of the USA and Switzerland. At the end of 1943 at the Tehran Conference the President of the USA Theodore Roosevelt raised, among other questions, the issue of the fate of Finland.

British Prime Minister Winston Churchill left a testimony in his memoirs concerning the negotiations on the part of the three allied leaders:

> This was how we left the discussions concerning the Polish question. Then the President asked Stalin if he was ready to discuss Finland. Could the Government of the United States do something to help pull Finland out of the war? Stalin said that the Swedish Deputy Minister for Foreign Affairs had told Madam Kollontai (the Soviet ambassador) that the Finns were afraid of Russian intentions to turn Finland into a province of Russia. The Soviet Government had responded, saying that they had no intention of turning Finland into a province of Russia unless the Finns forced them to do so. Madam Kollontai was then ordered to tell the Finns that the Soviet Government would have no objection to a Finnish delegation visiting Moscow. They did however request that the Finns make their position clear concerning their exit from the war. Here, in Tehran, Stalin had only just received the details of the Finnish response, which had been passed to him by Mr Bogeman. There was nothing in this response about the Finns wanting to break ranks with Germany. The response did though raise the question of borders. The Finns were proposing using the 1939 border as a basis for discussion, albeit with some concessions to the Soviet Union. Stalin thought that the Finns were not looking to enter into serious negotiations. Their conditions had not changed, and the Finns were already well aware of this. The Finns were still counting on a German victory, and at least some Finns were absolutely convinced that Germany would win.
>
> Roosevelt asked if there was any sense in the Government of the United States advising the Finns to travel to Moscow. Stalin answered that they were fully prepared to go to Moscow but that it would serve no purpose if they were to bring their current programme to the table.
>
> I said that in the first few days of the Russo-Finnish War I sympathised with Finland but turned away when I realised they had entered the war to fight against the Soviets. Russia

> should ensure the security of Leningrad and its approaches. The position of the Soviet Union as a permanent naval and air power in the Baltic region should be secured. The British people however would be aggrieved if the Finns were to become part of the Soviet Union against their will. Therefore I would be delighted to hear what Marshal Stalin had to say. I do not think it would serve any purpose to request indemnity. The Finns could cut down a number of trees but it is unlikely that anything would come of this.
>
> Stalin said that he did not need money but that the Finns in maybe five or eight years' time would be able to pay for the damage they caused to Russia by supplying her with paper, timber and many other materials. He thought that the Finns needed to be taught a lesson and he was full of resolve to seek compensation. I said that it seemed to me the damage that the Finns had caused Russia with their improper attack was far more than a poor nation like Finland could afford. I added: "That famous slogan was ringing in my ears again: "No annexations or indemnity." Maybe Marshal Stalin did not like me for saying it."
>
> Stalin with a broad smile answered: "I did not tell you I was becoming a conservative."
>
> It was then that I asked him what he wanted. Operation "Overlord" was on the horizon. We would like Sweden to have joined the war on our side by the spring, and Finland would have withdrawn from the war by then. Stalin said that this would be good.
>
> The topic of conversation then changed to territorial details: Vyborg ("Nothing doing about Vyborg") [in the original Churchill replicates Stalin's words "Nothing doing about Vyborg"–authors' note]; as well as the Karelian Isthmus; Hanko. "If the surrender of Hanko causes problems"–said Stalin–"I am prepared to take Petsamo in exchange." "A fair exchange," said Roosevelt.

In the American protocols for the Tehran conference this moment in the negotiations is described differently:

> [The] President [Roosevelt] said that according to the information he had the Finns were prepared to move the border back some distance from Leningrad but were hoping to keep Vyborg for themselves. Marshal Stalin at that moment interrupted with his own remark saying that this was not possible. After that the President continued saying that Hanko should be demilitarised and turned into a huge bathing beach.

In the Soviet version of the protocol of the meetings Stalin's words on Vyborg are completely absent. We return to Churchill's account:

> I said that the English want firstly that Russia be happy with her borders as they were, and secondly that the Finns are able to be a free and independent people and could live as well as they were able in these very uncomfortable regions. We do not want to put any pressure on Russia. Stalin said if that were the case the allies could turn up the heat on each other from time to time. Let the Finns live as they would wish to. Everything would be fine if they paid for half the damage they caused. Roosevelt asked if it was worth the Finns travelling to Moscow if they were not going to bring any concrete proposals, or any results, with them. Stalin said that if the Finns were not going to give any assurances that an agreement would be reached then this trip to Moscow would only serve the Germans, who would make good use of any failure. The same could be said of the aggressive elements within Finland, who are saying that Russia does not want peace at all.
>
> I said that this would be a lie and we would all testify to that loudly. "Fine" said Stalin "Let them come if you are insisting on it."

> Roosevelt announced that the present Finnish leadership were pro-German. If other leaders were in power we could achieve something. In Stalin's opinion it would be better if they were dealing with a different set of leaders, but that he would not object to Ryti. Let any one of them come and visit, even if they are the devil. He was not afraid of devils.
>
> I expressed the hope that Marshal Stalin would approach the question of Finland, duly taking into account the possibility that Sweden could join the war during the course of our joint offensive in May.
>
> Stalin agreed but said that he would not be able to deviate from a number of conditions.
>
> 1) The reinstatement of the 1940 agreement.
> 2) Hanko or Petsamo (at this point he added that Hanko was given to the Soviet Union as rent, but he was proposing to take Petsamo).
> 3) Compensation in kind of up to 50 percent of the damage that the Finns caused. The details of this compensation could be discussed at a later date.
> 4) A break with Germany.
> 5) The expulsion [when it is translated into Russian this becomes 'Internment] of all Germans!
> 6) The demobilisation [in the American protocol this is rendered as a reorganisation of the Army].
>
> As regards compensation I responded that it is easy to cause damage but not so easy to compensate for it and that it is a bad thing for any country to become a tribute to another. Stalin said that the Finns could be given the possibility of paying for the damage they caused over the course of five to eight years for example.
>
> I declared: "Experience shows that compensation on a large-scale is not possible."
>
> Stalin proposed occupying one of the regions of Finland if the Finns do not pay back the compensation, but if they were to pay it back then the Russians would withdraw over the course of a year.
>
> "I was not elected as a Soviet commissar" I said, "But if I were, I would advise against that. There are more important things to think about."
>
> We will support the Russians and are prepared to help them every step of the way, but we should bear the May battle in mind. President Roosevelt said that he was prepared to support everything that had been said (against large-scale compensation).
>
> Then Stalin asked: "Do you have any further questions?" The President answered: "There is still the question of Germany.."

Thus the three great powers in the anti-Hitler coalition agreed on the position concerning Finland. Stalin required a return to the 1940 agreement that Finland had violated, by aligning itself with Germany, as well as compensation for the half of the damage caused, and a clear break with Germany.

At this point let us move forward to the 2000s and recall that in contemporary Finland the historiography of the agreement between Stalin, Roosevelt and Churchill is suppressed. In all official dialogue that Finnish politicians and historians engage in that is timed to coincide with the anniversaries of the events of 1944 the Finns underline that in 1944 the USSR wanted to capture Finland in her entirety, strip her of her independence, and turn her into one of the Soviet Union's provinces.

Two months had passed since the memorable conversation between the three leaders and the environment at the Soviet-German Front had changed markedly. The forces of the Leningrad and Volkovsk Fronts had inflicted a defeat on the German forces just outside Leningrad and Novgorod and had liberated much of the Leningrad region and pushed the Germans back to the border with the Baltic region.

Such a significant change in the military environment in the North-West could only force the Finnish leadership to act on the diplomatic front. Just as they had done five years earlier the Finnish Government sent their ambassador Ju.K. Paasikivi as a negotiator. He arrived at the Soviet embassy in Stockholm to meet his long-term acquaintance, the USSR's ambassador Aleksandra Kollontai. Paasikivi, who back before the 1939–40 war had supported a compromise between the USSR and Finland, asked questions about the possible conditions for drawing up a peace agreement in 1944. The Soviet conditions were voiced again: a break with Nazi Germany; the expulsion of German forces in Finland; the repatriation to the USSR of those who as of 22 June 1941 were Soviet citizens; and the recognition of the 1940 state border by the Finns.

The grounds for Soviet diplomacy were underpinned by a series of attacks by long-range aircraft on Helsinki and Kotka. The Head of the Operations Directorate of the General Headquarters Shtemenko described these attacks delicately as follows: "Certain measures were taken, so to speak, to put psychological pressure on the Finns, to motivate them to come to the negotiating table." At the same time Stalin decided that in order to force the hand of the Finns to find a diplomatic solution the Red Army's main attack should be centred on the German forces on the southern shore of the Gulf of Finland. Shtemenko described this in his memoirs as follows:

> At about midnight on 14 February 1944 Stalin ordered the General Headquarters to tell the Commander in Chief of the Leningrad Front General Govorov that the city of Narva was to be captured no later than 17 February. "This requires both a military and a political context" Stalin underlined. "This is now the most important thing. I order you to take all necessary steps to liberate Narva no later than the date I have stipulated.

The Leningrad Front reached Narva after a fierce and bloody battle. The front did not have many forces left. The Germans had been able to beat back the Leningrad Front's first advance on Narva. As the Germans had been able to hold the line that ran along the Narva River successfully between February–March 1944 this had given the Finnish leadership some hope. The hope was that Finland would be able to come out of the war in more favourable circumstances than those put forward by the USSR.

The internal political environment in Finland did not support a peace agreement in February 1944 either. If the Finns were to accept the USSR's conditions then they would have taken their country on a completely erroneous path from 1941-44. In these years Finland was a *de facto* ally of Nazi Germany, although a treaty of alliance *de jure* had not been drawn up. The Finns were in no position to hand over Vyborg and the Karelian Isthmus without a fight. This would have meant that 25,000 Finnish soldiers who had died in the battles for the Isthmus and for Karelia in 1941 would have given their lives in vain. This would also have meant that all the Finns who had returned to their homes in 1942 would have to abandon them and begin their lives again in a new location for the third time.

Nevertheless, a Finnish delegation was sent to Moscow that was led by the same Paasikivi. At the very first meeting Molotov set out the Soviet conditions. Paasikivi, as he had done back in 1939, said immediately that he would not agree to anything and that he had come to Moscow to hear the Soviet requirements for peace in more detail. The very first point in the requirements–a demonstrable break in relations with Germany–led the Finns into an impasse. Paasikivi announced immediately that it would not be possible to meet this requirement since it would automatically lead to a war with Germany. At that moment, the Finns were more afraid of the powerful *Third Reich* than they were of the Soviet Union.

Given the availability of forces in Lapland and in the Baltic region it appeared to the Finns that the Germans could get to them quicker than Stalin could. As a result the negotiators left with nothing in place. Molotov pointedly remarked that judging by the behaviour of the Finnish delegation, Finland cared more about the interests of Germany than she did for herself. In April, the Finns sent their response that acknowledged the Soviet requirements as unacceptable.

The USSR People's Commissariat for Foreign Affairs made an official announcement, that the Government of Finland was not prepared to accept the minimal Soviet requirements and that it and only it, would be responsible for what happened next. Thus the politicians of Finland and the USSR were again not able to reach a compromise. The Finns again announced that the proposed Soviet terms were unacceptable and impossible to implement. Once again, as in November 1939 the words of the Soviet premier Vyacheslav Molotov proved timely: "We, as civilians could not reach agreement. Now the initiative will be passed to the military."

We will now turn our attention to the military aspect of these events.

2

Calm Before the Storm

In March 1944, Marshal Voronov, on the orders of general headquarters, conceived an overall plan for a military operation against the Finnish Army. His concept was that a powerful military alignment should be deployed against the Finns, which after completion of their military objectives would remain in the north-west and would then be sent to liberate the Baltic region. In April, the silence of the Finnish leadership was taken by Moscow as a rejection of the Soviet proposals for a separate peace. The military plans began to acquire an even more tangible and realistic shape.

The overall strategy for the Vyborg-Petrozavodsk Operation was eloquently described by Army General Sergey Matveyevich Shtemenko, (Chief of the Operations Directorate of General Headquarters) in his book *The General Headquarters in the War Years*:

> The concept of the operation on the northern flank of the Soviet-German Front encapsulated the idea of a consistent routing of the enemy. Now after 20 April the first attacks by Soviet forces were to be directed against the Finnish Army. The assumption at General Headquarters was that the Finnish Army, since they were not so well armed, and not so well trained as the Germans, would be defeated in a relatively short space of time.
>
> The Leningrad Front would carry out the first attack on the enemy's main forces. Its task was to break through the Finnish defence in the direction of Vyborg and to give the impression of breaking through to the Finnish interior towards the main political and economic centres, including Helsinki. In a secondary direction the front would send some of their forces to Sortavala to head along the northern shores of Lake Ladoga behind the lines and set their sights on the enemy, which had been on the defensive in Karelia.
>
> To carry out this operation the Leningrad Front was transferred from the 21st Army's reserves, which from the end of April had been commanded by the former Chief of Staff of the Leningrad Front, Colonel-General D.N. Gusev.
>
> Since the Finns had Soviet forces behind the lines it was unlikely that they would be able to feel they were in a strong position.

Thus the overall plan was as follows: to break through Finnish defences on the Karelian Isthmus and force them to weaken their alignment in Karelia and only then would the Karelian Front begin to advance. The ability of the latter to break through the Finnish defence raised questions, not only at Headquarters but the Commander of the Front Kirill Afanasyevich Meretskov was also concerned. Shtemenko described Meretskov's visit to Headquarters as follows:

> The Commander of the Karelian Front K.A. Meretskov very much wanted, in a report on the plan for the operation, to demonstrably show I.V. Stalin what a powerful, fortified area he would have to defeat. With this aim in mind he brought to Moscow an elaborately made

> model of the locality, as well as panoramic aerial photographs. Kirill Afanasyevich thought this would make it easier to explain to Stalin what fierce battles lay ahead, and to request additional forces as well as funds from Supreme Command.
>
> Since we had already carefully studied I.V. Stalin's character we tried to convince Meretskov there was no point in him taking these materials to the Kremlin: the Supreme Command did not take kindly to personal attributes and would not tolerate forecasts that favoured the enemy. Lieutenant-General T.F. Shtykov, a member of the front line Military Council was on our side. The Commander however did not agree.
>
> Kirill Afanasyevich aggravated this mistake at Headquarters itself: he began to demonstrate his model and his photographs until he had exposed the essence of the operation. I.V. Stalin listened to him pacing up and down the table, as was his habit. He then suddenly stopped and rudely interrupted Meretskov.
>
> "Why are you scaring us with your toys?" The enemy has clearly hypnotised you with their defences … I am beginning to doubt whether you would be able to complete the mission you have been assigned after all this."
>
> Meretskov then added fuel to the fire: after putting his "toys" to one side he immediately began to request heavy tank regiments and break through artillery. This really got Stalin worked up, another sharp outburst followed:
>
> "Do you think that you have scared us and that we are going to open our wallet? We are not easily scared."
>
> The Supreme Commander did not allow the Commander to finish his report and ordered General Headquarters to define the plan for the forthcoming operation and to establish the necessary forces as well as funds. He did put his plan forward again on another day but this time in the usual way. Stalin did not interrupt him, barely making any comments and he even allocated some additional forces to break through the enemy's defences. As we walked out of his office however he bid Meretskov farewell with these parting words:
>
> "I wish you success! Frighten the enemy yourself and do not give in to them.."

Kirill Afanasyevich himself did not avoid this issue in his memoirs either, but he was more sensitive in his description of the meeting with Stalin:

> On my way to the Kremlin I took with me a map of the topography of the Ladoga-Onezh Isthmus and once at Headquarters, by using the data from intelligence on the enemy's forces, I began to demonstrate how difficult it would be for our forces to operate there. I.V. Stalin did not like it when he was told that the enemy would start to act in such and such a way. He would often ask with some irony: "And how do you know? Has the enemy told you this personally?" The conscientious workers at the General Headquarters, who have been my long-term colleagues reminded me of this and tried in vain to talk me out of the concept I had described to them. It turned out however exactly as they had said it would. The Supreme Commander saw in my words an attempt to elicit additional reserves and refused to grant this. It was true that on receipt of a second report from the staff at Headquarters he did reconsider his decision and the reserves were assigned.

Both fronts began to make their preparations for the large-scale operation. Events on the Karelian Front to the east of Ladoga extend beyond the boundaries of this research. The Leningrad Front carried out preparations for the offensive operation very carefully. The front had the time, experience, personnel, and resources. By March–April on the Karelian Isthmus firing positions had already been put in place for the new batteries using the manpower of "local" artillery officers. Front line headquarters made use of unprecedented camouflage measures to hide the concentration of forces.

The deployment of new artillery units to the Karelian Isthmus took place in a period from 5–25 May 1944. In this same period artillery from the 23rd Army carried out planned adjustment firing as well as destroying the targets that had emerged in the course of reconnaissance.

In May 1944 Soviet aerial reconnaissance actually covered the Karelian Isthmus thoroughly and had photographed all the Finnish fortifications between Vyborg and Beloostrov. The location of firing points on the front line, the positions of Finnish artillery batteries, fortified construction work underway in the depth of the Finnish defences (during spring 1944 the Finns increased the pace of the construction of the "VT line"), all this was discovered and was noted in Soviet reconnaissance reports. The "VKT line" had not yet been photographed by aerial photography (moreover it only existed on paper), together with the "Salpa line" (this was situated north of the 1940 border line).

Finnish aerial reconnaissance of the Karelian Isthmus noted that movement along the roads was carried out by night and was sufficiently intensive judging by the tracks that criss-crossed the snow. It also noted that from 10 May all the Soviet units on the Karelian Isthmus had begun to observe complete radio silence. The Head of the engineering forces of the Leningrad Front Major-General Boris Vladimirovich Bychevskiy described these camouflage measures in detail:

> The Chief of Staff [the Head of the Leningrad Front M.M. Popov, author's note] paid a great deal of attention to the plan for the covert deployment of Gusev's Army to the Karelian Isthmus. It is no laughing matter to transfer 10 divisions "on the quiet," as well as around three thousand guns, tank units, and logistics forces! The task is even more cunning when you consider that all the deployments had to be made from the direction of Narva, including across the Gulf of Finland from Oranienbaum to Lisiy Nos. Just as had been done a year before, but now the white nights were upon us.
>
> Popov immediately imposed a "silencing lock" on all the telephones and radio equipment in 21st Army units. Flights over the Karelian Isthmus by the new aviation units were banned, as was any fire from the artillery units and battalions. In the Navra sector however constant reconnaissance battles were underway. The engineers were building 500 wooden craft, taking them down to the river and hiding them there. Nobody in the 8th, nor the 59th Armies was aware that all this represented no more than false preparations.
>
> Headquarters had stipulated that the operation would commence in the first half of June and so the deployment of the 21st Army under D.N. Gusev to the Karelian Isthmus continued in no particular hurry over the course of three weeks.
>
> The first to arrive quietly were the logistics units, as well as the corps headquarters troops, and engineers, who then settled into their pre-prepared locations. All the combat reserves had concentrated in the stores belonging to the 23rd Army on the orders of the Head of the Front's logistics units Major-General G.M. Savonenkov. The troops who supplied the armies were not supposed to move far. Toll gates appeared on the roads leading to the front line, and movement along them was strictly controlled. Telephones and radios were silenced.
>
> Externally the immediate battle area looked so peaceful that the commanders and soldiers who had arrived onto the Karelian Isthmus from the Narva and Pskov directions would initially look around in surprise. The inhabitants would work their plots calmly by day. No rockets howled away and in the evening accordions could be heard along with the patter of dancing. The ladies from the construction detachments sung such lively folk songs that they urged the soldiers to take off their tunics, put their caps askew and join in the dance.

Artilleryman Pavel Ivanovich Larin, who also arrived onto the Karelian Isthmus in the spring of 1944 with the 34th Separate High Command Reserve Very Heavy Artillery Battalion, also echoes Bychevskiy:

> The forces had been there for more than a year and had stopped firing at one another. This is strange for us: how is it that they are not firing at one another? I was a very good shot. The Commander of the unit received two sniper rifles, one of which he gave to me, the second he gave to another soldier, I forget who. We started to walk to the forward edge as free hunters. We would walk along the infantry's front line, and fire. Naturally, we would walk to our own observation post. We would observe everything from there, we knew the state of play: what was happening on the Finnish side. Where the fortifications were, what was happening with them, we could reconnoitre everything. If anyone approaches the infantry, you shoot and the Finns would begin to pound us there with mortars. The infantry would all but cuff our own brother one "Get out, it was nice and peaceful for us here." Right up until the half shelter next to the gun emplacement was hit and caught fire. It was summer, and warm. They didn't fire there anymore. Well damn it! Let the infantrymen hit them up!

Let us return to the memoirs of General Bychevskiy:

> A week later under the cover of darkness the heavy artillery under N.N. Zhdanov began to move. They took a number of routes around Leningrad towards positions that had been reconnoitred in advance and faded away, hiding in the forest expanses. Then it was the turn of the light artillery, after them came the road vehicles and tanks. At last it was the turn of the infantry to take up their forward positions. This was when the defensive work that the 23rd Army had done for the term of its involuntary sojourn came into play.
>
> The leadership were very accurate in their observance of the timetable for moving six divisions of the 30th Guards, and 109th Rifle Corps from Oranienbaum to Lisiy Nos via the Gulf of Finland. These corps were to be deployed in the principal direction of the attack, staying close to the Gulf of Finland. The white nights afforded just two to three hours of light twilight. The Baltic sailors however were very accurate in their execution of the operation. Small smoke screens created the impression of a fog. The trained companies and battalions were quickly offloaded from the holds of the self-propelled barges and tenders, hiding among the pines that were snuggled up alongside. When the sun, which had just dipped below the horizon, would come up again the shoreline would already be deserted.
>
> The reconnaissance section followed every move the Finns made very carefully, but nothing changed on their side. One of the Finns who was captured had indicated that they were awaiting orders from Mannerheim on a decision to allow up to 10 men leave from the company for a break to engage in agricultural work. Lists were already being drawn up.
>
> M.M. Popov was happy with such a clear testimony of how secretively the concentration of our attack alignment had been undertaken.

The deployment of artillery forces to firing positions that had been prepared in advance began on 1 June. The majority of the weapons had reached their firing positions by 6 June. Then the Soviet aerial reconnaissance photographed the firing positions that had already been occupied. Those batteries that the pilots had already identified were moved to a different location and fake positions were made out of the firing positions that had been discovered.

The Leningrad Front artillery commander General Odinstov recalled:

> The front line Headquarters developed and implemented operational camouflage measures with the aim of ensuring that the preparations for the operation on the Karelian Isthmus were perfectly concealed. The party and political work was undertaken in such a way that the intended target would not be revealed. The forces that had concentrated in the area around Ropsha were moved to positions that had been sought out in advance along a railway line in covered wagons and the trains did not stop at intermediate stations, as well as by sea–in the holds of transport vessels. During the course of the movement of the units singing was banned, and a complete silence was observed, it was banned for soldiers to fraternise with the local population. The forces moved around Leningrad. Units moved around this same city in small subdivisions along different routes, as the subdivisions of a local garrison would usually move around. At the outer edge, the existing rules of engagement were observed. No flights by new aviation units were allowed over enemy territory, and the new artillery units were not permitted to fire. At that same time, the forces that were located close to Narva almost within sight of the enemy would train in how to cross water barriers, so as to create the impression that an offensive was being prepared at this location.

The mobilisation of the rifle units to the Karelian Isthmus was carried out via Leningrad during the day, while individual trucks would mingle as much as possible with the movement of traffic on the streets and in doing so would try and not to draw attention to themselves. Some of the infantrymen travelled to the front line using Leningrad's public transport, such as the 187th Rifle Division, 97th Corps for example:

> In order not to draw attention from enemy reconnaissance on the eve of the operation subdivisions of the 178th Division from Strelniy and Ropsha travelled through Leningrad pretending to be ordinary passengers; then they moved in small groups, mingling with the city crowd, reached the right bank of the Neva, and from there they would travel to the upper reaches of the River Okhta, to their starting point.

The rifle units concentrated in forest expanses some distance from the front line. The mobilisation of tanks and infantry to their starting points for the offensive was to have been done at the last moment.

It must be stated that Finnish reconnaissance nevertheless observed the deployment of Soviet forces onto the Karelian Isthmus, based on reports from captured soldiers this was achieved by means of visual observation and by aerial reconnaissance.

This was the picture according to the reconnaissance section of the 18th Infantry Division as of 22 April: "The fact that the enemy is conducting engineering works south of the strongholds at "Joensuu" and "Bunker" in Mertuti and at Beloostrov close to the road is confirmed." This report was dated 6 May:

> The enemy is undertaking engineering work on the division's entire defensive line. The most active work is being carried out south of the Rajajoki estuary. The movement of enemy trains on 5 May 1944 was more pronounced than normal. Six trains were noted moving in the direction of Levashovo. In total over the course of a week 14 enemy train movements were noted, 14 on the mainline line and 1 on the Sestroretsk line.

For 13 May:

> They are communications trenches and trenches that are waist high; in addition to those branching out at an angle, they are somewhere around 200m from our own positions. The enemy's combat activity has increased over the course of the last few days, both in terms of the activity of reconnaissance groups and the firing activity on the part of infantry and artillery.

For 15 May:

> 10–12 May 1944 the enemy has opened up a number of new trenches and has continued to move their positions forward. Groundwork has continued along the entire length of the neutral territory, in spite of our considerable interdiction fire. On 14 May groups of enemy engineers continued their work. On 18 May work continued all night.

On 22 May 1944, the Finns concluded the rotation of their forces on the front, the 10th Infantry replaced the 18th Infantry Division. All the documents belonging to the Finnish divisions were burnt during the hasty retreat on 10 June 1944 but fragments of the Combat Journal for May have survived:

> The enemy in recent times has been very active in our sector. They undertook a number of raids to capture prisoners, and in many cases they succeeded in doing so; fighting reconnaissance was carried out by groups of soldiers up to a platoon and a company in number. From 11 May 1944 the enemy began to dig attack trenches from their own fighting positions towards our positions. These trenches are located approximately 100–200m from our positions, and in some locations this distance is at 70m. Movement on the enemy's side has intensified, especially by night. Observation platforms are being built right next to their positions, and groups of officers visit the front line and observe our positions. All the indications point towards preparations for an offensive.

The reconnaissance section of the 4th Army Corps however in its report entitled "A Report of the Enemy's Actions and those of its Combat Units" dated 2 June 1944 incorrectly interpreted the concentration of Soviet forces on the isthmus and again lapsed into complacency. All this despite the obvious preparations on the half of the Soviet side, which Finnish intelligence had been able to reveal:

> At the moment it is without doubt impossible to confirm that the enemy activity could amount to a strengthening of defences. If the information obtained from the sergeant captured on 28 May 1944 were only partly true, it is quite possible that the enemy is preparing for offensive operations on the isthmus. This possibility is also confirmed by the following observations:
>
> 1) Deployment of new infantry and tank units to the isthmus.
> 2) Reinforcement of artillery
> 3) Deployment of attack and reconnaissance aviation units from Petersburg and the re-direction of activity among aviation units based to the south of the city, to the isthmus.
> 4) Reinforcement of reconnaissance and espionage activity.
> 5) Deployment right up to the front line, that was noted from 25 May onwards and is being carried out intermittently.

6) Engineering work that has been recorded from the beginning of May and continues up to the present time, it could be said, is offensive in nature.
7) The testimony of captured Finnish servicemen of announcements concerning Finland's rejection of the Soviet peace efforts, which for the USSR, similarly, has become a priority issue.
8) Complete radio silence by the 23rd Army from 10 May 1944.

This same report also stated:

> It would appear natural that the enemy, in recognising the threat to its own logistics [that is to say the Leningrad Front's own logistics– author's note], would take steps to eradicate this threat.
>
> The suggestions however that the enemy is preparing an offensive on the isthmus cannot be ruled out … Units that have been deployed to the Karelian Isthmus have just come away from fighting and are completely exhausted, so they can hardly be considered capable of an offensive until they receive their reinforcements and have been able to reorganise.
>
> According to the information provided to us by the captured servicemen the enemy is to capture some border or other in the Beloostrov direction as well as some high ground in the centre of the isthmus by 22 June. On that basis it is possible to suppose that no general offensive can be expected before June.

The prisoner referred to here was a convicted soldier Sergeant Ivan Ivanovich Burlov who was injured and seized by the Finns in a fighting reconnaissance operation of 28 May 1944. Up until the time he had joined the 29th Separate Punishment Company he had served in the 113th Separate Signals Battalion, 108th Rifle Corps (according to Soviet information he had served in the 98th Rifle Regiment). According to Finnish information shortly after his interrogation Sergeant Burlov died of his injuries. Soviet information suggests that he was killed during a reconnaissance sortie and is buried in the area close to Okhta in the Pargolov district, Leningrad region.

The reconnaissance section at Finnish Headquarters considered that the Karelian Isthmus did present a threat but the Head of the reconnaissance department Colonel Aladar Paasnonen in a number of situations spoke of the danger of a Soviet offensive in different ways. One day he would acknowledge the danger of an offensive, and on another occasion he would speak of it with scepticism.

The twice-weekly overviews of the situation, which were put together by the reconnaissance department at Headquarters do not provide a clear assessment of the enemy's intentions either. If we take for example the text of a report dated 11–25 May 1944, which was the final report before the Soviet invasion: it is more than likely that Mannerheim based his decisions on reports such as these:

> <u>Units</u> The overall picture. The nature of the numerous exchanges that have taken place between units, across the various directions. On the Karelian Isthmus our aerial reconnaissance on 22 May 1944 confirmed large-scale deployments, which indicate significant changes in the alignment in the central part of the isthmus. …the aforementioned results in terms of aerial reconnaissance indicate the arrival of new units. The capture of a deserter who was captured by the Germans close to Narva must be linked to this information. He informed us that several infantry divisions had been deployed from there to the Finnish Front.

The Karelian Isthmus Movement that indicates local changes in units, has been noted in several locations, particularly in the western and central parts of the isthmus. On the roads leading to the north in the central part of the Karelian Isthmus aerial reconnaissance on 22 May recorded between 500–600 trucks, the majority of which, around 200–300, were on the road from Kujala to Peri and Warsala. The vehicles moving along the road to the front were loaded, as were many of the trucks moving away from the front. Evidently this is evidence of new units being deployed to the central part of the isthmus and it is possible that the advent of a new division between the 10th and the 142nd divisions. The Division evidently is the same one that was mentioned above in terms of their deployment from Narva.

Reinforcements and Forces
On the basis of the information received over the reporting period it would be accurate to suppose that the enemy, as they had done in the muddy season, had embarked on a large-scale reorganisation. The aim of this were augmentation, rest and recuperation and military training of units that have been weakened by protracted offensive battles.

Engineering work. Over the course of the reporting period the enemy has undertaken a considerable amount of engineering work on the isthmus… the enemy has also built new trenches in front of their front line (to the south and north of the main railway line, in the direction of the road to Mednoye ozero, Harvasuo, Lavosenmyaki), as well as building trenches that branch out to a point some 100–300m from our own positions.

The Enemy's Actions and Intentions
In connection with the dislocations and changes in the alignment the overall picture of the enemy remains mixed, and in connection with this any decision concerning the enemy's possible intentions is a complex one.

The enemy has freed up significant reserves in the northern part of the German-Russian Front, and it is possible that these could be used in an offensive against our own country, there is evidence of them being deployed to the Finnish Front (see point 1).

The enemy activity however does point to a continuation of defensive actions. Only on the Karelian Isthmus are there signs of preparations for an offensive. In connection with this particular attention must be paid to the offensive engineering works as well as to the arrival of additional forces, which has been confirmed with sufficient accuracy (this relates to the 1st Division). Taking into consideration however the information that the enemy has obtained concerning our own activities (including the arrival of German units onto the isthmus!) and the possibility of an offensive on Petersburg from the direction of the isthmus and the threat this poses to the overall situation, the reinforcement of defences on the isthmus would appear natural. Prior to this in the summertime the enemy alignment has been at a greater strength than it has in the wintertime. A possible secondary direction for the assault could be the Kandalakshkoe direction, but despite an intense enhancement of road repair work, the muddy season is currently preventing large-scale combat activity in that area.

Such a reassuring opinion was also supported by Mannerheim himself, who expressed his opinion in his memoirs:

> From the beginning of spring the enemy's reconnaissance activity has increased, and the artillery fire directed against our positions on the Karelian Isthmus has also increased. In May reconnaissance reports mentioned the changes in the composition of the enemy's forces, and the advent of new infantry divisions, as well as artillery, and armoured tank units. The advent of a new, and as yet unknown to us, Corps Headquarters was also established. This information however did not completely correspond to the information received from the Germans in which it was confirmed that some of these forces were located in the Baltic region.
>
> The composition of Russian forces on the Karelian Isthmus changes every spring. The Russians are in the habit of withdrawing their forces at this beautiful time of year for rest and recuperation, and to concentrate them in large camps that were located to the north of Leningrad. Maybe these deployments are taking place at the present time, since everyone was anticipating decisive operations against the Germans in the Baltic countries. The operational organs at Headquarters were also inclined to accept this point of view, and a similar point of view was supported by some of the officers at upper command level on the isthmus. The fact that the threatening possibility of an offensive from this direction had been underestimated was only partially supported, and we would be able to beat back an attempt at a possible offensive using the fortified positions that have been built over the course of three years.

It was at this point that the Marshal deluded himself. The "VT line" between May–June 1944 was only at partial combat capability. On the basis of incomplete and sketchy intelligence Mannerheim was behaving ambivalently. On the one hand in the winter and spring 1944 he signed orders on the start of serious preparations to counter a Soviet offensive, and on the other hand he sent some of his front line soldiers on holiday to do agricultural work. The situation with respect to provisions in Finland was lamentable. The majority of the men who were of working age were sunning themselves in the trenches on the front line. Sending Soviet prisoners of war to do agricultural work would not completely resolve this issue. In the period from 1941–44 Finland was not able to feed itself independently and relied on grain imports from Germany.

On 12 April Mannerheim signed a decree ordering spring leave for the period from 24 April–7 June 1944 for 9,500 servicemen. The infantry schools were ordered to send this same number of new recruits to the front line, and once the regular soldiers had returned they were to go back to combat training. On 30 May Headquarters took a decision to extend this leave for a week, up until 14 June. Servicemen from the country's far northern governorates such as Lapland, Oulu, and Kuopio had their leave extended for two weeks.

The acute shortage of labour in the agricultural sector led to the call up of those on the margins of military service who were born between 1909–24 being postponed by way of a decree issued by Headquarters from 5 May to 10 June. On 3 June Mannerheim signed an order on the retirement from the armed forces of *unter-offiziers* and privates born between 1902-03. Similarly, *unter-offizier* and privates born in 1904 were discharged from the artillery.

The assimilation of new types of weaponry was slow. By March–April 1944 the Germans had supplied their allies with new anti-tank weapons – *Panzerschreck* and *Panzerfaust*. These only arrived at the front however in April–May and only the 2nd Infantry Division received them on the Karelian Isthmus on the eve of the Soviet offensive. They never reached the 10th Infantry Division that was at the forefront of the Soviet attack. There were no plans to provide mass training on how to use the *Panzerfaust*, and right up to the 20th of June the Finnish infantry still did not know how to use them. As Finnish anti-tank gunner Valde Hamalainen recalled:

> From 21-27 May I found myself on anti-tank gunner courses in Tuusula. As I was reporting for duty the Major who was the course leader asked me why I was there again. He said there was nothing new for me to learn there. I answered that I had come there because I had been ordered to do so. He sent me along with Captain Pajunen to put together the first Finnish language training on how to use the *Panzerschreck.* We put it together but I do not know what happened to it, whether it was suitable or not.
>
> On these courses, despite what the Major said, there was always something new since we were trained in how to use new light but effective anti-tank weapons that had arrived in Finland from Germany: the *Panzerfaust* and *Panzerschreck.* This for me was an absolutely new weapon and I got to know it with great interest. We also carried out test firings from the *Panzerschreck.* The target was a trophy tank, a 33-ton "*sotka*," or in other words a T-34. We placed a thick sheet of cardboard inside the tank so we could see what effect the projectile would have, and what chance the crew had of surviving an attack.
>
> We fired from approximately 100m away. The first shot hit the tank's track, which flew off towards the forest with such force that it broke a 15cm birch tree that was standing 20m away like it was matchwood. The second shot was better and we ran over to have a look what had happened. A hole was clearly visible in the side of the tank. When we looked inside the tank to see what had happened to the cardboard we could not see it at all. When we looked around the tank more closely we saw that the cardboard was lying on the floor of the weapons compartment and had been pulverised into such small pieces it was as though an army of mice had chewed it to bits. Not one of the crew could have survived this, so this weapon really had lived up to its reputation.

The new German 75mm PAK-40 anti-tank weapons had also arrived at the front, which were capable of countering Soviet T-34s or KVs. Hamalainen had to enter into an argument with his own divisional command so that they left their men at the front to assimilate this new technology. The headquarters of the 2nd Infantry Division ordered Hamalainen to allocate a gun battery crew to go and build tourist cottages behind the lines!

Time passed. In early 1944 a commission arrived at the Karelian Isthmus from the operations department of the Finnish Supreme Command Headquarters. Based on the results of the inspection Mannerheim issued a successive order on the need to expedite the construction of the "VT line." In the order dated 10 May the Marshal's concern and frustration is palpable:

> 1. Despite the fact that many of my orders (No.1002/Op. 1/17 a/secret dated 22 February 1944, and No2153/Op. 1/28 g/secret dated 17 December 1943) underline the need to reinforce our positions at the present time, when we need to be ready to counter a large-scale enemy offensive, the situation again arises in which the inspectors that I have sent in confirm that there are shortcomings as well as alarming irregularities in the defence of the various sectors.
>
> 2. I know that in any offensive against us the enemy would base their calculations for success on the mass deployment of their material advantage. In connection with this if each commander is not using each moment of calm for training their men or leaves my soldiers I have entrusted to them without reliable shelter, then this would amount to dereliction of duty.
>
> I require all the commanders who serve under me to be absolutely resolute, and that they take full responsibility for ensuring that our positions would be ready to counter the pressure of an offensive, when the enemy has such a material advantage over us.

This was futile. Even this order that the Marshal had issued was ignored. On 30 May, some 10 days prior to the Soviet offensive the Head of the Operations Department of the Finnish Army's General Headquarters remarked in his diary:

> When I passed the fortifications behind the lines, the artillery positions, the locations where the reserves were stationed and right up to the actual front line itself, I did not see one soldier working on the construction of the defensive structures. I did however see a large number of soldiers sunning themselves and just lying about here and there. At this same time, an acute need to carry out this work was pervasive everywhere on the defensive fronts.

Meantime, on the Soviet side the most active preparations were underway for the general offensive. Throughout May and the beginning of June 1944 rifle and tank units in the 21st Army were engaged in enhanced combat training. Particular attention was paid to combat activity in forested and marshy areas and to overcoming an enemy's long-standing defences. Combat training lasted 25 consecutive days with 10 hrs of lectures and study per day! Cooperation was carefully worked out between the tanks and rifle formations.

Vladimir Ivanovich Trunin, a veteran of the 260th Guards Separate Heavy Tank Regiment recalls the breakthrough:

> The cartographers had picked out just this same site [as the location for the breakthrough–author's note] and we went there under cover of a tarpaulin. The entire network of agents that we had in Leningrad, that were under the Germans, had said that we had set off from just outside Narva. The fighting was also very fierce in that same direction, in Narva. Therefore the Finns and the Germans, had probably relaxed their guard. By night however when we conducted our manoeuvres, we were again deployed to Volosov, we would be loaded onto wagons and we would then creep in and cover ourselves with a tarpaulin completely, nobody would know who or what we were. We would be taken to Pesochniy under cover of darkness–that's it there–and then we would be offloaded. We arrived still under the cover of darkness. We arrived on the 10th reaching Beloostrov at 0900 hrs in the morning. We stayed in the woods, to the right of the Vyborg highway. That's how it was. We did not even refuel. We had enough fuel, 600l was enough.

The officer tank crews, who were to join the breakthrough, would themselves carry out reconnaissance of the Finnish defences and the combat paths for the tanks. On the basis of the information we received the instructions were given to the engineering units to clear the paths through the anti-tank obstacles and minefields, to take the launching equipment down to the rivers, and to the tank traps, and for building the assault bridges.

The engineers worked tirelessly. The 6th Engineering and Sapper Battalion removed 8,033 mines, destroying 4,692 mines on site (in total this amounted to 12,725 mines), and prepared 133 linear metres of bridge members, and received the crossing and engineering equipment from the 21st Army. During the course of the exercises the sappers in the battalion built a bridge across a water obstacle that was 15m long, and 4.5m wide, and with a carrying capacity of 60tonnes, in the space of four and a half hours. The reinforcements underwent a training course that lasted for 120 hrs.

The 7th Engineering and Sapper Battalion was engaged in road repairs in the area around Beloostrov as well as working to clear mines. The battalion removed 20,175 mines, destroying 536 mines on site (this amounts to 20,711 mines in total). The mine clearing work was undertaken at great risk, not only from Finnish fire, but also from the nature of the mines themselves. The neutral ground between the Finnish and Soviet positions represented a random overlap of minefields from different periods of time. The first minefields were laid back in autumn 1941. The maps of these minefields were not compiled with due care and the mines themselves had become overgrown with grass in the intervening three years. The sappers were not able to make use of probes and would feel each centimetre of ground with their hands.

The 8th Engineering and Sapper Battalion excavated 21 tank pits for the KV tanks in the 31st Separate Guards Tank Regiment that were to take part in the breakthrough and they also prepared and marked with poles the combat paths for the tanks. For the 260th Guards Heavy Tank Regiment, the 185th Separate Tank Regiment, and the 1,439th, and 1,222nd Self-Propelled Artillery Regiments the sappers cleared 30 pathways through the tank traps and removed 1,273 mines that were in the way of the combat paths for the tanks. They also excavated 26 firing positions for the self-propelled vehicles with niches for the ammunition.

The 9th Engineering and Sapper Battalion worked to repair and construct roads and prepared to cross the Rzhavaya Kanava, some 2km of ready elements (cribs) for the bridge that was 30 linear metres in length.

The artillerymen distributed the targets in advance between the different systems: the artillery and anti-tank regiments, the loaded forty-fives and ZIS-2s, would destroy the stone tank traps and the field guns would take out the barbed wire fencing and the minefields; the howitzers would destroy the trenches, and the earth and wooden firing points and would be used to suppress the mortar batteries. The armoured trains from the 23rd Separate Battalion were to pound the Finnish batteries, the location of which had been identified. All this was worked out in advance on specially constructed firing ranges.

Major-General Mikhalkin, the 21st Army artillery commander, observed:

> Never before had a combined arms army on our front had such powerful artillery firepower at its disposal. It was important too that it be used to the full. The Army's artillery headquarters worked a great deal and were under considerable pressure. We studied the enemy from every angle, created artillery groups, defined their specific tasks and in conjunction with the infantry carried out tactical exercises with live firing … Not only did we have to concern ourselves with the artillery units. The Front Line Commander Govorov, as he was checking up on the combined arms commanders ordered that they have a sound knowledge of the potential of the artillery and of the plan for the role of artillery in the offensive. It was around these important questions that I conducted training sessions with the corps and divisional commanders. I briefed them in detail on the objectives for the artillery when breaking through an enemy's in-depth, and long-standing defence. I also briefed them on the procedure for organising the interactions between artillery, infantry and tanks in the period when the attacks and the fighting are being supported to some depth behind enemy defences.. Similar training sessions were conducted by artillery commanders in the rifle divisions, for the commanders of the artillery, rifle and tank units.

Sergeant Viktor Pavlovich Kryukov, of 1,427th Anti-Tank Rifle Regiment observed:

> Leningrad's white nights. In our case they were acting against us. In the end we had to spend a week equipping our positions in sight of the enemy. We could only work under cover of darkness, and in that case time was of the essence. Over the course of that week we incurred heavy losses, and the majority of these were from wounds since the Finns would fire at us using the sound that we made as we excavated the ground. There were a number

of instances when owing to their lack of experience the soldiers would take a moment's lull as a temporary halt in the firing "in good faith" and draw themselves up to their full height to make their work a little easier. They would then be hit by a bullet or by shrapnel from a mine.

After the work had been completed our tracks could easily be traced, since the work would form embankments of fresh earth, which was a good reference point. We could not therefore hide our preparatory activities from the enemy.

At an observation post we would be safe from bullets or shrapnel from mines. A watch was arranged at these observation posts round the clock.

This phenomenon alone could enable a judgement to be made concerning the Finnish trenches and communications ditches. If you looked along the line of the communications ditches you would often see the tip of a bayonet. We guessed that this was a Finnish soldier who was walking the communications ditches at full height with his weapon back over his shoulder.

For the whole of May and the beginning of June small groups of Soviet ground attack aircraft would pass over the Karelian Isthmus escorted by fighters. The ground attack air divisions of the 13th Air Army carried out reconnaissance and photographic monitoring of targets in the period from 7 May – 8 June.

By 1500 hrs on 3 June, the Leningrad Front had issued an operational directive in which the armies were ordered to be at readiness to go on the offensive by 8 June 1944. On 5 June the headquarters of the 21st Army had issued order No.001 to the various units, which described the overall objectives of the offensive. Some of the armies were to be at readiness to fulfil this combat order by 8 June. (See table below for 21st Army artillery group composition by the evening of 8 June).

Composition of forces	97th Rifle Corps	30th Guards Rifle Corps	109th Rifle Corps
Length of the front for the advance	9,5km	6,5km	6,5km
Breakthrough front	4km	5km	3,5km
1 Echelon – 6 rifle divisions (34 battalions)	12 battalions	13 battalions	9 battalions
2 Echelon – 3 rifle divisions (33 battalions)	9 battalions	9 battalions	15 battalions
Reserve – 14 battalions	6 battalions	5 battalions	3 battalions
Tank regiments – 4 Self-propelled artillery regiments – 3 Engineering companies – 39 separate + 18 divisional Guns and mortars – 2 135 (without Air Defence System units, 45mm guns and 50mm mortars)			
Guns per 1km. of breakthrough front 2 135/12,5 = 170,8 = 171 guns			

On the night of 8–9 June, the 21st Army's final guns took up their closed firing positions.

See table below for 21st Army artillery at the start of the Vyborg Offensive.[1]

№	Designation of the system	97th Rifle Corps	30th Guards Rifle Corps	109th Rifle Corps
1	82mm mortars	162	243	162
2	120mm mortars	216	306	90
3	45mm guns	54	96	70
4	57mm guns	–	24	24
5	76mm field artillery guns	60	63	51
6	76mm divisional artillery guns	184	208	108
7	122mm howitzers	144	184	140
8	122mm guns	6	16	–
9	152mm gun-howitzer	48	90	36
10	152mm howitzers	32	32	32
11	203mm howitzers	6	20	12
12	Trophy 105mm guns	–	–	16
13	Trophy 150mm howitzers	–	–	16
14	37mm anti-aircraft artillery guns	–	–	–
15	76mm anti-aircraft artillery guns	12	10	–
16	85mm anti-aircraft artillery guns	–	36	20
17	120–130mm naval systems	–	13	19
18	152mm naval systems	–	5	10
19	180mm naval systems	–	7	15
20	280mm super heavy artillery	6	6	6
21	305mm super heavy artillery	–	6	7
22	356mm super heavy artillery	–	1	3
23	406mm super heavy artillery	–	1	–
Length of the front line for the offensive		9km	6,7km	6km
Breakthrough front		5km	6km	4km
Density per 1km of the offensive front		97,3 guns	182,2 guns	127,8 guns
Density per 1km of breakthrough front		175,2 guns	203,5 guns	170 guns

1 This does not include 50mm mortars.

The distribution of the 21st Army's artillery alignment on 10 June 1944

Organisational identity of the groups	Groups	The composition and number of guns and mortars in the group			Notes
		109 Rifle Corps	30th Guards Rifle Corps	97th Rifle Corps	
Rifle regiments	Close range	75 guns	183 guns	84 guns	
	Armour Piercing	216 mortars	297 mortars	216 mortars	
Rifle divisions	Anti-tank	148 guns and mortars	212 guns and mortars	168 guns and mortars	
Rifle corps	Special purpose	64 guns and mortars	264 guns and mortars	32 guns and mortars	
	Rocket-propelled	44 guns	74 guns	44 guns	
Army	Long-range artillery	52 guns	70 guns	54 guns	
	Guards mortar units	48 combat vehicles	24 combat vehicles and 432 heavy machine guns	24 combat vehicles	
	Mechanised cavalry group	84 guns and mortars	74 guns and mortars	84 guns and mortars	
	Anti-aircraft artillery group	32 guns	48 guns	12 guns	This group fired at ground targets
	Red Banner Baltic Fleet artillery	115 guns	11 guns	Out of range	TOTAL
TOTAL		878 guns, mortars, Guards mortar launcher combat vehicles	1,689 guns, mortars, Guards mortar launcher combat vehicles	718 guns, mortars, Guards mortar launcher combat vehicles	3,285 guns, mortars, Guards mortar launcher combat vehicles

On that same night from 8–9 June all the infantry's heavy weapons were brought up to their starting points, these were the close-range guns, mortars and heavy machine guns. From the battalions that were to go and storm the Finnish defences on 10 June, only one rifle, and an automatic rifle regiment were brought up to the front.

By the start of the Soviet offensive on the Finnish Principal defence line near Belooostrov there were 43,760 men from the 3rd and 4th corps. The reserve consisted of 31,380 men. In the area around Enso (Svetagorsk) and Laappeenranta, 100km from the front line, Lagus' armoured division was concentrated–this was the only mobile reserve in the Finnish Army.

The overall strength of the Soviet alignment reached 260,000 men, 630 tanks and self-propelled guns, and around 7,500 guns across all calibres. The three-fold advantage had been realised. Approximately 80 percent of all the forces and their equipment was concentrated In the direction of the main attack – along the Beloostrov–Kivennapa (Pevomayeskoye) – Vyborg road. Here the Soviet advantage was overwhelming.

Some 1,000 aircraft from the 13th Air Army were ready to support the offensive with air strikes. The Finnish Air Force on the Karelian Isthmus on 9 June could only make 33 ME-109 fighter planes available as well as 18 unreliably obsolete Brewsters. They were based at airfields in Suulayarvi, Heinjoki, and Kymi.

The number of targets that had been reconnoitred on the Finnish front line was so great that artillery preparation continued over two days. On 9 June this was due to continue for 10 hrs. The start of the Vyborg Offensive Operation was planned for 0715 hrs.

3

9 June: Ten Hours' Bombardment

On the morning of 9 June 1944, Finnish soldiers awoke in their dug outs at around 0700 hrs to the rumble of engines from the Soviet air armada. Ground attack aircraft and bombers from the 13th Air Army began to strike the Finnish positions. In the course of the raid Soviet ground forces marked their positions using white and green rockets.

Soviet aviation launched an enormous attack on the front line and on the targets behind Finnish defences. Target No. 21 (the area around lakes Pastorskoye and Svetloe) was struck by 70 bombers, whilst target No. 12 (Old Beloostrov, and the direction of the main attack) was hit by 82 bombers, and target No. 14 (Rajajoki station) was hit by 81 bombers. All the bombing was synchronised; there were 233 bombers over the Finnish positions at one time. The Soviet Air Force used their newest bomber aircraft the Tu-2 for the first time. After the bombers, some 90 ground attack aircraft attacked these same targets.

In the areas behind the Finnish lines around Kivennapa, Kiviniemi, and Valkjarvi on that same day were hit by 196 Soviet bombers. The stations at Rautu, and Raivola were hit by 77 bombers.

The most fortunate location on that murky day of 9 June was the city and railway junction of Vyborg. Some 600 Soviet Long-Range Aviation bombers (around 500 Il-4s and approximately 100 American-made B-25 Mitchells) were due to bomb this city on the night of 9–10. This ancient city was to be wiped off the face of the earth that day. A Soviet weather reconnaissance aircraft however that had flown over the city reported that conditions were far from favourable: the amount of cloud was at 10, the highest that it could be, with heavy rain, the southern edge of the cloud was 200–250m away, and visibility was between one to two kilometres. The mass attack on Vyborg was cancelled.

For five minutes prior to the start of the initial artillery barrage Soviet rifle units imitated the start of an attack, opening fire intensively from their guns. Machine gunners from pill boxes as well as the earth and timber gun emplacements in the Karelian Fortified District opened fire with 750 shells per gun. The aim was to draw Finnish infantry out from their shelters and then to hit them with artillery.

At 0800 hrs the army and naval artillery opened fire. The artillery of the 21st Army alone in the course of the five-minute raid used 17,274 shells and mines. After that Soviet artillerymen switched to a systematic destruction of Finnish defences. Ten hours of daylight were devoted to this task. The targets that the 21st Army's front line needed to hit were worked by some 240 guns with calibres ranging from 130 up to 406mm. Some of the artillery moved up to fire at close range. On certain front line sectors the 21st Army used some 50 shells per kilometre of front at close range!

Soviet artillerymen either exaggerated or played down the intensiveness of the bombardment, to completely unsettle the Finnish infantry.

The 203mm howitzers of 4th Guards Battery under Captain Ivan Ivanovich Vedmedenko moved up to fire at close range in the area around Beloostrov The mission was to destroy the artillery half-caponia in the Karelian Fortified Sector that had been provided to the Finns in 1941. Both sides had dubbed it the "Millionaire," in the same way as they had the pill boxes on the Mannerheim line. Vedmedenko opened fire from a distance of 1,350m. Of the 140 shells used 136 hit the target despite the fact that each shot would push a seven tonne howitzer backwards significantly, throwing up dust and sand in front of the firing position. In total on that day the 18th Guards Artillery Brigade destroyed two pill boxes and 23 gun emplacements made from earth and wood, firing 1,187 shells at the Finnish defences. For this achievement Captain Medvedenko was awarded the title of Hero of the Soviet Union.

Type of round, and calibre	**Usage, no. of pieces**
Mines	
82mm	6,702
120mm	6,793
Shells	
76mm, divisional artillery	8,991
122mm, guns	243
122mm, howitzers	4,736
152mm, gun-howitzers	2,390
152mm, howitzers	4,653
203mm	977
105/150mm, trophy guns	445
280mm	257
305mm	130
TOTAL, no. of pieces	**36,317**

The total number of shells used by the 21st Army's artillery on 9 June[1] (above)

From 1750 hrs to 18185 hrs Soviet fire was augmented, this was an artillery barrage with combat reconnaissance. After this was over the rifle companies from the 204th and 22nd Regiments moved forward with the support of the 2nd Tank Battalion, 220th Separate Tank Brigade. The battalion was armed with T-26 tanks, which were highly vulnerable to any of the Finnish anti-tank weaponry. The attack from the 1st Rifle Battalion, 22nd Regiment on the Finnish stronghold codenamed "Motor" (the Soviet designation for this stronghold was *Peschaniye bugry*" supported by 10 veteran tanks.[2]

1 This table does not include shells fired by the Red Banner Baltic Fleet.
2 "Peschaniye burgy" translates as sandy knoll–Translator's note.

Between 1810–1825 the Soviet battalion crossed the first trench and had broken through to the stronghold "Motor" supported by T-26s. Some particularly fierce fighting was noted on the right flank, but this had been suppressed by 1835 hrs. By 1900 hrs the mission had been completed, and the battalion began to establish itself in the areas that it had captured. The tank crews had paid a high price for this success: in all 10 T-26 tanks were lost. Three tanks had been burnt out, four were destroyed and the remaining three were stranded. The Finns claimed they had destroyed six T-26 tanks from the anti-tank "elephant-guns."

Tank crews of the 220th Brigade who went into battle in what were highly vulnerable vehicles, obtained valuable information for their tank crew colleagues. For all the tank crews that were to break through the Finnish defences by day at a later stage in the formidable KV tanks. During the course of the combat reconnaissance it was established that: 1) The Finnish anti-tank defences were weak: 2) The Finns had not put up any special anti-tank obstacles; 3) the terrain was negotiable even for the run down T-26s; 4) Finnish infantry conducts its anti-tank battles predominantly using close-range fire.

On 9 June Junior Lieutenant Mukhanov Nikolai Petrovich, the Commander of a tank in the 2nd Battalion, 220th Tank Brigade was killed in battle. Also killed were the Commander of a tank company in the 2nd Battalion in the 220th Captain Mikhail Yakovlevich Sharonov, as well as the driver-mechanic Senior Sergeant Aleksandr Mikhaylovich Zamyatin.

As a result of the battle for the stronghold named "Motor" the Soviet side estimated that Finnish losses as 70 killed, and more than 100 injured, and 12 taken prisoner. Six Finnish soldiers who were hiding from the Soviet artillery barrage in their dug out were caught out by the Soviet attack and were then surrounded and subsequently surrendered. In the end 26 rifles were taken, along with three "Suomi" automatic rifles, and one "elephant gun" by way of trophies. For the 1st Rifle Battalion, 22nd Regiment their losses were 40 men killed, 196 inured and 21 who were missing without trace.

On the shore of the Gulf of Finland the 6th Company, 203rd Rifle Regiment crossed the Rzhavaya kanava and climbed up to the "Yazyk" heights and had taken the first trench without firing a shot. This became possible thanks to powerful supporting fire: three whole armoured trains moved up to fire at close range: the "*Stremitelniy*" under Lieutenant Viktor Fyodorovich Lukashov, the "*Stoikiy*" under Captain Vasiliy Grigoryevich Kirillov, together with the 28th Separate armoured train under Major Pavel Stepanovich Rotobelskiy. Building on this success the Commander of the 109th Rifle Division General Stepanovich Trushkin put the 3rd Battalion, 381st Rifle Regiment into the battle and as a result the Soviet units took the "*Oryol*" and "*Chyornaya*" heights. According to Soviet information 11 men were taken prisoner in the course of the battle, from the 1st and 32nd (this was how it was rendered in the original text of the reports–author's note) Infantry Regiments. On the night of 9–10 June the second battalion in the Finnish 58th Regiment counterattacked the Soviet units on the heights on four occasions but were not able to achieve success.

Evening fell. On the night of 9–10 June the advance to the front line began for the actual attack alignment of the 30th Guards Rifle Corps as well as the heavy tank and self-propelled gun regiments.

The armoured tank forces of the 21st Army on the evening of 9 June 1944

Regimental Number	**Type of tank**	**No. of vehicles as of 10.6.1944**
31st Guards Heavy Tank Regiment	KV, KV-1S	15 (?)
260th Guards Heavy Tank Regiment	KV, KV-1S	25
185th Separate Tank Regiment	T-34-76	21
98th Separate Tank Regiment	T-34-85	21
394th Guards Heavy Self-Propelled Gun Regiment	ISU-152	21
397th Guards Heavy Self-Propelled Gun Regiment	ISU-152	21
1,222nd Self-Propelled Artillery Regiment	SU-76	36
1,349nd Self-Propelled Artillery Regiment	SU-152	11, 1 KV-1S
TOTAL		**157**

The tank alignment of the 23rd Army was weaker, which explains its auxiliary role in the attack:

Regimental Number	**Type of tank**	**No. of vehicles as of 10.6.1944**
46th Guards Heavy Tank Breakthrough Regiment	KV-1, KV-1S, «Churchill» Mk IV(?)	21
226th Separate Tank Regiment	T-34-85	21
938th Self-Propelled Artillery Regiment	SU-76	21
952nd Self-Propelled Artillery Regiment	SU-76	19
396-й Guards Heavy Self-Propelled Artillery Regiment	ISU-152	21
TOTAL		**103**

The front line's armoured tank reserve was as follows:

Number of the regiment	Type of tank	No. of vehicles as of 10.6.1944
1st Red Banner Tank Brigade	T-34-76, T-60, T-70, SU-26	34 T-34-76, 21 T-70/60, 4 SU-26
152nd Tank Brigade	T-34-76	
30th Guards Tank Brigade	T-34-76	
26th Guards Heavy Tank Regiment	IS-2	21
27th Guards Heavy Tank Regiment	IS-2	21
124th Separate Tank Regiment	T-34-76	21
220nd Tank Brigade	T-34-85, T-34-76, T-26, T-60, SU-76	
TOTAL		122

In the report on the combat activities of the 58th Infantry Regiment the events of 9 June are described as follows:

> The first few hours of 9 June 1944 passed as they usually would. Only in the defence sector close to the railway line, where the regiment's 3rd Battalion was on guard, did the enemy deploy in a number of areas under the cover of smoke screens. A group of enemy infantrymen some 60–70 men in number was noted as they advanced towards the front line. Nothing out of the ordinary was noted either in the "Bunker" defence sector, where the regiment's 1st Battalion had been. The enemy continued to work on the new trenches under the protection of an outpost. Judging by the explosions the enemy was engaged in mine laying [this is how it is rendered in the original–author's note]. Most likely the enemy wanted to actually hide their true intentions, either that or they were setting off their own mines. In front of the new trenches the enemy had set up a large number of barriers, evidently trying to show us again that their intention was defence.
>
> The enemy's artillery fire, which again did not differ greatly from any other day, had over the course of the last few days been more preparatory in nature. The previous evening a column of 100 trucks heading for the front had been noticed in front of the "Motor" stronghold.
>
> At approximately 0660 hrs on 9 June 1944 a powerful enemy air raid began, the main attack was on our neighbour to the left of us in the area around the Beloostrov road. At this time around 70 enemy bombers and ground attack aircraft flew from left to right over our defensive sector. They strafed and bombed our front line and the logistics areas behind the lines. The air raid lasted for approximately thirty minutes after which the enemy began to rain devastating fire down on us and a new air raid began. This time the enemy infantry began to move and occupied their forward trenches. We opened fire on the enemy with machine guns and artillery. The enemy made no attempt to go on the offensive but all the while its infantry was occupying the forward trench, and we also noticed movement behind the lines, and the infantry also opened fire with artillery and machine guns.

> The enemy's devastating fire immediately cut all the telephone lines, and we reverted to radio communications. On the morning of 9 June the enemy made a number of further air raids as a result of which the firing positions belonging to the regiment's 13th Company sustained direct hits. The enemy continued their devastating bombardment of our positions, and pill boxes were specifically targeted. They hit the positions next to the railway line hard as well as the Hastilyanmaki height. As a result of this six earth and wood gun emplacements were destroyed, all the trenches were damaged and the artillery correction points at Karki (Konchik) and Pohja were destroyed.
>
> In the "Bunker" defence sector a captured enemy pill box had collapsed under enemy fire, which served as a Command Post for the regiment's 1st Company. The Nila artillery correction point ceased to exist along with the pill box. The Pare artillery correction point in the ruins of the barracks at Aleksandrov had collapsed. Enemy infantry did not take the offensive into that sector at all.
>
> By that time the regiment's sub-divisions had lost almost all their heavy equipment. The majority of it had been destroyed over the course of two days by artillery fire and enemy air raids. In addition losses among the horses and among the personnel were so high that recovering the remains of the armament was not thought possible, the enemy was constantly trying to cut off the escape routes from the left flank....

The well-known Soviet academic Nikolai Nikolayevich Inozemtsev was a signals master in the 106th Howitzer Artillery Brigade in 1944, supporting the 23rd Army's offensive in an auxiliary attack sector. This is the entry he made in his combat diary for 9 June:

> The day of preliminary destruction. A mass of aircraft, "Ils", and Pe-2s flew in groups of between 30–60 aircraft. On the left flank the very powerful initial artillery barrage could be heard.
>
> Our batteries were firing wonderfully well. Shabrov, Ledentsov, Vnukovskiy, Gorenstein destroyed targets 18–20 using shells, with one, two, or three accurate shots. Close range fire works very well, the crews have coped with this artistically. The infantry is taking the heights at 182.5 and 123.2 almost without incurring losses, none of the pill boxes have been left in place up there and all the trenches have even been filled in. Some 14 Finns have been captured, who had been driven crazy by our artillery. All this took place in an auxiliary, diversionary direction.

From the Finnish side 9 June seemed like a realisation of hell on earth. Anti-tank gunner Captain Valde Hamalainen awoke to the thunder of the initial Soviet artillery barrage:

> At six I woke up because the building was shaking so much that I almost fell out of bed. Such a noise and commotion was coming from the street that I decided our building was coming under direct attack. I quickly got up to have a look what was going on. From the outside it was clear what was causing this terrible noise from the direction of the front line, where the enemy had gone on the offensive supported by a powerful artillery attack.

Artilleryman Pentti Talvenheimo also left a descriptive account of the ninth day of June from the Finnish perspective. He avoided being hit by the Soviet steel and survived to the end of the day, when he was able to write these lines:

My watch was coming to an end in the trench on the morning of 9 June, it was around half past five. The entire watch was looking out at No Man's Land from where a mist was slowly rising. I saw the face of war in the gaps in the mist–with barbed wire, the gash of the trenches, and the craters–it was a face I had known for so many years. A silence pervaded over the battlefield, which was broken only by a cuckoo in a tree near our stronghold. Soon the songstress had grown tired of calling and flew away to the south, without a glance at the front line drawn between human beings. The morning was clear and the day would be a warm one. The idyll of morning was broken by the advent of a bird of death on steel wings–a Soviet ground attack aircraft, an Il-2. It was as if death itself had landed to survey the field in which it was to reap its harvest. The ground attack machine passed along the road with its hard surface, turning behind our own lines it passed over them and in a shallow dive strafed the anti-aircraft gunner's positions not far away with rockets and flew over their heads. It then dropped small calibre bombs and departed back to its own lines.

I called through to the dugout and reported to the artillery reconnaissance scout that I thought the long anticipated offensive had begun. The artillery reconnaissance scout took my report seriously and hurriedly put on some clothes so as to come out into the trench. I had hardly left the telephone kiosk when I heard a commotion some distance away. The monotonous and heavy sound reminded me of the noise made by a swarm of bees. I looked through the stereoscope towards the edge of the woods beyond the enemy's front line and saw a large number of bomber squadrons coming straight towards us. I telephoned below once more and when the artillery reconnaissance scout picked up the receiver I told him tersely that a large-scale offensive had begun. As I said these words even I felt a shiver run down my spine.

I was sure of one thing. I had on a number of occasions in wartime managed to come through unscathed, but now fate had cast me and my colleagues to a place where my long tour of duty would end in death.

The artillery reconnaissance scout had hardly jumped into the ditch when the first bombs fell. They all exploded almost simultaneously. The ground shuddered and clouds of sand flew high into the air. Wherever you looked, everything was covered in a thick cloud of dust. My ears gave out from the noise and the hot blast waves threw us around the trench. It seemed like an endless number of bombs were raining down. Here and there the beams in the dug outs would be flung into the air, indicating a direct hit. The bombers turned over our heads and headed towards the Gulf of Finland, while the unit continued its journey to a point behind our own lines.

I prepared to enter the dug out and get to the radio, as a general volley of enemy artillery suddenly rang out. It was at this point that we witnessed really terrible destruction around the strongholds. It seemed like everything would be destroyed. The nervous tension though would soon ease and we would begin to get accustomed to these extreme conditions and it seemed that things were not all that bad. We could survive even in these difficult times. The air of panic eased slightly and turned into a desire for action.

I jumped through to the communications ditch and from there to the dugout and the radio. Masa Peltola tried to make contact but nothing came of it. I managed to get through to the battalion Command Post on the radio telephone, which we nicknamed the "tin whistle." Our radio-telephone was designated as a secondary channel of communication, but now I had to use it to communicate between two divisions. After a short dialogue, the battalion Command Post recognised us as Finns and it was thanks to this that we were provided with a good communication link with the commanders, who were very much in need of up to date reports. There was also an artillery officer there as well as a communications link to the batteries, which could provide covering fire for us. The telephony had been cut immediately after the bombardment began and no longer worked, despite all the efforts of the engineers. The initial artillery barrage lasted for another hour and a half. A very heavy enemy assault platoon transferred their fire onto our dug out, through the thunder we heard the swish of two heavy shells that came rushing towards us. We waited for them to bury us as the roof sheeting on the dugout would not take it. Guns firing at close range as well as tanks were beating up the firing points in our strongholds furiously, mortars would explode in the communications ditches.

In the first half of the day the enemy would congregate in front of our strongholds and go on the attack. At that same moment, the enemy transferred their artillery fire to areas behind the lines and to the flanks of the strongholds. We were protected by many layers of fire since the enemy had not yet attacked our sector. I forced myself to observe all this from our observation post so I was sat with the radio telephone and the artillery reconnaissance scout reported what was happening. One of the senior infantry sergeants was also using the radio telephone to report back, evidently he was the Deputy Platoon Commander in our stronghold.

The enemy unleashed a full-scale attack on the stronghold codenamed *Ostriyo*. They had probably not yet reached our communications ditches, which we could see from the flanks, since our artillery was putting up a fierce resistance. Sometime later they called off their attack. The artillery barrage also began to quieten down, although it would pick up again from time to time. We had a moment to breathe again. In the second half of the day the artillery fire resumed and rapidly reached what was for us an already familiar intensity. The enemy's infantry concentrated for the attack. Our artillery reconnaissance scout called in defensive fire but almost immediately he had to call it off, since he needed to redirect it to the area around the road. The attack on our stronghold had been beaten back and the enemy had ceased their attempts to capture it. Elsewhere we had not been so lucky, and the enemy had forced their way into several strongholds. *Ostriyo* was lost relatively rapidly. I saw groups of enemy infantry around the road. They were forcing a wedge into our defences at a distance of almost a kilometre. The enemy evidently remained happy with their initial success and as the twilight of the coming white night set in things quietened down. The situation was stabilising. The enemy's attempts to drive a wedge for a kilometre along the front line and also for a kilometre behind the lines close to the turn codenamed "Motor" put our stronghold in a very vulnerable position. The coming day did not promise anything good. The severe tests of the previous day had already drained the courage from the surviving defenders of our position and the gloomy prospects for the following day would certainly plunge everyone into an even deeper state of depression.

In the evening, a group of enemy sappers began to remove the mines in the area around the *Ostriyo* stronghold. The artillery reconnaissance scout sent me to the firing position and the gun that stood behind us, so we could open fire on this target. Since the target was not visible from the gun itself I agreed a simple system of hand signals with the scout to correct the fire. I ran to the artillerymen and reported the target to the crew commander, a lieutenant. A short time later our gun fired a burst and I waited for a signal from our artillery reconnaissance scout. At that moment heavy mortar fire rained down on our gun emplacement. They opened fire so quickly that evidently their artillery scout had noticed

> me running to this position. In the first break between the explosions I again returned to the Observation Post, since it was obvious that the gun was not going to fire any more.
>
> Late in the evening reinforcements arrived, in the shape of approximately a section in number of infantrymen under the command of a strong figure of a captain. To begin with they were billeted in our dug out with us, but then left when they found a suitable dug out in a gully close to a stream. We were brought supper by night and a new radio to replace the one that had broken. I knew nothing of this since I was already in a deep sleep on the plank beds after the trials of that day.

Finnish Headquarters all but failed to react to the start of the Soviet offensive, although according to Mannerheim's memoirs the thunder of the initial Soviet artillery barrage was audible both in the headquarters in Mikkeli and in Helsinki:

> At dawn on 9 June 1944 along a fifteen kilometre coastal sector a real storm broke out. After an air raid lasting an hour in which several hundred aircraft took part, such a powerful initial artillery barrage broke out, such as we have not witnessed before in either of our wars. It is only possible to imagine how powerful it was if one considers that it was audible at Headquarters, and even in Helsinki, that is to say at a distance of 220 to 270km. Despite the fact that the majority of the defensive lines were destroyed attacks were nevertheless beaten back along the entire front line. That evening after resuming the offensive the enemy managed with the support of tanks to capture several strongholds that had been moved forward and to hold them. This was prior to a lull in the fighting, as night had fallen.

Mannerheim wrote little of his actions on 9 June. The Headquarters and the Supreme Commander of the Finnish Army did almost nothing. Headquarters documents for that day devote a great deal of attention to the allied landing on Normandy, rather than the dramatic events in Beloostrov. Headquarters only ordered that the attacks on the strongholds codenamed "*Yazyk*" and "Motor" on the main defensive line be beaten back. The order did not differ much from those that Mannerheim issued in December 1939 after the Soviet forces had wedged their way into the Finnish defence. The only difference was the enemy. The elderly Marshal of Finnish forces had probably not fully realised what an arduous and glorious combat path the Red Army had trod in the ensuing five years of war and how much it had changed.

Back in 1943 German generals had informed the Finns that in their experience it would be impossible for them to stop a breakthrough of their defences in the course of a general Soviet offensive. From the point of view of the Germans the counter measures put in place after the offensive would be more important. These counter measures had not been taken by the Finnish Headquarters.

Frontline Finnish commanders attempted to respond. The Commander of 1st Infantry Regiment Vilyanen liaised with the headquarters of the 10th Division and requested reserves. The Commander of the division Sihvo in turn contacted the headquarters of the 4th Corps but received a negative response to his question concerning reserves. This same conversation took place between the chiefs of staff of the 10th Division and the 4th Corps. No promise was made of assistance. Late in the evening of 9 June Vilainen again telephoned his brigade commander and asked for just a single battalion for the area around Beloostrov. Sihvo replied: "Do not disturb the Corps headquarters at night." The headquarters were still acting in accordance with the pace of a positioning war without realising that they would before long have to run themselves, burning their documents and their comfortable cottage style dug outs.

By 2200 hrs Finnish time the headquarters of the 10th Division had prepared an order to the defences to withdraw back behind the lines, since the first line of defence had been almost totally destroyed. The officers were summoned to headquarters to relay the order back to the regiments. The Corps headquarters however vetoed the withdrawal. The order was never sent to the military units.

Sihvo himself was trying to get through on the telephone to Headquarters all night to report on the situation to Mannerheim. At 2300 hrs Finnish time the Headquarters Quartermaster General Lieutenant-General Airo picked up the phone. His response was terse and unequivocal: "The Marshal has gone to sleep, do not concede one inch of the trench."

This same 10th Division's reserve located close to Beloostrov consisted of the 1st Jager Battalion and the 2nd Battalion, 200th Estonian Regiment. There was little to counter the 30 battalions of 30th Guards Corps, which were aiming towards a breakthrough. Precious hours were slipping away.

At 2100 hrs an advance began of the majority of the tanks and personnel in the 21st Army towards the front line. From 0100 hrs on 10 June all the Soviet attack units began to march towards the front line. Even if the Finns had known the true scale of the Soviet plans it would already have been too late.

The murky and rainy day of 9 June 1944 had passed into history, but the worst for the Finns was yet to come.

4

10 June: Breakthrough

Following Sihvo's conversation with Headquarters in the evening he hardly had any other options left but to give the order for a counterattack and to liberate the strongholds that had been lost. The Fins tried four times to regain the stronghold codenamed "*Yazyk*" but without success. According to Soviet information the Finns tried seven times to regain the stronghold codenamed "Motor." The fourth counterattack was especially fierce, and after a battle fought at close quarters with extensive use of automatic weapons and hand grenades in the trenches the Finns succeeded in pushing back the 1st Battalion, 22nd Regiment a distance of 200m. After that, the severely depleted Soviet battalion was augmented at 2300 hrs by a company of sub machine gunners as well as by a rifle platoon from the 9th Company. The Finns succeeded in stabilising the situation. At 0500 hrs the 22nd Regiment transferred its positions on the front line to the 190th Guards Rifle Regiment.

In general, all the attempts made by the Finns to regain their positions on the night of 9–10 June were unsuccessful. The counterattacks had to be called off due to heavy losses.

The Leningrad Front made the next move. At 0230 hrs sappers from the 9th Engineering and Sapper Battalion in plain sight of the Finns began to draw up prefabricated sections of the tank bridge across the Rzhavaya kanava to the designated construction site. They carried the logs and boards some 150m from the Finnish positions. The Finns unleashed fierce fire on the sappers. Twelve men were injured, and the seriously injured medical orderly Shamarin became a casualty … The company laid low. The thirty-year old Private First Class Nina Genrikhovna Fyorodova set a personal example. At a cost of losses and heroic efforts all the materials together with the prefabricated elements of the bridge were delivered to the construction site by 0830 hrs. Thanks to the self-sacrificial actions of the sappers the bridge was already built by 0940 hrs and the "thirty-fours" from the 185th Tank Regiment had crossed it on their way into battle.

At 0600 hrs Soviet artillery again opened fire. In the space of two hours 20 minutes artillery from the 21st Army had spent 192,690 shells and large calibre mortars. The 13th Air Army again pounded the Finnish front line but this time using 172 bombers. A further 139 bombers attacked the areas behind the lines as well as the artillery positions.

In the course of the artillery barrage the Soviet Union's largest artillery gun, the 406mm gun fired its final shots from the Rzhev firing range. The "forty-fives" together with field guns fired on the Finnish positions at close range. Soviet anti-tank crews dragged the "forty-fives" up to the minimal firing distance, some 100–150m from the Finnish trenches. From Sestroretsk and from Dibuny station platform the batteries of armoured train Nos. 620 and 760, the "*Stremitelniy*" and the "*Stoikiy*" pounded Finnish mortar batteries. According to the memoirs of veterans from the 286th Rifle Division who had served in the reserves at Dubina, some of the shells from the armoured trains began to break off the tops of the trees where the division was stationed, which led to losses. The soldiers from the Karelian Fortified District withdrew their armament from the pill boxes and earth and wooden gun emplacements. Everything that could fire was aimed at the Finnish defence.

The consumption of artillery shells by the 21st Army[1] on 10 June was as follows:

Type of munition, calibre	Consumption, no. of pieces
Mines	
50mm	32 972
82mm	58 588
120mm	38 434
Shells	
45mm, Anti-Tank	24 946
57mm, Anti-Tank	1 765
76mm, Field artillery	10 760
76mm, divisional artillery	46 896
122mm, guns	1 887
122mm, howitzers	35 545
152mm, gun-howitzers	4 210
152mm, howitzers	1 831
203mm	207
105/150mm, trophy guns	1 373
280mm	151
305mm	–
TOTAL no. of pieces	**259 565**

The concluding accord in the initial barrage of Stalin's fourth attack was the simultaneous attack by 176 ground attack aircraft together with salvoes from heavy rocket mortars on the Finnish front line. In total 9,151 *Katyusha* shells and *Vanyush* shells descended on the Finns. As the Soviet officers noted after this "our units were conducting an advance on a sufficiently demoralised enemy."

The first to appear in the skies were Finnish fighters and they claimed seven bombers shot down, as well as one ground attack and seven fighters as a result of the numerous air battles. In terms of their own losses they listed a single "Brewster" with the identification code BW-365.

At 0820 hrs some of the 21st Army went on the offensive. The main attack was made by the 30th Guards Rifle Corps along the Vyborg road in Old Beloostrov. The 31st and 260th Guards Separate Heavy Tanks using KV and KV-1s tanks supported the guard's offensive. The self-propelled artillery

1 This table does not include artillery shells discharged by the Red Banner Baltic Fleet.

was represented by the 396th Guards Heavy Self-Propelled Artillery Regiment and the 1,439th Self-Propelled Artillery Regiment. The supporting corps for the artillery alignment was as described above; aside from the cannon artillery the guards were supported by the 276th Mortar Regiment and the 27th Mortar Brigade. Five sapper companies were responsible for providing engineering support to the offensive from the 17th Engineering and 52nd Separate Engineering and Sapper Brigades.

Advancing in the first echelon were the 63rd and 45th Guards Rifle divisions, the 64th Guards Division advanced in the second echelon. The most pressing objective for the guards was to capture the Finn's main band of defences and to advance to the boundary of the River Sestra in the area around Mainila. The 64th Guards Rifle Division joined the battle at a later stage; by the end of the day the guards were to have reached the boundary of the River Lintulan-Joki (Ptichey River), dug in and be ready to repel counterattacks. These measures were even superfluous, since on 10 June the 10th Infantry Division no longer had any available reserves.

The Finnish defences were overcome in just a matter of minutes. The Finnish units on the front line were suppressed and demoralised by a hail of fire that rained down on them from 9–10 June. The clouds of dust and sand raised up by the explosions of the shells, bombs and the rocket shells put much of the gun armament out of action. The anti-tank guns were for the most part destroyed, and the firing points were annihilated. Finnish artillery was all but inactive, the effect of mortar fire was assessed by the guards officers as being 'insignificant'. It was only the Soviet tank crews who recorded any fierce resistance in their combat documents. Hanging over all the Finnish positions was an enormous black–grey–yellow cloud of dust, sand, and earth.

The 190th Guards Rifle Regiment under Lieutenant-Colonel Afanasyev first forced their way into the Finnish trenches and then continued the advance along the highway towards Vyborg. The guard's offensive was so decisive that the artillerymen and supply carts could not keep up with the tanks and infantry. For their breakthrough of the Finnish defences in Beloostrov Afanasyev was awarded the Gold Star of a Hero of the Soviet Union.

The same situation was pervasive in the zone of attack for the 45th Guards Rifle Division, which attacked further to the left. The division's regiment momentarily overcame the Finnish defences. The first to attack from the 134th Guards Regiment was the company's *Komsomol* administrator Company Guards Sergeant-Major Georgiy Filipovich Yashin who was decorated with the Gold Star of a Hero of the Soviet Union for his actions in this battle. The regiments in the 45th Guards Division moved up to 15km crossed the River Sestra and captured the villages of Haapala and Pullinen.

By 0856 hrs the 1st infantry Regiment reported to 10th Division headquarters by radio that the Finnish defences to the north of the road to Beloostrov had been overcome and that they needed help immediately. At 0900 hrs it had become clear to 10th Division Command that the defences of the 1st Rifle Regiment had been overcome across the entire depth of the formation. The telephone lines did not work. The radio communications were poor, since the Soviet radio operators were raising an unbelievable amount of noise on the radio frequencies used by Finnish headquarters. The interception and suppression of enemy radio communications was the responsibility of the 623rd Separate Radio Battalion Special Purpose Detachment (OSNAZ) of the Leningrad Front–this was the precursor of today's Radio-Electronic Warfare (REB) and Radio-Electronic Countermeasures (REP) forces.[2]

The fact that the Finns did not have time to blow the bridge across the Pastorskiy ruchey and the River Sestra is testimony to the chaos that was taking place in the Finnish orders of battle at

2 Translator's note: The OSNAZ abbreviation expands to *Osoboe NAZnachenie* or Special Purpose.

the very height of the fighting. According to Finnish data the circumstances around the Pastorskiy ruchey played out as follows: sappers approached the bridge and prepared to blow it up, but behind the bridge was a 75mm gun manned by crews. The sappers saw that the infantry had begun to walk away to the right and left but not one soldier walked across the bridge to the area behind the Finnish lines. Suddenly Soviet KVs appeared on the road along with assault troops. The guns opened fire and were able to halt the first tank. Suddenly a lieutenant jumped onto the bridge in a dust-covered uniform. He had ran up to the sappers and asked without thinking: "Who are you?" "Mr Lieutenant we are sappers, we have been ordered to blow the bridge." The lieutenant waved his hand in the direction of the Oliumyaki and shouted: "Run! Run as fast as you can!" The Commander of the sapper group under Katay responded that they had to wait for *Fahnrich* Kussi, who would give the order to blow the bridge and the explosives had not yet been connected to the charges. The lieutenant called back "What the hell, can't you not see? There are none of our forces ahead of you? There are Russian tanks a hundred metres from here. Nobody is going to come and give you the order to blow the bridge." With these words the lieutenant himself ran off to get behind the Finnish lines. The sappers exchanged glances and ran after him. The guards captured the bridge intact.

The Soviet perspective with regard to this episode appeared somewhat different. Tanks accompanying the assault troops made up of sappers forced their way in front of the infantry and raced towards the bridge so decisively that the Finnish were not able to blow the fuses. The tank crews and sappers interrupted them and took the demolition specialists prisoner as well as taking the bridge across the River Sestra and Pastroksiy ruchey intact. The Deputy Commander of the 8th Sapper Battalion Senior Lieutenant Mikhail Nikolayevich Raud moreover personally captured two Finnish soldiers.

At 1025 hrs the headquarters of the 10th Infantry Division received a report that the Guards under Simonyak had captured the headquarters of the 1st Infantry Regiment in Olyumyaki.

At 1730 hrs the headquarters of the 10th Division began to destroy the division's barracks and the operational archive and set off from Kauhajoki (near Ilichyovo) to Rayvola (Roshchino). The 25th Chemical Warfare Company who found themselves to their cost at headquarters were given an order to cover the withdrawal to the east from Lake Kauhijarvi (this is now Lake Simaginskoye, Lake Krasavitsa).

By the evening of 10 June the Finnish defence was overcome at a distance of more than 15km behind the lines. An attempt by the Finns to organise a defence along the Sestra River had failed. The broken and demoralised Finnish units hurriedly withdrew back to the "VT line." The Soviet guards claimed they had captured 57 soldiers and one officer. By way of trophies the Guards Corps took 12 guns of different calibres, 11 mortars, and 22 machine guns, as well as 160 rifles, 12 automatic rifles and a large quantity of ammunition.

The Finnish 1st Infantry Regiment, which had taken the brunt of the attack by 30th Guards Rifle Corps, were to count their losses for some time yet. Some of the soldiers in the unit who had been shocked by the force of the Soviet artillery barrage had begun to disperse back on the night of 9–10 June. The assessments of the regiment's losses vary considerably. A trade-off evaluation of the overall losses today is as follows:

- 35 Officers
- 125 *Unter-offizier*
- 665 Privates

These are unprecedentedly high figures for the daily losses of a Finnish infantry regiment over the whole of the five long years of war. They constitute a little less than a third of the nominal strength of the Finnish infantry regiment. The majority of those who vanished without trace had either been captured or remain buried on the battlefield to this day, which over the course of 70 years has turned into a huge *dacha* settlement. As one veteran of the regiment said after the war was over: "We did not receive any order of any kind to retreat. Whoever decided to hold on, remains there to this day."

The 21st Army's losses in the piercing of the main line of the Finnish defence near Beloostrov were relatively light. The losses that they recorded are provided in the table below:[3]

Formation	30th Guards Rifle Corps			97th Rifle Corps			109th Rifle Corps			TOTAL
Division	63rd Gu. RD	45th Gu. RD	64th Gu. RD	178th RD	358th RD	381st RD	72nd RD	109th RD	286th RD	
Killed	45	84	4	7	44	11	24	206	4	429
Wounded	222	361	18	3	152	10	486	376	5	1 624
Missing without trace	–	–	–	–	–	–	–	–	–	–
TOTAL	267	445	22	10	196	21	510	582	9	2 053

As is evident from the table the principal losses were incurred by the Soviet divisions who attacked west of the breakthrough point and closer to the shores of the Gulf of Finland. Finnish officers of the 58th Regiment were able to retain some semblance of order and fought in their own sector. The 109th and 72nd Rifle Divisions had been ordered to finish off the regiment between the Gulf and the railway line to Vyborg in Beloostrov. The 109th Rifle Division's cemetery is located between the railway line from Beloostrov to Sestroretsk and a pill box in the Karelian Fortified District. On the majority of the graves the dates are always the same: 9 and 10 June 1944.

A group of unknown Finnish soldiers from the 58th Regiment, who had occupied a defensive position next to the railway bridge across the River Sestra put up fierce resistance for almost half a day. According to Bychevskiy, the events near the railway bridge across the River Sestra developed as follows:

> There was a hold up at the very start of the battle for the units of the 109th Corps under Major-General I.P. Alferov during the crossing of the River Sestra.
>
> A battle was already into its second hour by the time one of the officers from the Engineering directorate V.P. Andereyev along with the pontoon specialist Gulyanitskiy sent a report that up until that moment they had not been able to start work on the construction of the crib support bridges for the tanks. The deadline that was given was two hours after the start of the battle. The infantry, or to be more accurate, the Finns, are not letting our infantry cross the River Sestra. We, along with the Deputy Pilot M.A. Korol set off to see Gulyanitskiy. The situation there was unsuitable. The regiment on the right flank of the

3 Translator's note: I have employed Gu, RD to denote 'Guards Rifle Division' here for ease of presentation.

109th Division was laid low in the shores of the 10m wide River to a depth of just one metre. A group of brave Finnish soldiers had holed themselves up so well in the folds of the steep sided shoreline and the twists and turns of the river near the railway bridge that it was impossible to reach them using artillery fire. They were firing very accurately using machine guns and mortars and were in no mood to surrender. Gulyanitskiy and the Chief of Staff Kriventsov were becoming concerned. To the right the battle was still going on at a distance, but they were stuck fast.

"Kovalchuk is dead now, comrade General" Gulyanitskiy reported sadly, almost in tears.

"The former intelligence officer? A company Commander?"

"Yes, who was recently awarded his third order. Sergeant Ivanov was died with him. Five of our men were injured.

"How the hell did this happen?"

"He took it upon himself to drive the Finns out of their crevices. The bridge had to be built … Do you remember what happened near Kingisepp? We attacked them with grenades and cut them down with machine gun fire.

"This is the devil's work! So often I learn that our men have been killed and yet a few moment's ago we saw them alive. There is no need to check on them though. To approach or even crawl any closer to the river on the construction site of the two tank bridges and to start to lay down the structures that we brought up is impossible without putting ourselves directly in the path of machine guns to be cut down by fire. Finnish machine gunners and mortar crews found themselves in a particularly precarious situation. They were sitting somewhere right next to a sheer cliff. We were throwing grenades at them and offered them to a chance to surrender on a number of occasions, but they only responded with savage fire.

It took more than half an hour to restore the communications link with the artillerymen of the 72nd Division under Yastrebov, whose weapons were already behind the lines with the Finns who had dug themselves into the shoreline. After dozens of shots nine Finnish soldiers drew themselves up out of the crevices in the shoreline, raising their hands. There they found a further eight dead.

Only after 1400 hrs did the T-34 tanks cross the River Sestra in the 109th Division's sector under General N.A. Trushkin. A further two hours later the heavy, self-propelled artillery crossed again using a different bridge, and then a solid stream of vehicles and artillery from the entire Corps under I.P. Alferov crossed the river. On the evening of 10 June L.A. Govorov, A.A. Kuznetsov, G.F. Odinstov, P.P. Yevstignev and I were at the command post with D.N. Gusev. Reports were coming in from the corps commanders.

Simonyak reported that the 45th and 63rd Guards divisions under Putilov and Shcheglov were already fighting on a boundary formed of the two villages Kekkolovo and Mainila along the Vyborg road.

This meant they were advancing 15km per day! This was half way to the second Finnish line of defence! What's more the 64th Division under Romantsev had not even entered the battle yet. There was no need for them to at present.

The units of the 109th Corps under Major-General I.P. Alferov broke through the defensive line along the coast to a depth of up to 10km.

Dmitiry Nikolayevich informed Govorov that judging by the reports from those captured from the 10th Finnish Infantry Division our advance came as a complete surprise to the enemy. A few days prior to this 10 percent of the soldiers in the companies really had

> been released for agricultural work. Both yesterday's and today's artillery fire along with air strikes had wiped out almost a third of the men. The captured soldiers were "weeded out" of the forests in small groups; the enemy evidently had lost control.

The tank crews who had supported the advance by the 30th Guards Rifle Corps on 10 June 1944 sustained most of their losses from mines. In the 31st Guards Regiment nine combat vehicles had struck mines, but by evening eight of them had been repaired. In the 260th Guards' Regiment on 10 June a mine clearing tank was taken out of action, and seven tanks were destroyed or stranded.

During the front line breakthrough, the tanks did not encounter any fierce resistance, as Finnish reports recorded at the time: "The tanks opened fire on all the firing points that were firing at them." The only obstacle were the Finnish anti-tank mines set between 50–80m from the Finnish trench. This narrow section of the minefield was outside of the Soviet artillery's field of fire. Soviet sappers had not been able to work in this sector in advance of the offensive for obvious reasons, and some of the tanks fell victim to the mines. The terrain once it had been ploughed up by hundreds of tonnes of shells became heavy going even for the KVs.

Vladimir Ivanovich Trunin was a gunner/radio-operator in tank "630" of the 260th Separate Guards Heavy Tank Regiment:

> We had two mine clearing tanks in our regiment, these were KV tanks that had a fitting on the front...with steel cast wheels on an axle, with spurs on. This rotates when the tank is clearing mines and the mines explode, and the mine-clearing device is deployed again, making its racket. That's how it was... Before we could go onto the minefield however the bombers came over a second time. They dropped their bombs again. After they had turned away, they departed. We went straight onto the minefield. That's it. Two mine clearing tanks went in front of us. The width of these tanks was...well our width was 3,200. They would clear an area around four metres wide.

The combat journal of the 30th Guards Rifle Corps also notes that four SV-122 self-propelled guns were destroyed. [This is possibly an error in the document. In the summer 1944 the self-propelled vehicles that fought on the Karelian Isthmus were SU/SU-152s, and SU-76s]. As machine gunner Heimo Peltola, who is still alive today and who served in the 58th Infantry Regiment, recollected:

> It was just so terrible; it is impossible to comprehend the fire power that was there. It was not possible to make out individual shots, there was just a constant din. Add to that the aircraft. They bombed us with impunity, as we did not have an Air Defence System on the battlefield. Whoever came through this and saw it all has endured a great deal of suffering. For me personally this image has resurfaced in my mind's eye many times.
>
> My mate said: "They've got a close-range gun over there, fire at it. They've got more of those guns than we have rifles." The gun fired first. Peltola's ears became choked with sand. "Then it fired again, and all that was left of my mate was the lower half."

Artilleryman Talviheimo recalled:

> The following day, 10 June 1944 was the day of our offensive. By night our reserves did do something but did not see it through to the end. In the morning the flames of war were again burning with renewed vigour, burning body and soul with as much force as the flames of total war could burn in the direction of the main attack. The exhausted soldiers could not take this pressure and cracked. In the shape of a few hours the breakthrough expanded over

a few kilometres both in terms of depth and breadth. We were the first on the altar of the breakthrough since we had ended up on its flanks the previous day.

I awoke at nine in the morning on the plank beds in our dug out, as it was being jolted so violently from the volleys of bombs exploding close by. The dug out was shaking. A feeling of nervous tension had set in during the night's rest, and the awful reality of a new day caught me by surprise, but I soon got myself together and was able to act dispassionately. The artillery joined the barrage and it seemed that their entire 'riches' were raining down right on our heads. A Russian very heavy artillery platoon was firing more accurately than it had the previous day and the shells shook our dug out violently. The artillery reconnaissance scout telephoned below and gave the order to our battalion to open fire. The target was a group of enemy artillery reconnaissance troops who were adjusting the artillery fire that was aimed at us. A heated exchange of words began to the effect that as important as this was, the fire was needed elsewhere. I reported that if we did not take the Russian artillery reconnaissance crews out of the game then we would soon be shooting into the air along with the entire dug out. No sooner had I put an end to this argument, than it rained down on our positions more violently than ever. The outer lining on the hatches in the walls of the dugout hit me in the face and helmet. For a moment I began to black out. All I could think was that I would be thrown off myself somewhere with the bits of wood, stones and sand. My final thought was "That's it!" I had begun to feel some relief. My ordeal however was not over yet. To my surprise I saw that I was in one piece and safe and sound on the other side of the dugout. I saw that Masa Peltola, who had always put his colleagues first, and only then would he think of himself, had thrown some boards into a pile, thinking that I would be buried underneath them. We got into the communications ditch as we could anticipate that the next shells would finish things off and would obliterate our dug out completely. I was delirious from the hit that we had taken and had jumped out of the dug out without taking any weapons with me. I soon lagged behind the others and began to look for them. I thought that they could only get to the front line trench to adjust the artillery fire. At the Observation Post, though I was only semi-conscious, I encountered two soldiers not known to me, a lieutenant and a private. They looked at me in shock but when I explained to them that I had jumped out of a destroyed dug out they understood my situation. The lieutenant noticed that I did not have a weapon and gave me a hand grenade, since he himself understood that the offensive could begin at any moment. Happy with the fact that I was now armed I set off to the trench on the left to approach the end machine gun but did not encounter a soul on the way. A point blank shot from a close-range gun brought me down to earth and I went off in search of my group of artillery reconnaissance men. I looked into our dug out that had been so badly damaged and noticed that my colleagues were sat on the plank beds as though nothing had happened. I also sat down. We could not fight any more. We had no communications. The radio-telephone had been taken out of action, as it had fallen into the communication's ditch. We did not know that we no longer needed any communications since the enemy had broken through the defences and that our firing points had already been captured. At that moment fate began to single out even our small group. A soldier was brought into the dugout who had been blinded from his wounds, and a short time after this we found a soldier who had been heavily wounded in the chest near our dug out, with his last reserves of strength he had crawled up to us. He died when we were administering him first aid. We left this solider who had gone to his eternal rest on the plank beds in the dugout. Someone fell down onto the bottom of the communications ditch alongside us.

The fate of the group alongside us was of concern to our artillery reconnaissance scout, and he ordered me to check up on them. The path was for the most part over open terrain and was a very difficult one given this bombardment. At the beginning of my journey I encountered a strong figure of a Captain who had arrived under cover of darkness, and who had been experiencing problems with his subordinates. Some dead and heavily injured lay on the path and he was surrounded by around five of his colleagues. The Captain tried to explain to them that they needed to hold their positions but two soldiers at the most accompanied the injured soldier. The Captain called out as I passed by: "Have you seen what has happened?" I answered in an upbeat tone of voice that I had seen nothing of the kind and continued on my way. Keeping my ear to the ground I ran across the open terrain. A second later "*six inchers*" whistled through the air and their explosion shook the ground. I jumped into a depression in the ground, which to my misfortune was not very deep. The shrapnel passed over my spine and fell into the river, splashing water over me. In fits and starts I reached the Observation Post codenamed "*Pjare*." It was terrible there, since the barrack building, in which the Observation Post was located on the upper floor, had collapsed. A layer of bricks had covered the entrance to the shelter in such a way that it would have taken me hours to clear it. I began to look to see if there was any other entrance into the dugout and found a window. The dug out was empty. Our group had moved to another dug out without incurring any losses. The enemy very heavy artillery platoon had decided to demolish our dug out, and their shell landed on the roof. The ceiling held but the remains of the brick wall collapsed into the passageway in the dugout, blocking the path. An artillery observer from "*Glaza*" soon passed by and we quickly cleared away the path in the dugout. We noticed that he had a deep wound on his forehead, although he said that it was just a scratch. He only survived because the shell had failed to explode. I followed the artillery reconnaissance scout outside. The artillery fire was not so fierce against us anymore. Enemy infantry were evidently waiting for the ripe fruit to fall at their feet since it was not they who had started the offensive. Close to the road however their infantry were already behind our own lines. Who knows how they ended up there. Who knows how far they had got behind our own lines. The numerous batteries accompanied the infantry with a barrage of fire and were attacking the marsh behind our own lines. Fighters, ground attack aircraft, and bombers that were on their way back from a sortie flew over us. Some of them actually flew right over our heads as they reconnoitred the strongholds and sought out targets. I stood alongside an artillery reconnaissance scout on the roof of the dug out behind "*Glaza*." We could easily be seen from behind. A bomber flew over us at an altitude of a few dozen metres. The navigator looked directly at us. The aircraft shot over us and began to climb. It also began to turn with the engines howling. It soon pulled out at the requisite altitude to fly right over us. We understood what their thinking was and quickly got into the dugout. We saw how a huge bomb separated from the aircraft that had already started to free fall, the delivery address for this bomb was our dug out. For a moment we waited for the end to come but we survived by shear fluke. The bomb exploded next to the dugout but was not able to destroy it. The dug out shook violently and that was it. The enemy's successful breakthrough began to have an effect on the whole coastal defence sector. Owing to the threat of encirclement the 58th Infantry began to withdraw in accordance with the order they had received. The situation was unclear, and the enemy was undertaking local attacks carefully. In many locations their advance only led to them capturing empty trenches, and this was how it happened in our stronghold. The regiment was no longer able to put up any serious resistance since it was at minimal strength and in connection with this our withdrawal from the battle became a fateful one for many. As we were no longer able to slow the enemy advance our group of artillery reconnaissance men ended up with their backs to the ends of the communications trenches on the banks of the River Sestra. Enemy fighters and ground attack aircraft would constantly strafe the trenches along with the infantry who had captured our positions. The cleansing of our communications ditches had begun. Events followed one after the other at lightning speed. As a result our artillery reconnaissance scout was killed, and artilleryman Lavonen was taken prisoner. On the opposite side of the river I saw three soldiers with that same strong figure of a Captain who had remained to cover those withdrawing from the trenches but nobody was coming out of the trenches any more. Enemy artillery reconnaissance scouts, who were adjusting their artillery fire, saw us and the result was a fierce attack on the shore of the river. When this attack was over we withdrew back to the marsh, where I saw just three soldiers while the Captain was nowhere to be seen. I had no strength left anymore and I began to lag behind the others. The result of the fact that we had managed to escape from the enemy was a sudden nervous collapse, an endless tiredness gripped my whole body. I had been taken to the limit and was already prepared to give myself up to the mercy of the conqueror. The instinct of self-preservation however brought me to my feet and I soon came across a heavily injured Senior Sergeant who had been injured in the foot. My strength returned and I ran up to the small group of soldiers whom he had joined. I was given a automatic rifle with a disc shaped magazine from this unknown, deathly, and tired infantry Lieutenant and I felt safer with a good weapon in my hands. A short time after that we left for the edge of the village, which had been captured by the enemy, it is likely that this was Uusi – Alakyla. We turned west again and reached the shores of the River Sestra. The platoon crossed it, with bullets whistling around their ears. Our artilleryman Hanninen, who crossed the Rajajoki with another group, was then injured in the hand by a stray bullet. We passed the heavy artillery batteries and continued on with a Lieutenant-Colonel whom I did not know, and to whom I had to report on the situation on the front line. It was likely that nobody here understood what had happened on the front line and even a small report describing the actual state of play was very valuable. At some location I did not recognise a sentry grabbed my arm and pulled me, and one of my colleagues into a cellar, where doctors stood with syringes in their hands. Their patients were both the injured and the shell shocked. When I saw this I explained to the sentry that although we were dressed in rags we did not need medical assistance. "We are honest soldiers who are looking for our battalion, so we set, off–all the best." Later on I encountered a truck that was from our battalion, and which had brought us to the Kivennapi region, where the majority of our battalion were based. They looked at us there as if we were ghosts. They were all convinced that they had seen the last of us. The battle was over, but the war continued. We would have to come through many more tough tests before we would be able to stop this offensive. The rigid, single-minded leadership and stubborn soldiers were able to put an obstacle in front of this landslide that was destroying everything in its path. What seemed impossible in the midst of a hail of fire and the shocking events on the battlefield, now seemed possible after all.

Corporal Vejkko Kujala of 5th Company, 1st Infantry Regiment arrived on the front line with a company by way of reinforcements on the night of 9–10 June He arrived at a location close to the main road before 0300 hrs on 10 June, the junction of the 1st and 2nd Battalions of the regiment were located there. After 0800 hrs in the morning a messenger came running up to us and informed us that those capable of moving are allowed to pull back. Up until now it is not clear if this was a message from the company, battalion or the regiment. Kujala pulled back to the second trench at Pastorskoe Ruche, where he encountered the Battalion Commander Heikkinnen. The Battalion Commander ordered a defensive position to be taken up on this boundary. Kujala responded saying that to begin with the weapons needed sorting out. Heikkinen agreed and said: "Take up a defensive position a little further on, so that you have a chance to sort out your weaponry." Heikkinen's next phrase shocked the men: "I am going to stay here; I cannot fight any more." Heikkenen had been broken by the load that had been put on his shoulders by the offensive. Kujala asked the Junior Sergeant standing next to him to grab a horse that was walking around the alder bushes not far away. Heikkenen was put on the horse, although he protested: "What are you doing?" Kujala replied: "I am giving you an order, and if we see each other again you will be giving the orders." Heikennen managed to get back behind the lines on horseback ahead of the attacking wave of Soviet guards. By evening he had come to and had again taken up command of the battalion.

Sergeant Viktor Pavlovich Kryukov of the 1,427th Anti-Tank Rifle Battalion observed:

> In evening we were joined by our officer guests from the aviation forces who arrived at our observation post.
>
> For the combat crews of the guns this last element ahead of the offensive of the night of 9–10 June was the toughest test of their physical and moral qualities. They had to drag pre-prepared, combat guns into place in their firing positions. How were guns to be brought into position right under the enemy's nose. It was not possible to use vehicles. For one thing the slightest sound from the engine in the company vehicle and it would destroyed. Apart from that in certain locations the approaches to the firing points were protected by a marsh.
>
> The crews would bring the weaponry up to the firing points using their bare hands. If many of the crews in times past would have preferred to drag the guns during training exercises behind the lines sitting on top of the barrel to act as a counterweight, in a combat environment each of the crews preferred to simply drag the gun since mines were exploding close by all the time and they had to lie low. As a consequence the combat crews manning the guns remembered how much effort it took to move guns in a combat environment, which would be unthinkable under normal conditions. They just found the strength from somewhere.
>
> For a crew the pressure was at its zenith. The artillery observer was constantly looking at his watch to synchronise it with those of the pilots. The last few minutes were ticking away before the start of the offensive.
>
> The attack began. Immediately hundreds of explosions rang out around us from the shells of varying calibres that were shaking the ground. The carefully prepared artillery barrage had begun. I involuntarily opened my mouth so as not to go deaf.
>
> At that same time our aviation had begun to drop their fiery cargo. The first three missed their target and the bombs fell on our own positions.
>
> When the spotter contacted the pilots he was told that by then it was too late and the bombs had been dropped.
>
> The cannonade, without relenting in their fire power, would redirect their guns to the area behind the Finnish lines, and then again onto the enemy's front line. Nothing remained of the edge of the forest that stood in the Finnish defensive lines but roots. The trees would

be completely uprooted by the constant explosions and would actually end up with the roots uppermost.

From their distant positions the enemy would return fire against our own positions, but they did not have such fire power or concentration and in essence they did not do us any damage.

Forty minutes later when the fire from our own artillery had been redirected to behind the enemy's lines, the breakthrough Corps, the infantry regiment and the tanks went on the offensive. At that moment, the enemy's firing points would ring out. The attack was so decisive that the defences were overcome almost at the same time across the entire front. The active enemy firing points were hit at close range by our artillerymen.

Half of our regiment along with the advancing units set off for the town of Terijoke.

Guards Sergeant Major Aleksandra Fyodorovna Kochneva, Commander of the 134th Guards Rifle Regiment, 45th Guards Rifle Division:

> The artillery barrage was such a commotion, it is impossible to describe. Where had they got all those guns from? Such fire power was unleashed on the enemy. Our soldiers thought that the Finns had been on the defensive for three years, which would mean their defences were strong, which was why this hail of fire was rained down upon them. I do not know who could survive a hail of fire like this, it's enough to drive you crazy. The Finns came out from their dug outs, they were all shaking, and they said: "The Russians are firing shed loads at us!" This refereed to the rockets, known as *Andryusha*, that are fired in a volley, they burn everything. This was probably why they decided that we were firing shed loads at them. We took many of them prisoner.

Vasiliy Yakovlevich Tikhonov, 46th Rifle Division:

> By 10 June we had occupied a firing position in the area around Beloostrov. Operations aimed at liberating the Karelian Isthmus had begun. Our observation post was in front of the Sestra River. On 9 June, a two-hour artillery barrage began. The artillery rained down fire on the Finnish firing points that had been identified. This included the "millionaire" pill box that was in our sector. This had to be if not destroyed then at least suppressed. Close-range 152mm guns were moved up for that purpose. It was at this point that our command was crafty in their actions because after that once the artillery had quietened down, nothing actually happened. The day passed; the night passed. On the morning of 10 June our artillery rang out again. I witnessed all this from the Observation Post. There was a lot of enthusiasm and joy at witnessing our fire power. When the infantry went on the attack they encountered almost no resistance. We succeeded in advancing with minimal losses.

Albert Adolfovich Grinberg, the 168th Rifle Division:

> On 9 June in the evening we heard a commotion, the artillery barrage had begun. It was not only the field artillery that had opened fire, but the ships, and the forts, the earth beneath our feet shook. On the morning of 10 June the artillery barrage was repeated, and the offensive began. When we passed the front line there was not a blade of grass left alive, everything had been ploughed up. We passed the second line of defence again without entering into any fighting, the Finns had "dragon's teeth" there, which were solid lumps of granite that had been sunk into the ground to stop tanks. We saw a house that had exploded with walls that

> were two-metres thick. We also encountered defensive lines every two to three kilometres. We could only get through by staying on the road.

The Commander of the 1st Infantry Regiment Lieutenant-Colonel Viljanen later recalled:

> I moved to Novaya Alakyul to the so-called "General Pajari Observation Post.' The whole situation was clearly visible from there: slowly but confidently our infantry withdrew across the entire front; the Russians launched signal flares into the sky.
>
> I had to take the decision. I did not have any reserves left at all, just one single infantry formation. No other reinforcements arrived, not one of my commanders was communicating with me, even though I had sent three liaison officers with a request to whoever was in charge to contact us. The decision on what to do was mine alone.
>
> It would have been self-defeating to try and stop the Russians on the fields at Novaya Alakyul since behind them was an open, rising slope over a distance of more than a kilometre. If I had given the order to occupy a defensive position there nobody would have come out alive.
>
> I decided that events of such magnitude were happening that a few kilometres here and there really did not matter anymore.
>
> I had to take the entire decision myself. My decision was that: to pull back to the next water barrier. That was the River Sestra.
>
> Now, some 20 years later, I have thought about this many times–about what I would do if I found myself in that situation again. I would have taken that self-same decision. There were just no alternatives available.

The overall morale of the Finnish forces, who found themselves under the Soviet offensive in Beloostrov that swept away everything in its path was summed up an anonymous Finnish platoon commander in his research, which centred around the phenomenon of panic in front line units:

> When a soldier comes to after that awful artillery barrage and the air raid in Aleksandrovka and they are able to link these two serious thoughts together cognitively, the first thing that comes into their heads is the futility and the helplessness in this hell on earth. When the soldier sees that his colleagues are deserting the trenches, he does exactly the same thing. One by one they leave their positions and in their wake a short while later comes a huge crowd of soldiers running at speed who do not pay any attention to the machine gun fire, or the artillery fire and run as fast as they can to get behind the lines. They have one aim in mind–to get out of this awful place as fast as they can.
>
> There was no question of any evacuation of the injured and the dead in these conditions. Some 70 years later after the conclusion to these events in the area around the battlefield in Beloostrov and the River Sestra the remains of around 100 Finnish soldiers could not be found. Over the course of the dig that took place from 1991–2015 the remains of just a few dozen men were all that was discovered.

On the morning of 10 June Mannerheim's Headquarters began to react to Stalin's fourth attack. To begin with the Commander had planned to launch a counterattack using the forces of the 4th Corps and to restore the status quo. In the second half of the day however Mannerheim went back on his decision. Units in the 10th Division by that time had already lost the majority of their artillery and had withdrawn back to the north-west in complete disarray. On the recommendation of the Commander of the 4th Corps Laatikainen the order that had been issued by Headquarters was changed. All the Finnish units were to concentrate on the "VT line" and put up a fierce defence.

The breakthrough of the principal Finnish defence line that took place at lightning speed in Beloostrov created a condition in Mannerheim's headquarters that was close to shock. This was the first time in the history of the Finnish Army that it had been dealt such a blow. For the first time a whole Finnish regiment had buckled and fled, leaving their defences to be routed in a matter of minutes. As the German General Erfurt wrote in his diary: "The Marshal's cheeks reddened with shame over the behaviour of this Finnish regiment." Mannerheim himself noted in his memoirs: "The day of 10 June could rightly be called a black day in our military history."

In the first few hours of 10 June Headquarters had alerted a Jager regiment near Vyborg and a tank brigade under Lagus' armoured division in the area around Enso. The Jagers at that point were engaged in construction of the fortifications. The entire personnel returned to their barracks as fast as they could, where they were all issued with ammunition and grenades. The Divisional Commander Lagus' headquarters recalled all the divisional officers from their leave immediately.

The Jager Division had begun to prepare for an enforced march to the area around Kivennal–Lembolovo–Suurimyaki–Vuotjarvi. The objective: to concentrate behind the VT line and to prepare for counterattacks. The distance for this march was around 60km. According to the Combat Journal that has survived from the headquarters of the armoured division, the procedure for the advance was as follows:

> The first to advance at 0415 hrs was the Jager Brigade's Anti-Tank Division.
>
> At 1500 hrs the 2nd Jager Battalion would move off and the advance guard was to stop in Kivennapa.
>
> At 1700 hrs the 5th Jagers were to depart. Behind them at 1900 hrs the 4th Jagers were to move off. Closer to midnight the Jager brigade headquarters would depart, together with the logistics units and the 3rd Jager Battalion.

The armoured brigade moved away to the area around Vuotjarvi–Ipola–and to the south bank of Lake Muolaanjarvi–Ojnol–Kyyrola. To the north of Lake Muolaanjarvi on the road the Jagers and tank crews encountered the first fugitives. All the roads were choked with refugees fleeing the Soviet offensive on carts, on foot, on bicycles, whatever they could get their hands on. In contrast to autumn 1939 when the peaceful population was forced out of the border districts as threats were being exchanged, in 1944 the Finnish population of the Karelian Isthmus had to leave homes that had only recently been built, under a hail of Soviet shells.

Valde Hamalainen described the evacuation of the Kuortan clan from the area around the front line with eloquence. This story could be applied to dozens if not hundreds of families who had returned to their homelands in 1942:

> The Kuortan family, who were peaceful civilians, stood in the courtyard looking unhappy. They asked me straight away if they would have to run away or if they could stay. I ordered them to leave straight away and get as far away as they could as soon there would be nowhere for the civilians to go. They began to cry and make a fuss. They shoved their most precious possessions on a cart, like the sewing machine and sacks of flour, they harnessed the cow to the cart and opened the door of the barn, so the other cattle could scatter. This was how they had to leave the house they had only just built to the mercy of the war. The owner shouted out to us as he left, that we could slaughter the pig. After that the reigns were put on the horses and they too were led away and evacuated. Russian ground attack aircraft whistled in

> the blue sky, and the rumble of artillery was audible on all sides. In one sense their departure was worthy of a theatre.

A short time later the fleeing Finnish units appeared on the road: soldiers, who were in a state of shock as well as whole groups of soldiers, who had fled towards Vyborg with no weapons or equipment, who were telling all manner of frightening stories about the Soviet breakthrough in Beloostrov. In the vicinity of Kyyrola, the Jagers mocked these fugitives with comments such as: "So let's hit them with tanks and sort out the men from the boys." They did not know what awaited them just 72 hours later.

5

11 June: Jager Counter-Attack

11 June became known for the decisive way in which the Soviet breakthrough developed together with the advance to the "VT line," as well as for the arrival of the Jager Brigade from Lagus' Armoured Division. Soviet mobile groups were brought into the battle–these were tank formations with automatic guns on their armour. This did not pass without tragic incidents–a column consisting of a mobile group from the 1st Red Banner Brigade had advanced from Yappilya with the aim of capturing Terijoki. In the consist of this group were the heavy IS-27s of the Separate Guards Tank breakthrough Regiment. Not far from Terijoki the mobile group attacked tanks from the 98th Separate Tank Regiment that operated the brand new T-34-85 tanks (these were T-34s fitted with an anti-aircraft gun). In the heat of battle the tank crews mistook the IS tanks for German "Tigers" and approached them from the flanks, opening fire. Unfortunately, the attack was accurate and effective: one IS caught fire and two were taken out of action. In Terijoki part of the mobile group from the 1st Red Banner Brigade joined units from the 109th Rifle Corps that had been attacking along the shores of the Gulf of Finland from Beloostrov.

The Jager battle took place on that day when they fought the forward units of the 63rd Guards Rifle Division in the area around Polviselka–Matilla (Chaiko). The Jager Brigade was ordered to attack at 0030 hrs on 11 June. Their mission was to advance along the road from Kivennapa–Yappilya, and to reconnoitre the enemy's opposing forces and their numbers. The advance was to begin in the early hours of 11 June.

In the advanced guard of 30th Guards Rifle Corps was the 188th Guards Rifle Regiment under Guards Colonel Vasiliy Fyodorovich Davidenko, who was twice a Cavalier of the Order of Aleksandr Nevskiy. They were supporting a regiment from the 152nd Tank Brigade, 31st Guards Heavy Tank Regiment as well as the self-propelled guns of the 351st Guards Regiment. The obliterated Finnish units withdrew so quickly that by evening on 10 June the guards had lost sight of them. A company of KVs from the 31st Regiment with an automatic rifle and rifle company sitting on their armour were sent forward to reconnoitre the situation along the road from Yappilya to Kivennapa. The guards became embroiled in an engagement with Finnish anti-tank crews and the Jagers to the north of Lake Polviselnjarivai. After destroying the first rear guards the south of Matilla the tank crews descended on the anti-tank defences built to some depth. The Finnish Jagers–the anti-tank rifle brigades arranged their guns on the side of the road at a distance of two kilometres (the Finnish had twelve 75mm RAK-40 and 97mm RAK-38/97 anti-tank guns). They opened fire on the tanks at point blank range, from a distance of between 50–200m.:

> We set the anti-tank guns out as we did, so that the tanks as they advanced forward would not see them, and on the crest of a bend in the road so that they could also fire at the tanks

> from short-range. Three tanks that were sent into the attack along the road were destroyed (one of them caught fire). During the course of the action by the tanks the infantry did not support their efforts, and what is more they lagged behind the tanks, which is why the crew of tank No. 707 that was destroyed ended up being taken prisoner and were shot next to their tank, while the enemy actually removed the radio set from the tank. Our artillery by that time had not yet reached the designated boundary.

Fahnrich Berg, the Commander of the 3rd Launching Platoon, of the 7th Anti-Tank Rifle Battalion Company briefly described the first battle against the KVs of the 31st Guards Heavy Tank Regiment.

> The lead *"Klim"* closed in on us from the crest of a bend in the road. Lance Corporal Jokela, who was the aimer for the nearest anti-tank gun took aim and fired the first shot from a gun that had only just arrived in Vyborg. It ricocheted off. The *Klim* began to turn its gun towards Jokela's gun, since the tank crews had noticed the shoot of flame from the barrel. The Deputy Platoon Commander Sergeant Salmi and his crew lifted the frame of the gun since there was no other way to aim at a tank and ensure that the barrel did not drop down. The *Klim* nevertheless took aim. At that moment Salmi shouted to Jokela that he should be a bit more careful taking aim since it was at this point that we would sort out the men from the boys. There were just a few seconds in it. The shot rang out and scored a bullseye in the middle of the casing below the actual gun itself. The crew, who were thrown back a few metres by the recoil from the gun, returned to their weapon. The tank had been destroyed. One of the tank crew had managed to escape through a hatch in the underside, and opened fire with his machine gun, seriously wounding Sergeant Kirvyavainen, before he was bandaged up by the Jagers. The tank crewman was very surprised that his tank had been destroyed, since he had been told ahead of the offensive that the Finns did not have any guns that would be capable of piercing the armour of a KV tank.

Whilst the Finnish anti-tank crews began to fight their duel with the guards company KVs, the Jager battalions were attempting to continue the offensive. This did not progress well. The 2nd Jagers advanced forward through a dense forest almost as far as the River Lintulanjoki, while the 5th Jager were trapped on the road near a set of electricity power lines and were not able to move forward.

The Jager Brigade commander had not yet returned from his leave and he was replaced by Jager Lieutenant-Colonel Sandstrom. A company of KVs with their crew had appeared on the road at the same moment that Sandstrom and his Chief of Staff Poyhonen were standing on the road and trying to give the order to attack. Both officers had to slice down into a roadside ditch and wait for the Soviet tanks to pass them by. The Jagers and the guards mingled in the forest; the Finnish anti-tank guns began to thump away in the hills. Sandstrom caught one of the Jagers as they ran past and ordered him to make a bee line for Polviselka as soon as possible for some anti-tank grenades; they were not to be found there of course. The *Panzerschreck* and *Panzerfaust* weapons were not to be found there either.

Davidenko's guards and the tank crews regrouped and requested artillery support. At 1915 hrs (according to Finnish documents this was at 1800 hrs) the Soviet artillery barrage began and then came a new attack. Following a 25-minute artillery barrage the guards attacked the Finnish positions. The Jager Brigade began to pull back.

Concerning the withdrawal the 4th battery in the anti-tank battalion, the Jager Brigade was forced to abandon its guns. By way of trophies the regiment under Davidenko captured four anti-tank guns, three "*Komsomolets*" tractors (it was these that the Finns missed the most), as well as a truck that had been taken out of action. According to another Finnish report this battery was destroyed by Soviet tanks.

The Soviet tanks and self-propelled gun crews acknowledged the loss of eight combat vehicles on 11 June. The following officers were killed from the 31st Guards Regiment:

- Tank Commander Guards Lieutenant Anatoliy Sergeyevich Sergeyev
- Driver-Mechanic Guards Lieutenant-Technician Sergey Antonovich Karpov
- Platoon Commander Junior Lieutenant Andrey Petrovich Mikhaylov
- Platoon Commander Lieutenant Boris Alekseyevich Moryakov
- Tank Commander Ananiy Sergeyevich Sergeyev

The 152nd Tank Brigade, which had evidently also incurred losses in battle near Kuutersjelka (judging by the small fragments of the "thirty-fours" that even today can be found on the battlefield) but did not report its losses for 11 June but did report losses of 11 "thirty-fours" in the period from 10–13 June.

At 0215 hrs on 12 June, Jager Colonel Puromaa reported that the Jager Brigade had withdrawn from the battle and had concentrated in the area around Pamppala. The losses for the two Jager battalions over the course of a day of fighting were considerable: 25 killed, 167 injured, and 15 missing without trace, that is to say more than 10 percent of the initial compliment. The Finnish anti-tank crews lost two men killed, and 18 injured.

The fighting near Polvisekla the Jager Brigade lost around 600 bicycle troops and requested a further 800 (the official version says that these were burnt in a store in which they were kept). The brigades also immediately requested German *Panzerschreck* grenade launchers, two each per battalion.

Vasiliy Fyodorovich Davidenko, the Commander of 188th Guards Rifle Regiment remembered this fast paced battle as follows:

> It turned out that we were messing about there with a pill box, the Finns sent an entire battalion of troops against us on bicycles. When we approached this pill box at speed the Finns abandoned their bicycles and ran away. It was true that our Mortar Company Commander did fire into the glade where they were sitting. The Finns were scared and abandoned everything. What do I want to say? If this had happened back in the Finnish war, we would never have seen this, that the Finns would just abandon their bicycles and run off.

6

12–13 June: The VT Line

During the early hours of 12 June, the 30th Guards Corps with the tank crews advanced up to Kivennapa (Pervomayskoye). The guards and tank crews attacked Kivennapa without stopping, after capturing the incomplete long-standing defensive line on Linnanmaki mountain (today this is known as Staraya Krepost). Other units from the 21st Army joined the engagement with the enemy on the "VT line." All the Soviet units noted the presence of the pre-prepared defences with their well-equipped system of anti-tank and anti-personnel obstructions and long-term firing points.

The forward detachment of the 1st Red Banner Tank Brigade reached Kuuterselka at 0600 hrs on 12 June 1944. The detachment immediately entered into some fierce fighting, incurred losses and withdrew. Three T-60 tanks were burnt out, a further two T-60s were taken out of action, and the Finns destroyed another two "thirty-fours." At 1630 hrs the attack was repeated, and this time five IS tanks, as well as three T-34s and three T-60s entered the battle. The attack was again beaten back. Another "thirty-four" was taken out of action, as were two T-60s. Following these battles the 1st Red Banner Brigade withdrew from the battle and took some leave in the area around Puhtolovaya Gora.

During the course of these battles, a T-60 tank crew led by Lieutenant Nikolai Fateyev were burnt in their tank. Twenty years after the war Nikolai's father found the communal grave where his son was buried, and placed a touching epitaph on it–a father's farewell message to his fallen son.

Scenes just like this were repeated across the entire length of the Finnish front, where Soviet units approached the "VT line" and attempted to capture it without stopping. Preparations began to storm the line–this was in the shape of a combat reconnaissance mission, as well as preparing the initial boundaries for the offensive, and deploying the artillery.

On the edge of the Gulf, the 109th Rifle Division in their support of the tank crews in the 185th Regiment and the self-propelled guns of the 1,222nd Regiment approached the "VT line" on the evening of 11 June and attempted to attack the formation of Finnish forces without stopping. At 1400 hrs on 12 June the 381st Rifle and 602nd Red Banner Regiments in the division went on the attack after a short volley of *Katyushas* and an artillery barrage. The 2nd Battalion of the 381st succeeded in reaching the shore of the River Vammeljoki. The 1st Rifle Battalion crossed the river by wading through it and got caught on the bank but found themselves under a hail of fire from Finnish pill boxes. By evening on 12 June units from the 109th Rifle Division managed to clear the bridgehead fortification completely on the eastern side of the river and reached the principal line of defence on the road. The division's losses for 12–13 June were 186 men killed, and 622 injured.

The conclusion was as follows: Combat experience showed that attacking a heavily fortified defensive sector without stopping while the enemy is otherwise engaged causes losses, success is limited." This was what was noted in the Combat Journal of the Division regarding the events of 13 June 1944. It is hard to argue with this assertion.

Following the failure of the first VT line assault, the Commander of the Leningrad Front Colonel-General Govorov decided to transfer the direction of the main attack to the left flank of the 21st Army, closer to the railway line and to the Primorskoye road. The Artillery Commander of the Leningrad Front G.F. Odintsov recalled:

> The Front Line Commander on the evening of 12 June gathered the troop leaders of the 21st Army to a meeting at his Observation Point and announced his decision: he was to transfer the main attack to the Primorskoye road sector, onto the left flank of the 21st Army, and a part of the sector running from Metsjakula to Kuuterselka. This was to transfer the 110th Rifle Corps back into the army line up from the front line reserves and to actually regroup the main body of the artillery.
>
> This was a bold and far-sighted decision, which enabled him to outwit the enemy, and make a sudden attack on their long-standing reinforced concrete defences right where they would least expect it. They only had 24 hrs however to make this happen. In this short time they had to secretly redeploy an enormous amount of artillery to a new area (along the front line), this consisted of 110 battalions, and they also had to select their firing positions for them, identify targets, and carry out a topographical survey. Only if all this were achieved would it be possible to rely on the element of surprise in the attack.
>
> The Front Line Commander set the time for readiness for breaking through the second line of defence as 0700 hrs on 14 June. This deadline was dictated by the unusually difficult conditions for the deployment of artillery and for preparing forces for the attack.
>
> The machine of war gathered pace. I entrusted the Chief of Staff of the Artillery Forces General G.M. Brusseyev to identify targets for the naval artillery, and the headquarters officers were sent to join the 18th Guards and 106th Very Heavy Howitzer Brigades and to the very heavy battalions so that they could be alerted and deployed rapidly to move in the direction of Kuuterselka. I myself left to join the Commander of the Breakthrough Corps N.N. Zhdanov, whose comprehensive range of equipment would probably be the hardest to re-group to a new direction. The Corps Commander by the time we arrived had already marked out the routes for the deployment of each of the brigades, and for each battalion, and had personally familiarised himself with the timescale that had been developed for their commanders. Meanwhile the Chief of Staff of the Corps Colonel Gurevich had already sent a group of commanders to the road junctions where the Corps' units were to pass through …
>
> On the night before 13 June I left the artillery corps headquarters and headed along a country lane to meet the artillery units that were on the move. It was so light that it was possible to read a book. Sporadic artillery fire rang out on the front line. The country lane took us to a road junction. The senior officer at the command post reported: two brigades had passed the junction from the 5th Guards Artillery Division, these were the 17th Guards Artillery and the 95th Guards Howitzers. According to the timescale 30 minutes after that the 71st Light Artillery Brigade from that same division was due to pass by but the lead artillery regiment of the brigade was delayed. It did eventually appear. The Regimental Commander S.P. Milovidov explained: the brigade had been engaging the enemy at close range near Kivennapa, the delay had occurred as they were being withdrawn from the orders of battle.

I spent the majority of the night on the roads. Artillery fire flooded into the area around Metsjakula, Vahansaha, and Kuuterselka. The artillery units marched in an organised fashion, without making a fuss, and for the most part they were keeping to the timetable and observing discipline. There were no queues. At the crossroads and at the forks in the road, as well as at the bridges and on the narrow passes groups of officers met the artillery battalions and showed them where they needed to go next. At the end of their journeys they assigned them to firing positions and observations posts. In order to reduce the amount of time spent on preparing artillery fire the topographical batteries completed a survey of all the firing positions for the batteries as well as the observation posts in advance, set the coordinates for the targets and prepared the map boards for firing.

Late in the evening at the 21st Army's Command Post I received word of problems drawing up the ammunition on carts. This was happening when the plan was to expend 100,00 shells per day! The Head of front line artillery supply General Golubev had to be called to the Command Post; together with the Head of artillery supply for the Army he arranged for a single magazine of shells to be brought up from the front line stores straight to the active units.

On the morning of 13 June General N.N. Zhdanov reported: the artillery corps was ready in the new direction. Only the 40th Separate Battalion, of 305mm mortars had not quite reached their location yet. The delay was caused by the complexities of removing the mortars from their position–they needed a narrow gauge railway line to move around.

The Finnish disposition on the "VT line" was as follows:

- The sector from the Gulf of Finland up to the Leningrad to Vyborg railway line was defended by the Cavalry Brigade using the forces of the Tavast Cavalry and Nyland Dragoon Regiments;
- The sector from the railway line up to Kivannapa was defended by the 3rd Infantry Division using the forces of the 53rd and the 11th infantry Regiments;
- From Kivennapa to Korpiselka the defence was maintained by the 2nd Infantry Division using the forces of the 11th and 7th Infantry Regiments.
- The reserves: These were made up of the extremely shabby 10th Infantry Division that had lost its combat capability east of Vammeljarvi and the Armoured Division that had been divided into the Bjorkman combat group (north of Ahijarvi) and the Puromaa combat group (in the Pamppala district).

The auxiliary forces that had been hurriedly redeployed from Karelia, in the shape of the 3rd Infantry Brigade and the 4th Infantry Division, were still on the approach to us.

"With best wishes for your success in Karelia."

(Churchill to Stalin, 14 June 1944)

7

14 June: Kuuterselka Breakthrough

By the morning of 14 June in this new direction for the main attack everything was ready for the offensive. As it had been close to Beloostrov the artillery of the Leningrad Front had concentrated around 200 to 250 guns of middle and large calibres on a kilometre of the front line. The overall strength of the artillery alignment was 1,700 guns of 76mm calibre, or higher. In the course of two days of continuous work the supply units supporting the artillery had delivered more than 100,000 shells to the various positions.

The artillery barrage against the Finnish positions in Kuuterselka and Metsjakula began at 0800 hrs on 14 June 1944. This barrage lasted for one and a half hours. The Finns at some point had managed to slow the offensive by the 108th Rifle Corps close to the railway line.

At 1130 hrs in the morning the following report was delivered via a messenger from the 1st Battalion, 53rd Infantry Regiment:

> Sometime between 0700–0800 hrs in the morning an especially powerful artillery barrage began against our own district, but this was especially severe against the junction on the right flank, the 1st Company's positions. It was here that the enemy went on the offensive using large numbers of forces and attacked our positions. A Jager platoon was sent forward to assist together with any available headquarters personnel with a rifle in their hands but the enemy outflanked them in the area around my Command Post, where the entire battalion headquarters personnel are still heading into battle with a rifle in their hands. Behind the battalion's lines all the logistics personnel were told to get hold of a weapon and take up defensive positions. On the left flank an urgent call was put out for reserves but I could not make them available. At the moment it seems like the 2nd Company and the left flank of the 1st Company could hold on (communication with them has been lost). The enemy has got tanks. The situation is <u>very serious</u>, and we <u>urgently</u> require immediate assistance.
>
> Major Jahnukainen, 1000 hrs, 14 June 1944.

The towering height 98.6 in Kuuterselka was stormed by the 286th and 72nd Rifle divisions. The 286th Rifle Division adopted a three echelon formation. The first to attack the Finnish defences according to combat order No. 0031 was to have been the 994th Rifle Regiment supported by the 98th Separate Tank Regiment. In the second echelon were the 996th and 998th Rifle Regiments that were ready to build on the success of the plan.

The attack commenced at 0930 hrs. Following the end of the artillery barrage Soviet targets supported by the "thirty-fours" of the 98th and 185th Separate Tank Regiments and the SU-76s of the 1,222nd Novgorod Self-Propelled Artillery Regiment went on the attack. The armoured technology immediately came to a halt in front of the anti-tank dragon's teeth. The sappers were no longer able to clear paths through them quickly enough. The driver-mechanics began to look for ways to get around them. Finnish soldiers jumped out of their concrete shelters and opened fire furiously on the Soviet riflemen using all their weapons. The companies laid low in front of the barbed wire. It seemed that the scenes that had played out in the Winter War of 1939, when the infantry had not been able to advance on the Mannerheim line, and the Finns burnt out tanks deep inside their own defensive lines, would be repeated.

On the left flank the problems were exacerbated by the unusual behaviour of the Commander of the 994th Rifle Regiment. What actually happened remains a mystery but at the very height of the artillery barrage Lieutenant-Colonel V.K. Menkov left the Command Post with a radio and his orderly! The Corps' Command stripped him of his command of the regiment, and he was replaced by Chief of Staff Major F.T. Konev.

Times changed, however. The twenty-four year old Major Konev acted sensibly and with enthusiasm. The forward air controllers who were at the 286th Rifle Division's Command Post immediately called in an air strike by ground attack aircraft. An hour later, according to the testimony of surviving Finnish soldiers, "it grew dark with the numbers of Soviet aircraft" in the skies. The Finnish defensive structures could be seen clearly from the air and waves of Il-2s, line astern, attacked the heads of the Finnish infantry with rockets and bombs. The ground attack aircraft loitered in the skies constantly, not affording the Finns an opportunity to even raise their heads.

The 277th Ground Attack Air Division flew 361 sorties that day, and the main target were the Finnish defensive lines in Kuukerselka. The ground attack aircraft spent 378 hrs and 26 mins in the air. The division's combat aircraft operated in groups of between four to twenty aircraft. The intensity of this combat was such that the pilots did not leave their cockpits –after they landed the ground crew would fuel the Il-2s, load the guns, and would bring food for the pilot and gunner in their cockpits and the "flying tank" would taxi out again to take-off. The division's losses for the day amounted to just two aircraft, which were shot down by Finnish small-calibre anti-aircraft fire. According to Soviet claims seven air battles took place in the air over the Isthmus, in which the Finns shot down 18 Soviet aircraft for the loss of one *Messerschmitt*"(aircraft No. Mt-414).

As a result of the attack, Soviet by ground attack aircraft fire from the Finnish side diminished significantly, the Finns laid low or hid in their shelters. Taking advantage of this the gunners of the 994th Regiment went on the attack. After overcoming the barbed wire fence using raincoats, greatcoats, and jackets the infantrymen overcame this barrier and tore into the Finnish trenches. All the veterans of the 286th Division recalled Private Korablin, who had captivated them with his example. He was the first to run up to the barbed wire fence and began to cut it but heroically perished in the attempt. Vladimir Vasilyevich Korablin was posthumously awarded the title of Hero of the Soviet Union.

At 1045 hrs, the 1st Rifle Battalion. 994th Regiment broke through to the Finnish trenches. By 1110 hrs the 2nd Rifle Battalion had partially overcome the wire fences. The 3rd Battalion under Major Mikhail Ivanovich Lel, which had not been able to get through the wire barrier, incurred especially high losses. "All that was left was the absolute minimum" was how the situation was recorded in the regiment's combat yearbook. The Medical and Sanitary Division was not able to cope with the flow of injured, the heaviest losses were incurred by the 994th Regiment trying to cross the barber wire fence. The tank crews of the 98th Regiment on that day lost two tanks, which had been blown up by mines, and another three, destroyed by artillery. The first to pass through the dragon's teeth was the platoon led by Lieutenant Pyotr Grigoryevich Shevchenko.

The 72nd Rifle Division advanced to the right, the 133rd Rifle Regiment under Major Pyotr Yakovlevich Koleukho was not able to overcome the Finnish defences either on their first attempt. Ground attack aircraft and artillerymen inflicted another blow on the Finnish positions. The sappers of the 8th Engineering and Sapper Battalion–Sergeants Badayev and Sergeant Major Chyornykh were able to draw up to the dragon's teeth and blow a path through them using explosives for the tanks. The "thirty-four" under Company Commander Senior Lieutenant Vasilyev of the 185th Separate Tank Regiment (bearing the tactical number 958) was able to get through the dragon's teeth. Inspired by the success of the tank crews, the infantry moved forward and broke through the Finnish trenches.

Soviet journalists travelled to the area that was in the direction of the main attack. Lukinitskiy in his book "Leningrad In Action" described the capture of Kuuterselka as follows:

> Suddenly everyone saw a single tank that had broken through the dragon's teeth. Clawing, lumbering, and plunging downwards every now and again it crawled through the dragon's teeth. This was tank No. 958 under the command of Senior Lieutenant Vasilyev, who had taken advantage of the destruction of several of the dragon's teeth to look for a narrow, winding, path through them that only he could see. At that moment, the radio broadcast the third report: "I have found a path through, I am taking the path, follow me, order the infantry to attack."

The 187th Rifle Regiment, led by Major Yevgeniy Aleksandrovich Ryabkov, which had attacked from the direction of the marsh, was more successful. The artillerymen of the 16th Separate Anti-Tank Rifle Brigade who had beaten a log path through the marsh that was approximately eight kilometres long had brought their guns right up almost to the line of dragon's teeth itself. In the course of the attack they opened fire with such intensity and at close-range that the attack battalion of the 187th Regiment were able to break through to the Finnish stronghold straight away.

All the Soviet sources noted how fierce the resistance of the Finns had been, as they did the obvious Soviet advantage. Information in the Finnish archives on the battle is patchy and testifies to the difficult position that their 53rd Regiment found themselves in. The Regiment's Combat Journal was typewritten after the battle. From the dry entries the fact that the headquarters had gradually lost control over the situation on the battlefield is self-evident.

Luknitskiy described the overall sequence of events as follows:

> On foot..to the hill, on to the forest. A white house–with nobody in it. Onwards to the forest, and ahead of Kuterselka there are barracks–vehicles, people. A Command Post from the 72nd Rifle Division was found (this division was commanded by Major-General Yastrebov). Sentries. In the doorway stood a grizzled, dishevelled, unshaven colonel, his eyes bloodshot from a lack of sleep, he was fatigued beyond his limits. We asked him to give an update.
>
> "We are correspondents–"*Pravda*," *TASS*, "*Leningradskaya Pravda*!"
>
> "I can't, there is too much going on at the moment."
>
> "We just need 10 minutes …"
>
> "Okay, a little later on. If you are in agreement, you can have your 10 minutes but with interruptions…"
>
> From behind the colonel a ginger, tall, freckled figure in a greatcoat without epaulettes and without a peaked cap, and with a face that looked at first glance like he was drunk–in fact he was "intoxicated" from tiredness–wallowed out and said to us:
>
> "Were you coming to speak to me first?"

"And who might you be?" asked Lanskoy.

"I am Colonel Sibirtsev. Chief of Staff of the tank regiment. The regiment is fighting at the moment. You would be interested in that!"

Things became a little brighter for us, we went after him, he was leading us into the forest. A few fox holes, a raincoat under the pine trees, this was a small *dachka* in a few seconds flat, alongside was a working radio lying on the ground, and a couple of tank commanders were sitting around. This was the Command Post of the 185th Separate Tank Regiment, which was commanded by Lieutenant-Colonel Yunatskiy.

Then, in what was an exceptional explanation, which was intelligent, clear, and carried with it an understanding of the essence of what we needed, and in a rational, and comprehensive way using a large-scale combat map with the situation as it stood drawn on it, Chief of Staff of the regiment Serafim Mikhaylovich Sibirtsev told us about the battle for Kuterselka, which had been underway since dawn, and of the actions of this regiment, which consisted of T-34 tanks.

The battle is at its' zenith. Our forces are forging a strong path through the enemy's defences. This path starts at the Gulf of Finland, crosses the Karelian Isthmus, and continues to the north-east. The left flank of this path is the important stronghold of Metsakulja–and from there it runs into the gulf.

One of the most powerful of the successive strongholds in this line is the natural boundary and village of Kuterselka deep within the Isthmus.

The fortifications in Kuterselka are falling one after another. The efforts of the tank crews, who are acting in conjunction with the infantry, are highlighted here on this map in front of us, which was lying among the raincoats stretched out under a pine tree. S.M. Sibirtsev, who was receiving minute-by-minute reports from the radio-operators in the active tank platoons, was drawing lines with a red pencil that were cutting further and further into the square highlighting the area around the village of Kuterselka, on the edge of which we ourselves were standing. Above our heads ground attack aircraft were on the attack, diving, and air battles were taking place. All manner of guns were rumbling around the forest, and the chatter of the machine guns and the din of the bombs affected your ears so much that you had to introduce breaks into the conversation, and shout so as to make yourself heard.

The regiment's tanks crossed the Finnish lines without incurring losses, not one tank was lost, which is an astonishing success. We laid down on our stomachs onto the raincoats around the edges of the map, making our notes, and stopping every now and again to glance up at a manoeuvre of some sort in an air battle over our heads. I notice a *Messerschmitt* giving a long burst of fire, a white trail streaked out in front of the aircraft–tracer bullets.

After we had made our notes, and since we were afraid of missing that Colonel, we tore ourselves away from Sibirtsev. After promising we would be back we went to the 72nd Division's Command Post. Colonel Khikmat Zaynutdinovich Khakimov, who was a Tatar, and a kind, gentle and sincere person, and who was completely exhausted by the continuous–several days–of combat operations, still found it possible to talk. This was not just for 10 minutes either but for a whole hour and a half since in between saying a few sentences to us Khakimov was receiving and issuing orders: at this time the division was in the thick of the battle. A report came in that Lagus' fascist *Panzer* division had been sent into attack this division and was drawing closer to Kuterselka from Liykola.

German tanks had appeared to the east of Onka-Jarva… Colonel Sibirstev came in and said:

> "So they are already a kilometre past Liykola ... Well, in any case, we are ready aren't we?"
>
> "Our neighbouring troops are defending Mustamjaki ..."
>
> The usual feverish combat activity was prevalent at headquarters.
>
> We go to Mainila and look for the operations department. Finnish shells are falling. The black clouds of combat are again rising up two kilometres from us. Here though the sappers are busy building a bridge across the river. Our car is waiting for us.

After crossing the VT line, the 72nd Division, the tank crews of the 185th Regiment and the self-propelled gun crews of the 1,222nd Regiment continued their progress north towards Liykola. At 1400 hrs the Commander of the 72nd Division Colonel Yastrebov introduced his reserves into the battle–the 14th Rifle Regiment.

The Finns had to restore the status quo as soon as possible, but the forces in the area around the breakthrough were woefully insufficient for a powerful counterattack. The Commander of the 3rd Infantry Division, the hero of the breakthrough at Tolvajarvi in 1939 Major-General Pajarvi introduced his weak reserves into the battle in the shape of the 13th Separate Infantry Battalion and the 48th Infantry Regiment. This was futile. They would not be able to restore the status quo. The Finnish attack group–Lagus' armoured division–was concentrated to the north of Kivennapa. They had to march a distance of around 20km up to the location of the breakthrough in Kuterselka.

Between the Commander of the Armoured Division Ruben Lagus and the Commander of the 2nd Division Martola a dispute broke out over the scale of the attack alignment. According to the Combat Journal covering the actions of the armoured division, Lagus' position was as follows:

> It would be absolutely reckless to send that sort of a mass of armoured technology and Jagers to the Kuterselka road. When the enemy sees [from the air–author's note] a column more than 20km in length on the march, they will immediately attack close to the main road between Sahakyla–Metsjakulja. Then the entire combat group at Puromaa and the 3rd Division would be surrounded.

Lagus also thought that if all his tanks were burnt out on the ground from aerial bombing then there would be no more tanks left across the whole of Finland. As a result the Finnish military leaders accepted a compromise. The Jager brigade would be deployed as part of the counterattack as well as a battalion of attack guns with units acting as reinforcements.

The Puromaa Combat Group that consisted of the Jager brigade (the 2nd, 3rd, 4th Jager Battalions), as well as a battalion of attack guns, batteries of self-propelled anti-aircraft gun known as "Antti-Landswerk" and the 14th Separate Heavy Battalion moved forward from Kivennapa in the second half of the day on 14 June 1944. From the anti-tank rifle battalions it was only the firing platoon under *Fahnrich* Berg (with two guns) that became part of the combat group. The Jager Brigade again marched on their bicycles.

By 2200 hrs on 14 June 1944 the combat group under Puromaa had concentrated south of the village of Liikola (Tsvelodubovo). The area around Liikola was permanently at the mercy of Soviet aircraft and artillery:

> When the head of the 3rd Jagers' column reached the edge, the crossroads at Liykola was completely covered in smoke and dust. In this cloud the flames from explosions were clearly visible, trees had been broken like matchsticks, their crowns picked up by the blast waves and thrown into a field. Despite this the Jagers continued their advance to the concentration area along the ditches and along the road itself.

During the course of one of the raids on Liikola the Commander of the 53rd Regiment Lieutenant-Colonel Ravil was covered in sand in a crater after a bomb had exploded nearby, but the men who came to his aid managed to dig him out unharmed. It was here in the area around Liikola that the battalion of attack guns were given their combat orders:

The 1st Battery was attached to the 4th Jager Battalion and is to attack along both sides of the road. Their mission is to advance onto the fields around the village of Kuuterselka after which they are to immediately continue the offensive and reach the "VT line.":

The 3rd Battery, consisting of a single launching platoon (under Myulyumaa) was attached to the 3rd Jager Battalion and is to support the offensive along a path through the woods from Liykola up to Myulyu-oj. The rest of the platoons in the battery were to remain in the concentration area and prepare to take the place of the 1st Battery on the front line (it later emerged that the path was impassable for tracked vehicles, as a result of which the launching platoon under Myulyuma remained where they were).

The 2nd Battery in the battalion was to move westwards and cover the right flank of the combat group to the shore of Lake Vammeljoki. Zero hour was set at 2345 hrs.

The Finnish artillery alignment that was to have supported the counteroffensive (this was the artillery group under "*Nuoli*" ("*Strela*") after the surname of the Group Commander Major Nuolimaa), on paper represented a powerful force:

The 3rd Battalion, 16th Field Artillery Regiment comprising twelve 1917 model 152,m French howitzers (C 17 S), the Commander was Major Hallonblad;

The 18th Separate Heavy Division, eleven 1917 model Soviet 152mm howitzers (C 17 S), the Commander was Major Meter;

The 2nd Battalion, 8th Field Artillery Regiment, twelve 1917 model 152mm French howitzers (C 17 S), the Commander was Major Kallio;

The 14th Separate Artillery Battalion, twelve 1940 model 150mm German howitzers (15cm sFH 18), the Commander was Major Nuolimaa.

Subsequently the Light Artillery Battalion under Major Lempianen. However in fact the artillery group was blind and helpless. There was a catastrophic shortage of shells, the 14th Separate Battalion were forced to send trucks to Vyborg to collect shells (this is a distance of some 60km–author's note), and in conditions in which all the roads were thick with refugees, and ammunition deliveries were very delayed. The radio sets that the artillery reconnaissance scouts were using absolutely refused to work by night "due to the stress of weather." The cable link would momentarily fail under intense fire from Soviet artillery.

Soviet reconnaissance intercepted Finnish radiograms on the advance of Lagus' armoured division to the breakthrough area. All the front line units were informed about the counterattack that was being prepared.

According to all the Soviet sources and the testimony of Lunitskiy, and evidence provided by prisoners of war and other documents, the Soviet Command knew of the advance of Lagus Division from Kivennapa for the counterattack.

The Command of the 109th Corps undertook energetic countermeasures. In order to level the numbers of the Finnish tank attack the powerful armoured tank alignment had advanced to the area around Raivola to Kuuterselka by evening on 14 June:

- A company of tanks from the 98th Separate Tank Regiment (T-34-85s, no information is available concerning the numbers of tanks);
- The 31st Guards Separate Heavy Tank Breakthrough Regiment (11 KV and KV-1s vehicles);

- A company of IS-2 tanks (five vehicles) from the 27th Guards Tank Regiment under the command Guards Senior Lieutenant Usenko. These five Is tanks were in the mobile group under the 1st Red Banner Brigade and had already departed towards the area around Mustamjaki, but at around 2000 hrs they received an order to return to Kuuterselka and to be ready to beat back the Finnish counterattacks.

Evening fell and a calm descended on the front. Soviet gunners and tank crews were at rest in the forest near the road approximately three kilometres south of Liykola. The battle had died down. The tank crews of the 185th Separate Regiment, who had not left their combat vehicles for four days decided to take some rest away from their tanks for a while. The "thirty-fours" became empty. Any fighting with the scattered units of the 53rd Infantry Regiment had ceased. By all accounts, the commander of the 14th Regiment Lieutenant-Colonel Korolyov posted a small armed guard on the road, but the majority of the regiment were at rest.

It poured rain throughout 14 June; the temperature was cool. Twilight came. In the fields and in the forest a mist set in. The silence of this white night however was misleading. The Jagers and the attack guns had advanced up to their starting positions by 2320 hrs. At 2330 hrs eleven Finnish Ju-88 bombers from the 44th Air Regiment carried out a dive-bombing raid on Soviet units south of Kuuterselka. In total the Finnish pilots dropped 12,500kg of bombs (these amounted to seven high-explosive bombs of 500kg, as well as thirty-five 250kg high-explosive bombs).

The order for the remaining the bombers in the 4th Air Regiment to carry out a combat sortie is as follows:

> 2300 hrs 14 June 1944
> A night bombing raid:
> 2325–30 hrs 11 Blenheims, 2335–2340 hrs three Dorniers, three Blenheims, three DBs and two Il-4s, 2350 hrs four Blenheims. The target for all these aircraft was to be Kuuterselka.
> The approach to the target for all these aircraft was as follows: Kostelka–Kuuterselka and then a right turn, and a departure to the north before reaching Mustamjaki. Bombing is to be conducted, depending on cloud cover, from as high an altitude as possible.

The second group of bombers from the 4th Air Regiment dropped 17,600kg of bombs (these amounted to ten 250kg high-explosive bombs, eighty-four 50kg bombs, and eighty-six 12.5kg high-explosive and fragmentation bombs).

The artillery group under Nuolimaa carried out a 15-minute artillery barrage on Soviet units using four battalions. As the participants in the attack would later caustically remark from the Finnish side they did not even notice their artillery strike. Finnish self-propelled artillery crews only learnt of the aerial support after the war from books. Soviet officers on the other hand describe a "powerful" Finnish artillery barrage.

Cautious Finnish officers in the self-propelled artillery "divided" a battery of attack guns into sections. Of the 29 self-propelled guns that the battalion had at their disposal only seven vehicles from the 1st Battery actually went into battle.

At 2320 hrs the Finnish attack group consisting of the 4th Jager Battalion and the first battery passed the orders of battle for the 2nd Jagers, who had been laying low in the forest and quickly dug in.

At 2345 hrs Finnish artillery conducted another minute long artillery barrage, and the Jager Brigade went on the attack.

Soviet information concerning the battle in the forest is very patchy and meagre, and therefore the account that follows depicts the battle from the Finnish perspective. The attack guns advanced along the road from Liykola–Kuuterselka in a column, covering each other. The 4th Jagers advanced with them in the forest on both sides, and at some distance from the road. The vehicle in front was a self-propelled gun with the identification code Ps 531-19. The Commander was Lieutenant Sartio, a year prior to this he had returned from serving in the Finnish Volunteer Battalion of the *SS*. The driver-mechanic Corporal Olof Lagus, was the son of the Commander of the Armoured Tank Division. The crews of these self-propelled guns communicated with the 4th Jagers by radio via a signals officer, who would travel with the Jagers to the selected target. The Jagers and the self-propelled guns had gone about a kilometre without encountering any Soviet troops. Then a machine gun opened up against the Finns from a ditch on the opposite side of the road. The lead Finnish self-propelled gun quickly suppressed this fire. After that the Finns destroyed a Soviet anti-tank gun on the road. The lead StuG emerged onto a hillock and almost collided with a "thirty-four" standing on the road. From the turret that was askew and the dropping gun the Finns decided that the tank had been taken out of action in the preceding battle. The signals officer even reported this by radio across the Jager communications links. The first battery continued their cautious advance along the road. One of the self-propelled guns was advancing slightly ahead of the rest, while the three others were some distance behind, keeping the left and right sides of the road in their sights.

After moving forward some 50m, Lieutenant Sartio suddenly saw a Soviet T-34 on the roadside. The StuG moved round sharply through 90° and the first shell that Lagus fired at point-blank range set fire to a "thirty four." After that Sartio turned the vehicle's gun rapidly back to its stowed position. The burning tank lit up the twilight of a white night. The Finns noticed movement off to the right of the road. There in a small spruce forest stood a group of several T-34s. The Finns opened fire rapidly on the Soviet tanks. The gunner of the lead tank Olof Lagus claimed another two tanks for his tally. Two "thirty-fours" laid low and tried to escape from the battlefield but were destroyed by the Finns on the road. The first was destroyed by Lagus, and the second by the self-propelled gun with the identification number Ps. 531-3 commanded by Senior Sergeant Huhutainen, the gunner was Corporal Savela. By all accounts, the tank crews under Yunatskiy succeeded in firing just one or two shots in response and took the gun of self-propelled artillery vehicle Ps. 531-3 out of action. The result of the first engagement in combat involving the Finnish self-propelled guns of the 185th regiment, according to Finnish data was: Lagus–four tanks; Savela–two tanks.

One of those killed in the "thirty-fours" serving with the 185th Regiment was Vasiliy Terentyevich Vasilyev, who was a Company Commander from just outside Tula. According to Lunitskiy's information, his tank with the identification code 958 was the first to pass through the dragon's teeth defences in Kuuterselka. A front line photo-journalist had published a photo of him and his tank crew on the Primorskoye road at Terioki (Zelyonogorsk) in the daylight of 12 June 1944. The tank crews of the 185th Regiment had been constantly engaged in combat for four days and had not left their tanks–from the moment the tanks had gone into battle across the Rzhavaya kanava on the morning of 10 June. Unsurprisingly the tank crews were not able to mount any kind of a sufficient resistance against the Finnish self-propelled guns.

Hyytiainen recalled this short battle as follows:

> I managed to stop another "thirty-four," which was standing some distance away. The Russian tank did not catch fire but did not move any further. For some reason Corporal Savela did not record this victory. The enemy though had begun to wake up. A shell hit us, and the gun was taken out of action. The barrel was almost broken in half. Our "*Strumy*" was mobile but could no longer play any further part in the battle.

At that moment, the semi-automatic aiming system failed on Lieutenant Sartio's tank. The crew jumped out of the tank, inspected the fault and reported it to Command. Captain Kvikant ordered the unserviceable self-propelled guns to get back behind the lines and ordered a platoon of self-propelled guns under Lieutenant Aulanko onto the battlefield. As the self-propelled guns swapped places on the battlefield, the gearbox on Sergeant Nertamo's self-propelled gun (Ps. 531-4) was damaged. Aulanko also had to transfer to self-propelled gun Ps. 531-6 since on his "own" vehicle Ps. 531-5 the electric cables had been destroyed.

A few hundred metres beyond, his vehicle came face to face with a Soviet Su-76 of the 1,222nd Novgorod Regiment (the Finns mistook this for an ISU-152). Corporal Taponen's gunner fired first, and the SU-76 burst into flames. After that the Finnish self-propelled guns overwhelmed a battery from the 199th Anti-Tank Battalion, 72nd Division, which was standing on the road in a tactical formation. The Soviet artillerymen were not able to open fire and dispersed.

Finnish self-propelled guns continued their progress towards Kuuterselka. On the left flank a Soviet "thirty-four" appeared and opened fire but did not hit us. Taponen even destroyed this tank. The next moment a further "thirty-four" caught Aulanko's self-propelled gun in its sights. The Soviet shell hit the upper right hand front plate on the conning tower and broke through the armour. The shrapnel from the shell and the armour decapitated gun loader Paavo Havu. Taponen described this moment in the battle as follows: "Driver-mechanic Pentti Leppjakoski pulled the right hand lever towards him, and I pressed the gun's hand trigger. The gun did work momentarily, and the Russians again found themselves one tank down. Havu saved us all. He loaded the gun a moment before he died." Aulanko ordered the driver-mechanic to take the body of the deceased loader to the field dressing station and carry on with a new loader. Aulanko himself together with Taponen jumped out of their self-propelled gun and continued the advance on foot.

At 2330 hrs Major Okerman ordered the third battery in the battalion to advance to the concentration point and await orders. The 3rd Battery under Captain Kvikanta had by 0130 hrs on 15 June caught up with the 4th Jagers on the approaches to the fields around Kuuterselka.

At 0130 hrs Finnish self-propelled guns had advanced onto these fields. The lead vehicle was Kvikant's vehicle Ps.531-29, behind this was Ps.531-5 under Sergeant Ilmarli Koskiniemi, and then Ps.531-7 commanded by Sergeant Eino Vartina. The gunner in Koskiniemi's crew suffered a nervous breakdown, he jumped out of the self-propelled gun and ran back behind the lines. Koskiniemi noticed Corporal Taponen on the side of the road without a vehicle and took him on as gunner in his *pyatyorka*.[1]

The *semyorkas* were now leading this order of battle. The gunner Corporal Lauri Leppjanen was not aware of this, since he had not heard the radio conversations that the Commander of the self-propelled guns had entertained. Suddenly a "thirty-four" rushed out onto the road and attempted to leave the battlefield. Vartia issued an order to open fire. Lepjannen recalls this moment: "I asked, maybe this tank was one of ours? - "No this is a Russian tank, fire!" answered Vartia. I fired and hit the tank's engine compartment. The distance to the target was approximately 150m. The tank caught fire, black smoke rose up, and the fire lit up the local terrain."

Following this, the *semyorka* set fire to another "thirty-four" and managed to destroy a KV tank. This heavy Soviet tank did not catch fire but was no longer able to move and took no further part in the battle. Just ahead of the fields on the side of the road was a heavy Soviet tank. It was not firing, possibly because the crew had abandoned the vehicle. The Finnish self-propelled guns fired in unison and the tank caught fire. As they drew closer to this tank the Finns identified it as an

1 Translator's note: Here *Pyatyorka*, which literally translates as "fiver", refers to the designation for the type of self-propelled gun.

IS-2. As they advanced onto the fields the Finnish self-propelled guns turned onto a line to the left of the road.

Finnish self-propelled guns claimed they had destroyed up to nine T-34-76 tanks; Major Yunatskiy elected tactfully to remain silent about his losses in the course of this battle. Soviet guard's tank crews noted that at the time the heavy KVs and IS-2s had gone into battle Yunatskiy only had two combat capable tanks left. By all accounts, these two "thirty-fours" chose to abandon the battlefield and headed in the direction of Rayvola.

Finnish artillerymen meanwhile were taking desperate measures to set things up for the artillery spotters. The 2nd Battery, 14th Separate Heavy Battalion was to be supported by the 3rd Jager Battalion. The Battery Commander Lieutenant Oker-Blom was forced to travel to the front line on a motorbike and verbally reach agreement with the Commander of the 3rd Jager Battalion on where he was supposed to direct his attack. There was no other communication between them. The 14th Separate Battalion was responsible for adjusting the artillery fire for the whole of the artillery group. The divisional signal's officer Lieutenant Vuorinen travelled to the front line on motorbike again to establish communication. In the area around the crossroads at Liykopa he was observed by Soviet ground attack aircraft and was shot by strafing from their guns.

Lieutenant Similia, the Commander of the 1st Battery, 14th Battalion, adjusted the artillery fire from a self-propelled gun. He had the only working radio set and it was Major Hallonblad in his crew who received his radiograms for him. In the semi-darkness of a white night Simila opened the hatch so as to discern the target more clearly. A mine exploded on the armour of the self-propelled gun and Similia sustained around a hundred wounds in his side from shrapnel. After that the Finnish artillery fell silent completely since they had lost their "eyes" on the front line. Over the entire course of the battle for Kuuterselka the Finnish artillery had fired 1,981 shells.

A fierce battle raged in the forest though between the Jagers and the gunners of the 14th Regiment under Lieutenant-Colonel Korolyov. According to the memoirs of the Finnish veterans, the 4th Jager Battalion went on the attack with a battle cry that was more reminiscent of the battle cry of the barbarians or the cries of wild animals. As one veteran of the 2nd Jagers recalled: "I have never heard such awful swearing in my entire life."

The strength of the Jager attack discouraged the wearied and depleted ranks of Soviet gunners. A thick fog descended on the forest, and the Finnish and enemy lines could no longer be discerned, it was impossible to see where the hand grenades were falling. In the chaos of the constant chatter of the machine guns, shouts in Russian and in Finnish, as well as the orders of battle for the 14th Rifle Regiment and the Jager Brigade mingled with each other. The Regimental Commander Lieutenant-Colonel Vasiliy Ivanovich Korolyov was injured in the leg, according to the entry on his commendation list he did not abandon the battlefield (according to other sources he did leave the battlefield). He was replaced by Deputy Regimental Front Line Troop Commander Major Mikhail Stepanovich Komlev. Major Sergey Fyodorovich Lavrentyev, who was one of the battalion commanders was killed, and many other officers were injured. The regimental command had been destroyed, and a chaotic retreat began.

The majority of gunners in the 14th Regiment withdrew in disarray to the fields around the village Kuuterselka. Some of the troops took up a circular defensive position and continued to diverge away from the Finnish Jagers that were advancing forwards. A small number of soldiers were captured. In the words of those who survived the battle with the Jagers there were young conscripts amongst those taken prisoner, as well as seasoned veterans. They were all shocked at the ferocity of the Finnish counterattack.

According to the testimony of tank crews from the 31st Guards Regiment the headquarters of the 72nd Rifle Division lost its command and hurriedly retreated back to Rayvola. The artillerymen of the division together with the Commander of the 211th Mortar Regiment that was attached to it, Lieutenant-Colonel Georgiy Mikhaylovich Shepelev had to stop the runaway 14th Rifle Regiment. As a result of the withdrawal of the infantry his mortar gunners found themselves face to face with the Finnish Jagers. Shepelev had fought in the Polish Campaign of 1939 and in that conflict he had not lost a second of time. On his command the regiment took up a circular defence, covering all the access routes to his own positions with mortar and rifle fire. After that the officers in his regiment stopped two retreating "thirty-fours" under Yunatskiy and two anti-tank guns, ordering them to fight to the last with everyone else. Shepelev reported to his Brigade Command about the Finnish breakthrough by radio, as a result of which the 219th Mortar Regiment that stood in a gorge south of height 98.6, turned round and prepared to fire. Shepelev also liaised by radio with the guard's mortars and on three occasions he adjusted the fire for the "*katyushas*" around the Finnish orders of battle.

The Commander of the 9th Howitzer Artillery Brigade, 72nd Division Lieutenant-Colonel Vasily Uvarovich Golovastikov, who had served in the Worker's and Peasant's Red Army Air Force since 1922 did not let the grass grow under his feet either. He sent two batteries in his regiment to fire at close range, while he gathered together the headquarters officers along with the artillery officers who were not at their guns to beat back the Finnish attack on foot.

All this time the remaining mass of artillery, which had crossed the Finnish defensive line near Kuuterselka had already stopped and stretched out into columns, as they prepared to support the advancing units on the next Finnish defensive boundary. The 35th Self-Propelled Howitzer Brigade had already turned towards Mustamjaki and the road was thick with tractors, self-propelled howitzers, and trucks.

When on the crest of the heights the forces of the 3rd Jager Battalion appeared to the right of the column the Commander of the artillery platoon Lieutenant Aleksey Pavlovich Benevolenskiy ordered the heavy howitzers to turn right 90° and fire on the Jagers from close range. The first to open fire was Sergeant Boris Yakovlevich Mamutin's crew.

The result of these manoeuvres, the Finnish self-propelled guns and the Jagers were met with a hail of Soviet artillery fire almost head on. Golovastikov and Shepelev personally ordered their officer groups to launch a counterattack. Several times the battle descended to unarmed combat. Lieutenant-Colonel Mikhail Konstantinovich Pigarev was killed in this battle together with Major Grigoriy Grigoryevich Petrov, the Deputy Political Instructor of the 9th Howitzer Artillery Regiment. For his part in this battle Shepelev was awarded the title of the Order of the Red Banner of Combat.

On the left flank the 3rd Jagers, 133rd Regiment were fighting off fierce attacks, while on the right the 187th Regiment were doing the same. The Commander of the 187th Rifle Regiment Lieutenant-Colonel Mikhail Danilovich Chyornysh was fatally wounded. Despite the fact that in the division's documents he is listed as having distinguished himself particularly well in this situation, he did not receive any kind of an award for his actions. The Lieutenant-Colonel died that same day in the division's field hospital and is buried on the upper banks of Lake Raivolanjarvi in a communal grave. All the deputy commanders were injured and their places were taken by the Chief of Staff of the Regiment Lieutenant-Colonel Vasiliy Vasilyevich Titov. Many other officers were killed. Among them the veterans would remember Captain Aleksey Alekseyevich Khrustalyov, the Commander of the Mortar Company. When the mortar gunners had run out of ammunition, Khrustalyov gathered his men, and ordered them to launch a counterattack using their own personal weapons and to die a hero's death. As Viktor Pavlovich Kryukov of the 1,427th Anti-Tank Artillery Regiment recalled:

> Night … of sorts, and then it was over. Heavy artillery began to fire from behind Finnish lines. Command had taken the decision: the unit was to be moved closer to the road and to the enemy's defences. The Chief of Staff had taken command of the regiment–the Regimental Commander had fallen ill.
>
> When I walked in this direction, I saw soldiers who were walking away towards the forest in small groups. I came across a soldier on the way whose jaw had been ripped off. He could not speak, and tears poured out of his eyes. He did not know where the enemy was or which direction he was supposed to be going, where the infantry had gone, or where he could get help. I could not do anything to help him and just showed him where it would be safe for him to get away and where he could get help–this was the direction in which the infantry had gone. The soldiers could not go far in the forest however since 300m beyond the forest was a lake and the entrance to the road was already blocked. Walking back 300m along a country road I suddenly heard a bullet fly past me. I immediately got down into a ditch. Suddenly I saw a senior sergeant running towards me from a small ruined house. I hailed him and suggested he hide in the ditch since someone somewhere was firing. He answered me saying that somewhere was an enemy sniper and he had already exchanged fire with him.
>
> A short period of time went by, and he, the senior sergeant, sunk down to the ground–he had been hit by a bullet from the sniper sitting up in a tree.
>
> The enemy's bombardment of the forest expanse using artillery grew stronger. Some of the shrapnel from the shells and mines reached me. I even picked one of these fragments up. By crawling on my stomach along the shallow ditch on the side of the road, I reached the location where we were supposed to dig in and take up a defensive position.
>
> This location was ideal, a small house and a barn ready-made. Barbed wire and enemy anti-tank obstacles were located no more than 100m from us.
>
> A trench next to the house itself served as a shelter for the commanders. This was a poor location however from which to observe the enemy's lines. I chose a separate pit for myself and began to carefully dig down deeper. It was in this location that four of our anti-tank guns had been hidden, using the folds in the terrain, these guns were being dug in deeper.
>
> An infantry captain and lieutenant crawled past me. I heard the lieutenant advise the captain: "Let's stop here. It's safer and we have something to defend." The Captain flatly refused and advised it would be better to crawl to the forest.
>
> I passed this conversation on to the Chief of Staff. I told him that two officers had shot their soldiers and were retreating back behind the lines. The Chief of Staff ordered them to approach him in the trench. The Captain shook his hand and wanted to leave. He was given an automatic weapon and told to get back and fight. The Chief of Staff confiscated their documents–he did not arrest them. In a manner of speaking they have got it coming to them.
>
> Unexpectedly from the direction in which our principal units were based a tank emerged. It headed straight for our battery. Since it was a good target and we were able to open fire on it but would not have escaped with our lives, our battery gunners put the frighteners on it. The tank would not have had a clue we were there, and we trained our

weapon on him. The tank turned towards the barn, or more accurately towards the shed, passed underneath it and carried it on its armour.

The tank needed to find a path through the obstacles. It approached the Finnish defensive obstacles and turned along the line of defences, but it had only gone a few metres when a loud explosion was heard. The tank caught fire and remained where it was. Even though the Finns were firing constantly it was difficult to tell whether the tank had hit a mine or had been destroyed by a gun.

This moment galvanised the Finns, and they attacked us with a battle cry.

It would have been more than foolish to open fire with the guns that we had since all our ammunition was armour piercing. Our artillery crews and some of the soldiers who had joined them opened fire on the Finns. We in our pits were well protected from the bullets.

I momentarily felt fear because when I had tried to open fire from my automatic rifle nothing had happened. It was as if I was without a weapon even though I had three full magazines for my Shpagin sub-machine gun, which amounts to 70 cartridges in the magazine. After looking over my weapon my saving grace came to me when I realised that in the narrow and freshly exposed trench it had become blocked with fine sand.
Having detached the disc shaped magazine I worked the bolt manually several times. I then replaced the disc shaped magazine and the automatic weapon duly began to fire.

A second of our tanks appeared from out of the edge of the forest. It was running in to intercept the Finns. Thus the Finnish raid began to die down. The surviving Finnish soldiers crawled back into their shelters.

A terrible fate befell that tank – it burst into flames, only one man jumped out of it. He crawled, as though on all fours, to a location 100m from us. A narrow copse shielded him from the enemy's gaze.

Evidently the tank was full of fuel when it had gone into battle and was also fully armed, since a number of explosions rang out from inside it. Clouds of thick black smoke streamed away from the vehicle after these explosions.

Once again our wider front did not make itself known. Not one shot rang out from our side. We knew though that not two to three kilometres from us were hundreds of our tanks and guns.

A short time later we noticed three people running towards us from our own side. We let them know about our location, and they crawled towards us. They were a Lieutenant-Colonel and two Sergeants. They had a radio with them. They were reconnaissance soldiers. After getting the latest from us on the situation that had unfolded they surveyed the forward edge of the Finnish defences. They confirmed, as they say in reconnaissance speak, the coordinates and passed this information on to their command by radio.

We now continue the narrative from the Finnish perspective:

At 0215 hrs the 3rd Battery of self-propelled guns received an order to replace the 1st Battery on the front line. They only had two vehicles left, which became engaged in a duel with Soviet artillery on the battlefield. The Finnish self-propelled guns claimed they had destroyed eight Soviet guns at close range, of which three were heavy anti-aircraft artillery guns. Three Soviet trucks appeared on the right of the battlefield carrying ammunition. The Finnish self-propelled guns opened fire from a distance of 200m and destroyed all three of them. The Finns also claimed they had destroyed a tank that had been standing behind a wooden storage building.

Soviet artillery continued to rain fierce fire on the advancing Finns from close range. The self-propelled guns under Commander of the 3rd Battery received two direct hits and were taken out of

Mannerheim inspecting construction of fortifications in Vammelsuu, 12 October 1942.

Building an AT-obstacle. The rocks were so large that a 5-ton truck could only carry one stone at a time, 12 November 1943.

Finnish concrete AT-obstacle line ready at Siiranmäki, 18 May 1944.

Typical view of Finnish covered battle trench, Vammelsuu, 18 May 1944.

A rustic HQ dugout of 6th Infantry Regiment known as the "Winter Palace" in Beloostrov (Valkeasaari). The Finns had to abandon them in great haste on 10 June 1944.

Parade of the Armoured Brigade of the Finnish Army in Enso on 4 June 1944 (Marshal Mannerheim's birthday and Day of the Finnish Army). The Armoured Brigade still used light T-26 tanks of all versions in large numbers in 1944.

The most formidable and modern part of the Armoured Brigade was the Assault Gun Battalion equipped with German StuG III assault guns, 4 June 1944.

Finnish assault gun crew. Note that Finns replaced the German MG-42 with the Soviet DT machine gun. Also note the insignia of the Lagus Division on the right sleeve of the gunner, 4 June 1944.

Column of supply trucks of the Armoured Brigade on parade, 4 June 1944.

View of Finnish defences somewhere around Uusikirkko from the air, 14 June 1944.

View of Finnish defences from the air, Kuuterselkä on 12 June 1944.

The grand offensive begins. Multiple M-30 rocket launchers and KV tanks of the 31st Guards Heavy Tank Breakthrough Regiment ready for action in Beloostrov (Valkeasaari), 10 June 1944.

Tank with turret number 700 "Suvorov", 31st Guards Tank Heavy Regiment, and Guards of the 63rd Guards Rifles launch their attack, 10 June 1944.

Tank with turret number 641, 260th Guards Tank Heavy Regiment, moves out with supporting infantry from the 63rd Guards Rifles, 10 June 1944.

10th Infantry Division headquarters after Soviet air strike, 9 June 1944.

Air strike on Vyborg railway depot, presumably 15 June 1944. Image taken from a Soviet bomber.

Air strike on area of Neuvola, June 1944. Image taken from a Soviet bomber.

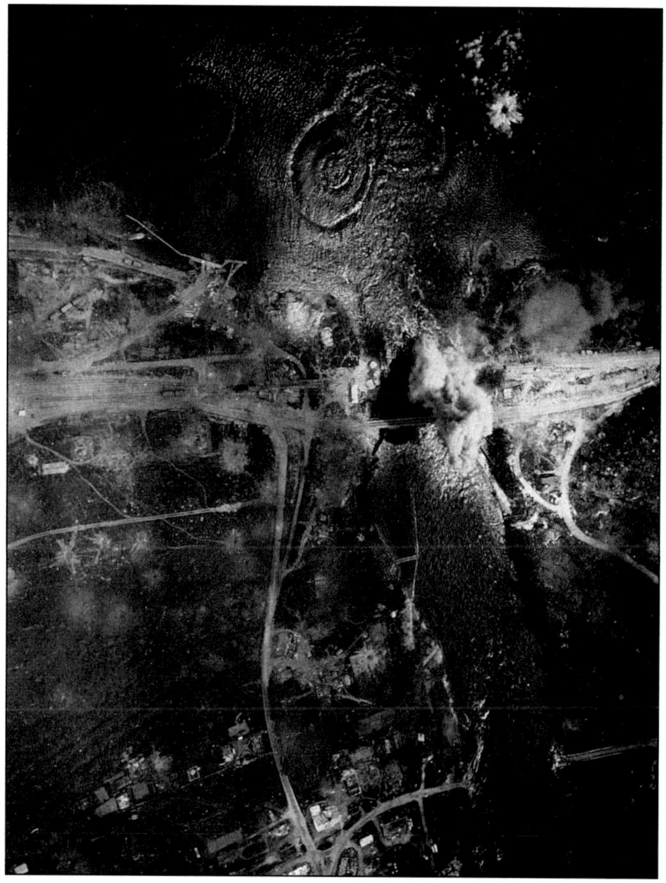

Air strike on Kiviniemi Railway Bridge, eastern Karelian Isthmus, June 1944.

A Soviet KV tank with mine-roller moves out, presumably in Beloostrov (Valkeasaari).

Heavy Soviet artillery passing through the Finnish obstacle line in Beloostrov (Valkeasaari). Note a Lend-Lease Allis-Chalmer DW-10W tractor and a Soviet 203 mm heavy gun, 10-11 June 1944.

Soviet AT-gun crew towing their 45 mm gun across Vammeljoki River. The poster on the left states, "Forward towards Vyborg!", 15 June 1944.

Finnish PAK-40 AT-gun from Lagus Division in firing position at Polviselkä, 10 June 1944.

Finnish officers in a field briefing at Polviselkä, 10 June 1944.

An image that became a symbol of heavy fighting in 1944. A Finnish infantry squad and a Maxim MG crew under Soviet artillery fire in trench at VT-Line. 16 June 1944.

A series of photos taken from the rear gunner seat of an Il-2 Shturmovik at Siiranmäki. One can see obstacle lines, Soviet armour ready for assault, trenches and a burning village. The air strike was delivered by 4 Il-2s from VVS KBF 7th Guards Diving Ground Assault Regiment. The regiment commander, Hero of the Soviet Union Guards Major Alexey Mazurenko personally led this attack. 10:30 AM, 14 June 1944.

Soviet troops (presumably 46th Rifle Division) advancing on light SU-76 self-propelled guns along Koivisto Road. After 15 June 1944.

Knocked out Finnish StuG III in Kuuterselkä. Apparently, this is StuG Ps-513-17 that was immobilized, abandoned by crew, and blown up. After 15 June 1944.

Knocked-out Finnish StuG III Ps-531-29 in Kuuterselkä. According to the Finnish sources, this StuG was destroyed by a Soviet T-34-85 and abandoned by the crew. After 15 June 1944.

A famous Image showing Finnish troops retreating on the Karelian Isthmus, 11 June 1944.

A very well-camouflaged Finnish PAK-40 AT-gun in Summa, 18 June 1944.

The last Finnish civilian to leave Vyborg, 20 June 1944.

A staged image of attack by T-34s of the 152nd Tank Brigade and infantry in downtown Vyborg. After 20 June 1944.

Colonel Kemppi, commander of the 20th Infantry Brigade, in his HQ in the basement of Osuuspankki Bank, 20 June 1944.

action. As a result on the battlefield there were only three serviceable Finnish self-propelled guns–two were ordered to withdraw from the battle (one owing to an engine failure, and the second from the weapon had failed). Repairing the self-propelled guns on the battlefield under heavy Soviet fire was tantamount to suicide.

By 0518 hrs the *Nuoli* Artillery Group had used up all their ammunition. Major Eriksson telephoned the Head of Artillery in the 4th Corps Colonel Sippola to solve somehow the issue with the supply of ammunition, but Sippola did not even try to engage him in conversation. By all accounts this was linked to the fact that the Head of Corps Artillery had not long before this happened received a false report from Colonel Klehr that according to information coming in from the main group of artillery reconnaissance troops, Kuuterselka had succeeded in fighting off the Russian advance.

At 0445 hrs it had grown sufficiently light to allow Soviet ground attack aircraft to appear over the battlefield. Despite this the Commander of the 3rd Jagers Major Hyunninen decided to take things to a conclusion, even if it would be at the cost of all his subordinate's lives. At 0700 hrs the 3rd Jager Battalion made its last attack near Kuuterselka and was able for a time to occupy part of a trench in a switching position on the "VT line." At 1000 hrs the Jagers were still at the heights and were trying to purge the trenches. The self-propelled gun commanded by Sergeant Halonen was providing covering fire for them but he then ran out of fuel.

Those who came out of this battle alive recalled:

> The dead from our 53rd Regiment began to end up into our trench. A pair of officers were lying there whose collar insignia had been cut away–this meant the Russians were also engaged in collecting badges. Our machine gun with its full magazine was lying there in the position in which it had been abandoned. It seems that here the fighting was not so intense..

At 0540 hrs some of the Jagers began to go on the offensive. To the right Soviet tanks along with their infantry launched a counterattack and pushed the Finns back to the forest. As Corporal Heikki Hyuvamaa, of the Battalion's 3rd Battery of attack guns recalled:

> I went back to Liykopa from the stone storage building on foot. On the way I saw a field strewn with our fallen soldiers. The Russians were firing their guns and fighter aircraft were taking to the skies. I had lost the magazine for my automatic gun somewhere along the road. I could not remember where and how I was to find my battery. Sometime later a truck stopped on the road and took me to Parkkila. I had not managed to fire my self-propelled gun once. This was a terrible disappointment. All I could remember was how badly our Command had worked. There had been no cooperation with the Jagers. I did not see a single Jager.

Sulo Vuorela from the 3rd Battery recalled:

> He was a true dog of war that Halonen. He said: "We had only just reached the summit of the heights and the Russian tanks were there in front of us on a plate. Load the last armour piercing shell!" Driver-mechanic Yakkola replied: "If you want to go then let's go, but we will not come out alive." I noticed a KV on the slope leading up to the heights and immediately fired. I hit the tank but the shell was a fragmentation round, we had loaded the wrong one by mistake. The enemy however was not able to respond to our shot straight away. Evidently the fragmentation round had also knocked them senseless. Halonen, who had been in the

> gunner's position replacing the injured loader Poskipart loaded the last armour piercing round. I fired and pierced the tank–the KV began to emit smoke.

Viktor Pavlovich Kryukov, 1,427th Anti-Tank Artillery Regiment:

> The dawn was already in full swing when an idea came to us: we should check the trailer that was standing on one trailer wheel and carrying the soldier's field kitchen boiler. Two of our soldiers crawled up to the boiler from the opposite side to the enemy and began to unwind the lid. It turned out that the boiler was full of edible *kasha* that had been abandoned by some unknown unit. We did not have any mess bowls with us and we ate off of a tile. As soon as we had sunk our spoon into the *kasha* and put it where it was meant to go we experienced some very pleasant sensations.
>
> We noticed a look of confidence on the face of our Lieutenant-Colonel. This was our kinship with the principal forces from whom we had been cut off. In the breaks between firing from the Finnish artillery, the hum of engines reached our ears. All this gave us strength.
>
> From the start of the artillery barrage ahead of the first breakthrough I had not slept for seven days.
>
> Suddenly from our direction we saw our own aircraft, to begin with three, then a further three, and then a few more, they were moving in the direction of the Finnish positions. The sky was criss-crossed by fire from our artillery guns. The artillery barrage had begun but this only lasted a few minutes. In our area, which had seen us cut off from the road, a chorus of countless Russian voices shouted "Hoorah!" and the tanks began to move. The enemy began to retreat, answering back with artillery fire from afar.
>
> It became more difficult for one of the batteries in our regiment, which was some distance away on the other side of the road. They were on the threshold of being captured by the Finns. It was only thanks to the composure and courage of our gray-haired Captain, the Commander of our Battery (whose surname I have forgotten) that we were able to hold out against the enemy.

After 1000 hrs the situation on the battlefield had evidently turned in favour of the Soviet side. The Finnish combat group had not been able to complete their combat mission. The Finnish losses were so high that Major-General Lagus suggested to the Commander of the 4th Corps that the offensive be called off. Laatikainen accepted this proposal. At 1030 hrs Puromaa's combat group received an order to withdraw from the battle and to take up a defensive position on the Isthmus between Lakes Suulajarvi and Onkijarvi.

Sometime after 1100 hrs, the withdrawal of Finnish self-propelled guns began. At 1145 hrs Finnish officers gathered next to the self-propelled gun commanded by Captain von Trojla. It was Lieutenant Aulanko alone who began to report the situation, as a Soviet shell exploded nearby. The shrapnel wounded Captain von Trojla fatally in the head and injured Lieutenant Aulanko and Senior Sergeant Liimatt. The next shell penetrated the armour of von Troijla's 'machine' and this too had to be left on the battlefield.

The last to withdraw from the battlefield was the self-propelled gun under the command of Corporal Taponen from the 1st Battery. This tank carried a section of reconnaissance soldiers on its armour along with the bodies of the fallen Finnish self-propelled gun crews.

At 1300 hrs reinforcements reached the Soviet side. The 381st and the 602nd Red Banner Rifle Regiments, from the 109th Rifle Division arrived by the rail along the line running from Leningrad to Vyborg towards Kuuterselka. After gathering together all the forces into a fighting force the Soviet units again advanced forward. By 2300 hrs Soviet forces were already in Liykola. The battle for Kuuterselka was over.

8

Outcome of the Kuuterselka Battle

The Kuuterselka battle ended in a resounding Soviet victory. Despite the initial success the Finnish counterattack had collapsed and the battlefield fell to the Soviet units. The Finn's second line of defence, the VT line, which had been under construction for three years, was breached in the course of three days. The time had come to reap the fruits of victory–to write victorious and excusatory reports, as well as recommendations for awards.

Major Yunatskiy, the Commander of the 185th Tank Regiment in his report missed out some unpleasant details. He accused the infantry from the 72nd Division of deserting their position and underlined his role in beating back the Finnish counterattack: "..It was only by dint of me assuming responsibility for the Command of the IS tanks that saved the situation."

The report on the actions of the 31st Guards Tank Regiment draws a somewhat different picture. In the words of the guard's tank crews from the moment they arrived on the battlefield all that was left of Yunatskiy's 185th Tank Regiment were two combat capable "thirty-fours" and the regiment would not have been able to participate in the battle on the strength of these tanks.

The 1,222nd Novgorod Self-Propelled Artillery Regiment was very up front in reporting its losses. The regiment lost four self-propelled Su-76 guns that were burnt out; and seven self-propelled guns needed repair following the battle. The 3rd Battery in the regiment, which had remained to cover the withdrawal of the 72nd Rifle Division on the road north of Kuuterselka had lost all their combat vehicles. The Commander of the Battery Senior Lieutenant Glushko was burnt in his tank, and a further five self-propelled gun crews were killed in other tanks:

- Nikolai Afanasyevich Trushchev–SU-76 gunner
- Pyotr Ostapovich Ganzin–SU-76 loader
- Ivan Semyonovich Kiyayev–SU-76 gunner
- Aleksandr Maksimovich Kislitsyn–SU-76 loader
- Serapion Petrovich Smirnov–SU-76 commander

Lauri Yantti described the condition of the 3rd Jager Battalion and the overall losses among the Armoured Division as follows:

> On their evening journey to Lampalle the formation of the 3rd Jagers looked unusually sparse. I looked at the pale faces of those who had come through a fierce battle with tears in my eyes. These were the last survivors of what had recently been a large battalion. The battalion's losses amounted to 236 men. Each of those who had survived the battle had lost a comrade. The mood for everyone was downbeat. The voice of Battalion Commander Major Hyunninen was also shaking, as he mentioned the fallen Jagers in his speech as well as all three of the fallen company commanders. When he continued however he again spoke like

a strict military commander. The battalion had abandoned such and such a number of rifles, automatic weapons, biscuit pouches, binoculars. "It is categorically forbidden to abandon weapons and equipment" he said–"the Finnish Army cannot afford this."

Some 1,500 men arrived in Kuuterselka from the ranks of the armoured division, both the injured and the fallen. What soldiers they were! Conscripts who had been preparing for war for years; they were at the peak of their combat capability. Undoubtedly it could be said that the best soldiers in the armoured division in Kuuterselka had gone to a better place. The losses in the officer corps were shocking: 40 men, of whom 10 had been killed. We had been dealt the first heavy blow. The armoured division never really recovered from this....

Contemporary assessments of Finnish losses are significantly lower than the figures cited by Yantti in 1955. Nevertheless, the losses for the Finns were heavy. According to the assessments given by contemporary Finnish researchers the Jager Brigade, which prior to the battle had 3,000 men, lost 624 men in the course of seven hours of fighting. After their fighting around Kuuterselka the armoured division was withdrawn back behind the lines for a holiday and for reinforcement.

Of the 29 Finnish assault guns that participated in the counterattack five were lost outright and they remained on the battlefield and were left to the advancing Soviet units. A further 15 self-propelled guns were taken out of action due to failures and sustained combat damage. The Finnish battery of attack guns claimed 17 tanks and self-propelled guns destroyed in the course of 15 June 1944.

Assessing the losses among Soviet tank crews is complicated, since Lieutenant-Colonel Yunatskiy and the other officers preferred to keep silent about them. Nevertheless an assessment can be made of the number of combat vehicles in the 185th Regiment concerned, based on the fact that at 0800 hrs in the morning of 18 June 1944 the regiment advanced forward from Pekjarvi station towards Leypyasuo with just four "thirty-four" tanks. Fragmentary information concerning losses and victories is set out in the table below:

Claims for tanks destroyed in the tank battle for Kuuterselka were as follows:

Soviet	**Claims**	**Finnish**[1]	**Claims**
185th Separate Tank Regiment Lieutenant N. K. Sitnik	2 SPG	Private S. Vuorela	1 T-34, 1 KV, 1 SU
31st Guards Heavy Tank Regiment	3 SPG	Junior Sergeant L. Lepyannen	2 T-34, 1 KV
A Company of the 98th Separate Tank Regiment	0	Corporal O. Lagus	4 T-34
A Company of the 27th Guards' Heavy Tank Regiment	14 tanks, 9 SPG	Junior Sergeant Haampajaki	2 T-34, 1 SU-152
1,222nd Self-Propelled Artillery Regiment	2 SPG	Corporal O. Savela	1 T-34

1 These claims for victory are provided based on the book *Finnish Armoured Tank Divisions 1919–1969*. In other sources claim figures are higher, such as those provided by Erkki Kakela.

1st Red Banner Brigade	14 tanks[2]	Corporal O. Taponen[3]	1 T-34, 1 KV, 1 SU
Hero of the Soviet Union Rusanov	1 tank from the Anti-Tank Company's line up		
TOTAL	31 tanks, 14 SPG	TOTAL	14 tanks, 3 SPG

Acknowledged losses:

The Soviet side	**Acknowledged**	**The Finnish side**	**Acknowledged**
185th Separate Tank Regiment	No data	Irrevocable losses	5 StuG III vehicles
31st Guards Heavy Tank Regiment	1 KV destroyed by friendly artillery fire		
Company of the 98th Separate Tank Regiment	0	Taken out of action for technical reasons	15 StuG III vehicles
Company of the 27th Guards Heavy Tank Regiment	1 IS burnt out, 2 destroyed		
1,222nd Self-Propelled Artillery Regiment	4 burnt out, 7 required repair		
TOTAL	**15**	**Total**	**20**

The following account was taken report written by the Finnish Attack Gun Battalion on the battle for Kuuterselka:

> Losses: a) in terms of personnel: killed, one officer (Lieutenant Mullumaa) + two *unter-offizier* + one private. Wounded: two officers (Captain V. fon Troyl, who died later in hospital, and Lieutenant Aulanko) + three *unter-offizier*, and 15 privates; b) materiel losses: five self-propelled vehicles, three of which were blown up by their crews, and another two with serious damage that were left for the enemy.
>
> Ammunition expelled: 470 armour piercing shells, and 360 high-explosive fragmentation shells.
>
> Trophies: despite all our efforts we did not manage to evacuate any trophies from the battlefield, owing to the retreat by our forces everything was left to the enemy. There were only two or three serviceable tanks left, while for anti-tank guns the figure was one and a half dozen.

2 Since a company of IS 27 tanks from the Guards Tank Regiment formed part of the Mobile Group in the 1st Red Banner Brigade, the victories for their brigade have also been included in the figures.

3 In Finnish documents these victories are attributed to Corporal T. Yuomoy, however according to data provided by the Finnish researcher Erkki Kakela the gunner in the battle for Kuuterselka was actually Taponen.

> Enemy losses: a) 11 T-34 tanks, three KV tanks, and three self-propelled guns b) other losses: 26 anti-tank guns, one field gun, three trucks, one cart, and a large number of infantry soldiers.
>
> Tactics: the reason why the enemy had not been able to halt our advance was the overwhelming advantage in terms of military equipment. The enemy's artillery, which was even adjusted from aerostats, was of decisive importance. The enemy made active use of field artillery at close range in the anti-tank role. In terms of the way the enemy's tanks were used a centralised control was hardly in evidence. At the end of the battle the enemy's tanks moved around the battlefield carefully from shelter to shelter, using the folds of the terrain, they would for the most part attack from the leeward side of a hill. After they had fired they would quickly retreat back into their shelter.
>
> Summing up the experience of the battle: our artillery fired very little in view of their small numbers, there were instances in which our units would fire. The reason for this was that the telephony communications had been taken out of action right at the beginning of the battle. Adjustment of artillery fire was for the most part conducted using a 30-watt radio set from inside our own self-propelled guns. However since our officers really had no idea of how to do this (the artillery reconnaissance scout that had been attached to us had been injured), almost no artillery adjustment was actually carried out in the first battle.
>
> There was no cooperation between the Jagers and the self-propelled guns on the battlefield. This was linked to the fact that no exercises had taken place that practised cooperation. The divisions should have had Jagers assigned to them and they would have been specially trained for operations in open terrain. The reason why our self-propelled guns almost always came out the victors in tank duels was that the crews were trained to move very quickly (small exercises would take place on a daily basis that drilled weapon handling), and also that the gunners in these self-propelled guns would aim their weapons very carefully, and were able to be fully reliant on them.

From the Soviet artillerymen's perspective, N.N. Inozemtsev described the Finnish counterattack as follows:

> Between 0600–0800 hrs a group of Finnish automatic riflemen left the marsh and moved forward to the advancing troop's flank and counterattacked in the direction of height 96.2. The large amount of artillery altered the orders of battle and they were not able to open fire. The Divisional Commander telephoned Tishenko.
>
> "I am putting you in charge of the Kuuterselka sector–height 96.2."
>
> We will be opening fire on these sectors. The Commanders of the 1st and 2nd Battalions along with the commanders of the batteries and the reconnaissance troops are to defend their positions with gun and machine gun fire. The commanders of the operations platoons advanced forward, but there was no way to communicate with them. The Commander of the artillery division asked to open fire on 96.2, the Finns had allegedly driven our forces out of there.
>
> The Colonel orders:
>
> "Open fire–one battalion! Open the aim by 300m. Belikov came running up to us (he was in charge of the radio at our Observation Post):
>
> "Comrade Sergeant Major, I had a message from Safonov, he cannot get through to Shulga.
>
> "So he should tell you and report the situation directly."

"I am on 96.2. The situation has improved. Fire 800m further north. Find out who out of those heavy guns is firing at the heights, take them out now, they are firing right at us!"

The Colonel shouted down the telephone:

"Shulga, cease fire immediately! Open the range 800m."

Safonov, after he had subsequently learned that it was his own division that was firing on him, flew into a rage. For a long time afterwards he would share his impressions of being hit by 203mm shells, his own shells to boot.

Several of the generals came to this location. The situation quickly re-established itself. At 1400 hrs the enemy gathered their wounded and began to withdraw. Tanks had entered the breakthrough in the direction of Mustomyaki. By 2000 hrs our troops had advanced some six to seven kilometres. Liykola was captured.

Thus the powerful Finnish defensive band in the sector running from Mustomyaki–Kuuterselka had been breached. We were moving forward with the Artillery Commander. We inspected the defences in Kuuterselka. Everything has been done steadfastly and resolutely. There are six lines of ditches. Five rows of strong granite dragon's teeth and the heights of the stones are between one and a half to two metres. These have been placed in a deep tank trap that cannot be seen from the ground based observation posts. The trench is lined with tree logs and is two and a half metres deep, with open firing points and shelters in every three recuperation recesses, and with a stone for the dragon's teeth every 10–15m. Immediately behind the first trench there was a second with strong pill boxes and guns set to fire at close range. In the immediate vicinity of this trench were concrete large calibre shelters designed for between 15–20 individuals. They could only be destroyed by direct hits from heavy bombs. On all of the open locations and in the particularly important directions there were pill boxes with a one point eight to two metre capability, these had armoured canopies. Over a kilometre of the front line just on the forward edge there were five or six of these pill boxes as well as 10–12 concrete shelters. Some 200–300m further on was a second line, which was almost analogous to the first. This was where the narrow gauge railway ran.

The Finns had not managed to complete these powerful structures. Some of the pill boxes stood under construction, and everywhere there were stores housing cement and dug outs in which the stone revetments had yet to be added, and hoists lay set out on tripods. In the forest were small, collapsible plywood houses for the workers.

In each of the trenches, and especially lying in between them, were a mass of bodies. The open firing points had been hit at close range and by mortar fire, some of the pill boxes had been destroyed by the "assault vehicle guys" but for the most part the structures were intact. The Finns had caved in under the barrage of rockets, the large-scale bombardment and the powerful artillery barrage and … had fled. They immediately came under artillery fire once they had started to get back behind the lines, and they were also bombed by Il-2s. There was almost nobody left to mount a defence on the second line itself.

Having forged their way forward the "IS" tanks had decided the fate of the battle and had driven the completely demoralised Finns back to the village of Kuuterselka. After a massive air strike by our aircraft, particularly ground attack aircraft, the powerful stronghold had been completely occupied by tanks, self-propelled guns, and infantry.

The second Finnish line of defence on the Karelian Isthmus was the strongest of all those we had seen, and much more heavily armed than the "Mannerheim line," but it was breached in less than 12 hrs albeit with minimal losses on our own side.

That's a civilised army for you, advanced technology and Russian valour!

9

Storming of the Siiranmyaki Height, 12–15 June

There are few military history specialists remain in Russia who recollect the battle for height 171.0 (the former Finnish village of Siiranmyaki). For the Finns this is the only bright period in the first stage of the battles in the summer of 1944. The storming of the height with the long-standing Finnish structures lasted for three days and ended in its capture, however the units of the 23rd Army were not able to move further north.

The 381st and 281st Rifle divisions stormed the heights with the support of the tank crews from the 46th Separate Guards Heavy Tank Breakthrough Regiment, the 226th Separate Tank Regiment, the 952nd Self-Propelled Artillery Regiment and the 396th Guards Heavy Self-Propelled Gun Regiment.

In defence of the height stood the reinforced 7th Infantry Regiment under Lieutenant-Colonel Adolf Ehrnrooth of the 2nd Division. This division did not fall within the direction of the main Soviet attack and withdrew back to the "VT line" in a more organised fashion. On the other hand the 281st Division had approached the height when they were already heavily thinned out– the 1,062nd Regiment in this division had transferred to a two battalion line up. The 2nd Rifle Battalion in this regiment was disbanded due to heavy losses.

The Soviet units had reached the height by evening on 12 June 1944 and for two days they prepared for the storming operation: artillery was concentrated, and the sappers reconnoitred the approaches to the height. In the course of the battles on the approaches to the height the 281st Rifle Division took prisoners from among the men in the 7th Rifle Regiment and the 3rd Volunteer "Compatriot Battalion." The Karelians who had fought in this battalion had declared under interrogation that they had been conscripted by force.

The commanding height of 171.0 towered over the surrounding fields like a natural fortress. The approaches to this were protected by concrete and granite dragon's teeth and a fence made from barbed wire three or four stakes deep: on the summit full size combat trenches were built, as well as machine gun firing points, and armoured machine gun turrets, and concrete anti-tank gun positions. Even here however the Finnish fortification builders had allowed the same mistake to be made as they had in the construction of the Mannerheim line, and had even made it worse: there was only one trench on the summit, the Finnish defence had no depth to it.

It was Ehrnrooth's combat group that was responsible for the defence of the sector, which incorporated height 171.1. The main regiment in this combat group was the 7th Rifle Regiment. The 4th Fortress Battalion (which was analogous to the Soviet separate anti-tank machine gun battalion) as well as Malinen's detachment also formed part of this group. For anti-tank defence Ehrnrooth had two machine gun companies–the 3rd RAK-40 and the 6 "forty-fives".

The Finnish artillery group incorporated five battalions, which had been formed into Aalto's artillery group under the command of the Commander of the 24th Light Battalion Major Paul Aalto. When necessary Ehrnrooth could call upon his neighbouring group on the right flank–this was Meri's artillery group. In total 11 divisions, or 132 guns, were ready to support the defence of this height.

The immediate defence of the height was entrusted to the 1st Battalion under Major Eino Kuvaja of the 7th Infantry Regiment. Further west the 4th Fortress Battalion stood at the defence of the height, as well as the 1st Battalion under Lieutenant Colonel Omar Toppola from the 6th Infantry Regiment. All that was in Ehrnrooth's reserve was the 2nd Battalion, 49th Infantry Regiment, but where necessary he could call up reserves from his neighbours on the right flank, where the fourth battalion was located.

The breakthrough of Finnish defences about Siiranmjaki had afforded the 23rd Army an opportunity to continue their advance along the road from Valk-jarvi and further towards Pasuri, disrupting the lateral lines of communication, as well as attacking Rautu and posing a threat to the right flank of the 15th Rifle Division to the east of the Karelian Isthmus.

13 June

According to Finnish information, the 281st Rifle Division on that day attacked the height, but these attacks were easily beaten back. In the Combat Journal of the Division, as well as that of its regiments no attacks on the height were recorded for 13 June, but there is a mention of an attack by day in the Combat Journal of the self-propelled gun crews in the 938th Regiment.

The 46th Guards Tank Regiment sent one KV on a reconnaissance mission. Only the one tank bearing the turret number 684 approached the line of dragon's teeth. The tank's crew, which were commanded by Guards Junior Lieutenant Roman Ilyich Petrov had been given an order to draw fire towards them and to force the Finnish anti-tank guns on the height to fire.

The Finns rained a hail of fire down on this tank. The vehicle sustained six direct hits and was taken out of action. In order to confuse the enemy and to imitate the loss of their combat vehicle, the tank crews donned gas masks, and let off a smoke grenade inside the tank. The crews relayed to their comrades by radio where the Finnish anti-tank guns were, and from where the machine guns were firing. The Finns claimed they had destroyed two KV tanks and two T-34s. In the Combat Journal of the 226th Separate Tank Regiment no losses in materiel are recorded for 13 June.
During these 24 hours the 816th Artillery Regiment, 281st Division spent 467 shells of 76mm calibre, and 349 shells of 122mm calibre on the Finnish defence. By the end of the day the entire artillery of the 98th Rifle Corps had been drawn up to their firing positions. The plan was to use a large part of the divisional and regimental artillery firing at close range.

14 June

In the early morning Soviet ground attack aircraft carried out a bombing and ground attack assault on the height. At 0800 hrs the artillery began their assault, raining fierce fire down on the height and the nearby areas behind the lines, cutting off the Finnish infantry reserves from the height. The artillery barrage lasted for 30 mins. The artillery salvo on the height ended with the traditional salvo of "*katyushas*." At the same time as the "*katyushas*" were attacking the 396th Guards Self-Propelled Gun Regiment moved up to the open firing positions to fire at close range. At 0955 hrs the advance began.

The 381st Rifle Division advanced on the front line that was two and a half kilometres west of the height without the support of armoured vehicles. The 1,263rd and 1,259th Regiments knew how to break into the Finnish trenches and to capture their small sector. At 1400 hrs the Finns made two counterattacks and drove the Soviet battalions out of their positions. According to incomplete information the losses of the 381st Division in the first twenty-four hours of these battles amounted to 100 men killed and 250 injured. Two battalion commanders from the 1,263rd Regiment were killed in the fighting: Captains Iosif Yefimovich Dubasov and Savva Prokhorovich Nazarenko. The division was not able to achieve a great deal of success.

The 281st Rifle Division administered the main thrust of the attack on Siiranjami heights using two regiments. The 1,062nd Rifle Regiment on both sides of the road from running from Suurkyulya to Vuotta supported by "thirty-fours" from the 226th Regiment. The 1,064th Rifle Regiment supported by KV tanks from the 46th Guards Regiment and the SU-76s of the 938th Self-Propelled Artillery Regiment. The first to move across the fields to attack were the tanks of the 46th Guards Heavy Tank Regiment, as well as the sappers. Tank 684 commanded by Petrov which was spending a second day standing next to the dragon's teeth, was revived and began to open fire. The tank was hit again more than once, and Petrov and his radio operator, Guards Private Vdovkin, were killed. Guards Junior Lieutenant R.I. Petrov was posthumously awarded the Gold Star of the Hero of the Soviet Union. He is buried in a communal grave in Olshaniki. Guards Private Nikolai Nikolayevich Vdovkin was actually listed among those missing without trace by mistake. He did not receive any award.

By midday, the riflemen together with the tanks and self-propelled vehicles had reached the dragon's teeth but had not found a way through. Although the majority of the "forty-fives" and field guns in the 281st Rifle Division had advanced forward to fire at close range, the fact that they were firing at enormous boulders meant their fire was ineffective. The advance was came to a standstill. The 1,062nd Rifle Regiment reached the south-western slopes of the height under fierce fire from the Finns and laid low. On the right flank the 1,064th Regiment also laid low close to a line of fencing. The Finns alerted and mobilised their reserve–the 2nd Infantry Battalion, 49th Infantry Regiment received an order to take up a defensive position along the northern shore of the Kulmala-oja stream, two kilometres north of the main defensive line.

The commander of 46th Guards Regiment ordered the tank crews to forge paths through independently. Some tanks remained at the dragons' teeth, the rest had departed and had begun to fire intensively at the Finnish firing points. At 1415 hrs the Commander of the 4th Guards Company Lieutenant Sokolov forged the first path through the dragon's teeth in his KV tank. This success can be explained by the fact that Sokolov's driver-mechanic was Guards Senior Sergeant Boris Yeliseyevich Shmelev, who was the most experienced driver-mechanic in the regiment. To begin with the crew tried to demolish the dragon's teeth by firing from their main tank gun. The dragon's teeth however turned out to be very large and strong. The Finns tried to fire at the tank. The direct hits from the shells took the KV tank's gun out of action. For two hours whilst he was under fire Shmelev rammed and uprooted the granite blocks that were more than a metre in height. He managed to push the dragon's teeth out of the way and was the first to reach the height. All this time the fire from this tank was covered by other KVs, SU-76s, and ISU-152s. Three batteries of "hunters" fired 30 shells each at the Finnish trenches and pill boxes from a distance of between 200–300m from the dragon's teeth. Behind the lead KV commanded by Sokolov an SU-76 commanded by Lieutenant Mussa jumped into the path that the KV had created on his own initiative. A fourth SU-76 became caught in the dragons' teeth owing to an error on the part of the driver mechanic.

By 1500 hrs the sappers had cleared additional paths in the Finnish defensive obstructions. With the support of the armoured vehicles battalions from the 281st Rifle Division broke through towards the height. The battle in the trenches was in full swing. The tank crews fired at the Finnish machine gun nests from close range, as well as at the folds of the trenches using guns and machine guns. The Finnish anti-tank defence on the height was suppressed, and the Finns just did not have anything with which to match this firepower. The local Finnish counterattacks were not crowned with success, but the commanders of both companies–Captains Kiiskinen and Walden– were injured. Lauri Karl Gustav Walden, the son of the Finnish Defence Minister, disappeared without trace on the way to the dressing station. He was not captured. The veterans of the 7th Infantry Regiment agreed that he had been killed by a direct hit from a shell or from a salvo of *Katyushas*.

According to Soviet sources, by 1700 hrs almost the entire height had been captured. The situation on the left flank, which was where the 1,062nd Rifle Regiment were coming under fierce fire, was more serious. From the edge of the forest west of the height the Finnish sappers and machine gunners were firing using diagonal fire all the approaches to the height, preventing any reinforcements from getting through and inflicting heavy losses on the regiment. Finnish fire from all types of weapons was so fierce that the evacuation of the wounded from the battlefield was impossible.

The commander of 7th Rifle Regiment Lieutenant-Colonel Adolf Ehrnrooth had no intention of giving up the height. Almost immediately his combat group began a series of furious counterattacks. The 2nd Battalion under Lieutenant-Colonel Larko of the 49th Regiment launched a counterattack after 1700 hrs and by 1810 hrs he reported that the height had been purged completely. After that the trenches on the height changed hands several times. According to Finnish information at 1830 hrs the Soviet side went on the attack again supported by four KVs they re-conquered the height and had reached its apex. After 2100 hrs there were more than 10 heavy tanks on the summit.

At 2100 hrs Soviet tanks and infantry following an artillery barrage began to advance from the summit of the height to the north in the direction of Kulmala-oja. The tanks descended onto a minefield; the infantry was halted by fierce fire. One "thirty-four" caught fire, and another two set off mines and also caught fire.

At 2150 hrs, Finnish artillery opened fire on the height with a fierce barrage, some of the Soviet armoured vehicles were destroyed by the "*faust gunners*" of the 14th Company, 49th Regiment that had arrived just in time, and Lieutenant-Colonel Varko was able to raise his battalion for the counterattack. By 2330 hrs Varko reported that the entire height with the exception of the 50m trench sector was in Finnish hands. The height in its entirety was scattered with the bodies of the fallen. At midnight, the Finnish reported that the whole height was in their hands, but the soldiers of the 1,064th Rifle Regiment had momentarily recaptured it. Varko did not give up and again counterattacked at 0020 hrs and again at 0130 hrs with the support of artillery. At 0153 hrs the Finns announced that the last KV tank on the height had been destroyed. By way of trophies the Finns captured two "forty-fives" and five machine guns. At 0220 hrs a further two KV tanks appeared on the height and banished the Finns. All night the Finns did not relent in their attempts to recover their lost ground. In one of the counterattacks *Fahnrich* Tuomas Gerdt from the 12th Separate Battalion and a Cavalier of the Mannerheim Cross was injured. The counterattack broke down due to Gerdt's injury and the fact that the Finns had used up all their hand grenades.

Both sides had incurred the heaviest losses. The Siiranmyaki height itself is not that high, the battle was played out over short distances and had often turned into hand-to-hand fighting. On the night of 14–15 June the Finns carried out an exchange of sub-divisions on the height. To be accurate however, there was almost nobody left to replace. From the 2nd Company, 7th Infantry Regiment only six soldiers remained, while 15 remained from the 3rd Company. The 4th Fortress Battalion as well as Malinen's detachment had also all but disappeared in the course of twenty-four hours of fighting. The anti-tank guns were taken out of action, but in the battle on the height the

Finns were the first to effectively deploy the *Panzerfaust* weapons. For his destruction of Soviet tanks on 14 and 15 June the nineteen-year-old Private Seppyanen was awarded the Mannerheim Cross.

Soviet records do not allow claims for losses to be either confirmed or refuted. The guards from the 46th Regiment only incurred one irrevocable loss in terms of a single KV tank. In the course of a day the 226th Regiment lost one tank that had been burnt out, and two that had been taken out of action, and a further two "thirty-fours" became trapped in the dragon's teeth. The self-propelled gun crews of the 938th Regiment operating the lightly armoured SU-76 vehicles suffered the most– nine of them were taken out of action on the height itself, and a further three on the approaches to the height. The report on the actions of the armoured tank forces of the 23rd Army assesses the losses in the battles for the height as six SU-76s, one SU-152, one T-34 and one KV, which is evidently less than the losses recorded in the regimental documents.

The following episode is testimony to the intensity of the battle on the height and is described by the artillerymen of the 281st Division. Senior Lieutenant Sergeyev from the 816th Artillery Regiment, as he was checking the positions of the close range guns, noticed that all the rifle regiment gun crews were suffering from fatigue. The Divisional Commander ordered all the division's remaining guns to be brought onto the height to fire at close range. Sergeyev had to gather a crew together from volunteer riflemen, and in the end he managed to draw one gun up to the height to fire at close range. From the Combat Journal of the 281st Rifle Division:

> Under fire from the artillery barrage the Finnish infantry drew right up to the trenches but were beaten back by automatic and machine gun fire and grenades, they lost men killed and wounded. According to the testimonies of Finnish prisoners of war Finnish command had deployed a fresh battalion from a tank division from Vyborg to the area around Siiranmyaki …

According to Soviet sources, the battalions from the 1.062nd and 1,064th Regiments beat off up to six Finnish counterattacks. In the last Finnish counterattack, according to the assessment by Finnish officers, up to a battalion of Finnish infantry took part. By the evening the 1,062nd Regiment had incurred such heavy losses on the height that it was withdrawn back to the second echelon of the 1,064th Regiment. It was to be replaced the 133rd Separate Artillery and Machine Gun Battalion of the Karelian Fortified District, but at that time this Battalion was occupying a defensive position to the east, in the area around Korpikyulya, and only appeared on the height by the morning of 16 June.

The 1,064th Regiment in the battle on 14 June incurred the heaviest losses in the division. After a day's fighting the following remained to serve in the division: In the 1st Rifle Battalion: there were 42 men, in the 2nd Battalion there were 108 men, and in the 3rd there were 50. Only eight men remained in the regimental battery, and in the anti-tank battery only six remained. The battalion and company commanders were all injured. The Regiment's Political Instructor Major Lazar Grigoryevich Aizenberg, and the commanders of the rifle companies Captain Grigoriy Sergeyevich Yeliseyev, and Lieutenant Vasiliy Pavlovich Vorobyov, the Battalions' Komsomol organiser Lieutenant Semyon Kirillovich Goroshko, the Deputy Battalion Commander Senior Lieutenant Ismail Khisametdinovich Khisametdinov, the commanders of the anti-tank gun platoons Junior Lieutenant Aleksandr Ivanovich Chikin, and Lieutenant Pavel Leontyevich Printsevich, the commanders of the rifle platoons Junior Lieutenants Nikolai Mikhaylovich Dvortsov and Junior Lieutenant Sergey Sergeyevich Pudov were killed.

Combined losses for the 281st Rifle Division were 232 men killed, and 582 wounded. The Finns claimed they had destroyed seven KVs and three T-34s on the night of 14–15 June. The outcome of that day was that Soviet units captured the height. By way of constant counterattacks however and heavy artillery fire of 14 June the Finns were able to halt the further advance of Soviet units to Vuotta. The Commanders of the 98th Corps decided to leave the armoured vehicles on the height to support the rifle units and to mobilise their reserves–the 438th Rifle Regiment, 177th Rifle Division to continue the advance.

During the course of a day of fighting the artillery from the 2nd Infantry Division spent approximately 8,540 shells, which had a significant impact on the course of the battle. In all of the Soviet documents the strength of the Finnish artillery is emphasised.

15 June

On the night of 14–15 June both sides were engaged in preparations for the forthcoming day's fighting. Both sides evacuated their wounded and drew up fresh forces. By morning on 15 June Finnish infantry had received their *Panzerfaust* weapons–these were modern anti-tank weapons, which enabled them to effectively combat Soviet armoured vehicles.

The commander of 281st Rifle Division moved his command post up to height 171.1, into the orders of battle of the 1,066th Regiment. The division regrouped and prepared to attack northwards. The Finnish side also prepared for a new day's fighting. From the morning Ehrnrooth's combat group had been subordinated to the 2nd Company from the 2nd Battalion, 7th Rifle Regiment. At 0715 hrs the Soviet artillery barrage began, Finnish artillery responded, after starting a counter artillery barrage aimed at the height. The cannonade from both sides lasted for two hours. The Finns managed to fend off the Soviet morning attack. After going on the attack at 0740 hrs the 483rd Rifle Regiment had only moved some 200–300m and had fought off Finnish counterattacks twice at 0930 hrs and 1120 hrs.

Soviet command had decided to move up the heavy self-propelled guns of the 396th Regiment onto the height in the morning. On the command "Herons–forward! No retreat!" the 396th Guards Heavy Self-Propelled Gun Regiment in its full compliment of 20 ISU-152s went into battle. On the height the self-propelled guns had to fire at almost point blank range as they fought off attacks from Finnish infantry:

> Bozhok ordered the driver-mechanic: to move 30° in the direction of a trench. The driver-mechanic turned his vehicle, and the gun pointed along the trench in which a great number of Finnish soldiers were hiding. After lowering the gun to its maximum, comrade Bozhok opened fire. Many of the Finns merged with the earth and stones and shot into the air, while those who survived just sat there like deaf ducks, deafened by the blast wave. Sometime later the reconnaissance crews of the 1,066th Regiment reported that they had only taken 32 deaf Finnish servicemen prisoner, but there were many more who had been seriously wounded.

By the midday were ready to carry out their attack. Between 1125–1130 hrs Finnish bombers dropped 48.5tonnes of bombs on the height. Following a short artillery barrage the Finnish infantry went on the counterattack targeting the height from the north and west. The 2nd Battalion, 7th Regiment under Captain Raassina attacked the flank of the Soviet alignment from the west. The Battalion comprising a Jager platoon and three companies amounted to around 350 men. In a ferocious attack the battalion succeeded in getting up to the height and in clearing out some of the trenches but was stopped by Soviet armoured artillery fire. The Battalion's losses for 15 June were around 120 men.

The Finns had succeeded in pushing the Soviet units back to the height but were not able to capture it in its entirety. At 1515 hrs the next Soviet artillery barrage began and at 1520 hrs four "thirty-fours" from the 226th Regiment began to attack in the direction of Kyulmya-Olya jointly with the 483rd Rifle Regiment. The Finnish sappers and chemical weapons troops were ordered to take up a defensive position along the Kyulmya-Olya stream. In total the narrow Finnish line held 130 soldiers. By 1800 hrs the Soviet advanced guard had reached the stream where the Finns had gathered all their available reserves from the 1st and 3rd Battalions of the 7th Regiment. It was to this same place that the Regimental Commander sent a temporary combat group of 100 soldiers from the logistics sub-divisions. Lieutenant-Colonel Ehrnrooth did not lose his composure and tersely informed his subordinates: "We have been ordered to hold the defensive position, and we will defend it to the last man."

The Finns also managed to destroy two tanks in the battle, and the Soviet gunners were cut-off from their tanks by enemy fire. According to Finnish records they succeeded in cutting the advanced guard off from the main forces in a flanking manoeuvre and by 2040 hrs they had recaptured all the positions they had lost on the height. Soviet records show that the Finns launched around 12 counterattacks, and furthermore the final counterattack had to be fought off by officers as well as soldiers, who were at the divisional Command Post on the height itself.

In total the 281st Rifle Division lost on 15 June, according to incomplete records, 118 men killed, and 290 wounded. On that day, the Finnish artillery fired 7,300 shells. As a result of a direct hit on his Command Post by a shell the Commander of the 38th Heavy Artillery Brigade Colonel Ivan Semyonovich Khrutskiy was killed.

16 June

Despite all the efforts by the Finns to recapture the height, Soviet tank crews together with a severely depleted infantry held onto it until reinforcements arrived. On 16 July 1944 the exhausted Finnish units were ordered to withdraw back to the River Vuoksi. The battles on the height continued meanwhile, though not with the same level of intensity as they had before. On that day, the 1,066th Regiment lost its commissar. Major Kalin Denisovich Ponomaryov was killed on height 171.1. Moreover, the 3rd Army Command ordered that the depleted 381st and 281st Rifle Divisions be pulled back to the reserves. The battle concluded with the withdrawal of the Finnish forces to the north. The Soviet forces did not pursue them.

The veterans of 7th Regiment left some vivid recollections behind of the battles for the height. Only two of them are cited here. Heikki Peltovaara, the Commander of the section and the signals officer for the 10th Company, 7th Infantry Regiment, recalls one of the counterattacks on the height:

> My section also received reinforcements, two young soldiers who were born in 1926.
>
> Suddenly I heard the beat of engines in the skies. I noticed ground attack aircraft, flying almost at tree-top level towards us from the direction of the village. I dived into a ditch, and lay down, stretching out fully. A burst of machine gun fire passed through the place where I had been standing and covered me in earth. With a howl that was growing ever louder the ground attack aircraft passed over us, and the links from their machine gun belts rained down on me. Cries of help could now be heard constantly.
>
> I saw our Company Commander, Captain Pentti Ruuskanen, he was several metres away to the right. He shouted: "Everybody get down! Do not get up!" At that very moment a powerful explosion rang out from his direction, and everything was covered in smoke. A shell from a *Katyusha* exploded next to the Captain. His legs were blown off; his injury was fatal. His signals officer died alongside him.

I decided that soon there would not be one square metre of ground left here that had not been touched by a shell as the salvos were falling on the road itself. I ran forwards keeping to the left of the road, since it was a bit quieter there. Junior Sergeant Kuyvamyaki was running alongside me with a rucksack on his back–he had only just got back from leave. Something exploded at the top of a tall fir tree on the edge of the marsh and the crown fell to earth. Kuyvamyaki cried out that he had been injured in the hand. We had though escaped the zone of the main artillery barrage. Kuyvamyaki left for the dressing station behind the lines.

This was how our first counterattack ended in failure. The immobile barrage of fire lasted for approximately an hour and had its effect–our company was scattered. Many, including the company commander, had been taken out of the game. Those of our company who were still alive had gathered at the edge of the forest, where it was sufficiently quiet. The artillery as before was attacking the road, and only the odd shell would reach us. The sound of rifle fire would shortly be heard from the front, along with cries of "hoorah!"

We formed into disparate groups and advanced towards the height. I walked at the head of my section. Since the Russians had broken through our defences on the height, we carefully approached the edge of the forest, having formed into a line. We emerged into a field and prepared ourselves for an attack. When we surged forward the Russians were nowhere to be seen, we were separated by the Siiranmyaki height. I ran forward across the field as fast as I could go. At that moment we cried "Hoorah!" at the tops of our voices, we could already see the enemy. Bullets were whistling through the air, exploding bullets cracked alarmingly.

I could see the retreating Russians in the distance. I jumped into a metre long shell crater in the field and opened fire from my automatic weapon. We got caught up on the height itself, and this was why our second counterattack was successful. The top of the height was behind us, but the breakthrough had been halted.

The clank of tank tracks was soon audible on the height, and the alder thickets began to sway. We did not have any adequate weaponry to stop a tank. In the next shell crater however was a young lad (he had been born in 1926) who was from the last batch of reinforcements, Private Sairanen, I knew that he had an anti-tank grenade with him. I beckoned him over to me. The tanks were already close and had begun to toast us with fire from their guns. The field was peppered with exploding shells. Our thin line on the summit of the height was floundering. I noticed that the vehicles were starting to move towards the edge of the forest and further towards us. Private Sairanen, who I had called over to me, ran around the field with an anti-tank grenade in his hand. Shortly though there was a flash of an explosion where he had been standing and he disappeared in a column of smoke. Either shrapnel or a bullet had hit the anti-tank grenade.

On my right I saw another young soldier born in 1926, who had joined my section in Vuottaa, Private Pitkyanen, who was running in front of a tank. At that moment he fell down onto the ground. This young soldier had been cut down by machine gun fire. I decided that it was also time for me to get back to the forest since there was nobody left on the battlefield apart from the enemy tanks, and the last of our soldiers had disappeared to the sound of gunfire from tanks. I did manage to reach the forest safely.

For Captain Valde Haimalainen commander of the anti-tank gun batteries, who had been fighting since 1939 and had survived the battle for Summe in the succeeding Soviet-Finnish War, the battle for the height would be the last in his military career:

12 June 1944
I received orders to bring all the guns up to a position on the Siiranmyaki height, which was partially fortified. This work however was never completed. This was where we paid the price for the soldiers who had been sitting around twiddling their thumbs for years and had not been building adequate defences.

Some of my guns were deployed on the height, and I was very dissatisfied with the positioning for the guns. They had no depth to them, and they were all positioned on the height's southern slopes. In addition they were all more or less in a line. If they had to retreat just one step away from these positions no other positions had been built for them. We burnt our buildings in Saarenmaa so that the enemy could not make use of them. We had not however burnt down the garage on the edge of the forest.

I quickly gathered our battery together. Tiilikainen was ordered to take up a defensive position on the southern edge of the field at Saarenmaa. Wilhelmson's position was on the eastern edge of the height, a concrete position had been cast for a gun and shelters had been built. The firing position was next to the wrestling hall where I had trained so many times. I ran between Tiililkyainen's and Viljhelmson's guns, checking that everything was okay. We had four guns left, the other two had been buried on the main defensive line in the course of the enemy artillery barrage.

I spent the night in the Company Commander's tent …

13 June 1944
I decided to move away to stay on the height. I wanted to be closer to the battlefield since there were better prospects there to actually engage in combat, than there would be behind the lines. Since there would be no question of me staying in a tent I had to find a dug out of some kind where I could stay. On the slope of the height not far from the trench was a small, but strongly built bunker. This was where Captain Kiiskinen lived with his folk. Even though it was already cramped in the bunker, Kiiskinen allowed me to stay there, as he understood that I had to stay somewhere. The location was suitable since it was located between the two platoons.

That entire day was spent bringing the positions up to scratch, we camouflaged them and did other necessary work …

So many enemy soldiers were killed on the field in front of us in one day that it resembled a marsh with a mass of hillocks. I very much regretted that none of the infantry officers had demolished any of the observation towers that stood on the highest point on the hill south of Siiranmyaki during the course of the retreat. It was from those same towers that Anna-Liisa had monitored the situation in the air along with other members of the *Lotta Svard*. I was often in those towers and I knew that Siiranmyaki and all our defences were visible from them and the enemy would know them like the back of their hands. Even the slightest movement on the height would be perfectly visible through binoculars. The excellent conditions for adjusting artillery fire against our own positions were an invaluable gift from us to the Russian artillery reconnaissance scouts. In the course of the hurried retreat the idea of destroying these towers had not even crossed my mind.

Towards evening I was caught in a rain shower and was wet through but I had no change of clothes. I had to spend the night in Kiiskinne's bunker in clothes that were dripping wet and this bunker owing to its concrete walls was cold, like a tomb. I had nothing to feed the stove with and the smoke would have given away the position of our bunker–thanks to those who had not demolished the towers as we were retreating. There was no room to stretch out in the bunker, but half awake, I did at least manage to lean on something. Kiiskinen sat by the telephone receiving reports, issuing orders and ordering the artillery to fire on menacing sectors nearby. He was so busy that he probably did not get a wink of sleep the whole night. At last that cold and wet night was over, and a new, bloody day dawned. That day saw the blood of many of my comrades in arms spilt – and mine too.

14 June 1944
That morning I ran to my Command Post. I could not have known at that moment, that I was going there for the last time. On the way back I bumped into my former Commander, Captain Markku Hassinen, who was standing on the roadside with a smile on his lips. This would be the last time I would see him too–Hassinen died in Vuosalmi from shrapnel wounds to the stomach that he had sustained when he got up from a trench to gaze out at the battlefield. We spoke a few words between us but we were both in a hurry and had no time for long drawn out conversations. I had to get back immediately to the Battalion's Command Post on a ridge that was a few kilometres away from the front line as I had been summoned there. In a deep depression in the earth I met Captain Laamanen. He said he had been made the liaison officer between the infantry and the anti-tank crews so I was to send all my orders to my superiors through him. He also told me that the artillery platoon under Captain Olasa had been subordinated to me, he also had heavy anti-tank guns in his company. It seemed that my responsibility was increasing sharply, as it had been at the end of the Winter War, when the entire anti-tank defence of Vyborg consisting of 12 guns had been subordinated to me. I was happy because I had more guns and more personnel once again.

Along with my signals officer Remes, a Lapland lad, I set off again for Siiranmyaki. On the way we suddenly came under attack from a fierce artillery salvo. The shells exploded all around us at almost the same time. We had to jump into a ditch, which luckily was sufficiently deep. On the edge of the culvert, which was right next to us, several shells exploded, and we were covered in earth. I personally was in an excellent mood, which rubbed off on Remes. I said to him that the shells were not going to hit us anyway, so that he would not be scared. My signals officer told me calmly that he was not scared. Since it seemed that the artillery barrage would go on for some time, we decided to make our shelter a little deeper, so as to while away the time. We had to sit together in a crouching position for half an hour before the barrage let up sufficiently for us to shake off our clothes and continue our journey. On the way I encountered one of the gun platoons that were now in my command. This platoon was commanded by *Fahnrich* Kuisma.

On reaching the height I was told that the enemy had attacked our positions on the edge of the field and our infantry was planning to launch a counterattack under the command of Lieutenant Sippola. I left my signals officer there and took a grenade in my hand, which did not even have the fuse inside I noticed later. I went into the counterattack along with the infantry since one of my gun was there and I wanted to help my men. The Russians retreated from our positions with sufficient ease. Among those killed during the counterattack were Lieutenant Sippola, a Cavalier of the Mannerheim Cross, he had been shot in the temple.

I set off to get a sense of the situation on the height. A fierce battle had been fought there. Our gun on the left flank had already been destroyed, and dozens of Russian tanks were already snarling around on the height. Lieutenants Urho Vilhelms and Uuno Kaksonen approached me. I gave them orders and we defused the situation with a few pleasing drags on a cigarette. The battle that was thundering away above our heads was of no concern to us. After that two of my good friends climbed up the slope of the height. They almost reached their positions when a shell that exploded next to them cut down both Vilhelms and Kaksonen. This was how two of my good mates in the Army met their end right in front of my eyes.

I tried to reach my friends, but the enemy had already broken through our defences. When I went to the crest of the height the Russians were passing between us in an endless column. Pastor Laaioki, who had actually performed my marriage ceremony, rushed past me, a pistol in his hand. I emptied a whole magazine at the advancing Russians, but my automatic rifle was powerless against an enemy armada. With a heavy heart I had to leave my fallen friends on the southern slope of the height, next to the crest of the mount, and withdraw. There was nowhere to take shelter. There was just open terrain and the advancing enemy for dozens of metres around us. It is possible that a single Finn firing an automatic gun was for them a very modest target, since they did not return my fire, and I managed to get away.

I withdrew back to the bunker. To my amazement I saw Captain Kiiskinen lying in a pool of blood in a vest next to the door of the bunker. What had happened? I decided that he must have jumped out to try and save himself and our artillery had undershot and the shell had exploded right at that moment as Kiiskinen had jumped out. I left him just a few dozen minutes ago when he was giving orders in the bunker and had ordered artillery fire. Now he was lying in front of me seriously wounded. In battle things change quickly.

No one knew yet what had happened to the commander in the bunker. I immediately called for help. We lifted Kiiskinen onto a stretcher and took him to the dressing station. He was in a great deal of pain, he would pray out loud, then cry, then complain. We could only help him by carrying the stretcher as fast as we could. As we reached the road we saw a driver with an ambulance wagon. I ordered him to take the Captain to the field hospital urgently. Kiiskinen was later awarded the Mannerheim Cross. He really had earned that award.

I continued my journey to the Battalion Command Post. I received an order there via Laamanen from my superiors to destroy the enemy tanks that had broken through onto the height …

Our task was to pull the gun up along the side of the height that we had defended and on to a suitable firing position along a road through the forest. We had turned onto this road since it was our only possible route. It turned out that the entire road was peppered with craters, and fallen trees, and had turned into a fluid like mush. Our gun weighed 1,850kg and the wheels were small for the weight of the gun. Since it was very heavy to lift and we only had a few men, we had nowhere near enough strength. I left the soldiers under the command of Kuisma to pull the gun forward and set off with Remes to call on the infantry for help, they were on the crown of the height about 400–500m away. At that same time I decided to reconnoitre a firing position. At around 1500 hrs I arrived at Captain Walden's Command Post, which was on a slope, approximately 70–80m north of the summit of the height. I asked a soldier who had run past me in a crouched position, I was hoping that Walden was going to detail one of his men to help with pulling the gun. I was told that he had only just left for the first aid post, so that his injured hand could be bandaged. Later I found out that Walden had disappeared without trace on the way to the first aid post, evidently form a direct hit from a bomb or a shell. I decided to go after him.

There was a small clearing to the right of the bunker that was a few dozen metres wide. The enemy had managed to hold onto its southern edge, in a small wooded area that was overgrown with bushes on the summit of the height. It was there that several enemy heavy tanks stood in a line with their guns trained in our direction. Aside from the tanks this small wooded area was full of elite Russian infantry. Our infantry could not launch a counterattack until the tanks had been destroyed. Then I realised that our artillery would not be able to fire at the tanks since they were actually very close to our own positions. Therefore it was up to me to destroy these tanks.

On so many occasions in the Winter War I had encountered tanks and escaped unscathed. I had not felt any of the respect of which tanks were worthy. Since I had to act fast in to the bargain, I was not going to wander among the bushes. I thought that since Walden had passed this way, I too would make it through. I went straight across the clearing, bathed in sunlight, past the line of tanks, but all the time I kept my eyes on them. My signals officer was wiser and did not follow me.

When I was in the middle of the clearing a tank gun roared. I did not hear the explosion but I felt a sudden, very sharp pain as though my whole body had been shattered. I threw up my hands and fell face down. My whole body was burning as though it had been torn into pieces by red hot tongs. I could not comprehend at that time where I had been hit, it seemed that my whole body had been injured. I did not make a sound, death as it came closer seemed to me like a friend. Now it was my turn to follow in the footsteps of all the other injured men. My will to survive however got the upper hand and I tried calling out meekly for help, as the strength was leaving my body, draining out of me along with the blood that was mixing with the earth of Siiranmyaki. I knew though that none of my comrades could help me, nor would they summon up the courage to help me here, on the brink of death. Only God could help me! A short time later I passed into the merciful darkness of a delirium, I had lost consciousness. This ended my pain and suffering.

Later on I came across an artillery reconnaissance scout, who had become a witness to these events. He recalled that my gun had been severely delayed (I do not know if the soldiers managed to drag it to the position or not) but the enemy had suddenly gone on the offensive across the clearing, in which I was doubled up in a pool of blood. The tanks had crossed the clearing and had nearly run over me. The infantry that had come after them had ransacked me. They turned me over onto my back, ripped off my collar insignia as keepsakes, and took my belt, pistol and the watch from my wrist. They had not fortunately taken my wedding ring from my bloodied hand, since it was still on me, as was my hand. After that they had left my "body" and continued on their way on the trail of the tanks. My signals officer had been injured in that battle.

Private Seppyanen managed to destroy the tanks that had broken through using a *Panzerfaust* weapon and our infantry had launched a counterattack. For this achievement he was subsequently awarded the Mannerheim Cross. The Russians had been held back for half an hour, after which they returned with more reinforcements and again pushed our troops back. In that half hour period somebody, most likely medical orderlies, had come and removed me from the battlefield. I was taken onto a stretcher and then initially to a first aid post, and then after a tetanus injection I was taken to a field hospital. A label was placed around my neck, on which was written: in a full state of shock. Fortunately, Ahti at that time was on three month's leave and he did not get to see his lacerated and dying brother placed onto the operating table.

The overall losses for the 98th Rifle Corps during the course of the storming of Siiranmyaki and the height to the west were 3,784 men, of whom 887 had been killed. Losses for the Finnish 2nd

Infantry Division were 873 men, of whom 164 had been killed, 760 injured, and 49 were missing without trace.

As of today, a sole Finnish memorial has been erected on height. Built in 2004, it is constructed of concrete and granite. In connection with the construction of the cottage settlement known as *Karpikyulya*, the trenches in the vicinity, where 1,064th Regiment had broken through to the height, were employed as a spoil dump. As of 2016 the height does not have a designated cultural heritage status.

10

Battle on the Gulf of Finland Shore and 1st Red Banner Brigade Raid

The events occurring between Rayvola and the Gulf of Finland, which decided the outcome of the whole of the battle on the "VT line" are often hidden behind the epic battle on the white night of 14–15 June 1944 near Kuuterselka and the bloody battle on the Siiranmyaki height.

On the evening of 12 June the Commander of the 21st Army introduced the 108th Rifle Corps under Lieutenant-General Tikhonov (the 46th, 90th, and 314th Rifle divisions) that were fresh from lave, into the battle. The objective was to augment the army's orders of battle in the Primorskoye direction. The 109th Rifle Corps under Alferov moved to the right and began to prepare for the storming of the "VT line" along the railway line to Kuuterselka.

The 108th Rifle Corps adopted a combat formation made up of two echelons and in addition they began to storm the VT line. The 46th Rifle Division under Borshchev attacked in the first echelon, along with the 90th Rifle Division under Major-General Lyashchenko. The 31st and 260th Guards Heavy Tank Regiments were due to support the offensive by these rifle units, along with the 1,439th and 1,238th Self-Propelled Artillery Regiments. In the second echelon was the 314th Rifle Division under Colonel Larionov.

The Corps' artillery alignment was imposing:

> The artillery bombardment group comprised the 85th and 95th Heavy Howitzer Brigades, the 18th Super Heavy Guards Howitzer Brigade, the 40th and 32nd Separate Super Heavy Artillery Battalions, and the 3rd Heavy Howitzer Brigade:
>
> The 1,324th, 1,325th, and 1,326th Light Artillery Regiments from the 71st Light Artillery Brigade all fought at close range and were joined by field artillery, as well as the anti-tank battalions in the rifle units:
>
> The counter-mortar activity group consisted of the 1,227th, 1,085th, and the 1.211th Howitzer Regiments from the 67th Brigade.
>
> The 127th Gun Artillery Brigade and the 138th Corps' Artillery Regiment were attached to these divisions.
>
> The 398th, 858th, 96th Artillery Regiments as well as the 254th, 534th, 251st, 257th, and 276th Mortar Regiments along with the 29th Guards Mortar Regiments fought in the sector of the Corps' offensive.

On the morning of 14 June, after a powerful artillery barrage lasting one and a half hours, units from the 46th and 90th Rifle Divisions went on the offensive between the Vyborg–Leningrad railway line and the shore of the Gulf of Finland. The principal attack was inflicted on the centre. On a signal fired from a red flare battalions from the forward regiment's attacked as far as the river.

Corporal Pentti Ratia of Tavast's Cavalry Regiment observed:

> Anything that could was firing at us. Aviation, heavy artillery, even the Kronstadt forts. My dug out was on the Marina Gora. I sat in the dugout after tucking my head into my shoulder. Each nearby explosion from a shell was like a tree log hitting my helmet. I got to thinking: "This is it for you mate." I saw how a shell hit the church and the dome fell to the ground, just like it was a little football..

The artillery barrage was powerful, but it was in this very area that the structures that made up the VT line were almost 100 percent complete and the Soviet forces encountered fierce resistance. In certain locations Soviet forces succeeded in crossing the river and capturing some of the trenches, but they were not able to advance any further.

In the sector of 46th Rifle Division's advance, the situation by 1600 hrs had unfolded as follows: the 1st and some of the 2nd Rifle Battalions from the 314th Rifle Regiment had crossed the river just down from the bridge; the 2nd Battalion from the 314th Rifle Regiment had gained a foothold on the left bank. These battalions succeeded in breaking through to the first Finnish trench. The remainder of the battalions were as before on the eastern bank of the river. The commanders of both regiments–Majors Fadeyev and Melnikov were wounded. The Division's 176th Regiment advanced to their starting positions to repeat the attack. In the course of a day's fighting the division had lost 140 men killed, and 571 wounded. Three batteries from the 1,238th Self-Propelled Regiment reached the river and opened fire from this location since there were no fording points suitable for the SU-76s.

In the sector of 90th Rifle Division's advance the situation was complex. At 0300 hrs the 266th and 173rd Rifle Regiments occupied their starting positions for the attack. In the course of an artillery barrage lasting one and a half hours the supporting artillery fired 26,617 mines and shells, but the majority of them were not able to inflict any significant damage on the gun emplacements in the "VT line" with their thick walls. In total one hundred and sixty five 122mm shells were fired. Just 10 minutes prior to the end of the artillery barrage the regiments went on the attack and began to ford the river Rayvolan – Yoki. The 286th Regiment succeeded in crossing the river and advanced forward a distance of one and a half kilometres. The regiment's 3rd Battalion came under fire from the flanks, and sustained 30 percent losses in terms of its personnel, and did not cross the river. The 2nd Battalion from the 173rd Regiment crossed the river in a decisive speed march and succeeded in breaking through to the first trench in the "VT line." The Regiment's 3rd Battalion came under such fierce fire that it had to lay low on the eastern bank of the river, with no possibility of advancing forward. The day's objectives for the divisions and regiments remained unfulfilled. In the course of a day's fighting the 90th Rifle Division had lost 701 men killed and wounded.

Eleven KV tanks from the 31st Guards Heavy Tank Regiment and the self-propelled guns were not able to support the infantry effectively due to the fact that the fording points had not been reconnoitred beforehand, neither had the enemy's tank traps, mines, and anti-tank guns. In this situation the commanders of the 8th Engineer's Battalion made a name for themselves as heroes. Under deadly Finnish artillery fire Battalion Commander Major Bobykin and Company Commander Senior Lieutenant Raud crossed the river together on pontoons and measured out a tank crossing point across the river. Raud was shot in the chest and died on his way to hospital. Unfortunately on 14 June 1944 this did little to help the situation at hand.

Despite this difficult situation on 14 June, the Finns held out. They only lost a small proportion of their strongholds. It appeared that the cavalry brigade had managed to hold out and that the situation was under control. This however was certainly not the case. On the cavalry brigade's left flank events took place that would lead to a complete collapse of the Finnish defence.

The 1st Battalion, 53rd Infantry Regiment that had been defending the VT line near the railway bridge across the Vammel-Yuka, following a morning attack by the 456th Rifle Regiment, of the 109th Rifle Division they had been driven out of the first trench. The Battalion Commander Yahnukainen gathered everyone together who was to hand–logistics and signals personnel, and drivers and managed to beat off almost all the positions. The 6th Jager Battalion came to his assistance, they were one of the few Finnish reserves located on the western side of the Isthmus. In the second half of the day the 456th Regiment again went on the attack and again captured a segment of the Finnish trenches. A short while later Major Yahnukainen ordered his Battalion to begin to withdraw to the north, justifying his actions by breaking through the defensive line in Kuuterselka. The left flank of the dragoon regiment remained unsettled. Subsequent events began to unfold at the speed of an avalanche.

The 21st Army Command immediately took advantage of the breach in the Finnish defences in Kuuterselka. At 1615 hrs on 14 June a mobile group from the 1st Red Banner Tank Brigade, which had been standing at readiness in the area around Pukhtolova Gora received an order to enter the breach, strike and hit Mustamyaki (Gorkovskoye) railway station and advance further to Uusikirkko with the objective of getting behind the lines of the cavalry brigade and cutting off the Primorskoye road.

The Brigade's raid preparations took 35 mins and they went into battle at 1650 hrs. By 1930 hrs the tank crews, carrying the motorised infantry on their armour passed Mustamyaki and the Syuryainen-Myaki farmstead. The tank crews were constantly supported by ground attack aircraft from the 227th Ground Attack Air Division. Over the course of the battle for the complete lifting of the siege of Leningrad ground attack aviation began to provide effective support to the tank crews as they advanced. In one of the brigade's tanks was the best signals officer from the ranks of the Air Force–a pilot from the 943rd Ground Attack Air Regiment Senior Lieutenant Aleksandr Fyodorivich Razgulov. He called in an air strike from a group of between four to 12 Ilyushin aircraft by radio and skilfully guided them onto the target. Our pilots first and foremost were acting to suppress the enemy's anti-tank guns. Razgyulov was especially successful in working with the squadrons led by Parshin and Polyakov, who had already proved themselves very well in battle back in January 1944. In a single sortie the ground attack aircraft made around five or six approaches on the target, demoralising the anti-tank gun crews and assisting the Soviet tank crews to destroy them.

In comparison with the events of the previous January, the communications system had been optimised between the air controller and the airfields. The waiting time had been reduced as had the number of links in the chain of command for ordering an air strike. The ground attack crews also noted that in the Vyborg Offensive Operation the ground units serving in the Leningrad Front identified themselves for the pilots much better than during the battles for the lifting of the siege of Leningrad. The tank crews made widespread use of target identifying signal flares and lines of tracer bullets from their tanks' machine guns, which was much appreciated by the ground attack aircraft pilots.

At Mustamyaki Station, tank crews captured some of the guns from Hankipokhya's artillery group. After that they encountered almost no resistance. The Finns had been taken by surprise. In Neuvola the tank crews attacked warehouses as well as the logistics belonging to the Cavalry Brigade and the artillery units. The Combat Journal of the 16th Heavy Battalion was burnt along with the headquarters trucks, a copy however has survived, which was written by the Battalion's Adjutant after 14 June:

> When the tank column broke through to Neuvola, a column made up of our 2nd Battery also broke through from a secondary road to the main road, A tank, together with five machine gunners opened fire on the column as a result of which the first tractor left the road and entered a roadside ditch, and Lieutenant Paysalo fell face down onto the ground from the vehicle. The tank column laid waste a truck that was travelling on its own back from Sahakyla, and the fourth gun from the 3rd Battery was run off the road by ramming it, in the forest the tank column passed three guns from the 3rd Battery, and destroyed a truck belonging to the Battalion's dressing station near the Vammeljarvi bridge and according to witnesses three tanks that passed our column made up of carts without firing a single shot went on to Leistila, there they turned round and opened fire on the column. Our logistics units had withdrawn back to Vammelyarvi an hour before this happened.

The tanks rammed and destroyed the trucks, and the stockpiles of military equipment, as well as pushing the guns off the road and firing at anything that moved. At 2025 hrs (according to Finnish records the time is given as 1930 hrs) Soviet tanks broke through to the courtyard of the Cavalry Brigade's headquarters, which was located in the picturesque Vaamelyarvi estate on the banks of the lake that bore its name. At first the Finnish officers mistook the tanks for their own but a burst of fierce fire that broke out in an instant dispelled all their doubts. In the panic that ensued the brigade headquarters succeeded in setting the mansion house in the estate on fire and scattered. The cavalrymen reached the area around Uusikirkko through the forests and marshes and continued on to the north.

Soviet tank crews at first thought they had destroyed nothing less than the headquarters of the 4th Army. In total in this raid the 1st Red Banner Brigade had captured 15 automobiles, 60 trucks, 150 bicycles, up to 25 guns, one banner, three seals bearing the coat of arms, 10 radios, 20 telephones, and up to 200 rifles and 250 horses. Amongst those killed, according to calculations made by Soviet tank crews, was a Finnish Lieutenant-General!

However, the most important thing was not the valuable trophies captured by the tank crews, but something quite different. The Cavalry Brigade's left flank was left open, and the logistics had been destroyed. The Nyland Dragoon and Tavast's Cavalry Regiments, which had been on the front line, stated the following: on the evening of 14 June communications with headquarters had been lost and were not re-established. Signals officers sent to headquarters returned and reported that the headquarters building was on fire, and the place was crawling with Soviet tanks with infantry soldiers sitting on their armour. The regiments did not have any way of contacting command. In this situation the regimental commanders took a decision at their own risk: in the early morning of 15 June they would begin to withdraw in small groups, making their withdrawal as covert as possible for the Soviet forces.

As a result, by the morning of 15 June the "VT line" from the Vyborg–Leningrad railway line up to the Gulf of Finland had been abandoned <u>in its entirety</u> by the Finnish forces. The Finns had no reserves left at all in the western part of the Karelian Isthmus with which to counter an attack.

The only mobile reserve hat was capable of mounting a counterattack was Lagus' armoured division, which was located 30 km to the east of the location of these events. The Jager Brigade at that moment was fighting in Kuuterselka and was not aware that the battle had been lost.

The entire Finnish defence in the western part of the Karelian Isthmus had collapsed. The 90th and 46th Rifle Divisions climbed aboard their SU-76s and went in pursuit of the retreating Cavalry Brigade. By 1200 hrs on 15 June the 340th Rifle Regiment had captured the station at Ino, and without encountering any resistance, had begun to advance along the Primorskoye road towards

Vyborg. The Cavalry Brigade at that time was retreating along a parallel course, avoiding the road. The Finns were justifiably concerned about attacks from Soviet ground attack aircraft.

Following the failure of the counterattack in Kuuterselka Finnish Command thought as they had before that the main attack from the Soviet forces would be made along the road in the direction of Liikola–Vierumyaki–Kyuyurelya. It was to there that Lagus' units retreated and from where they took up their defensive positions. The 4th Corps Command and Headquarters did not immediately see that the 21st Army had carried out its main attack through a gaping breach west of the railway line. It was there that the fresh 152nd Separate Tank Brigade was heading, which had replaced the exhausted 1st Red Banner Brigade that had incurred heavy losses.

Following the war, this catastrophe gave rise to a war of words between the 3rd Infantry Division Command and the officers of the Cavalry Brigade. The famous Finnish historian, writer and officer Wolfgang Halsti, who in the summer of 1944 had been the Chief of Staff of the 3rd Infantry Division, in his post war books blamed the Cavalry Brigade for the collapse of the defence and lay all the blame for the defeat on the shoulders of the unsanctioned withdrawal by the cavalrymen. This gave rise to heated written responses from the officers in the Cavalry Brigade, who in turn blamed the 53rd Infantry Regiment and the 3rd Division for allowing the breach in the defences in Kuuterselka and Sakakyulya, which led to a routing of the logistics units and of the Cavalry Brigade headquarters. "A victory has many authors, but defeat is always an orphan."

A decade later Colonel von Essen, the Commander of Nyland's Dragoon Regiment, described the events of the 15 June as follows:

> Discipline in the regiment remained high, despite the losses and exhaustion. On the day of the breakthrough on 14 June I, with the help of my heroic signals men spent the whole day in communication with the regiment's subdivisions on the front line. The regiment held their positions despite the furious Russian advance. In spite of the heavy losses, the regiment succeeded in inflicting heavy losses on the enemy, destroying two tanks. We withdrew from the main defensive boundary only when I had given the order to withdraw at my own risk.

Cavalry Captain Vartiainen:

> I went through the entire defensive sector. Tavast's regiment up to the sector under the Nyland's Dragoon Regiment and back again. I know the conditions that we had to fight in on the "VT line" on the night we abandoned it well. I had to climb out of trenches a countless number of times since they had been completely destroyed. The logs that reinforced the sides engulfed the trench in a crosswise pattern and it was impossible to move around inside. In two of the trenches the sludge and water was at such a level that feet, hands and heads of the fallen were only partially visible. There were dozens of dead lying in the trenches, I did not check the trenches branching off and the communications trench, but I think that there were dead lying in those too. The deepest trench sector that had been destroyed was 300m in length, and there were a number of sectors that were 100–150m long. The stronghold that had sustained the most damage was near the railway bridge, this was the stronghold under Lieutenant Viinamyaki of the 4th Troop, Nyland's Dragoon Regiment. I saw two unexploded eight-inch shells in the dugout, which had broken through the parapet of the dugout. There were an enormous number of unexploded small calibre shells in the area.

Colonel G. Ehrnrooth:

> As far as I knew, we did not have any reserves on the whole southern part of the Karelian Isthmus, the 1st and 6th Jager Battalions, which had been attached to the Cavalry Brigade, had already been mobilised in the area around Lempala–Sakakyulya–Mustamyaki, therefore it had been almost impossible to stop a breakthrough of our defences to a considerable depth. The only pretext for holding the defensive line in Vammelsuu would have been "fight to the last man in honour of the Tavast Regiment," which would have provided a moral, but a not very realistic basis for defending the Karelian Isthmus.

Boris Vladimirovich Bychevskiy, the head of the Leningrad Front's engineering force:

> It was already dark when the officers from Army headquarters arrived from the 108th Corps. We learned from them the reasons for the disappointing results from the first day of fighting for the 46th, and 90th Divisions. The centre of the position in front of the bridge on the Primorskoye road from Vanhasar up to the Gulf of Finland turned out to be complex, and sacciform. This emerged in the course of the actual attack. The ground attack aircraft from the division's regiments overcame one six row belt of two-metre high granite tank traps, and 300m further on there was another one, which was hidden in some bushes. The barbed wire fences laid in five rows of steaks was also fixed in place using ties. It is difficult to shoot these away even from close range. Approximately twenty pillboxes that were destroyed and captured on the eastern bank but beyond the river in an area that was overgrown with bushes there is barely a dozen of these pillboxes, including artillery examples. This sector was being defended by the remains of the Finnish 10th Infantry Division that had retreated, as well as units from the 1st Bicyclist's Brigade, and the 2nd Coastal Defence Brigade. This defensive centre turned out to be a very powerful one against which to achieve a breakthrough without an initial artillery barrage.

Corporal Toivo Hoffren after the war wrote a fictional story, which though it exaggerated Soviet losses and Cavalry Brigade achievements – not to mention some glaring factual errors – it does provide a good impression of the two-day battle:

> Either the builders of the Mannerheim Line turned a blind eye to a huge mistake, or they had not finished its construction before the start of the last flare up, we just never got to the bottom of it. The trenches were well built and strongly reinforced, the shelters for the personnel consisted of strongly built bunkers made of concrete and armour, but there were no communications ditches leading to the logistics areas behind the lines. We spent two days excavating them ourselves. In front of us, at a distance of between fifty or sixty metres the enemy had gained a foothold on the bank of the Vaameljoki.
>
> The whole night the enemy rained unrelenting fire down on us, which did not actually inflict much damage. The sentries stood their guard as usual and the new recruits were taken on patrol singly so we had three pairs of eyes, instead of two as before. Inside the walls of the Vammelsuu public school, some 200m from us our enemy was celebrating something, judging by the sounds that were reaching us from there. On the edge of the wood, a little further on, the "thirty-fours" had been lined up in a row, like taxis in front of the old bus station in Helsinki. In the forest, further on still, the hum of engines could be heard, and the loud voices of the commanders carried far across the battlefield.
>
> A new recruit who was standing alongside us by the name of Unto, who had sparkling eyes, was gripping his rifle. His face was pale with worry, and his very large helmet was constantly sliding down in front of his eyes. There was something touching about this thin

body, these nervous thoughts, driven only by a fear of the leadership. These lads would stand to attention meekly as soon as they saw a corporal. For us, seasoned soldiers, this was something new. It would almost come to it that we could not help but polish the faces of these new recruits for the time that they were with us. We knew that we could never get accustomed to a peaceful life. To force us to stand to attention before some sucker, or to take orders from some sleazeball would be tantamount to a suicide attempt for the individual giving the order. On the other hand our "*Kaiser*" had no time for stupidity, we had to be true to her until the very end. The *Kaiser* we had grown to love was a 75mm anti-tank gun, which we had received three weeks previously, and which in the last few days had set fire to five Russian tanks. German steel in Finnish hands was a dangerous enemy.

"But is our artillery going to get the chance to fire?" I gave the recruit a look in passing. Something was tickling his throat. I looked at Yorma, who was greedily smoking through a copper cigarette holder made from a shell casing at the foot of the trench.

"Maybe we don't have any artillery left any more, or they are trying to find new guns to replace those we have lost. They need to do something soon, and where, damn them, are the reinforcements?" I felt that this lad was shaking as he stood by my side, looking out at the old school.

The enthusiasm of these young lads enlivened our marches with their pleasing voices. The serious lectures given by the old Feldwebel Jagers and the slogan: a Finnish forest soldier is invincible. In these five days though we came across something the old lecturers had not encountered before. Now heavy automatic weaponry played a role, which in previous wars had been the preserve of a sharp pair of eyes and a good rifle. Since we evidently did not hold the advantage in firepower on our side of the Vaamelyoki, the hum of the marches seemed to us like a twist of fate.

At 0200 hrs Raymo came to see us, along with our Platoon Commander Kuparinen to relieve us. The weight of responsibility on his shoulders was such that I left an indelible impression on his whole being. He did not utter a word, he just quietly jabbed with his fist.

"Keep your eyes peeled! They are clearly no newbies. They will want to wet our whistles; it would be easier to fight a bunch of drunkards."

"Well yes. I don't know what will happen at all. They promised us reinforcements, but they haven't arrived. Artillery. Damn the artillery. Where is out famous artillery?"

"Maybe all our gunners are holidaying on Lake Saima."

This was Yorma's black humour.

"Hold your tongue. If we are going to withdraw from here, where will we stop? Eh, what's there for us?"

In the distance and off to the left a sub-machine gun rang out from one of our outposts, interrupting Raymo's speech. In response to this bursts of tracer bullets were pouring out of a machine gun on the edge of the forest.

"Give the ruins of my damned school a few bursts. We will get rid of somebody no doubt."

"Get out of here and try and get some sleep. And stay down lad if you want to get back home on your own two feet."

The new recruit all but crawled between us back to the bunker. It was probably terrible for him. It was terrible for all of us. It began at 0400 hrs in the morning. Thousands of guns were bellowing, spewing out tonnes of steel at once. The door only burst open once, when Kuparinen ran in after Raymo.

List of Maps

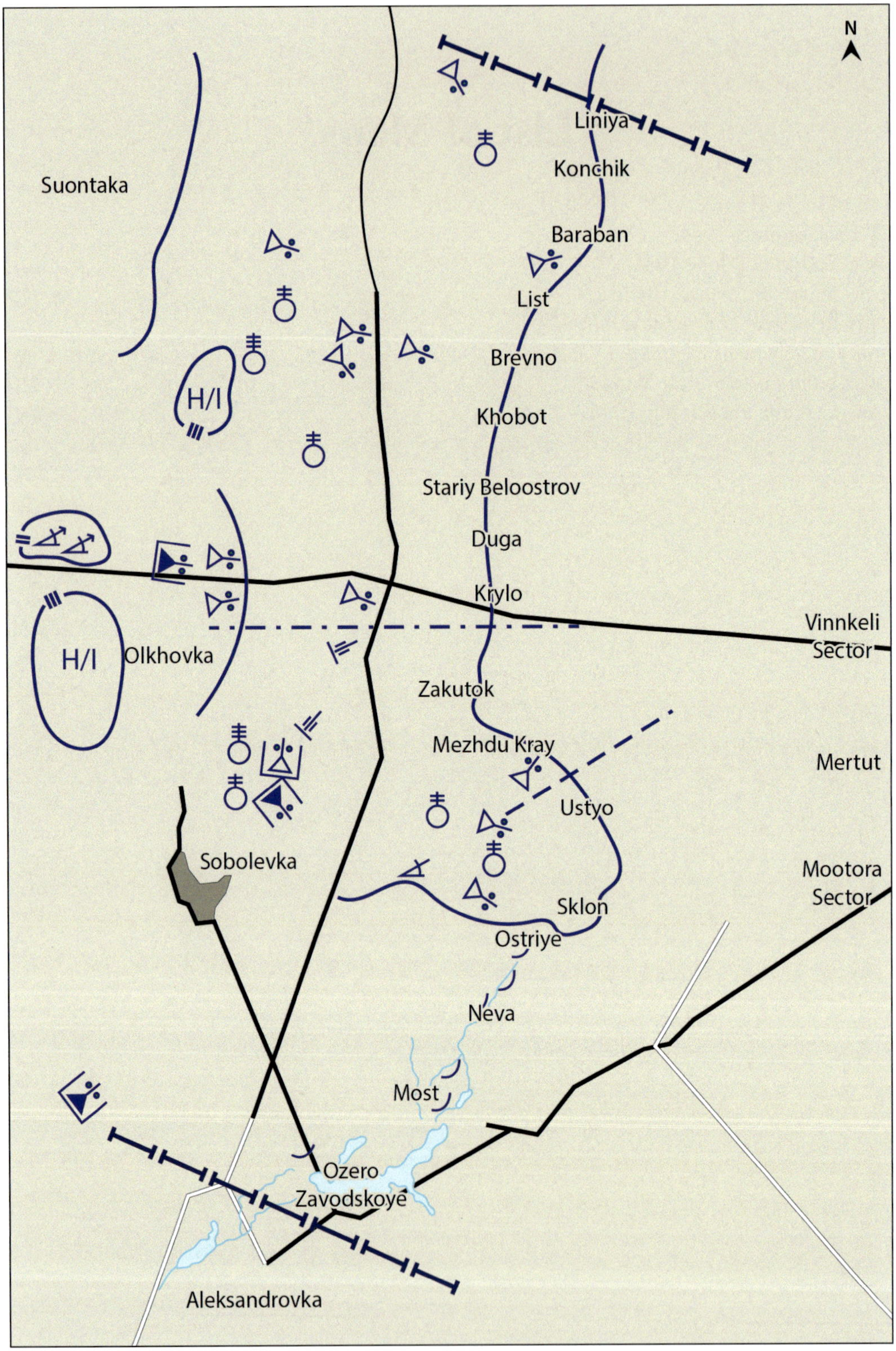

VT Line, summer 1944.

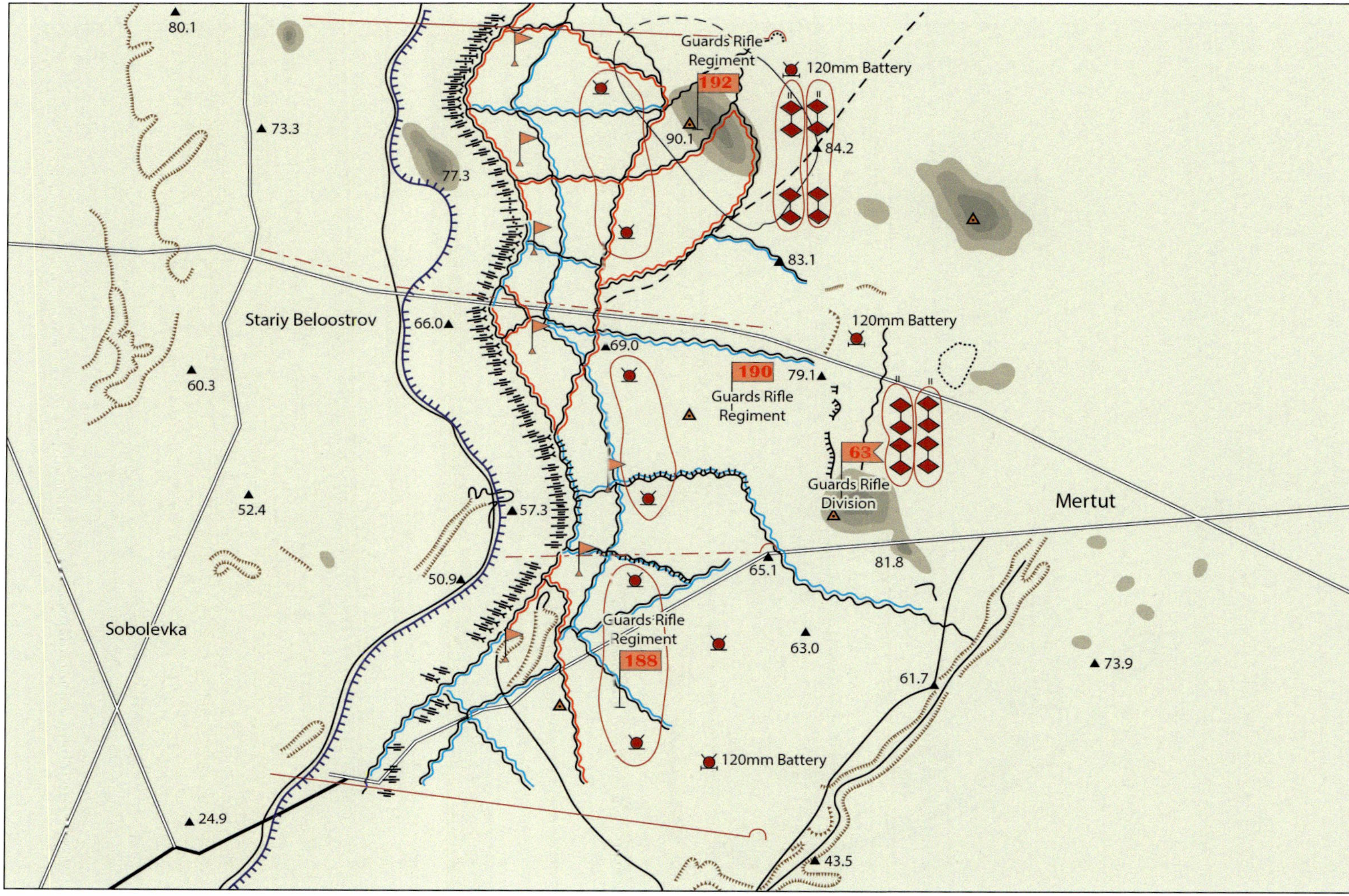

Soviet build-up, 8 June 1944.

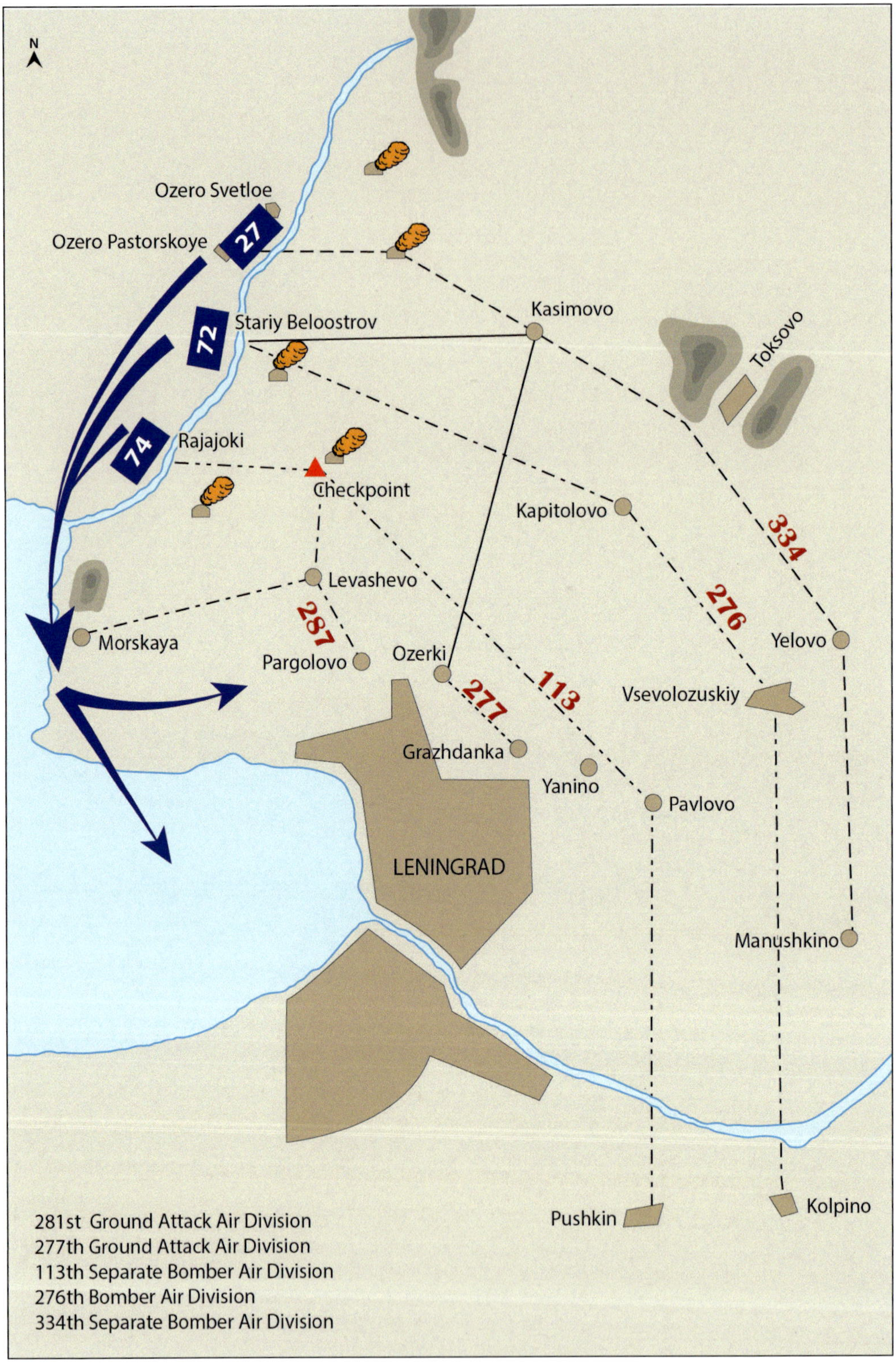

Soviet air assault, 9 June 1944.

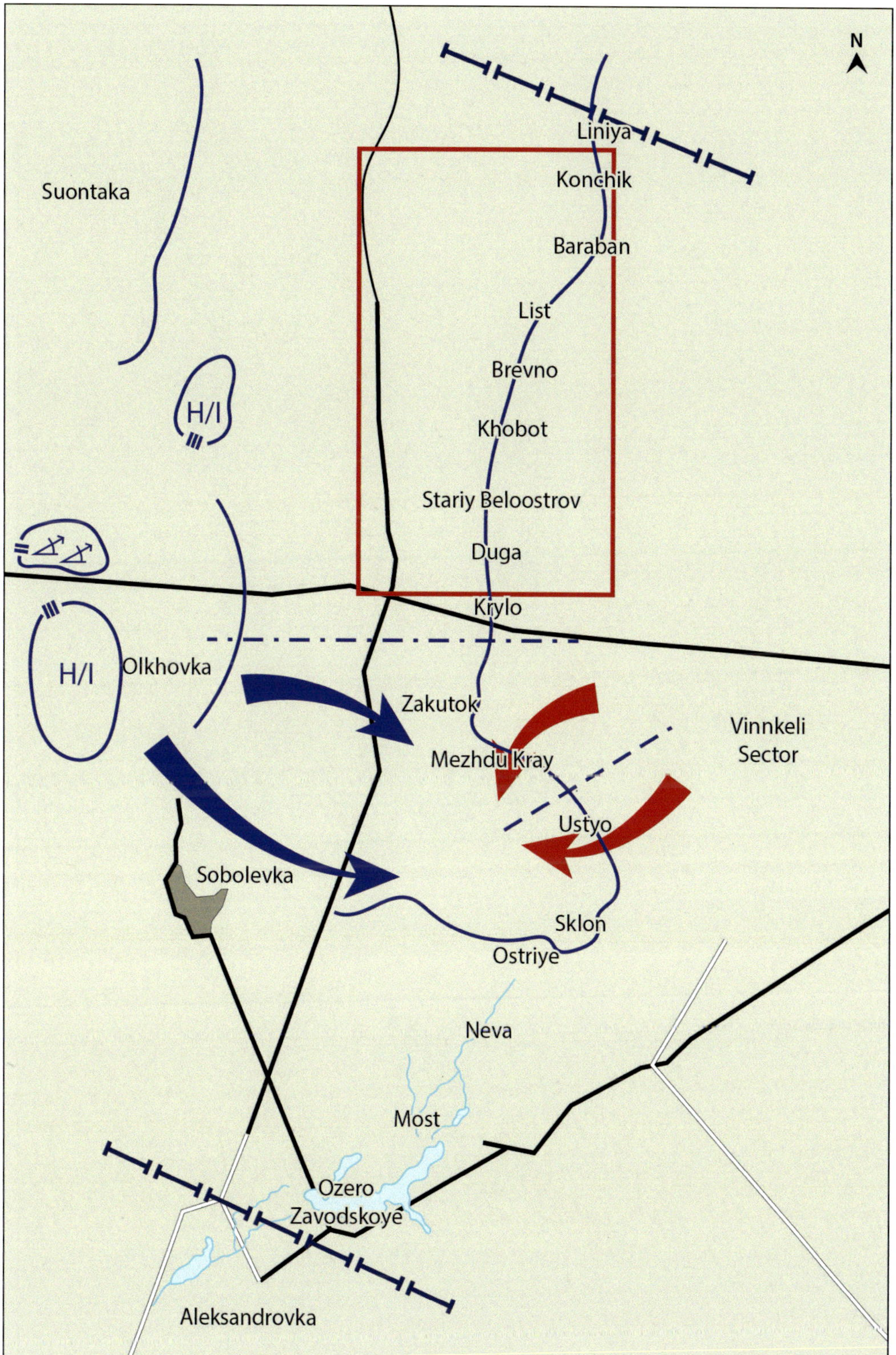

Stariy Beloostrov and vicinity, June 1944.

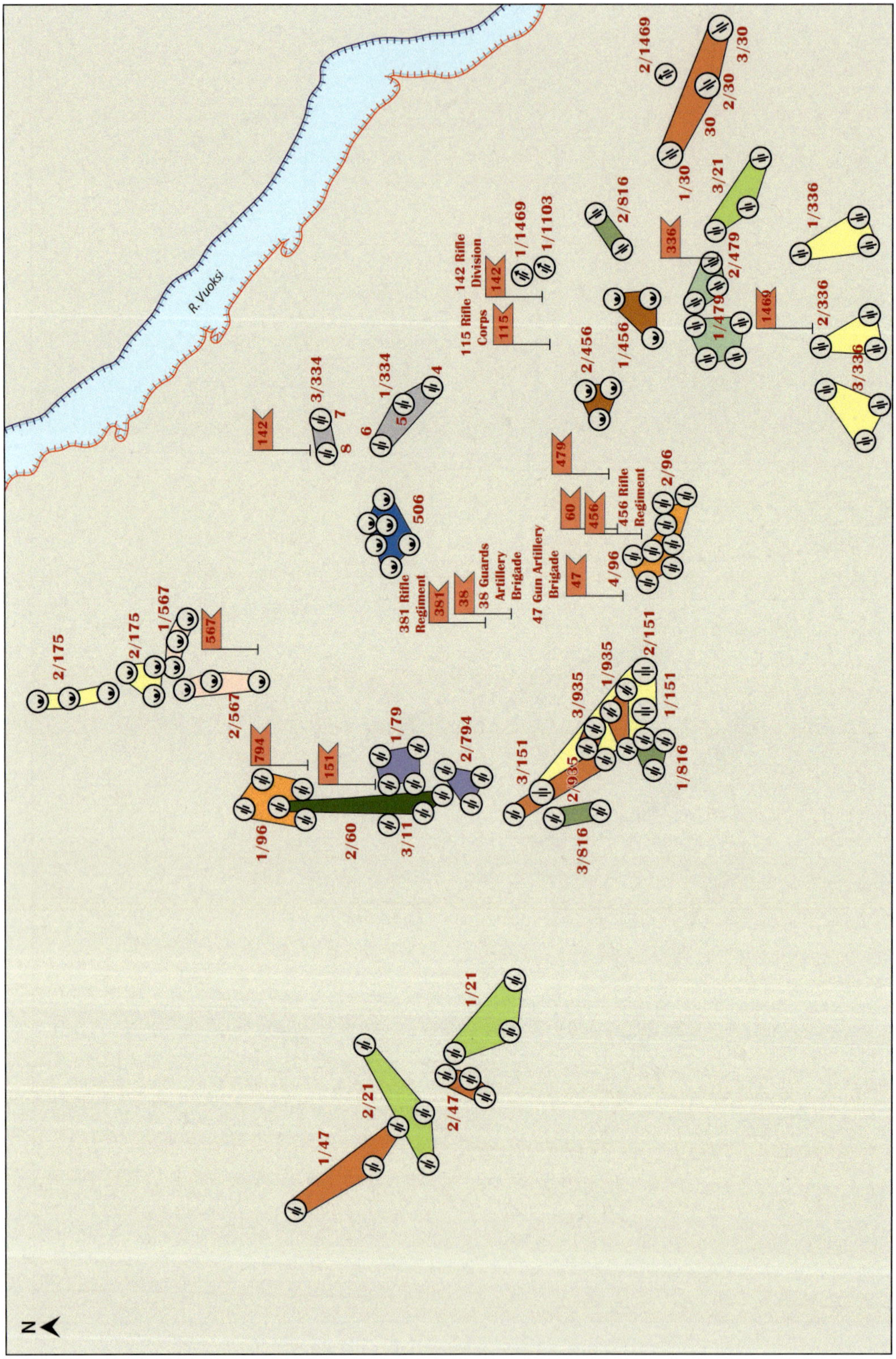

Finnish deployment west of the Vuoski, July 1944.

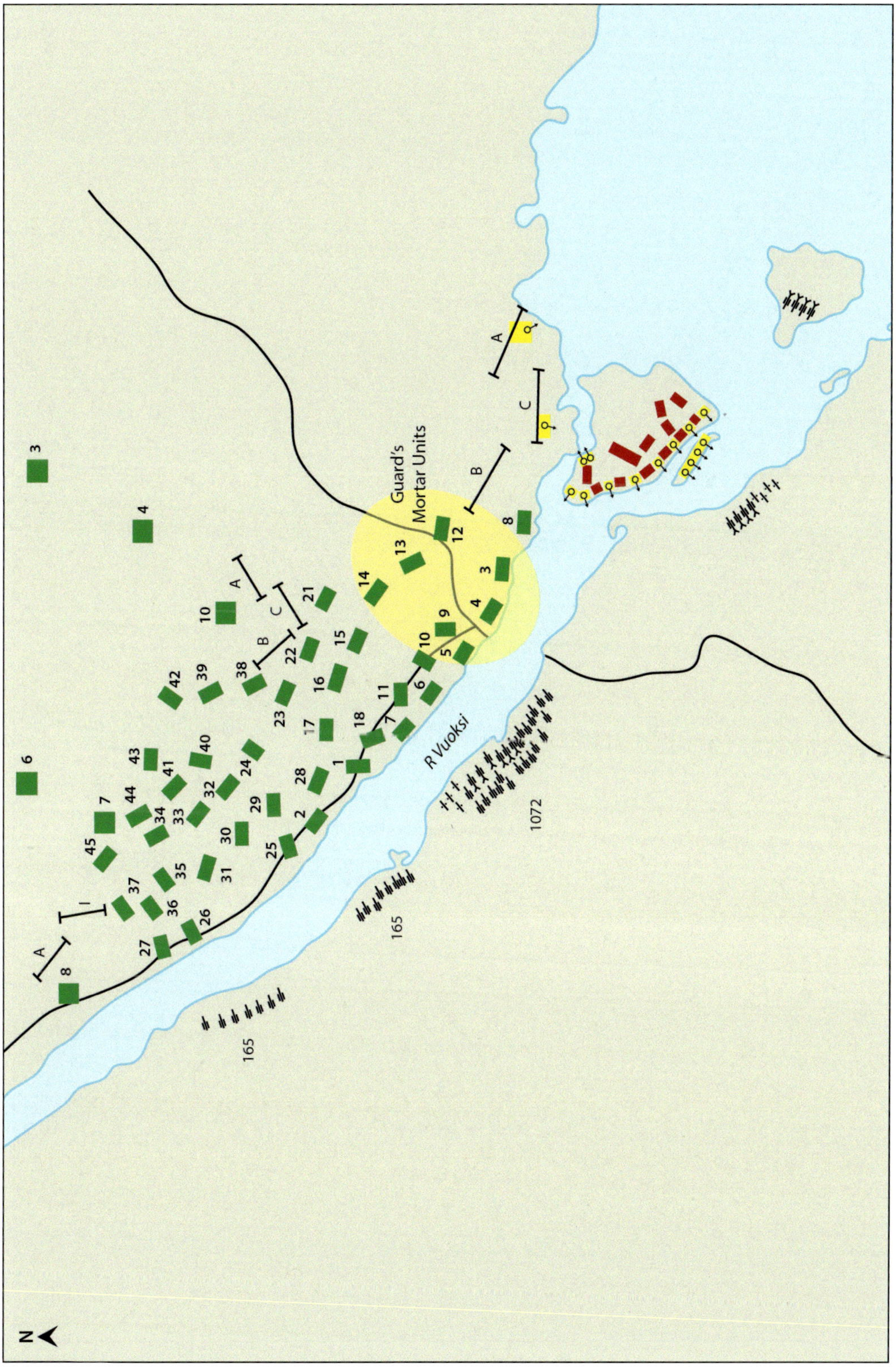

Soviet build-up east of the Vuoski.

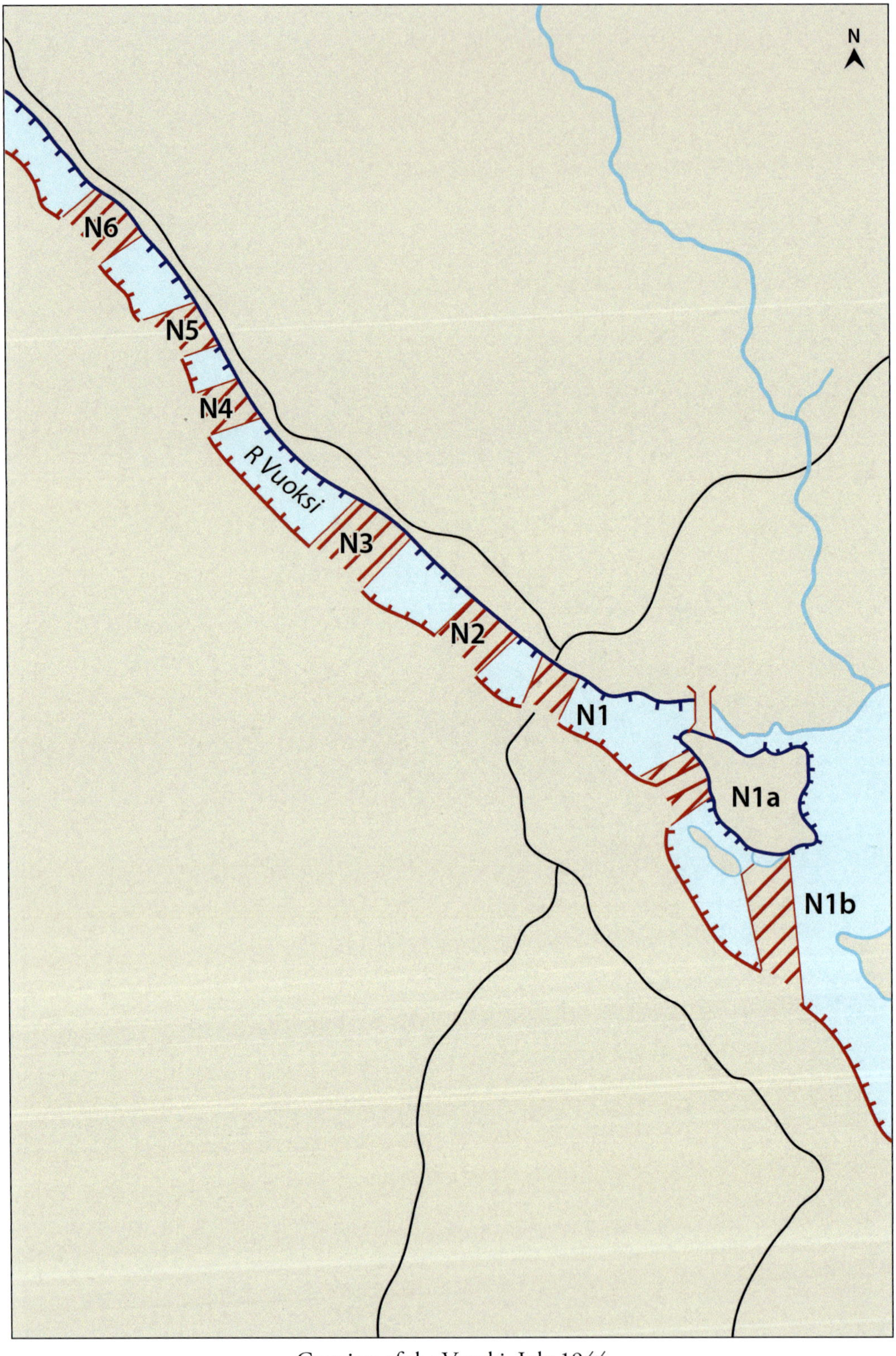

Crossing of the Vuoski, July 1944.

"The left flank is ready. Everyone–without exception, the trench has collapsed once. The entire salvo landed right next to us–Kuparinen gasped–drawing himself up to his full two metres in height in the bunker. It was true, everything around us was roaring and howling. There was no point in trying to count the individual explosions. It sounded like rocks being offloaded from the bed of a lorry into empty steel tins. It was an awful sound, and the bunker shook under the terrifying power of an explosion. We just looked at each other. The new recruits jumped to their feet, one of them cried out. Am awful flood of swearwords rang out. Everyone reached for their weapons, it was easier if you had a weapon in your hands.

"That was an eight inch shell. Do they want to turn our bunker into an air ship or something?"

I took refuge in a corner and tried to defuse the atmosphere a little with my ironic observations. I looked at Raymo, who was standing by the side wall, and, without taking my eyes of him, I looked at the vibration sensor, which had been fixed to the table. Our powerful bunker was shaking, like a mattress on the sea. The vibration meter was giving some awful readings. The telephone began to ring, but when we picked up the receiver there was nobody there. Somewhere it was warm, but it was not cold in our bunker either. The telephone had failed, that was clear to us. We were ignorant as far as anything else was concerned. We had already become accustomed more or less to this storm of steel but this noise it seemed would do our heads in. The only one among us who looked calm was Yorma. He had leaned against the back door and sitting on his haunches was steadily filling the magazine of his automatic weapon. Now and again he would look around at each of us, as though he was assessing us or drawing his own conclusions. The enemy fire it seemed was only getting stronger. The explosions from the "eight inch" shells grew more frequent. The devastating fire from the guns destroyed everything on our line that had been built by the hand of man. It was strange what thoughts came to mind. One minute I was revisiting my childhood, the next I was back in the present. It was all moving in a single stream. Everything I had achieved, everything I had done. I remembered my father, who had left in due course for Russia, and it was because of him that my colleagues were teasing me at the beginning of the war.

_"Don't have any secrets, otherwise papa will take you prisoner!" That was going round in my head at the time, but reason got the better of me, and the image of my mother. The thunder though continued. The artillery barrage had already lasted for one and a half hours. It was now half past six. A thick dust lay all around the bunker in the light of a carbide lamp. Nobody uttered a word but written on everyone's faces–was an extreme level of stress, we all knew what would happen once the artillery barrage let up. It was what we feared most of all. The attack. Would we come out of this battle alive, or would it prove to be our last? The new recruit who had cried out had also calmed down slightly. It was obvious though that he would not be leaving the bunker for a couple of hours yet. Five days with hardly any sleep, and explosive gases mixed with dirt that had eaten into our faces made us look like lepers. There was no longer any water in the bunker, what we had was just enough to quench our thirst. Our bunker with its thick walls shook once again. It seemed like the enormous power of the explosion had turned it upside down. There were three thousand explosions per minute per hectare, the Ivans were setting a record that would hold for a century. Raymo's face was pale, like that of a ghost. His bright eyes looked at everyone in turn, as though he was asking them a question, but he did not utter a word.

"Eh, guys, they are redirecting the barrage!" someone's voice screamed out. I do not know who it was, but everyone got to their feet. They all rushed to the exit. The artillery was still thundering but the shells were falling on the logistics areas behind the lines. I was the third to jump out. Raymo was the first to jump out followed by one of the new recruits. The external door at the end of a short corridor was missing. It had flown off somewhere, and the trench, which began just beyond the door, was also missing. Outside it was just crater on crater, here and there fragments of logs, which until very recently were whole logs that had reinforced the walls of the trench. At least all three of us were able to get outside. I dived into the hollow just a few dozen metres from the bunker and glanced at what was there beyond the river. Enemy infantry were advancing from the edge of the forest like a murky oncoming wave out at sea. Wearing their greatcoats that had been ripped open, some 400–500 soldiers were running towards the waters in an ungainly horde. The machine guns kept firing, but they were not aiming at anything, but the machine guns were raining down deadly fire from the edge of the forest. The Ivans that had run half way got right down, even though the bullets were passing way over their heads. Do they really put their machine guns behind their attacking forces? That thought went through my head, and then something quite different appeared. Ten metres away stood our "*Kaiser*" bereft of a crew. Where was everyone else? Why were they not manning the gun? I looked at the bunker. A soldier was standing in the doorway and right on the threshold a wall half a metre in height rose up that was made of small fountains of earth. That terrible artillery barrage had exposed our bunker but the enemy had not driven anyone out of the bunker with their machine gun fire. If anyone so much as stuck their nose out, they would immediately be sent to kingdom come. Raymo shouted something but I could not hear over that hellish noise, I did see though how one of the new recruits jumped out through the door. He was still in the air when a burst of fire got into him. His body was cut in half as though he had been cut with a penknife, and he fell to the ground lifeless. I tried to get to the gun but had hardly gone a few paces when Kuparinen and Kyuyuronen rushed past me. They had nevertheless managed to get out of the bunker. I ran after them at full height, firing as I went with my machine gun. I did not know if they were killed by my own bullets, but anyone that had reached the edge of the river had fallen to the ground. At that moment the "*Kaiser*" opened fire. The guys had set a record for bringing a gun up to a firing position. I do not know if they took aim or not, but in any case the incoming fire from the edge of the forest died down. At that moment we saw tongues of flame coming from near the old school, the Russian guns had joined the game firing at close range. It was evident soldiers were running across the hills in the distance, this was the infantry that had climbed out of their digs. There was a constant deafening roar, through which the sharp and piercing explosions of the gun cartridges cut like a knife. I changed the magazine on my automatic weapon as though I was in the heat of battle. "Nobody reasons in war they just load and fire" was a thought that crossed my mind, there was no need to aim in this case. Just prop the gun up on the ground and pull the trigger. We just had to get the targets out of the way. It was awful, it seemed like the whole world was coming down on us. The enemy artillery had stopped firing at the logistics areas behind the lines and had begun to fire at close range. Their attack had petered out. The enemy soldiers were running under the protection of the forest like hares that had been smoked out of their burrows. Our position was worse though. We had hunkered down some 40m from the bunker in terrain that was reminiscent of a giant's potato field, while all around was a high wall of sand, while dark shadows rushed here and there, or doubled up, like birch bark in a fire. I did not hear the explosion, just a din that lifted everyone off the ground. I came to in the bunker. I was lying on the floor, on my back, Yorma was pouring water into my mouth.

"You're a strong guy!" I did not hear his words but from the movement of his lips I could tell that Yorma was speaking. It suddenly became very amusing to me. Everything around me just became so funny. At that same time I began to frisk myself, but I did not find a scratch on me. I had been covered with sand. A shell exploded right next to my crater and covered it with sand. Only my head was poking through the crater when the guys had pulled me out and taken me into the bunker. I had gone deaf. I was alone. I could not hear a thing, but the bombardment was still going on, which was evidenced by the way our bunker was shaking. Somebody put a cigarette into my mouth. I looked up. It was the new recruit Unto who was standing there. What sort of new recruit was he now? He was dirty, sand was flaking off his uniform and his face was as pale as death, but with two piercing blue eyes. The childish expression on his face, that he had worn just a few hours ago, had gone forever. One of his colleagues had been lost and he was lying by the door of the bunker. A burst of machine gun fire had stitched him full of holes, like a sewing machine. Another of his colleagues had also been taken out of the game and was rolling around in the corner overcome with embarrassment after he had come undone. What sort of a picture had they painted for these guys when they shut the door of the training classroom and they had begun their journey to the front? I do not know who they were, but they all fell, and he was left alone amongst us, unknown soldiers. I put my hand on his shoulder and he ended up lying on the ground next to me. I gestured to him to take the mess tin with the cold peas porridge still inside but he just shook his head. It was strange but none of us wanted to eat. None of us wanted to sleep even though we had gone without sleep for several days. The hell continued outside but I could no longer hear it. The bunker was shaking so violently that it seemed it would collapse at any moment and everyone was looking at the doorway as though in anticipation of something. Rifles that were ready for battle were pressed between our legs, and our hands were holding onto the gun barrels. Our rucksacks had been piled up in the corner. We had thrown just a bag of ammunition onto our shoulders, which we had not taken off even for a moment. Once again everyone in the bunker had got to their feet. Each of us was trying to be the first outside, me included. I got up from the back wall and dived towards the doorway. I flew outside like a bullet from a gun and a tall column of sand rose up in front of me. A shell once again exploded right next to me but this time it served only to accelerate my motion through the air, throwing me some distance from the door. It appeared that Kuparenin had been struck by a bullet or something in the back. To begin with he could walk on his own two legs, but then it was as though he had fallen onto the gun. The "*Kaiser*" was in action again and damn it we seriously needed it now. The "thirty-fours" had gone on the attack. They were advancing across a wide front, firing as they moved forward. Were they not firing at us though? What the hell! The tanks were hitting our dug outs on our own side of the river. One after another rocks would be blown sky high. What next? Enemy soldiers were running from the edge of the forest towards the tanks in their green greatcoats. They were around 10 in number and they were carrying boxes of ammunition. The tanks had run out of ammunition and they were carrying new loads of ammunition. I did not feel anything. I turned my automatic rifle towards the enemy soldiers who were running some 50m away from me. I pulled the trigger and three of them were no more. Three men had been killed who personally done no wrong to me, and what is more they were defenceless. I began to feel slightly-ill, I was completely overcome by this emotion and then I saw another two running towards the tanks. Such a crash rang out to the side of me that even with my concussion I could still hear it. The flames from the explosion almost burnt my face. It was Unto who was firing, his lips were moving and forming some words that I could not make out. My hands were moving automatically. Load, fire. This lad though was firing very accurately. After every shot a drunken enemy soldier would fall to the ground in his greatcoat that had been torn open. The bank of the Vammelyoki in those early morning hours represented an awful sight. There were around a dozen enemy tanks on fire. This bank of the river was covered in the bodies of the fallen and they were also to be found on our side of the river. More and more tanks though were moving forward from the edge of the forest and the "agriculturists" took up arms against them. Wave after wave of ground attack aircraft flattened our defences, shamelessly firing at anything that was still alive in the overturned dugouts. Kuparinen had long since run past me. He had died right before my eyes. He had been hit again from on high but he had still tried to get back to the gun. He was happy–for him the war was over.

We had to run between the bunker and the trenches a further seven times until our enemy was able to ford the Vammelyoki. Ahead of the former tank trap more than 20 tanks were smouldering, the fallen were piled up in a heap. They kept on coming and coming, however. The field was completely covered in a dark mass of soldiers in a dark green, woollen uniforms, they clearly were not drunk! They were new, fresh soldiers! The formidable KV tanks appeared from beyond the river with their powerful guns. Steel continued to spew out in ever increasing volumes. Damn it though we only withdrew back to the field, to the edge of the forest. It was there that we dug in once more. For many this was the last act of their lives. We performed the last rites for them in absentium, their bodies still lay on the battlefield. The Nyland Dragoon Regiment to our left were driven from their position and had departed at 1000 hrs on 15 June. The signals officer who had feared for his life had not been able to reach us, after he had alluded to this hellish artillery barrage. It was only at 1600 hrs, instead of 0400 hrs in the morning that we heard the shout "Get out if you are able! Our rendezvous point–Uusikirkko." The enemy was already behind the lines and suddenly attacked from this point. Their artillery evidently were not aware that their infantry were already behind the lines since they continued to bear down on us mercilessly. Both our soldiers and their soldiers died from this barrage of fire. It seemed some of our soldiers had gone out of their minds as they headed straight for the enemy's line of fire. The injured also remained there in the field, among those who had dug themselves in. I saw many pairs of pleading eyes, many of them it seemed had put a gun to their heads. The hell at Vammelyoki had come to an end. This storm of steel, which would be impossible to imagine even in your nightmares had broken though our famous line of defence. We had come through a test, which had left indelible scars on our souls and on our thoughts. The Tavast Cavalry Regiment had stood firm to the end, and along with them–their cavalry troop. The guns were left where they were. It was only the gun aimers who had gone crazy who removed the locks from the guns when the enemy had all but turned their guns in our direction. The locks were thrown into the Vammelyoki. At around 0600 hrs in the morning we met Colonel von Essen and some other officers at a crossroads where four roads converged. The shabby officers who stood before us were clearly not capable of serving as an inspiration for him. This slave driver however, who had once sworn at us so loudly told us in a quiet voice to go to the coast since the enemy's tanks were already on the road that led to Uusikirkko. In a few hours' time we would be surrounded, and this for the enemy would be a great

> achievement. We now walked silently through the forest. A bird was singing somewhere. Life went on. It had to go on. On the feast of St. John the Baptist in 1944 the entire Finnish people had heard the thunder of the steel hell at Vammelyoki over the radio. The sounds of the battle were recorded 10km behind the lines, but it was possible to understand from these sounds what was happening at the front.

Junior Sergeant Pentti Piiparinen Lappenranta:

> This is your story. It might as well though belong to anyone of the thousands born in 1919 or in 1920, and who had worn government issue clothes for five years. For me, the author of these lines, the war had already come to an end in the last few days of June. News of your death reached my hospital in September. Your journey came to an end in the forests near Ilomansti, where you had begun your journey. Near Velivaarvi or Loukhivaarvi, were you started out in 1941. Everything had come full circle. You had a long journey to make, up to the banks of the Onega, and back to where your path began. Where you began this journey was where you were to end it. May the silence be kind to you after all these terrible years of war.

Konstantin Simonov had also visited this same sector of the VT line and left his own romanticised description of the battle:

> The astonishing success of Colonel Borshchev's units in this direction had begun from the third day of the breakthrough of the second Finnish line in the area around Meste-yarvi. The breakthrough of this line had taken 16 hrs in total. The difficulty lay in the fact that the troops had been ordered not to let the pace of the advance slip, and in essence, just a day had been given over to preparing for this attack right in front of the line. Both the short timescale, and the exceptional natural camouflage of the Finnish fortifications had prevented any serious reconnaissance of the line by battlefield reconnaissance troops. It also prevented an opportunity to add any further details of any significance to the previous information gathered by aerial reconnaissance. Thus, when in the morning after a powerful two and a half hour artillery barrage the troops went on the attack, they were not able to capture the line straight away. Apart from the many pillboxes that had been reconnoitred, and which were attacked by artillery directly, dozens of gun emplacements had also appeared before the division 's front line.
>
> Major Melnikov's infantry under fierce fire had succeeded in fording the river but were halted at the foot of a steep slope, next to the pillboxes themselves. In places the infantry found themselves so close to the pillboxes that it was impossible for heavy artillery to continue firing, pulling the infantry back however, since they were just a stone's throw from the pillboxes, would have been inappropriate, and would have been linked to heavy losses.
>
> The divisional commander in this sector took the decision to suppress the fire from the pillboxes by using self-propelled guns firing at close range. The subsequent day and night operations were successful thanks to the self-sacrificial work of the self-propelled gun batteries and the brave march by Major Melnikov's infantry in the centre. As soon as the first pillboxes had been silenced by close range fire, the infantry would climb decisively up the slope, which incidentally, as Colonel Borshchev described it, was in this location, so steep and precipitous that it was "just like in Izmayl, if only we could put ladders up." The infantry scrambled up the slope and forced their way into the first of the pillboxes. Meanwhile to the

right Major Zimina's regiment, which had not been able to ford the river the evening before, scaled the slope and in a narrow sector, which had been suppressed by artillery, captured all the pillboxes to some depth. After the first battalion had broken through the rest of the battalions forced their way through the narrow bottleneck in the breakthrough, and after cutting through the whole line like a knife, began to spread out to the left and right behind it. The Finns demonstrated this time that they were highly sensitive to the threat of an encirclement even when they were sitting on a fortified line. As soon as our battalions began to spread out behind the line once they had broken through the Finns began to abandon the pillboxes one after another in Major Melnikov's regiment's sector, where they were still holding out. Having taken advantage of the nervousness of the defenders, Melnikov and his regiment began with some confidence to attack the pillboxes using infantry one after another in the centre of the defensive line. He was injured in this battle but his regiment in the course of several hours had occupied a line in his sector that extended all the way back.

This was the beginning of the end for the Finns. As our forces broke through and then retired the flanks, and again broke through and again retired the flanks, our forces had by morning purged the entire Myatsikulya defensive line. Naturally, it was not only the decisive actions on the part of the infantry, and not only the anxiety that stemmed from the threat of a deadly retreat that forced the Finns to abandon their powerful defensive line so quickly. In truth the work of our artillery had a huge role to play. I inspected the Finnish positions after the attack and I have to say it was an unforgettable sight. Apart from anything else the Finns just had not been able to hold out psychologically. Far from all the pillboxes had been damaged and destroyed, but there was not one of them that had not suffered a direct hit. All the earth around the pillboxes was full of craters. The barbed wire had been mixed with the communications cables and was rolled up into clumps. Not one of the communications cables were intact; they had all, even those that were buried deep underground, been severed in the first half an hour of the artillery barrage. All the garrisons had been disconnected. The communications ditches and dug-outs which had even been built with a number of logs or boards overlapping one another had been transformed into a mound of logs, earth, and boards.

According to the testimony of prisoners of war, despite the fact that the line consisted for the most part of concrete fortifications and despite the fact that in a number of places the garrisons had simply fled following the breakthrough, saving their own lives, the Finns lost up to 60 percent of their entire complement of personnel on this line. They were overwhelmed by enemy fire, stunned by the speed of the onslaught, and by the awful prospect of certain death that was drawing ever closer.

When you speak to the commanders now, shortly after the incident, and you explain everything–both the psychological and the military reasons for the decisiveness of our successes, opinions differ in respect of the attitude to the Finns: some say that the Finns are not the same as they were in 1940, that their will to fight has reduced significantly, and that they don't have the determination and resolve they once had. Others say that overall the Finns have not changed very much. They all however agree on one point. Whether the Finns themselves are the same or not is a question of secondary importance. The main thing is that we are not the same as we were in 1940. The combat experience that our officers gained over the course of three years of the Great Patriotic War, and the knowledge of how to manage our forces, and the skill in taking advantage of any small, piecemeal gain in order to develop it rapidly into a large-scale, overall success; decisiveness in the riskiest encirclements and flanking manoeuvres, and the capability to orientate around the battlefield and change a decision in a very short space of time depending on the environment–all this coupled with the materiel within the breakthrough units that has grown over time has ensured that in every given scenario we have enjoyed an incomparably greater degree of firepower for the same numerical strength of forces.

Immediately after the breakthrough at Mesme-yarvi, the units under Colonel Borshchev moved further along the coastline, hunting down the retreating Finns. In less than two days some 40km were covered from the second to the third line.

11

VT Line Breakthrough and Post-War Contemplations

Following the war, participant generals and historians contemplated the question: why had the Karelian Isthmus, the gateway and the key to Finland turned out to be so lightly defended and so obviously unprepared for its own defence? Why did the main lines of Defence and the "VT line" fall so quickly?

Lennart Oesch, who had the opportunity to observe the actions of the Commander of the 4th Corps Laatikainen, attempts to provide a detailed answer to this question in his memoirs. In his long and scrupulous analysis Oesch was critical of the fact that Laatikainen had spread the Corps' forces out. In Oesch's opinion Laatikainen allocated a great deal of his forces on his left flank in the defensive belt belonging to the 2nd Division. There in the area around Kivennapa–Siiranmyaki there was a high density of forces, a powerful artillery alignment, and the reserves were concentrated in the immediate vicinity of the front–in the shape of Lagus' armoured division, which had been divided into two groups. As is evident from our narrative a powerful artillery alignment was an important factor in the battle on Siiranmyaki height, where the Finns had succeeded in holding out until 16 June.

Within 3rd Infantry Division's defensive belt the situation was much worse. Just two battalions defended this winding 11km defensive sector that extended from the railway line up to Kuuterselka. The breakthrough sector itself in Kuuterselka was 6km wide and was defended by just one battalion from the 53rd Regiment. Two Soviet divisions fought against this battalion and were supported by two tank regiments and one self-propelled regiment. Artillery from the 3rd Division was also significantly weaker than in the 2nd defensive line.

Thus Laatikainen was anticipating an attack on his left flank in the area around Kivennapa–Siiranmyaki. Despite the fact that on 12 and 13 June the Finns had clearly managed to intersect the redeployment of Soviet forces to the area around Kuuterselka–it was just impossible to covertly redeploy such a large number of forces in a short space of time–Laatikainen did not react to this in any way. He ignored a report from the Chief of Staff of the 3rd Division Holsti, who had reported on 13 June in plain text that a Soviet offensive was due to begin shortly. As a result for the entire day on 14 June when in Kuuterselka a fierce battle was raging, the Finnish reserve–the armoured division–stood idle in the area around Ahiyatvi and Pamppala.

Oesch asserts that Laatikainen was mistaken in his assessment of the importance of the direction from the perspective of the possibility of an offensive developing there–only one road ran from Siiranmyaki to the north towards Vuotta. At the same time the breakthrough in Kuuterselka enabled the 1st Red Banner Brigade to march to the west along a lateral route via Mustamyaki and to threaten to cut off two main roads–the Srednevyborgskoye and the Primorskoye.

Oesch was also of the opinion that the allegations levelled at the Commander of the 3rd Infantry Division Payari, who, according to the testimonies of some officers (including Lauri Yantti) tried to restore the position using just the forces of his own division and did not request any assistance from the Corps Commander, were unjustified. In his argument Oesch cites a report written by Payari to Mannerheim dated 10 June. This report was quoted by Wolf Halsti in his post-war works: "Additional forces need to be deployed to the "VT line" as soon as possible, and I reported to the Commander of the 4th Corps that I can probably repel the first Soviet attack, but in no way could I counter a large-scale offensive. The 3rd Division's defensive belt needs to be halved, otherwise the defence just won't hold out."

Oesch was sharply critical of the counterattack that was carried out solely by the forces of Puromaa's group, but at the same time is of the opinion that it is difficult to predict if the forces of the entire armoured division would be sufficient or not in order to liquidate the breakthrough from Kuuterselka to Sahakulya. He leaves the question of the critical position of the Cavalry Brigade to one side. This is sufficiently characteristic of Finnish military history literature–which concentrates on Kuuterselka and on Siiranmyaki, and furthermore the threat of encirclement together with the loss of the Cavalry Brigade, are ignored.

The next question was why were such vast resources and military might concentrated in the occupation of Eastern Karelia, where grandiose defensive lines were constructed in amongst the Taiga? Oesch attempts to explain this as Mannerheim's personal decision and by his desire to use all his available forces to retain Eastern Karelia for Finland. Let us recall Mannerheim's bombastic words in 1941:

> During the war for independence in 1918 I took my oath to protect the Finnish and Belomorsk Karelias, that I would not replace the sword back in its scabbard until Finland and Eastern Karelia were free. I took this oath in the name of the Finnish Peasant Army, counting on its brave soldiers and on the selfless nature of Finnish women.
>
> The Belomorsk and Olonets Karelias waited 20 years for this promise to be fulfilled, for one and a half years Finnish Karelia that had been devastated by the Winter War, awaited its rebirth.

In point of fact, the dream of a greater Finland and the attempt to "stake out" captured territories in Soviet Karelia could explain the huge resources and military might that were invested in the construction of fortifications on the Masel and Olonets Isthmuses. The successful defence of the Finnish Army on the Mannerheim Line from mid-December 1939 to 11 February 1940 evidently, had convinced the Finnish command of the belief that both in 1944 and in 1945 Finland could sit it out behind its new powerful defensive lines, and negotiate favourable peace terms for itself.

Oesch also highlighted a meeting that took place at Mannerheim's Headquarters on 3 February 1944. Aside from Mannerheim also present at the meeting were the President Risto Ryti, as well as members of the Government: Rangell, Witting, Walden, and Tanner. It was at this meeting that the following, among other things, was said:

> A normal relationship of trust needs to be developed with the Soviet Union. If we have to give up Eastern Karelia to do it then this should not be a barrier to peace, however much the wider circles within our country may resist it. Eastern Karelia should, nevertheless, remain in our hands wherever possible as a shield for future negotiations.

One could sit at length and speculate on the reasons for the breakthrough of the two Finnish defensive lines, but this fact has to be acknowledged: in the first stage of the Vyborg offensive operation Soviet Headquarters, the General Staff and Leningrad Front Command were able to covertly redeploy a powerful attack alignment, they achieved the element of surprise and completely outplayed their Finnish opponents in Mikkeli.

The chief of the fortification section at Headquarters General Hanell was in a difficult position. He had to explain somehow why the new defensive line, which had taken three years to construct turned out to be unfinished and why the Leningrad Front had broken through it in something like three days. Hanell asked the commanders of the infantry regiments that had been defending the "VT line" to send in their reports.

Two days prior to his death, Colonel Valbek sent in his report, the Commander of 49th Infantry Regiment had fought on Siiranmyaki height:

> The VT line
> To Major-General Hanell, fortifications section Supreme High Command
> 2.7.1944
> <u>Concerning Combat Experience on the VT line at Siiranmyaki</u>
> The details set out below are in respect of the 2nd Battalion, 49th Infantry Regiment's battles in the course of the counterattack by the battalion, and in the battles for the stronghold on Siiranmyaki between 14–16 June 1944.
>
> The combat positions: there is no depth, and no intermediate defensive boundary, in connection with which we had to fight in a clearing behind the Siiranmyaki stronghold as the enemy succeeded in clearing the trenches. In the clearing a number of foxholes were dug, which do not provide the necessary protection from shrapnel from shells that explode in the canopies of trees. There is no way of redeploying the personnel around the trenches.
>
> In order to correct this situation,. We tried to advance forward onto the field, but the numerous enemy tanks that were manoeuvring on the battlefield itself put a stop to these attempts by maintaining a constant vigilance.
>
> The potential intermediate boundaries should certainly be linked by communications ditches in order to prevent a purge of the trenches, and the communications ditches should certainly be fitted with gun emplacements and anti-tank defences, These issues were noted by previous Finnish units who occupied these positions.
>
> <u>Anti-tank Defence</u>
> The lack of positions for anti-tank guns–is a glaring error (there was no time to build these) as is the absence of pillboxes immediately behind the principal defensive line, and on the principal defensive line itself. In connection with this enemy tanks, on passing the forward line of obstructions, were able to operate on the battlefield with impunity, which made it much more difficult for our infantry to fight as they are supposed to.
>
> <u>Machine gun Positions</u>
> The location of machine gun emplacements is good and they are able to perform their function,
>
> <u>Barriers</u>
> The stronghold itself had already been lost, so the battalion had to fight in the surrounding area, where there were no anti-tank barriers. The enemy's attack on 16 June 1944 that was aimed at capturing the trenches was carried out from the southern side of the trench using the elimination method, so it is impossible to assess the significance of the barriers in terms of the battle the battalion actually fought. The same could be said for the anti-tank barriers.
>
> <u>The Combat Trench</u>

> 1) The cut-and-cover trench proved to be perfectly suitable for combat and provided good protection from intense enemy artillery fire, the covering over the trench also held out against enemy fire.
> 2) The depth of the trench it turned out, based on feedback, to be "very deep," but this only served to reduce losses from artillery fire.
> 3) The straight sections of trench were also very long, and this led to unnecessary losses, especially when the tanks were firing. (The tanks fired using their guns at the bends in the trench, and the shrapnel would fly into both of the branches either side). The impact of enemy artillery fire on the sectors that featured long straight sections, was also considerable. This became the principal drawback in the open part of the trench.
> 4) The open trench was unsuitable for combat owing to its unnecessary width and its large straights sections, which led to high losses from artillery fire. In addition this trench could not survive a direct hit, and in many locations it was levelled.

The Commander of the 53rd Infantry Regiment Ravila observed:

> In the sector where the breakthrough was recorded such a mass of artillery had been concentrated that we could not have conceived of previously. At the very same time huge numbers of ground attack aircraft were carrying out air strikes. In addition a number of ground attack aircraft appeared over our own front line for the first time. The damage they inflicted from their attacks in actual fact was modest; more significant however was the effect on the morale of our forces.
>
> Enemy infantry continued to go on the attack until such time that the artillery fire had been redirected deeper behind the lines; this practice, which is opportunistic and acts to minimise losses–is a characteristic trait for Russians. In an instance such as this the defending forces have no time to climb out of the trench in order to counter the attack with their own small arms fire. As soon as the defensive line has been breached they would immediately proceed further into the breach itself, without paying any attention to the flanks as they extended out. Enemy artillery fire was also, as it turned out, capable of using their entire forces to cover the flanks of an advancing wedge and inflicted heavy losses on our counterattacking forces.
>
> A Russian advance could be compared to an autogenous gas cutter, which is able to cut through the thickest armour. As soon as the breach has been achieved, additional forces are able to join the battle as they pass through it.

It was these thoughts that a German major tried to communicate to Finnish generals in January 1944. These words however were ignored, and the Finnish officers, similarly, did not acknowledge fully how much their enemy had changed since 1941 and that the character of combat operations themselves had changed. In reality it could be said that from 1941 up to 1944 the Finnish Army, the Commander-in-Chief, as well as headquarters, and General Headquarters had been blissfully unaware and had held out hopes–firstly in terms of the victory of fascist Germany, and then that they would be able to sit behind their "VT line" as they had succeeded in doing in the previous war.

No sooner had the Finnish Headquarters feverishly tried to take some action to stabilise the position on the Isthmus, than the Soviet Supreme Command Headquarters were handing out medals. Stalin rated Grogorov's achievements in breaking through two Finnish lines highly. On 18 June in Moscow Shvernikov awarded Govorov the Marshal's star. The title of Hero of the Soviet Union was awarded to many of those who had participated in the breakthrough. The award of other orders was widespread in the USSR. The units of the Leningrad Front who had participated in the breakthrough of the VT line were given the honorary designation of "Leningrad" units. Soviet successes were broadcast widely in the Soviet and world press, despite the fact that the Western world's attention was focussed on the landings by allied forces on Normandy.

On the front line meanwhile a rapid advance by Soviet forces had begun towards Vyborg. The echelons along with their reinforcements from the Olonets and Masel Isthmuses were already mobile, but over the course of 15-16 June the Finns were able to mount only a limited number of combat capable forces against the Soviet mobile groups. Leningrad Front Command in turn had introduced the armoured tank reserves of the 21st Army into the battle. The subsequent few days were characterised by very fast-paced battles on the approaches to Vyborg.

12

A Head-on Battle: Introduction of Finnish Reserves, 15–19 June

In the Finnish camp by 15 June, some important reshuffles had occurred. It had become clear to Commander-in-Chief Mannerheim that the decision to disband the Group Headquarters on the Isthmus in March 1944 had been an incorrect one. Against the backdrop of a modern war and a situation that changed by the hour Finnish Headquarters were not able to provide effective command of the two army corps on the Isthmus. The outcome of this was the reformation of the group on the Isthmus, and the appointment of General Oesch as Commander.

General Lennart Oesch, who was born in Pyhajarvi and described himself as someone who "had a Swiss passport but at heart was a Finn," was a member of Mannerheim's inner circle. He was a loyal and experienced General whom Mannerheim trusted and whose opinion he was predisposed to listen. Mannherheim had recalled Oesch from Petrozavodsk in a telephone call. He arrived on the Karelian Isthmus and by 15 June had begun to get up to speed with things on the front. The position of Finnish units was, to put it mildly, unnerving. The VT line had been breached, and it had not been possible to restore the situation by way of a counterattack. Against the backdrop of the situation that was unfolding Oesch took the decision to withdraw to a line running from Vyborg–Kularsaari–Taipal, pulling back some 50–60km to the north. He had to defend his decision in a long telephone conversation with Mannerheim. The Marshal, as he had done in the Finnish War, had insisted on a solid defence and did not want to concede a metre of land without a fight. Oesch however succeeded in convincing Mannerheim that on 15 June 1944 Finnish units in the central part of the Karelian Isthmus were not capable of maintaining a defence and were in urgent need of rest and recuperation. This could only be achieved if they were to withdraw over a long distance. The Finns hoped that Soviet artillery would not be able to catch the mobile groups and provide effective covering fire for the advancing Soviet units. If the logistics units fell behind the Soviet attack alignment would lose its strength.

As a result, Mannerheim approved Oesch's decision; and on that same day the Finns began to withdraw back northwards, covering themselves with powerful defensive forces. Oesch described the events of these critical hours and days in detail in his memoirs:

> The breakthrough of the "VT line" mobilised all the defensive units on the Isthmus. The situation was not changing by the day but by the hour. It became difficult to command combat operations on the Isthmus directly from headquarters in Mikkeli, if not impossible. The division of the formations on the Isthmus into two army corps, which were directly subordinate to Headquarters, and which had taken place in spring 1944 had been an incorrect

decision. Back then in the interests of enhancing the level of responsiveness and control, as well as planning the defence of the Isthmus as a whole, retaining a unified command made sense, that is to say either an Army to defend the Isthmus, or a group. Between this unified command and the divisions the two intermediate levels in the corps would be retained, the 3rd and 4th army corps. Organising things in this way would have been more forward looking.

Now when the redeployment of new units to the Isthmus had begun, when one defensive line had been broken, and the second was ready to come under enemy attack, the situation forced–and once again this came upon us very quickly–the creation of a new level of command and required the appointment of a commander. He would need to be in the immediate vicinity of the front line and to cooperate closely with corps command to keep abreast of the situation and to organise a defence.

In the afternoon of 14 June the author of these lines, who at the time was the Commander of the "Olonets" Group received at his own headquarters in Aanislinna (in occupied Petrazavodsk) an order to transfer my authority to Lieutenant-General Talvela, and to leave for the Isthmus immediately, and take up command of the 3rd and 4th corps. That is to say the entire forces on the Isthmus–with the exception of the Headquarters reserves.

When in the role of a newly appointed Commander I arrived at midday on 15 June at the headquarters of the 4th Army Corps, which was situated in a group of Russian dugouts in Yulya-Kuusa my headquarters still did not exist. In the afternoon only a few officers arrived to assist me from Headquarters. There could be no question of setting up a command post, since there were no working telephones, cables or any other equipment for a command post. I began to make sense of the situation based on reports that were arriving from the headquarters of the 4th Army Corps. The situation was very unclear. Confirmation was received of the fact that a breakthrough had occurred in the second half of the day. The breakthrough had already been expanded and Russian units were rushing towards Kannelyarvi and Uusikirkko. The armoured division, which had counterattacked in Kuuterselka, had been withdrawn from the fight after a long battle. No information was available concerning the units of the 3rd Division, which had fought in the area around Kuuterselka and Sahakyla, the Cavalry Brigade had withdrawn along the coast of the Gulf of Finland to the west, and the 10th Division was to have defended the railway line in the area around Rieskyarvi–Vammelyarvi. The situation continued to change, but in a way that was anticipated, without any nasty surprises, since these had already happened, at least at that moment they had.

I had been studying the situation for several hours by the time the Commander-in-Chief called and asked the new Commander for his opinion, on whether the sections of the "VT line" could be regained in a counterattack. My response was that it would be impossible with these units, which had been forced, in the presence of the enemy's Commander-in-Chief to abandon the "VT line" and which continued to withdraw back towards Vyborg, while reinforcements had not arrived by 16 June, to regain the "VT line", and the counterattack would be senseless. The Commander-in-Chief asked if the Mannerheim line from the last war could be used as a new defensive line. The response to that was as follows: the Mannerheim line was situated in close proximity to the current theatre of operations, the withdrawing units and the reinforcements that were arriving would not be able to take up positions on this line, and in addition the Mannerheim Line had been all but destroyed in the last war. The front, on which it was possible to attack the Mannerheim Line, extended over a greater

> distance than the "VKT line." Furthermore the terrain on the Mannerheim line was much more accessible for tanks, which for us were the enemy's most dangerous branch of the armed forces. I suggested pulling our forces back to the "VKT line," and fighting a rear guard action using powerful defensive forces, whilst retaining their combat capability. The reserves would get there in time and we would have time to organise a defensive boundary.
>
> The Commander-in-Chief approved the proposal put forward by the Commander of the units on the Isthmus. Thus the first order issued by the new Commander became an order to retreat, but one that would retain strong defensive forces. On the morning of 16 June the corresponding order was issued: to use defensive forces to provide cover and withdraw to a line from Muurila–Kuolemajarvi–Hatjalahdenyarvi–Kakyarvi–Perkyarvi -Muolaanyarvi–Yuskyarvi–Kirkkoyarvi–Purmusyarvi–Valkyarvi–Rauma–Kosela–Ladoga. By the early morning of the following day a follow up order had to be issued to withdraw to a line from Vyborg–Kuparsaari–Vuoksi–Suvanto–Taipale, that is to say to the VKT line. It was on this line that the units were to mount a fierce defence and not take one step back.

It was during these critical hours outside of Vyborg that the first echelons of the 4th Infantry Division began to arrive from the Onezh Isthmus. On the move were the 3rd, and 20th Infantry Brigades. On 16 June battalions from the 5th, and 20th Infantry Regiments were offloaded at the Kamara station, they then set off for the front line on a speed march. In connection with the breakthrough in Kuuterselka both regiments prepared to take up a defensive position in the area around Suulayarvi but almost immediately it became apparent that these boundaries could not be defended. As a result the order for the occupation of defensive boundaries that was given to the 5th Regiment in the course of the march to the front line changed three times! By evening the regiment's battalions had reached the station settlement at Perk-Yarvi and had received orders to take up a defensive position on a boundary from Mikkelin-yarvi to Lavoinsuo–this was the southern edge of the station settlement at Perk-Yarvi. In the area around marker 66 an advanced guard of the 5th Regiment ran straight into a forward detachment of the 358th Rifle Division, which were travelling on the armour of the 98th, and 185th Tank Regiment's "thirty-fours" towards Vyborg.

Towards evening, a battery of self-propelled guns along with the 2nd Jager Battalion arrived to assist the 5th Regiment. The Jagers, infantrymen, and self-propelled guns launched their attack on this boundary and were noted by Soviet artillery observers from an aerostat. The artillery raid on the orders of battle of the Jagers dispersed the Finnish battalions. Since they had been badly depleted in Kuuterselka the 2nd Jager Battalion had lost their combat capability. Out of all the regiment's officers only the head of supply and the battalion's adjutant were still alive after the battle, and the latter was injured. From 14–17 June 1944 the losses among the officer corps in the 2nd Jager Battalion were at 90 percent.

The 3rd Battalion of 5th Infantry Regiment, which had come under artillery fire, had simply fled. This can easily be explained by their providence. The battalion was formerly the 20th Separate Punishment Battalion known as the *Chyornaya Strela* and consisted of prisoners who had been called up to serve on the front line, instead of sitting in prison.[1] According to a number of rumours that were circling, on seeing the firepower the Soviets had at their disposal some of the former prisoners formed a gang and headed away from the front line. After hijacking a lorry, the desperate deserters found themselves caught in a shoot-out with military police close to Lappeenranta and as a result they were confined on a group of islands in the Saimaa lakes, where they remained until the end of hostilities.

1 Translator's note: "*Chyornaya Strela*" is Russian for "Black Arrow".

In this head on battle between Perk-Yarvi and Lounat-Yoki, the Finnish self-propelled guns destroyed a T-34-85 from the 98th Separate Tank Regiment. By all accounts it was in this very regiment by fatal coincidence that the Commander of the 385th Rifle Division Colonel S.A. Vrublevskiy, the Division's Deputy Political Commissar Colonel A.D. Kireyev, and the Divisional Commander's Adjutant Senior Lieutenant V.Ya. Kutyr served. All three of whom were killed. The colonels are buried in Bogoyavlenskiy cemetery in Leningrad, and the twenty-five year old Senior Lieutenant Kutyr lies to this day in an unmarked grave on the battlefield, in a pine forest close to marker 66.

To the east of the railway line on 16-17 June, Lagus' Armoured Division was fighting in the area around Suulayarvi and Kannelyarvim holding back the Soviet divisions. At 1630 hrs on 17 June the Commander of the Armoured Division Colonel Bjorkman reported on the condition of his brigade to Lagus: losses in the battles close to Suulyarvi ran to seven or eight 'Vickers' vehicles. One "thirty-four" had to be sent to Varkaus for repair. Just seven or eight combat capable T-26s, plus the "thirty-fours" remained. A KV broke down and was still undergoing repair in Yonal. The battalion of self-propelled guns were still not up to strength following losses sustained in Kuuterselka. At 1900 hrs on 17 June at Armoured Division headquarters an urgent message arrived from Corps headquarters: Soviet tanks had broken through the Finnish defences between Hatjalahdenjärvi and Kaukjärvi, the infantry, who were panic stricken, had fled. Major Rasi and the Commander of the Jager Brigade Puromaa were despatched from armoured division headquarters to sort out those who had fled.

Later that evening, at 2345 hrs, the Commander of the 4th Infantry Division Major-General Autti called and requested two "thirty-fours" be sent to him urgently, since to the north of Kaukjarvi in Leppyaniemi some nine Soviet T-34s had appeared. The response from the Soviet tank crews was negative: just four 'thirty-fours" were left in the formation and all of these had only just gone in for servicing, so they would not be available for combat. The tank crews asked if the 4th Division had received their *Panzerschrecks* and *Panzerfausts*, and if they had indeed received them why they could not be used in combat? Autti responded saying that the division had only received these weapons two days ago, and nobody knew how to use them yet.

Lieutenant-Colonel Frey, chief of staff of 4th Infantry Division, telephoned back a short time later and again requested tanks, declaring that if they did not materialise then the entire Finnish defence would collapse on the western side of the Karelian Isthmus. After a short discussion the Armoured Division reluctantly allocated two 75mm PAK-40s from the 4th Jager, which advanced to the area around Summy and covered the road to Vyborg.

The situation grew worse in as much as Lagus ordered the Division to prepare for an urgent withdrawal and called his officers to a meeting at 0315 hrs. At this meeting Lagus ordered them directly not to engage in combat on the "VKT line" and to withdraw beyond the Saimaa canal. The reason for this, in the General's opinion, was that it would be impossible to hold Vyborg. The Commander of the 4th Corps Laatkainen agreed with the conclusions of his subordinate and immediately underlined that Vyborg must be held at any cost, out of prestige.

It was during this meeting that Lagus issued an order for the Armoured Division to withdraw behind the lines away from the battle for some leave, and also to allow for reinforcements and repair of the materiel. The Jager Brigade and the four combat capable StuG III were to withdraw to the area around Liimatta–Karhusuo, while the self-propelled guns with their 13 unserviceable attack guns withdrew to the area around Portinhoikka.

At 0950 hrs on 18 June when part of the division were already on the march Laatkainen telephoned Lagus and informed him of the order for the 4th Corps: the Armoured Division were, as soon as the units reached the assembly areas, to immediately advance to the front line and take over a defensive sector from the 10th Infantry Division and the Cavalry Brigade. In response to Lagus' order Laatikainen passed on the following disappointing news:

> I don't have any forces to hand; I need time to clarify the situation and gather together all the commanders of the different branches of the armed forces and the supply troops, so that the forces can be sent to the right places. The value in combat of the Jager Brigade is very small, there are around 2,400 soldiers in the formation, and losses in the Finnish officer corps exceed 60 officers. It is with these small battalions that we are meant to hold a defensive sector for a whole infantry division and a cavalry brigade. The paths through the forest between Rokkala and Summa can become dangerous. I am only able to send four attack guns, and one T-34 as well as Vickers tanks from the armoured materiel I have available.

Nothing, however, could be done. At 1048 hrs Lagus informed Puromaa that the 10th Division was completely demoralised, and only 200 men each were left in the cavalry and dragoon regiments, so aside from the Jagers there was nobody to hold the front line. Puromaa responded immediately that after the head on battle near Perkjarvi the 2nd Jager were in such a state that that they could only be sent to the front line a day later.

By 19 June, Soviet units were already some 10–15km from Vyborg. An attempt by the Finns to slow down the Soviet units on the boundary of Rokkalanyarvi using the forces of the exhausted cavalry brigade, and the Jager brigade, as well as several light Vickers tanks led to nought. The "thirty-fours" of the 152nd Brigade, which were moving along the Primorskoye road, swept the weak Finnish defences away as well as the very depleted lines of the dragoons, the cavalrymen, and the Jagers. A tank battle between the Vickers tanks against the T-34s in the area around Rokkalanyoki ended with a predictable result. Two tanks were lost, and another was destroyed by mistake by Finnish anti-tank crews, who were not expecting to see any of their own tanks. Following the battles of 16–19 June General Lagus ordered the tanks be sent into battle in small groups, while the light Vickers tanks were to be used very sparingly. As information was received that the enemy had heavy tanks the Vickers were immediately sent back behind the lines.

On the afternoon of 19 June, the armoured division withdrew from the battle and passed through Vyborg to the north. The Jager brigade formed a small encampment in Esplanade Park in the centre of the city. At a meeting of the commanders at 1750 hrs Lagus heard a disheartening report on the condition of his elite combat formation:

> Colonel Puromaa: the units are so exhausted that they are only able to go into battle again after rest and recuperation. The 2nd Jager Battalion is in a particularly bad condition.
>
> Colonel Bjorkman: as far as the armoured materiel in the armoured brigade is concerned–only two T-34s and 12 "Vickers" tanks are combat capable.
>
> Major Okerman: the tank evacuation and repair point–north of Kanaoya.
>
> Major Valanne: bicycles to replace those lost will be delivered only between six and eight hours from now.
>
> Colonel Klerikh: special shells are available in Hanhiyoki, and also in Yustila.

Overall the withdrawal to the VKT line was more or less successful. The artillery of the 10th Infantry Division was partially pulled back and saved. The remains of the Cavalry Brigade withdrew beyond Vyborg and stationed themselves in the area around Tervajoki for rest and recuperation. Two battalions of the 58th Infantry Regiment ended up cut off from their own lines by Soviet tank columns that were on their way to Vyborg, but they did manage for the most part to get out of the pocket, by taking advantage of their overall confusion. The main contingent broke through to Karhusuo to the east. According to the memoirs of surviving officers the Finns were most fortunate – the mass of Finnish infantry crossed the road at that same moment that Soviet tanks commanders had gathered for a field meeting.

On that day 19 June that was so full of dramatic events echelons from the 20th Infantry Brigade Onezh Isthmus arrived into Vyborg led by Colonel Armas Kempli. They were offloaded at Tali and Tammisuo stations and marched to Vyborg. In the afternoon, the brigade began to occupy defensive positions on the southern edges of the city. The view of Vyborg astonished the reinforcements as they arrived.

Vyborg, which everyone knew as a centre for pre-war tourism, looked like a ghost town. The glass had been blown out in all the houses in the centre–the result of the explosion of a train carrying ammunition on 15 June 1944. On the night of 14–15 June the railway depot in Vyborg was bombed by 72 Il-4s from the 8th Long-Range Air Corps, which had dropped approximately 83tonnes of bombs on the target.

The civilian population was nowhere to be seen. The city was evacuated between 15–16 June. The last barges had been loaded in the port, which had taken the loads from out of the wholesale warehouses. The city was crawling with looters, who had robbed abandoned flats and shops. The majority of soldiers were unarmed. The subdivisions of military police were nowhere to be seen in the city.

The newly arrived battalions from the brigade passed through this abandoned city to its southern and south-eastern edges and occupied defensive positions. The supply of defensive positions then began, which left a great deal to be desired. The order of the day from Marshal Mannerheim was read out to the Finnish units on the front line:

> Our forces have occupied defensive positions on the so-called "VKT line." It is here that the enemy advance into the interior of our country must be stopped. It is for this reason that I ask that a fierce defence of this line be mounted. In particular I would emphasise that any breakthrough of this defensive line would weaken our potential for defence and thus threaten the future of our country and our people. I know that the construction work on this line in places never got underway, or has only just begun, but I am certain that a Finnish soldier, when necessary, would make use of the features of the terrain and the Finnish spirit to create an impenetrable defence.

Nearer the evening a stream of retreating Finnish soldiers poured through the 20th Brigade's positions. To begin with they were rank and file soldiers and then whole subdivisions led by officers made their way into Vyborg along the main road on the Isthmus (Leningrad road). The retreating troops were very demoralised. In conversations with soldiers from the 20th Brigade they painted a gloomy picture of the Soviet advance: "Tanks are moving forward, they are right on the bend in the road;" "Russians are advancing and sweeping away everything in their path, they can't be stopped." This had an immediate, and dramatic effect on the morale of the soldiers. "I think that for many of the comrades in arms by evening it had become clear that we were the last of the Mohicans that were still fighting, and the rest of the soldiers had already escaped back to their villages for the harvest" was how Corporal Kotilainen described the condition of his forces.

Brigade officers had information that the Finns were holding out defensively in the area around Summy and that the distance to the Soviet units was less than 20km. At 2100 hrs the stand down signal was sounded for the battalions. The break was brief. The Commander of the 3rd Battalion Lieutenant-Colonel Sorri had earlier sent reconnaissance groups to the south-east along the Vyborg road. On their return the reconnaissance troops reported that on the approaches to the city they had come across the retreating 25th and 58th Regiments. Both regiments were moving swiftly in the direction of Vyborg in utter disarray and had completely lost their combat capability. Even the officers in the retreating regiments did not know where the Command Posts for their battalions were. At 2300 hrs at 20th Brigade headquarters a message came through that the forward Soviet units were in the area around Sainio some 10km from Vyborg. An alert was sounded in the brigade as well as a call for full combat readiness. All the companies had taken up defensive positions in their unfinished trenches. The mood was downbeat. The soldiers of the 2nd Battalion were in a particularly bad mood, as they had taken up a defensive position near the main road on the Isthmus, close to Ristiniemi cemetery.

The 2nd Battalion commander composed a farewell letter to his father, sealed the envelope and wrote on it in his native Swedish hand: *Att öppnas efter min död* (Open after my death*"*). The night passed with nervous anticipation as final preparations for battle were concluded before sunrise.

Colonel Kempi's headquarters was located in the basement of a bank on Torkel Street (now Prospekt Lenina, *dom* 12), today a branch of Sberbank. Major Bjokman's command post was situated to the north of the Ristimyaki cemetery. Major Kirma's was based in a wooden structure south of Batareynaya Gora.

It subsequently emerged that night that the brigade had more serious problems than the demoralisation of officers and men. The 20th Brigade had taken just one and a half loads of ammunition with them from Svir. In 1944, a load of ammunition in the Finnish Army consisted of: 45 rifle bullets, 350 automatic rifle bullets, 600 sub-machine gun bullets, and 1,200 heavy machine gun bullets. A load of ammunition for a light battalion consisted of 1,200 shells, and for a heavy battalion of 480.

A standard Finnish artillery attack would require the use of 40 shells. That is to say in the evening of 19 June the artillery had just enough shells for 10 artillery attacks–"this is nothing" armoured division artilleryman Captain Yantti, remarked in his memoirs.

The 40th Heavy Battalion had left their reserve of shells at Svir station, and the officers were promised that at Yessolya station a train would be standing that would be carrying supplies of shells. On arrival at Yessolya it turned out there no train was there waiting for them, nor were there any shells. The Directorate of the 20th Brigade arrived in Vyborg on 18 June and immediately began to demand that their armament be brought up to three load of ammunition, but the required forms that needed to be filled in to submit a requisition for the supply of ammunition were missing. As a result the requisition for one load of ammunition was only drawn up on 19 June and was sent to the appropriate authorities. By evening however on 19 June no response to the requisition had been forthcoming, and Lieutenant-Colonel Arra, the Head of Artillery for the Brigade on the night of 19–20 June began to call the artillery supply section in the 4th Corps. There they confirmed to him that he could come and collect one load of ammunition for the entire brigade in Rautakorli (a set of tunnels to the north of Vyborg).

Colonel Kemppi thought that one load of ammunition was woefully insufficient because the bridges north of Vyborg could be destroyed in the course of the offensive and requested three loads. This was a complex undertaking: on the night of 19–20 June Lieutenant Heikel, the Head of the brigade's ammunition supply section was despatched to wake the officers in the Corps' headquarters and request three loads of ammunition. The last thing Heikel wanted to do was to wake the colonels and he ignored this instruction. In order to be absolutely certain Lieutenant-Colonel Arra went personally to the headquarters of the 4th Corps. At midnight he awoke the Artillery Commander, Colonel Sipoola and the Head of the Artillery Supply Section Major Kayante from his bed.

The drowsy officers tore strips off Arra telling him that he could not requisition three loads of ammunition at once, but they did make a promise to him of sorts that there was a possibility that three loads could be collected "at first light" on 20 June. At least this was the impression that Arra had. The official requisition for the promised three loads of ammunition at 20th Brigade headquarters would be backdated to the morning of 20 June.

13

Vyborg Catastrophe, 20 June

At 0300 hrs the 20th Brigade's battalion commanders received a message that the brigade's entire artillery had reached their firing positions and the groups of artillery reconnaissance troops had had left for the front line and the had established radio contact with the artillery batteries.

At 0330 hrs the first of Lagus' self-propelled guns arrived–these were drawn from a separate tank company in the armoured brigade. They were German StuG IIIs, as well as five BT-42s manufactured in Finland. Two self-propelled guns from the first platoon immediately took up their firing positions near the main road on the Isthmus. One vehicle took up a position in the area around the racecourse, while the remaining two–on the railway lines in the depot.

Lagus ordered that the principal and reserve positions for the self-propelled guns be prepared under the protection of stone built buildings, and also informed the Commander of the Separate Company Lieutenant Sepel that firing the 114mm shaped charge howitzer (*Hochladung*, they are also described in the documentation as "special German shells") from the BT-42, would penetrate the armour of Soviet KV tanks. Subsequent events demonstrated that this was most definitely not the case.

By 0500 hrs the Brigade's Sapper Platoon had blown the bridge over the railway line south of the station. The buildings that were obstructing the line of fire for the platoon's forward companies were destroyed by demolition. At the same time units from the 90th Rifle Division, the tank crews of the 152 and 30th Guards Brigade reached the southern edges of Vyborg. Artillery as well as the logistics troops had been drawn up to the city.

At 0530 hrs the Soviet advanced guard appeared ahead of the Finnish positions. Fires had broken out resulting from the demolition of the buildings around the depot. Using the smoke as a screen Soviet infantry was able to get closer to the enemy and appeared in front of the 5th Company like a bolt from the blue. In the final shoot out the Soviet soldiers gained a foothold amongst the heaps of logs, ruins and boulders.

By 0600 hrs three *Panzerschreck* grenade launchers had been delivered to the second battalion, as well as three rounds for them. How these were to be used–nobody in the battalion actually knew. The "forty-fives" arrived but the 75mm heavy anti-tank guns had failed to materialise. The one PAK-40 gun had not been delivered to where the Soviet units had carried out the first strike–but along with two "forty-fives" it had taken up a position east of the railway line, not far from the municipal prison.

At 0730 hrs the Finns noticed a mobile group from the 1st Red Banner Tank Brigade–some 50–70 tanks on the road. According to Finnish information, they managed to set fire to three tanks using heavy artillery fire. However four Soviet KV tanks from the 31st Guards Tank Regiment however had been blown up by mines on the road.

In the direction of the Primorskoye road, Soviet units appeared in front of the positions only at 1030 hrs. At 0840 hrs the last units of the Jager Brigade passed through the Finnish positions as they were retreating, leaving the defenders a large number of rifle bullets and mortars. At 1300 hrs the Finns announced that they had destroyed three Soviet tanks in front of their positions. These losses are not confirmed in Soviet sources.

The first half of the day was spent in a fire-fight. By 1300 hrs it appeared that the first attack on the city was spent. On the morning of 20 June the Finnish brigade had incurred minimal losses–no more than approximately 30 injured soldiers. By that time however in the Brigade's 2nd Battalion the ammunition had begun to run out. The mortar gunners could be sent home since almost all the mortars had been fired. The soldiers on the front line had a clear view of the concentration of Soviet armoured materiel to the south of their own positions. A KV tank from the 260th Guards Regiment advanced towards Finnish positions along the road. This tank was blown up by a land mine but the crew did not escape. A Finnish "forty-five" opened fire on the KV on the road, which a moment later led to the death of the crew. Attempts to destroy the KV using the *Panzerschrecks* were unsuccessful.

The situation with respect to ammunition and the Soviet preparations for a fresh attack, which were taking place in full view of the Finns, drained the soldiers of their will to fight. "We could see how the political commissars with their white gloves were commanding the infantry to take up positions on the armour of the tanks."–phrases like these appeared in the memoirs of Finnish veterans. It is true that fear always exaggerates things.

Attempts to supply ammunition to the front line failed miserably. The Head of the Brigade's Artillery Supply Section Lieutenant Heikel went around the headquarters all night long, trying to secure bullets and shells. He decided not to go to the headquarters of the 4th Corps and headed straight for the ammunition store in the Rautakorpi tunnels. He was not given anything from the ammunition store, but he was able to call Corps headquarters from there, where the response he received was as follows: "We will put your requisition together in the morning." On the basis of the subsequent conversation Heikel thought that he had verbal permission to take 200,000 rifle, and 200,000 automatic rifle bullets. At 0330 hrs he returned to Vyborg, with great difficulty he put together a train formed of carts and set off again for the store. The Head of the ammunition store Captain Rautamaa refused to issue the bullets, since he had not received documentary confirmation from Corps headquarters.

At 1000 hrs Kemppi had to send Major Nurmi, the Head of the Operations Section of Brigade headquarters, to the ammunition store since they had already ran out of bullets. Nurmi managed to secure from the miserly foreman at the store just 100,000 rifle bullets and 100,000 automatic rifle bullets. No heavy shells were issued at all.

At 1115 hrs Captain Salven, a messenger arrived at Kemppi's headquarters from the armoured division, to establish cooperation. Kemppi informed him that artillery support had just at that moment ceased. Salven immediately reported this to the Head of the Operations Section of the 4th Corps Lieutenant-Colonel Pesoniusu. He promised to sort it out.

In order to solve the problem with the supply of ammunition Mannerheim's Headquarters itself had to get involved. At 1215 hrs a telegram was sent from there to brigade headquarters. A group of brigade ammunition supply personnel were sent to the ammunition store for the third time already, taking with them the telegram and their automatic weapons. It was there that they finally received their bullets and mortars. They were still not issued with heavy shells, since it turned out that the shells in the store were for 1938 model howitzers and not 1937 models. Captain Rautmaa set off immediately to obtain this ammunition from Simola station, but it was too late already.

By 1300 hrs the long awaited 75mm German anti-tank gun had finally been delivered to Torkkeli Street but without a crew. It seemed that the front line was only just being supplied with ammunition, while the brigade continued to fight, but at that moment events took what was for the Finnish side an unexpected and tragic turn.

At 1230 hrs Soviet artillery opened fire. Fires broke out and the entire telephony network was disabled. It was especially difficult to maintain communications between the 2nd Battalion and Brigade headquarters. A messenger had to run a distance of two and a half kilometres along the city's deserted streets under fire. At 1245 hrs Major Bjokman decided to move his Command Post 500m to the north away from the cemetery to a stone dwelling and establish contact. The 6th Company took the withdrawal of the headquarters as a signal for the overall advance.

At 1340 hrs *Fahrnich* Kastren, the Commander of the 2nd Platoon, 6th Company glanced back and saw the battalion headquarters officers that were pulling back towards the city. The Finns also noticed that both the self-propelled BT-42s had left the battlefield, one was towing the other vehicle. According to the Finnish self-propelled gun crews, BT-42 vehicles were damaged and were not able to take any further part in combat. At that moment a shout rang out from Private Mannelin, who was standing next to Kastern: "The battalion is retreating, that's an order!" This shout became the straw that broke the camel's back. *Fahnrich* Kastern, without checking if it was an order or not, ordered his platoon to retreat, and did not pass the order on to the neighbouring 3rd, and 4th Platoons. Only after that did Kastern look to the left and see that the 1st Platoon was holding the line once more. He ran over to them and asked the Platoon Commander Captain Aspola, if there really had been an order to retreat. Aspola responded saying that he had not heard anything of that sort. *Fahnrich* Kastern ran over to his own platoon to cancel the order, but it was too late. A panic ensued in the battalion; soldiers were breaking their necks to head for the centre of the city and the castle. On seeing these soldiers running away the machine gunners and mortar gunners abandoned their positions. Soldiers were abandoning their weapons and running as fast as they could back behind their own lines on the pretext of the lack of ammunition.

The commander of the 2nd Battalion Bjokman knew nothing of this, since at that same time he was engaged in moving his Command Post 500m to the north and had forgotten to inform his platoon commanders of this. When a messenger who had been sent by Captain Aspola arrived at the location of the old Command Post he found it deserted.

It was only 20 mins later that from Batareynaya Gora a messenger arrived and informed them that the battalion had fled. Bjokman thought that the neighbouring 4th Battalion under Major Kirma had fled. He had no way of contacting the 4th Battalion. At that very moment, a messenger ran up to the Command Post and informed him that there was nobody at the Platoon Commander Captain Apola's Command Post, and almost the entire 6th Company, and the reserve 1st Company had fled back behind the lines. The Battalion Commander was taken aback by this news and made him angry. He sent his adjutant Lieutenant Sirkka to stop those who had fled on Batareynaya Gora, and the messenger Lieutenant Lehtinena–to stop the soldiers at the castle. It was too later however as two platoons from the 6th Company were running away faster than the officers could catch them.

At 1425 hrs the heavy division reported that all 460 shells had been fired at the enemy and the battalion was sitting without any ammunition in Herttula. The 20th Light Battalion was still firing from the Monrepos Park.

Bjorkman found himself in a difficult situation. He had no way of contacting his neighbours, and the line to brigade headquarters had also been cut. The 6th Company was running back behind the lines, leaving a gap in the defence. With no way of ascertaining the actual state of affairs on the front line quickly, the Battalion Commander took his decision. At 1430 hrs he ordered via his messengers to pass onto the 5th and 7th Companies an order to retreat, but he forgot to tell them where the new defensive line would be. Bjokman sent a lorry carrying ammunition that had finally arrived back to the city. The Major's confusion was passed onto the messengers–they left the battalion headquarters but did not have the courage to join the companies on the front line. As a result the 5th Company remained in their positions at the cemetery up until 1530 hrs, when the "thirty-fours" of the 1st Red Banner Brigade had already reached its boundaries. The 7th Company had no knowledge of the order to retreat either.

Having issued the order, Bjokman dashed to the Batareynaya Gora in order to check to what extent his officers had succeeded in halting the escape. It was there that he encountered two self-propelled BT-42s and noticed that the entire infantry had long since fled. Bjokman ordered one of the self-propelled guns to go to Papulu, and the second to go beyond the bridges close to the castle and hold a defensive line at that location. The self-propelled gun that had departed to Papulu, became caught on the railway lines closer to the railway station and was abandoned by its crew. Following this, the unhappy major, who had not taken the trouble to look what was happening in the battalion's positions (the Soviet advance had not even begun yet) ran to the brigade's headquarters.

When Bjorkman, who was out of breath and wet through with sweat, arrived at the bank, Colonel Kemppi dictated the order once again. He interrupted this to open up to Major Konyak, who was shocked, and dumbstruck at the grief that Bjokman poured out to him. Kemppi did not understand the situation either, meanwhile he made the following decision: the reserve battalion under Captain Malinen, which had been augmented by the Jager platoon in the 3rd Battalion, and a company in the 4th Battalion, should counterattack and regain the 2nd Battalion's positions. Kemppi thought that Soviet units had broken through the 2nd Battalion's defences and was not aware that the Battalion had simply abandoned their positions and fled.

At 1455 hrs Kemppi reported to Laatikainen via Headquarters (there was no direct communication link with the headquarters of the 4th Corps, by all accounts): "The defensive line has been breached at Ristimyaki. We are going to counterattack. We are running low on shells. I request that these be delivered to the gun emplacements urgently."

At 1550 hrs Kemppi thought that the city could still be held and issued an order to a sapper company and a signals company to take up a defensive position in the Old town near the bridges, but this was already a very unrealistic assessment of the situation. A complete collapse of the brigade had begun.

At 1600 hrs the 1st Battalion under Captain Malinen had set off for the front line to launch a counterattack. A company under Captain Suutarinen went to the 6th Company's positions, and were immediately either injured, or killed, after which his company fled.

At 1630 hrs the Finns had succeeded in beating back a Soviet attack on Ristimyaki cemetery but Soviet tanks and infantry began to encircle the 5th Company under Laasko via the 6th Company's positions that were abandoned. The company began to withdraw and encountered a company from the 1st Battalion, who were led personally by Captain Malinen. Having become intermingled with each other the Finnish companies abandoned their positions and fled back behind the lines. Malinen attempted to halt the exodus with a pistol in his hand but was unsuccessful. At that moment, another strange incident occurred: Captain Malinen transferred command to Captain

Laasko, and yet disappeared from the battlefield himself, saying that he was tired and needed to rest. Nobody saw him any more after that.

At 1710 hrs Colonel Kemppi sent an urgent telegram to corps headquarters. "I request a fresh battalion to assist." This telegram may as well not have been sent. At 1725 hrs Soviet tanks and their crews moved towards the city along the *Krespostnaya Ulitsa* and the *Leningrad road.* On the corner of the Leningrad road and *Ilyinskaya Ulitsa* the only tank battle to take place in the city's 700 year history occurred. A T-34-76 commanded by Lieutenant-Technician Naumenko from the 2nd Battalion, 1st Red Banner Tank Brigade, went head to head with a BT-42 self-propelled gun commanded by Captain Sippel, the Commander of the Separate Tank Company. According to Finnish records, Sippel fired two shells at the "thirty-four," missing the target both times, it was then that he understood that the 114mm shells were ineffective against Soviet armour. After that his self-propelled gun (with the tactical number 717) turned around, hurried away from the front line along the Leningrad road and turned right, onto *Ilyinskaya Ulitsa*, and it was here that the "thirty-four" commanded by Lieutenant-Technician Naumenko caught up with it. A Soviet shell fired from a distance of some 50m penetrated the turret. Captain Sinnel and tank crewman Sorvisto were killed. Driver-Mechanic Virtanen, who had been injured in the back, was able to escape from the badly damaged vehicle and return to his own lines.

The 4th Battalion of the Brigade at that time was still holding a defensive position on the south-western edge of Vyborg. In accordance with an order a proportion of the battalion had crossed from the cape of Pappilanniemi and had taken up a defensive position on Havi embankment.

At 1715 hrs, as the 4th Battalion Commander was talking to Colonel Kemppi on the telephone, Captain Pusa, the Commander of a gun company politely informed him that Soviet tanks had parked outside the headquarters building. The conversation had to be interrupted and the officers set off towards the castle apace under a hail of Soviet bullets. On the streets of the Old town the headquarters officers became disorientated and the elderly Major Kirma became detached from the others. After that nobody saw him again. His relatives still search for his burial site to this day. According to returning ex-prisoners of war, Kirma spent the night in a cellar and died on the city's streets on the morning of 21 June in a skirmish with a Soviet patrol. Two of the battalion headquarters' officers were found the next day in Lappeenranta some 50km from Vyborg.

At 1723 hrs the 20th Light Battalion were moved from their firing positions in Monrepos and set off back behind the lines. In the course of a day's fighting they had fired 2,075 shells.

At 1730 hrs the lead "thirty-fours" were already on *Krasnaya Ploshchad* next to Brigade headquarters. The headquarters personnel had fled. Kemppi was in such a disorientated state that he decided to stay in Vyborg forever. According to one Finnish legend, whenever a soldier would ask Kemppi where he was to set up his defensive line, Kemppi would answer: "In Tornio! Set up your defensive line on the Swedish side of the River Tornio!"

Nevertheless Kemppi's adjutant Lieutenant Virtanen managed to convince the Colonel to leave the bank building itself:

> On a mission given to me by Colonel Kemppi I went into the city to reconnoitre the situation, and in the centre of the city I discovered enemy tanks. Using circuitous routes under fire from artillery and a bombardment I reached *Krasniy Kolodets* square and entered the courtyard outside the bank. An abandoned lorry was standing there into which the personal effects from the headquarters had been loaded. It was into this lorry that I had previously loaded my suitcase. I rushed into the cellar (the headquarters was housed there), and it was dark inside. Smoke was coming from the cellar, none of the headquarters staff were there anymore. I climbed a steel staircase into the building of the bank itself. Colonel

> Kemppi was on his own in there. I gave him my report as was customary, to which Colonel Kemppi answered: "I am not a Commander any more, I no longer have a brigade under my command, my headquarters staff have also gone." I suggested he should leave but all the Commander would talk about was staying in Vyborg. Finally he agreed. We left via a back entrance, and occasionally holding hands we crossed the courtyards, and emerged onto *Severniy Val*. Enemy tanks were firing from the direction of Torkkeli Park.

Kemppi and Virtanen reached the bridge near the castle at 1740 hrs. After looking up at the tower in the castle the Colonel said: "Somebody run up there and take down the flag. It would be shameful to leave it to the enemy." *Fahnrich* Myakinen, a Company Commander from the 4th Battalion heard this order. He ran towards the castle. The flag was removed at 1745 hrs under fire from Soviet field artillery that was attacking the castle tower at close range. All this time Virtanen was keeping an eye on the bridge, where Soviet tanks had yet to appear.

According to legend Myakinen gave the flag to the Brigade Commander with the words: "Mister Colonel here is the flag; the order has been completed." "After all that I am no longer a Colonel" came Kemppi's dejected reply. This same flag can be seen today in the branch of the Military Museum of Finland in the Fortress of Suomenlinna.

At that same moment, the last of the Finnish infantry were running across the bridge near the castle. The majority of them had no weapons, and those that had weapons had no bullets at all. The brigade officers with pistols in their hands tried to slow their progress and organise at least some kind of a defence.

At 1750 hrs the bridges near the castle were blown sky high, the wooden structures of the bridges caught fire. The brigade officers proved unable to slow down the infantry, who were running in all directions. In the supreme military court the Commander of the 4th Corps Laatikainen used this fact to support his allegations against Kemppi: "The fact that the enemy advance could not be halted even for one second beyond the bridges near the castle, where they could have been stopped using minimal force, is testimony to the fact that brigade command had lost control of the situation and of their subdivisions."

At that same time, on the embankment of the old town beyond the castle, Soviet tanks and infantry appeared. A fire-fight began. Soviet artillery attacked the Finnish flanks near the castle via a partially destroyed railway bridge, and again a panic stricken exodus began. This was only stopped near the *Kammeniy Most* (known today as the Saimaa Canal).

This exodus turned out to be fateful for the families of those seriously injured in the 20th Brigade, who were lying in the military hospital to the north of the castle. In order to rescue them they would have needed to have been moved just two and a half kilometres to the north, beyond the *Kammeniy Most*. There was however nobody available to organise transport in the chaos of the exodus from the city. Military Doctor Otto Salonen and Military Nurse Eyno Varola remained with their patients. After 20 June 1944 nobody saw either of them alive again. They did not return to Finland in the course of the prisoner exchange after the war. The circumstances of their deaths remain a mystery to this day. Kaple Autio, who was taken prisoner in the hospital, announced in the 1990s that everyone who was in the ward was shot on the spot by Soviet machine gun fire. Autio himself was only saved because he had hidden under the body of a big Finnish medic.

In 2004 Corporal Vilno Myulyuniemi recalled what he had seen in the hospital on that fateful day:

> When I arrived at the dressing station, Doctor Salonen and Military Nurse Varola were standing on the street in jumpers. The doctor was racked by nervous tension. I asked Varola

why the dressing station had not been evacuated. He responded saying that anyone who was able to get away, including the medical staff, had already left.

The doctor had done all he could to get the injured that were unable to walk, away from the dressing station but he had received no assistance even from brigade headquarters. I asked the nurse how many injured patients there were in the hospital and he answered seven patients. The doctor had given them a sedative and they were sleeping, a doctor does not abandon his patients, and I was not about to abandon the doctor.

I looked through the wall made up of sandbags that had been built to protect the dressing station, and I saw a Russian detachment of some 50 men heading for the dressing station. I said to Varola that they were Russians and it would be safer for everyone if I were to "disappear," since in accordance with my orders it was time to head for the bridge near the castle. At this Doctor Salonen said that it would be best if there were no armed soldiers in the dressing station.

By the evening of 20 June 1944, all that stood between the victorious Soviet units in Vyborg and Helsinki was a thin grey line of Finnish soldiers who had been suppressed by a defeat. A German 150mm howitzer from the 14th Separate Battalion, and the crew commander was the Commander of the Battery Captain Lauri Yantti. For two hours the road to Helsinki was more or less open. Why did the Soviet units not continue the offensive immediately, taking advantage of the obvious panic among the Finnish soldiers? Soviet tank regiment archive documents record that the offensive was not continued immediately because of the absence of the necessary fording equipment to cross the narrows of the Saimaa canal.

Captain Yantti recalled these dramatic hours:

At 1320 hrs the battalion received an order from the Artillery Commander of the 4th Corps to immediately advance to the area around Herttuala. It was there that we were to receive an order to occupy the pre-prepared firing positions to support the troops defending the Vyborg units. We did not have the slightest idea that the infantry and artillerymen had deserted the city in a panic. We soon had reasons to suspect though that something was amiss with the 20th Brigade.

At a crossroads in Rapattile we saw a strange, abandoned camp. Entire boxes of brand new knee high boots, underwear, and office files had been upturned onto the ground. There was nobody there at all. Unsurprisingly a few minutes later our artillerymen were sporting the new boots even before the officers arrived. They grabbed the new underclothes from trucks that were standing in the forest. These trucks had been left in a very neat row. The bodies of these trucks were full of gas masks, harnesses, expensive coils with telephone cables–anything linked to the brigade's logistics. Only the drivers were missing. When I arrived and had begun to look around this place in amazement my gaze fell on a piece of paper from an office file that the wind had blown under my feet. There was good news on this piece of paper, which at that moment did nothing to cheer me up:

"The price of cinema tickets can be reduced from four marks to two marks."

What was this abandoned camp telling us? It would soon become clear.

The 14th Heavy Battalion, which in accordance with their orders had been transferred to come under the artillery commander of the 20th Brigade, continued to march towards the firing positions in Herttuala. At 1645 hrs on the Vyborg–Lappeenranta road the acting Battalion Commander Captain von Numers jumped out onto the road in front of a column, and waved his hands franticly, interrupting our onward march. Lieutenant-Colonel Arra had only just informed him of the shocking news of the collapse of the defence in Vyborg. According to the information he had, all the bridges were still intact. The blasting of the *Kamenniy Most* had also been unsuccessful (a second attempt to blow the bridge under Sergeant Puputti was only partially successful). The fact that the Russians could appear at any moment on the Tienhaara headland was written on the faces of the artillery commander, as well as on the faces of the other officers. Lieutenant-Colonel Arra had already reported what had happened to the headquarters of the 4th Artillery Corps and to the headquarters of the 10th Division in Yustila. Despite this, the arrival of six-inch howitzers in the battalion had been a godsend to the artillery commander, who had been desperately seeking assistance. At that moment I was leading a column and the battalion commander asked me to send a single howitzer near to the *Kammeniy Most* to fire at close range under the command of an officer and not to let enemy tanks cross onto the Tienhaara headland at any cost ...

..Firing at close range–it's no easy task; it is best to head off yourself. What can you do. I handed over the battery to my deputy, Lieutenant Blyumenthal. We shook hands as we parted. And then: "The first gun, march!" The artillerymen drew their helmet straps onto their chins...we covered these five or six kilometres in a rush, as if we were rushing towards a fire. As before a group of fugitives were walking towards us, some on foot, others on horses or in vehicles. They were signalling desperately to one another. They were also in a hurry but were moving in the opposite direction to us. They were running away lightly equipped, most of them did not have a rifle, someone had boots on...and someone else was walking along the side of the road with one leg in breeches. The deafening sound of aircraft engaged in an air battle roared above our heads ...

On our bank in the area around Tienhaari, officers from the 20th Brigade had begun to stop the brigade's soldiers who were running away. In the coastal forest areas there were around 100 very traumatised soldiers.

Colonel Kemppi arrived onto the Tienhaara headland along with the last of his soldiers. He affirmed the plan for the brigade headquarters officers–to take up a defensive position on the headland and strengthen it with guns firing at close range, and despite the fact that he could clearly see the fractures in the brigade's will to fight, he said that he would go and report to the headquarters of the 4th Artillery Corps in Kavantsaari ...

At 1730 hrs we arrived on the bank. Under a fierce hail of shells we had carved out a trench for the howitzer and shelters for its crew. We aimed the barrel of the howitzer towards Sorvali on the opposite side of the bank.

A short while later the last of the soldiers from the 20th Brigade made their way away from the coastal bank, led by their Commander Captain Kokkola. Major Virri ordered them to hold a defensive position there. Prior their departure to Kavansaari Colonel Kemppi ordered the brigade's subdivisions that had lost their combat capability to gather together in Tienhaara. This company also went, maybe, by mistake? When I asked Captain Kokkola the reason for the withdrawal, he quoted the order given by Colonel Kemppi. One of the retreating soldiers had given the steadfast artillerymen their most treasured possession–a bucket of jam, which they had carried with them from Vyborg itself. After treating themselves our artillerymen were ready to carry out their combat mission, and their duty.

Was there anyone left on the Tienhaara headland? "Ah!" yes there was. Aside from our heavy howitzer in an area of coastal scrub a section of infantry held a defensive line and were more heavily armed, with a sub-machine gun. These troops were commanded by *Fahnrich* Pitkyanen (he remained the only officer to be awarded a decoration for the Battle of Vyborg). I also with great difficulty managed to stop a single BT-42 self-propelled gun and force it to join the firing position (was this *Fahnrich* Kaakinen's self-propelled gun?). There was also a 75mm anti-tank gun, which Lieutenant Alfors' crew had dragged from Vyborg through their own efforts. In addition there was a pair of "forty-fives." That was all. They took up their firing positions and set their field of fire. They decided that their lives were not going to be taken without a fight.

> The firing grew in intensity. Minutes seemed more like hours. The tension became almost unbearable. The howitzer had already been loaded with an armour piercing shell. I was told that the driver-mechanic on the BT-42 had discovered that the firing pin had failed on the howitzer and he had "gone for spare parts." As far as the future of Finland was concerned this was probably the most critical moment, since the road from Vyborg–Tienhaara and further on to Helsinki was almost unguarded …
>
> Nobody could see at that time however, but the only thing that could be heard from the direction of Vyborg was a quietly whispering wind..
>
> Vyborg for the Russians was a solid lump that needed to be digested. The advance across the *Kamenniy Most* had not been undertaken immediately. Our "forces," that had been defending the bridge for about two hours, handed over part of the defence to the 20th Separate Battalion under Major Penttilya …
>
> What for Vyborg had been a fateful 20 June came to end. Vyborg had been irrevocably lost. When late in the evening we skulked around the coastal scrub with Major Pentillya, agreeing on the sectors allocated for defensive fire, we noticed something interesting. Against the backdrop of the night sky the first Russian silhouette was clearly visible–a sentry in a greatcoat on the cliffs of Sorvali, looking just like Peter the Great. He was an easy target. If you wanted it–you just believed, but if you didn't–no need, we did not fire at him. That night though we really did open fire on Torkkeli Park, where our Jagers had been resting under the cover of foliage on the morning of that day.. Our aerial reconnaissance had reported that now the park was crawling with Russian regiments…

In reality there was no continuation of the advance. The Finns, who had held a defensive position in the area around Papula, heard the sound of marching and voices coming from Vyborg's *Krasnaya Ploshchad*. The units of the Leningrad Front had fulfilled the first objective of the Vyborg offensive operation brilliantly and had reached the line from Vyborg–Vuoksi in the course of 10 days. In the Soviet-Finnish War that had taken place five years earlier it had taken the Red Army 105 days to cover this distance. Soviet Command had calculated that the Finnish resistance had finally been broken and that the pursuit of the enemy could begin from 21 June.

The fact that Vyborg, which for Finns was a symbol of Western influence, had fallen so quickly was a national shock. Ekvist subsequently observed: "Without Vyborg Finland is an invalid of a country." The city had been held in the Soviet-Finnish War, by the time the armistice had come into force on 13 March 1940 Red Army units had only reached Batareynaya Gora. The Finnish flag had been removed from the castle tower at 1500 hrs that day in a ceremonial atmosphere and with full military honours. On 20 June 1944 the flag had to be rescued from the castle tower in a hurry.

Mannerheim only devoted one paragraph of his memoirs to the fall of Vyborg, and writes of the fall very guardedly:

> On 20 June, the enemy's 21st Army went on the offensive between Vyborg and Vuoksi and achieved considerable success. Vyborg had fallen after a short battle, which in its intensity bore no comparison to the battles in the final days of the Winter War for this ancient city.

> The fall of Vyborg was a cruel blow to the fighting spirit of the forces, and also entailed the loss of an important stronghold, which should have held out against the considerable forces of the enemy. In addition the enemy gained a trampoline from which they could cross the Gulf of Finland. After the battle however the Russians were not able to proceed any further, despite the number of large scale advances they had undertaken, since it was in this direction that the 10th Division under Colonel Savonyousi, and the 17th Division, which had just arrived from Eastern Karelia under Major-General Sundmana, had organised a powerful defence.

The 20th Brigade's flight from Vyborg and the loss of the city in the space of just a few hours gave rise to a conspiracy theory. The theory states that allegedly the generals at Finnish Headquarters had agreed ahead of time to relinquish Vyborg and hold a defensive position in a much more advantageous boundary–the Saimaa canal. Mannerheim, naturally, knew nothing of this plot. The omissions and inconsistencies in the memoirs of several of the generals at Finnish Headquarters serve as the basis for this conspiratorial version of events, together with Lagus' statement that it would be impossible to hold Vyborg. The fact that Laatikainen had not contacted the brigade at all that day, as though he had forgotten about them and abandoned them to their fate, also supports this theory.

An analysis of 21st Army and 20th infantry Brigade losses resulted in the judgement that no significant battles had actually taken place in the city itself. Despite what the Finnish authors have written about heavy losses inflicted by Soviet units in the storming of the city these are not confirmed by Soviet records. On 20 June 1944 the 21st Army lost 174 men killed, and 665 injured. There were no recorded instances of anyone missing without trace. The principal losses had been inflicted by the 358th, and 372nd Rifle Divisions, which had begun the storming of the Finnish defensive VKT line east of the city.

The 90th Rifle Division under Major-General Lyashchenko, which according to official Soviet records "had fought for almost six hours in the outskirts, and in the streets of the city," had lost in total just three men killed, and 33 injured. The 314th Rifle Division, which in Vyborg had "fought for every street and every house," had lost just five men killed, and a further 64 who were missing without trace.

According to the first reports the Finnish Army's 20th Infantry Brigade lost 19 men killed, 101 injured, and 419 missing without trace. Subsequently a large proportion of those who had been "missing without trace" had again returned to their unit. Such inconsistencies in the losses on both sides confirm once again that no significant battles actually took place in the city itself.

A contemporary assessment of the 20th Brigade's losses is as follows:

Killed	85
Died in hospital from their wounds	4
Died in captivity	15
Returned from captivity	47
Missing without trace, most likely taken prisoner	4
Deserted	6
Fate unknown	1
Total	**162**

The fall of Vyborg had brought the military career of Colonel Armas Kemppi to a dramatic end. He was removed from his position as a Brigade Commander, was arrested, and accused of complicitly handing over the city to the enemy. The court sentenced the former Colonel to three months in prison. The colonel's will to live had been broken. He died in 1949; despite the fact that he had known Kemppi for a considerable time, as well as the requests and favours from colleagues, Mannerheim did not send Kemppi's widow his condolences following his death. The commander of the brigade's 2nd Battalion, Major Bjokman, decided he would not await the court's judgement and shot himself on 21 January 1945.

The veterans of the 20th Brigade avoid the subject of 20 June 1944 in their memoirs. Only a small number of eye-witness accounts remain of the last day that Vyborg was in Finnish hands.

Private Korhonen, 5th Company, 20th Infantry Brigade:

> The Company Commander Captain Laasko gave a speech yesterday in which he had again reiterated military discipline. He described a scenario to us that was more optimistic than was actually the case. A German *Messerschmitt* squadron was to provide cover for us from the skies, while our Air Force, according to Captain Laasko, was stronger than that of the enemy. He warned us not to go into the cellars to feast on jam. The local inhabitants could be poisoning the jam like they had done in the previous war. The day before this we had paid a visit to the cellars of the *Valio* company to feast on their marmalade, and our stomachs had been grumbling all that time.
>
> Now the enemy was literally raining down bombs on us. A whole sea of fire was roaring in front of our eyes. Enemy infantry went on the attack, but we managed to beat them back following a fierce battle. The shortage of ammunition was critical, which could not fail to have an effect on the will to fight. It was for these same reasons that our artillery was not firing. The attack guns were supposed to attack the road and prevent enemy tanks break through to our positions. At midday the self-propelled guns withdrew, one was towing the other behind it. All that time the enemy was batter out defences, while they had more infantry on the edge of the forest than there were ants in an ant's nest.
>
> The tracks of the "thirty-fours" began to clank along the cobblestones that made up the road on the Isthmus. At this we all felt a shiver run down our spine. I remembered my mother. We had a couple of *Panzerfausts*. They were brought to us right at the last moment, and nobody knew how to use them. A look of horror had appeared on the faces of the soldiers: their pale faces, covered in layers of dirt from constantly "kissing the ground" resembled the faces of the dead. I had trouble recognising the faces of my friends.
>
> The tank did not pass us by like we wanted it to but parked on a small square between the cemetery fence and a small house and began to fire right and left. The soldiers in the platoon that had been deployed, and who were stricken with horror, were shaking on the ground some 15m from the tank. They were so stricken with horror at what they were seeing that they were not even able to flee.
>
> We could see that the 6th Company was beginning the withdrawal. The company's messenger arrived with an order from the battalion commander to withdraw. That cannot be! I don't believe it!
>
> At that moment, the reserve battalion under Captain Malinen appeared behind our positions and opened fire on us by mistake. We tried to explain this to the commander, that our troops were still in their positions and that they should stop firing! He tried to force his soldiers to reconnoitre the situation, but since all they were doing was just lying on the ground and shaking, I suggested to my colleague that we move forward. By jumping

> over headstone after headstone we moved forward. We noticed that our own troops were still where we had left them, but they were a little more able to open fire. At 1600 hrs we reported this to Captain Malinen, who stood with a pistol in his hand on the cemetery fence and was trying to raise his troops to go on the attack under the threat of being shot, but in vain.
>
> Suddenly I saw a huge mass of infantry on the road. Then I noticed that the last of our soldiers were gathering their things and crawling in through a window in the railway depot and jumping out the opposite side. I also jumped to my feet. I was only able to catch my breath somewhere outside the city and I thought that the war would soon be over. The war however continued.

Corporal Pauli Kotilainen, in the Jager Platoon in Captain Malinen's Battalion recollected:

> We arrived at the northern bank of the Ristimyaki near the railway depot and dug in. The enemy artillery fire grew ever more intense. At that same time the sound of tank engines from the direction of the road on the Isthmus was growing ever louder. The heavy tanks that we had feared so much were coming for us. We climbed onto the hill itself, on which were enemy machine gun positions. Our troops were by and large already holding a defensive position, but a withdrawal had already begun from the right flank. Our "forty-five" opened fire with a few shots on the hill but was soon silenced, after receiving an angry response from Soviet KVs. The lads from the anti-tank platoon tried to destroy the tanks to the right of us using the *Panzerschreck* weapons, but they were a significant distance away. The *Schreks* only worked over a distance of 150m, and nobody in the battalion up until their arrival into Vyborg, had heard sight nor sound of this weapon at all, and nobody had any idea how to use it. The enemy artillery in front of us had not yet been especially active. However artillery, and tank fire from the right hand side of us near the road made our situation a much more difficult one.
>
> The situation was gradually becoming a little more nerve wracking. We could hear the sound of the tank engines as well as small arms fire from within the city itself. The thought of encirclement was probably unnerving many, and suddenly, before one could get one's head around the fact that something very important had happened, the situation degenerated into complete chaos. Panic ensued. Soldiers rushed at breakneck speed towards the depot on the slope of Ristimyaki hill. Some officer or other with a pistol in his hand was trying in vain to stop the men running away. They were just acting on their instincts. Someone had fallen, killed by an enemy bullet just a second away from reaching the slope that would have been their saving grace. The background music to all this was the threatening roar of Soviet tank engines and the sharp shots from the tanks' guns that cracked like whips. A swarm of enemy aircraft circled above us, adding their share to the overall chaos. From the opposite side of the railway line in the area around Karjala, wooden houses were burning brightly and one after another columns of black smoke rose into the sky.

On the Gulf of Finland's northern banck, Finnish artillerymen could clearly see the castle tower, and witnessed the lowering of the flag:

> I recall the rapid withdrawal from positions north of Uusikirkko as though in a fog. I looked at the battalion officer and I thought to myself, was it really just two days ago that he travelled to the area around Summy in his car on a reconnaissance mission and had almost been run over by an enemy tank? Was it really only two days ago that we had tried, firing our

six-inch howitzer at close range, to stop enemy tanks in the area around Kauk-Yarvi on the Keibel headland? It would be quicker to wait for soup to boil, I was tired of sitting around here. On the other hand from the direction of the front line, nothing of any concern could be heard from Rotanpesya, so we could actually sit around. The drops of water from water columns thrown up into the air by exploding shells sparkled brilliantly in the sunset, and every now and again something would be thrown into the air–a piece of shrapnel or a bit of a rock or something. A junior sergeant who was standing next to me, and watching the battle through his binoculars, woke me from my thoughts.

"There was a flag flying on top of the castle just then, but it's not there now."

"What are you saying? I saw the flag just a moment ago, let me have a look."

The flagpole was empty and the flag was missing. Maybe the conditions were so still that the flag had drooped down. No, the flag was not there. Our observations drew the attention of others, who were approaching us. I was offered a mug of soup and a bread roll with jam but I didn't feel like taking them. If the flag has been removed–what does that mean? A terrible thought was creeping into my head, had Vyborg been relinquished? It could not possibly signify anything else–how and when had this happened? From the expressions on the other soldier's faces it was clear that this thought had entered their heads too, although nobody dared say it out loud. I ran to the telephone:

"What has happened in the city, the flag has been lowered from the castle tower?"

"We don't know anything." A response such as this only gives rise to negative thoughts.

Alongside us in the garden of an estate I could see excitedly an old acquaintance, a battalion commander. Had he heard something? No. He was calling the artillery group headquarters: "Do you know anything?" They did not. At that moment a frightening bang rang out, the air shook and waves were crossing the Gulf from the south. From the area around Sorvali a huge column of smoke was rising up from an explosion. What on earth was that? In any case, something had happened that required action and not thought. We were sending groups of artillery reconnaissance troops back to the front line in the direction of the city! The battalion commander sent a reconnaissance group there on rafts. On approach to the southern bank they were strafed by enemy infantry.

Sometime later a flag appeared again on the flagpole on the castle tower in Vyborg, but it was not ours. An artillery reconnaissance soldier from Huusniemi reported that the conquerors were celebrating their victory in Mon Repos, songs and music could be heard. (Extract is taken from the Artillery Officer B. Laurla's in *And The People Fought* (6/1964)).

A patriotic Finnish defender of Vyborg, Lieutenant-General Harald Ekvist, set out, as was his custom, his thoughts about the loss of the city in his diary: "It is not surprising that Bjokman and Kemppi's nerves had got the better of them. Both of them are chronic alcoholics, and I had warned the Marshal about this!"

14

The VKT Line Battle Begins, 21-22 June

The first round of the battle on the Karelian Isthmus had come to an end. The result of this battle was a victory for the Leningrad Front. The Finnish Army had incurred a defeat near Beloostrov, Kuuterselka, and had shamefully relinquished Vyborg. The condition of Finnish units which had fallen under the weight of the Soviet offensive, left much to be desired. Many Finnish soldiers had become demoralised, and military discipline had been severely shaken.

Soviet tanks had caused horror and panic amongst the Finnish infantry. As in the previous war, the Finnish anti-tank defence had not been able to put up a sufficient rebuff to contemporary Soviet armoured technology. At the beginning of the war from 1939–1940 in the Finnish Army there had been just 100 "Bofors" anti-tank guns, which were capable of effectively countering Soviet armoured technology. At the beginning of the fourth Stalin attack there had been 110 German PAK-40 guns in the Finnish Army, which were able to penetrate the armour of almost all the allied tanks. A large number of the "Bosfor," as well as the trophy "forty-fives" and "Lahti-Solaranta-39" guns by 1944 were very weak. It is surprising but after four years of war the Finnish Army would again encounter these same issues that they had in 1939 on the Mannerheim Line. The situation was exacerbated by the fact that from 1940 onwards the strike capability of the Soviet Air Force had grown, and the small arms, anti-tank, and artillery units had gained experience and endurance in the course of the toughest battles against the Germans.

For the first time in the Finnish Army mass desertion had taken place. According to an emotional assessment written by Lauri Yantti, the "pinecone guard" or the "Saimaa weekenders" (as deserters were dubbed by Finnish soldiers) amounted to up to three divisions. This assessment seems highly exaggerated; however, the issue of desertion really did manifest itself in the Finnish Army in the summer of 1944.

On 22 June, the Commander of the Tank Division Lagus visited Laapeenrantu and saw the chaos in the city for himself: the city was overflowing with deserters, and abandoned semi-automatic guns were lying about in restaurants and cafes.

Major Mikkola reported to Major-General Lagus that the soldiers of the 1st Infantry Regiment were not digging themselves into their positions any more: "We will have to leg it again soon anyway." The soldiers had not seen the regimental officers for some considerable time. In the area around Yustily some enterprising Finnish soldiers had begun to trade in officer's binoculars. On 24 June Lagus sent an order to all the battalion commanders in the division, which contained the following words: "Demand unquestioning observance of military discipline."

The loss of fighting spirit, disintegration, and the general disorder in the forces on the Isthmus was a cause for concern among Finnish Command. On 22 June 1944 Lieutenant-General Laatikainen sent the following order to the units in his corps:

> Front line units, having fought their rear-guard action, and investing super human efforts, have lost their combat capability. The utmost attention must now be paid to enhancing combat capability on the "VKT line." The commanders are to remain in their units as much as possible and are to personally monitor the strict execution of orders. Commanders are to visit the front line as much as possible, monitor discipline among soldiers, and help them to believe in themselves. There is a great deal of testimony of how soldiers succeeded in reducing their feeling of being overawed when confronted by powerful Soviet tanks. Personal heroism and courage, with which our soldiers achieved success fighting tanks whilst incurring minimal losses on our own side, did much to enhance the will to fight as well as boosting a soldier's belief in their capability to beat back an attack from a numerically superior Army. These examples, as well as lectures in military training provided at any given opportunity, will help us to scale down our difficulties. Laatikainen.

Such a gloomy situation, however, only really concerned the 10th Infantry Division, Cavalry Brigades, the 20th Infantry Brigade, as well as individual units in the armoured division. By around 20 June on the front line near Vyborg fresh Finnish units appeared. A permanent flow of reinforcements came in from the Olents and Maselga Isthmuses.

The reader should be reminded: on 10 June 1944 Mannerheim issued an order for the redeployment onto the Karelian Isthmus of the 20th, and 30th Infantry Brigades, as well as the 4th Infantry Division. On 12 June the 3rd Brigade completed their loading onto a train and set off for Salla on the Karelian Isthmus. Some 25 minutes after military train 6101 had started its journey it was attacked by a pair of Soviet aircraft (the Finns recognised them as "Hurricanes.") The locomotive was destroyed, and some of the bullets and shells entered the leading carriage. Brigade Commander Colonel Yosse Olavi Hannula was killed and the head of brigade headquarters Major Rinne was slightly injured. As he had known Hannula personally Lieutenant-General Harald Ekvist lamented the General's death bitterly, he had great admiration for him as a military historian.

On 15 June when the Finnish defence had collapsed on the "VT line," Mannerheim issued an order to redeploy the 11th, 17th, and 6th Infantry Divisions to the Karelian Isthmus. In order to enhance the effectiveness of the leadership of the troops themselves, the headquarters of the 5th Army Corps was transferred from the Olents Isthmus to the area around Vyborg. On 15 June Mannerheim also ordered preparations to be made for a withdrawal from the stronghold on the southern bank of the Svir. The Finns abandoned their long-standing reinforced defences that had been built around Podoporzhye without a fight. Overall the Finns redeployed from the Olents Isthmus more than half of their forces–this was the estimate made by Headquarters in Moscow.

The dramatic events of 20 June in the ancient city of Vyborg have overshadowed in historical literature what were no less significant events east of the city. The storming of the VKT line by units from the 97th, and 109th rifle corps on 20 and 21 June was unsuccessful–the fresh forces of the 3rd Infantry Brigade did not descend into a panic as the 20th Brigade had done in Vyborg and greeted the attacking forces with organised fire. For the first time the Finns began to use their *Panzerfaust* weapons widely.

On 21 June 1944 units in the 21st Army received an order for them to transfer to pursuing the retreating enemy. The 26th Guards Heavy Tank Regiment left Vyborg in a tactical formation and headed to the north-east, engaging the enemy in combat on the move near Tammisuo

Station, without having reconnoitred the enemy positions. The situation turned out to be a highly unfavourable one for the guard's tank crews. The presumption that the Finns were demoralised and were deserting turned out to be incorrect. The guards ran into a pre-prepared defence behind a quarry and a railway line. The tanks that were moving directly towards Tammisuo were set on fire by the *Panzerfaust* weapons, as well as anti-tank guns. The tanks that had turned to the right beyond the crossing and had moved along the line of the Finnish defences, were fired upon using *Panzerfausts* weapons aiming at their right flanks. As a result of the first battle one IS caught fire, a further nine were destroyed and another tank was blown up by a mine. It is evident from documentary records that the tank crews did not realise straight away what weapon had been used against them, they called the *Panzerfausts* "cumulative anti-tank guns."

During the second half of the day, the tank crews went on the attack once more, and this was again unsuccessful. In combat the Finns set fire to six IS tanks, and 11 tank crewmembers were either killed, injured, or were recorded as missing without trace. The heavy IS tanks turned out to be helpless against Finnish infantry from the 3rd Brigade, who had dug in on the edge of the quarry amongst the boulders. The limited speed of rotation of the turret, as well as the low rate of fire from the IS tank's gun and the lack of infantry cover proved fateful for the tank crews in this battle. The crew serving under Company Commander Senior Lieutenant Kharlov were all killed in the course of this battle and were posthumously awarded the title of Heroes of the Soviet Union.

East of Tammisuo, in the area around the height of Mustamyaki, the situation for the Finns had turned out to be worse. The 1st Battalion, 3rd Brigade reported the following: "At 1615 hrs the enemy again went on the attack following a terrifying artillery barrage. They are no communications. It is impossible to control the battle. The different companies are scattered. The remains of the battalion are attempting to hold Mustamyaki." Nevertheless, it was with great difficulty that the Finns succeeded in holding their positions. This same situation was repeated the following day–the Finns did not run away, nor did they shudder. The Soviet forces in turn drew up their artillery and rained a hail of fire down on the Finns. As Ekvist had feared the Finnish infantry began to incur very heavy losses on the rocky terrain, which prevented them from digging in. By evening on 22 June the losses for the 3rd Infantry Brigade had reached such a level that the Brigade Commander Colonel Hannterya proposed pulling his troops back some three or four kilometres to the north. In the evening of that same day the 72nd Rifle Division with the support of IS tanks and the four "thirty-fours" that remained in the formation of the 1st Red Banner Brigade broke through the defences of the 48th Regiment in the area around the Tali Station and captured the railway station itself, which contained an important railway junction. During their withdrawal the Finns managed to blow up the bridge over the small Tali River. Some five or so days later this was to become known as nothing less than an "accursed" bridge.

The battle for Tali Station took a heavy toll on the 109th Rifle Corps. After advancing towards the apex of the attack the 72nd Rifle Division actually lost its combat capability. Reports do not speak of rifle regiments but of the remains of these regiments. Amongst those who fell in this battle was an eighteen year old combatant from the Novgorod region Vasiliy Sukhov from the 72nd Rifle Division. At a critical moment in the battle when a company commander had been injured, Komsomol member Sukhov took it upon himself to command the company. He was injured twice and twice refused evacuation, despite the fact that the second injury was serious – his jaw had been blown off. Sukhov died in a field hospital and was buried along with his colleagues in a mass grave in the settlement of Kirillovskoye. He was posthumously awarded the Gold Star of a Hero of the Soviet Union.

Between 21–23 June 1944 the 1st Red Banner Brigade in the course of the battle for Tali station lost its best forward air controller–Senior Lieutenant Razgulov. He was seriously injured and died in a field hospital. Tank Company Commander Captain Rabazov and other tank crews. After Tali station had been captured there were only two mobile "thirty-fours" in the 1st Red Banner Brigade. The brigade withdrew from the battle and headed back behind the lines to receive reinforcements.

Simultaneously, the latest attempt to negotiate and armistice between the USSR and Finland came to nothing, and this will be discussed later. The Leningrad Front began to prepare for the second phase of the Vyborg Offensive Operation, the aim of which was to reach the Laapeenranta–Imatra line. The guard's heavy tank regiments that had rested and had received reinforcements advanced towards the front. Govorov's attacking fist–the 30th Guards Rifle Corps under General Simonyak also advanced to the front line from the area around Kahari. They were ready to begin the second round of the battle.

In addition to the Finnish reserves that had arrived from Karelia, another important combat unit had appeared in the Vyborg direction. On 16 June the German *Kuhlmey* Air Wing redeployed from Estonia to airfields near Imatri and Laapeenranty. From 17 June German fighters and fighter-bombers began to carry out combat sorties over the Karelian Isthmus. The first attacks using Ju-87 dive-bombers were conducted on 20 June. The number of combat sorties and the tonnage of bombs dropped by the German air wings are equal to, or higher than the same figures for the Finnish Air Force in the summer of 1944.

German aviator Rudolf Gerndt describes his last combat sortie over the Karelian Isthmus:

> *Oberleutnant* K.F. Koch was shot down on after me over the Karelian marshes on 23 June 1944 and sank in the bog along with his parachute! We fired at the tankers that were refuelling the "thirty-fours" directly on the front line. Koch and I made between four or five passes, and we hit the targets since we could see the tanks had caught fire. Since we accelerated by at least 600–700km/hr in a dive their "quadruple" mounted guns always missed.
>
> They then caught onto this, but Koch did not want to stop bombing the enemy at all. My Fw 190 F-8 sustained a direct hit in the fuel line running from the fuel tank in the port wing and caught fire, I decided to put this fire out using a manual fire extinguisher. I had been hit as I was pulling out of a dive and then I noticed that my control cables had been severed. I tried to climb as much as I could on full power so I could bail out, but I could only get to 300m. At this altitude the engine died and the aircraft stalled and entered a spin. Taking into account the fact that the aircraft had gone out of control, as well as the small flame that was licking my left thigh, I had to act quickly, since the ground was coming towards me rapidly and everything was happening much more quickly than in this narrative.
>
> I opened the cockpit, as a result of which the small flame was open to the air and I found myself sitting in the midst of a fire! My face, hands, and legs were burnt as I, constrained by my straps, managed nevertheless to free myself from them, and "plop!" I was in the air. At the last moment! I saw my aircraft hit the ground as I was sitting on wet grass in a forest clearing and shook the moisture off the grass to cool down. The parachute had opened some 30m above the ground. It had been so hard to grab hold of anything, to free myself from my straps, and pull the parachute rip-chord with hands that were bleeding from the burns. I had taken my gloves off a few moments before bailing out as my hands had become hot. If I had not done this, my hands would not have been so badly-burned. When I bailed out my helmet had come off, I had lost all my hair, and the fire had left deep scars on my face ...

15

Combat Reconnaissance on the Saimaa Canal

On the northern side of the modern day *Druzhba* bridge on the Siamaa Canal, beyond the filling station, an enormous boulder rises up. A memorial plaque can be seen on this boulder in three languages from the veterans of the 61st Infantry Regiment in the Finnish Army, which had fought in these locations between June–July 1944. In Finnish literature and in the war film *Framam framsta linjan* ("Beyond the Front Line") made in 2007 the fighting on the Saimaa Canal is depicted as a large-scale battle, full of drama. A Finnish language text in Wikipedia also describes a large-scale, almost epic battle. Let us try and define the course of events, and how these events are described in military documents belonging to the Russian Ministry of Defence.

With the passing of the evening of 20 June 1944, when the Finnish Front failed to collapse due to the sluggishness of the Soviet side the situation on the canal became more relaxed. Reinforcements arrived but the Soviet side did know show any signs of activity. It would appear that the Finnish defenders on the Saimaa Canal could breathe a sigh of relief, since the direction of the main Soviet attack by the 21st Army had clearly shifted towards Tali station.

On 22 June, however, at 0400 hrs a rare, and disturbing bout of enemy fire broke out on the Finnish positions in the area around the *Kammeniy Most*. At 1030 hrs the enemy fire intensified sharply, and Finnish artillery reconnaissance personnel noticed the concentration of Soviet infantry in the opposite bank. By 1230 hrs small Soviet subdivisions were able to cross the Gulf near the *Kammeniy Most* and dig in on the small islands in the Gulf. According to some Finnish documents, it was only a few Soviet soldiers that were able to cross the gulf itself by wading through, while other documents mention up to two companies of soldiers made it across. The Finns began to prepare a counterattack, and at 1250 hrs a message arrived, that the artillery barrages had worked in the favour of the Finns and that the bank had been purged. In the second half of the day the Soviet artillery attack on the Finnish positions on the canal intensified, but no attacks followed it. The night of 22–23 June passed in a rare artillery duel.

At 0840 hrs on 23 June "the sky was smashed into pieces" as Lauri Yantti wrote. A Soviet artillery barrage began in the course of which the whole telephone network was interrupted on the front line. A fording of the canal followed the artillery barrage in the area around *Kammeniy Most*, Herttuala and Sammonsaari. Soviet units however did not encounter what were by then the disjointed and demoralised soldiers of the 20th Brigade, but fresh soldiers, from the 61st Infantry Regiment that had only just arrived from Svir under Lieutenant-Colonel Marttinen.

Despite fierce fire from the Finnish side by 1040 hrs Soviet infantry managed to cross the canal and dig in on both sides of the railway bridge. West of the bridge on the bank of the Gulf there were just one platoon of Soviet infantry, and they were immediately pushed back to the canal by a Finnish counterattack.

The 19th Red Banner Rifle Regiment crossed the Saimaa Canal. This formation had distinguished themselves in the Soviet-Finnish War by their crossing of the Taipaleenyoki on 6 December 1939. A laconic entry in the 90th Rifle Division's combat report is depressing reading:

> After the artillery barrage, which continued for 30 mins, the 19th Red Banner Rifle Regiment set about fording the Gulf in the area around /3591-b/ in small groups and as a single battalion using rafts. After launching four rafts onto the water carrying three personnel the 3rd Rifle Company were met by fierce machine gun, and defensive artillery mortar fire from the enemy gun emplacements that had not been taken out, as well as from the batteries on the forward edge and behind the defensive line. Three of the rafts were hit and sank without reaching the opposite bank, one raft did make it to the bank but nobody got out of it. The assault using the four active rafts ended with the death of their courageous occupants.
>
> Out of the 21 enemy rafts that had been prepared for the crossing–apart from those that had been actively used–14 had been destroyed. By way of an order issued by the Divisional Commander further action to cross the Gulf was stopped and was not revisited again.

The attack of the 372nd Rifle Division on Leeppyasaari was also forced back by the Finns. Attempts however to cross the canal did not stop there. At 1045 hrs General Lagus allowed the light "Vickers" tanks to cross the canal for a counterattack. At 1120 hrs Lagus ordered the entire armoured division to advance to the area around Hanhiyoki and to be ready to carry out counterattacks, both in the direction of Kamenniy Most, and Yustila–Portinhoykka. Tanks however were not used on the Finnish side. At 1232 hrs Lieutenant-Colonel Marttinen reported that the entire coastal line was in Finnish hands once again.

At 1400 hrs Soviet bombers struck the "Finnish" side of the canal, while on the Soviet bank the Finnish artillery reconnaissance troops had noticed that Soviet infantry movements had intensified. The Finns launched a powerful artillery attack on the possible locations where Soviet infantry may congregate. This activity was not followed by attempts to ford the canal, and the Finns calculated that they had succeeded in scattering Soviet infantry on the "Soviet" bank.

The next attempt to cross the canal began at 1530 hrs, but this was beaten back by the Finns. Following this, a calm descended on the Saimaa Canal, although Soviet Command came up with plans to continue the advance on Helsinki, orders were issued on 29 June for the creation of a mobile group based on the 220th Tank Brigade, which had only just received the new T-34-85 tanks and had concentrated in the area around Vyborg. These plans however remained on paper. Both sides dug in and remained on the defensive until the armistice was signed on 4–5 September 1944.

16

The Ryti–Ribbentrop Pact, 23 June

With the fall of Vyborg, the military situation for the Finnish side looked sufficiently bleak. How the Soviet advance could be stopped and how Marshal Govorov's breakthrough into the central regions of the country was to be turned around was not altogether clear. The redeployment of forces from Olents and Maselga isthmuses had still not been completed, and whether or not there were enough forces to slow down the next phase of the Soviet advance–that question was still open. The will to fight for the Finnish units following the completion of the first stage of the battle for the Isthmus was clearly not at its peak. A few undertook to argue the point that the first stage of the operation from 10–20 June ended in a resounding victory for the Leningrad Front. It was for this same reason that in Soviet historiography it was acceptable to put a full stop o the story of the Vyborg Offensive Operation on the evening of 20 June 1944, when the red flag was raised on the Vyborg castle tower. In reality this was just part of the battle; but after the fall of Vyborg the politicians already had an opportunity to really put an end to the war and to restore relations between the USSR and Finland back onto a peaceful footing.

At the same time that fierce fighting was underway amongst boulders and crags near Tammisuo and Tali, no less dramatic events were unfolding on the diplomatic front. The fall of Vyborg shattered the Finnish government's faith in a successful outcome to the war, and they decided once more to clarify the conditions with the Soviet Union in accordance with which Finland could exit the war. Against the backdrop of Soviet military victories and the forthcoming Karelian Front offensive via Svir, which was to begin on 24 June, this enquiry that was put to the Swedish Embassy in Stockholm, appeared strange, if not presumptuous and inappropriate. The Soviet response was sufficiently aggravated and was interpreted by the Finnish side as a demand for unconditional surrender. From the authors' point of view this explanation looks more like an attempt to justify double-dealing that been orchestrated by Suomi's upper leadership. Thus the Soviet response, which Mannerheim cites in his memoirs, went as follows:

> Since the Finns have deceived us several times, we want the Finnish Government to relay a message that has been signed by the President and the Minister of Foreign Affairs, stating that Finland is prepared to capitulate and to approach the Soviet Government with a request for peace. If we receive this information from the Finnish Government, Moscow is prepared to accept a Finnish delegation.

In reality Finland's previous attempts to lay down the peace process had clearly been interpreted by Stalin as deceit and a lack of willingness on the part of the Finns to actually find a peaceful resolution to the situation. The demands in the written request asking for peace against the backdrop of future events appear logical for the Soviet side. On the other hand if the USSR demanded Finland's surrender, why would they then call for a Finnish delegation to Moscow? The declaration "readiness to capitulate and to approach the Soviet Government with a request for peace" is not the same as declaring "we demand unconditional surrender," this was precisely however how the Finnish leadership interpreted the Soviet response. From the authors' perspective this was done once again to highlight the Soviet demands as unfeasible, excessive, and to continue the war, after having approached Nazi Germany for urgent military assistance.

On 22 June 1944, without any warning or any formalities of protocol the Minister of Foreign Affairs in Nazi Germany Joachim von Ribbentrop flew into Helsinki. He requested of the President of the Finnish Republic written guarantees that Finland would not agree a separate peace with the USSR. Ryti signed a letter to this effect, although it was clear that the Finns had no intention of fulfilling this request. Finland needed military and economic assistance there and then, and Ryti was prepared to sign new papers in order to receive it. They did indeed receive the help they needed, and it played a key role in the battle for Vyborg Bay and in the fight for Tali-Ihantala.

17

Tali-Ihantala
Greatest Battle in the History of the Karelian Isthmus

Everything that could be fired, has been fired
From both sides. Anyone who fought in this
battle can be proud of themselves to the end
of their days.

(Captain Gunnar Laatio, 35th Infantry Regiment, Finnish Army)

After rest and marked celebrations of the capture of Vyborg, the units of the Leningrad Front embarked on the next step of the offensive operation. Within the confines of this phase the Soviet units were to break through the Finnish defences, cross the Saimaa Canal and advance to the Lappeenranta–Imatra line. In doing so they would set up the pre-requisites for a final march westwards to the Kotka–Kouvola line, to the eastern shore of Lake Kymi-Yoki.

The 30th Guards Rifle Corps – Marshal Govorov's attacking fist, which had rested and received their reinforcements, advanced to the front at Tali station (now Paltsevo). The concentration of the corps at their starting positions began at 2300 hrs on 24 June and ended at 0430 hrs in the morning of 25 June. Tanks, self-propelled guns, and artillery arrived at their starting positions early in the morning of 25 June. The artillery in the 30th Guards Rifle Corps took up their firing positions at 0330 hrs in the morning.

Within 30th Guards Rifle Corps on 24 June there were 22,665 men; there were 7,002 in the 45th Guards Rifle Division, 7,017 in the 64th Guards Rifle Division, and 7,041 in the 63rd Guards Rifle Division.

The Guard Corps advanced in two attack alignments. South of Lake Leitumonjarvi (now Lake Maloye Krasnokholmskoye), from Tali station the 45th Guards attacked westwards, up to the fork in the road at Portinhoikka and further on at the sluice gates at Yustila on the Saimaa Canal. The 27th Separate Tank Regiment (equipped with the new T-34-85s) supported the 45th Guards Division's advance together with the 397th Guards Heavy Self-Propelled Gun Regiment (equipped with ISU-152s). This was the principal direction for the corps attack. North of Lake Leitimontyarvi on the right flank of the corps, the 64th Guards attacked to the north-west in the direction of Ihantala. They were supporting a division of KV tanks as well as "Churchill" tanks from the 260th Guards Separate Heavy Tank Regiment.

Combat order No. 0028 issued by corps headquarters dated 24 June 1944 set out ambitious goals for the offensive on 25 June:

> The 30th Guards Rifle Corps with the 27th Tank Regiment, the 260th Tank Regiment, the 394th, and 397th Guards Heavy Self-Propelled Artillery Regiment, and the 211th, 219th, and 227th Mortar Regiments, the 94th Anti-Tank Artillery Rifle Regiment, the 106th Heavy Howitzer Artillery Brigade, the 85th Howitzer Artillery Brigade, the 127th Gun Artillery Brigade, the 1,157th Corps Artillery Regiment, the 17th Gun Artillery Brigade, the 24th Guards Motorised Rifle Regiment, the 1st Guards Mortar Battalion, the 84/17 Sapper's Brigade, and two divisions of the first echelon (the 64th and the 45th Guards Rifle divisions) are to destroy the enemy from a pre-equipped, naturally advantageous position in a band running from marker 32.0 (4106) near Sarela farmstead, and, are to principally attack the left flank in the direction of Yuliveden-Kyla, Yustila, Myakelya, and Kananoya, and destroy their personnel and armament, keeping the objective close at hand, and whilst on the move, cross the Saimaa Canal using whatever is available, and capture the highway from Surmyalya, Yustila, and advance to the boundary running from marker 75.4 (5288) at Lake Lautsenlampi, marker 65.0 (4590).
>
> Subsequently, after having drawn up armament, forming an alignment, further the advance in a north-westerly direction, cutting off the highway from Nyuma–Lautala and advance to the boundary: Nyuma, Kyarkisilta, and marker 78.3 (5276), ensuring in doing so that the army reserves are deployed and introduced into battle in the northern, and south-westerly directions.

The terrain north of Vyborg is difficult for an advance. Aside from the forests and marshes that characterise the Karelian Isthmus there are mountains, cliffs, and ground strewn with boulders that serve as additional cover for defending units. The presence of cliffs and rocks strengthens the impact of artillery fire on personnel, who are outside of their shelters by orders of magnitude–fragments of rock are added to shrapnel from mines and shells that can hit infantry soldiers.

The Soviet artillery barrage commenced at 0700 hrs on 25 June 1944. For those same Finns, who two weeks earlier had experienced an artillery barrage for themselves in Beloostrov and had survived, the storm of artillery fire on 25 June in Tali turned out to be no less severe. This is not surprising, since the Artillery Commander of the Leningrad Front General Odintsov had again concentrated an artillery alignment in the direction of the main attack consisting of 900 guns, and 24 heavy rocket launchers. This meant a density of 230 guns per kilometre of front. The artillerymen of the Leningrad Front near Tali station repeated the hail of fire that had been used in Beloostrov and Kuuterselka.

21st Army's Tank alignment at 0800 hrs on 25 June:

109th Rifle Corps Sector			
Unit		Type of vehicle	Quantity
98th Separate Tank Regiment	This unit has combat capable tanks	T-34-85	7
1,439th Self-Propelled Artillery Unit	-//-	SU-152	8
	-//-	KVS-1[1]	1
In the 30th Guards Rifle Corps' sector			
The 27th Separate Tank Regiment	-//-	T-34-85	21
260th Guards Separate Heavy Tank Regiment	-//-	KV-1	7
	-//-	Churchill	3
394th Self-Propelled Artillery Regiment	-//-	ISU-152	19
397th Guards Self-Propelled Artillery Regiment	-//-	ISU-152	21
	-//-	SU-57	4
97th Rifle Corps sector			
The 1,238th Self-Propelled Artillery Regiment	-//-	SU-76	15
108th Rifle Corps sector			
The 124th Separate Tank Regiment	-//-	T-34	15
A mobile group consisting of the following:			
The 30th Guards Tank Brigade	-//	T-34	32
	-//	T-60	6
	-//	T-70	3
27th Guards Separate Heavy Tank Regiment	-//	IS-122[2]	13
	-//	SU-57	2

1 As per the original document.
2 This is as per the original document.

The artillery barrage halted an hour and a half later, and at 0830 hrs the guards went on the attack. In both directions the attacks by Soviet units broke through the Finnish defences in both directions.

East of Lake Leitimoyarvi soon after the beginning of the offensive the Finnish orders of battle made up of the 28th Separate Finnish Battalion on the front line were crushed; units from the 64th Guards Division had advanced to the farm on the Kalliopelto outcrop in the space of half an hour after the start of the offensive, by 0900 hrs. At that same time the guards captured the Aniskala farmstead:

> Bandaging materials were in danger of running out, since even a single soldier needed a great deal of bandages. I used almost everything on one soldier, a shell had exploded next to his foxhole in the crown of a tree, and he was mangled beyond all recognition. A single large piece of shrapnel had almost cut his leg off above the knee, and I applied a tourniquet and a splint. He had to bandaged from head to toe however, he was so cut up. The stretcher bearers needed to craft the torniquet and splint from poles and straps since there was nothing else to hand. He was taken to a dressing point, but I do not know if he survived beyond that. He was conscious throughout, despite his terrible wounds. His comrade, a Junior Sergeant, who was in that same foxhole stood up on his knees and stared out onto neutral territory. When I asked him something, he did not respond. It was as though his eyes were not seeing the world around him anymore, even though he looked like he was alive.
>
> The weather at the time remained wet, and the foxholes that were in the fields, were half full of water. It was very unpleasant to remain in those foxholes all day and all night. That was how things were on 24 June in the area around Tali Station. The night of 24–25 June was relatively quiet. All the signs however pointed to something highly unusual happening on the enemy's side. The sound of engines could be heard all night long from the direction of the enemy, engines starting, and the rattle of tracks and other sounds, which indicated preparations for an attack. Artillery fire from the enemy's side was weak and actually more annoying than anything.
>
> It would have been possible to take a nap somewhere in the trench, and the physically and emotionally exhausted soldiers who did not get a wink of sleep all night would not be disturbed–despite the conditions that were totally unsuitable for this, nature took its course.
>
> Night turned into day. When the clock hands turned 0700 hrs, it was as though the rainy skies had been smashed into pieces and the entire underworld had been unleashed and had descended upon the hapless sons of man on earth.
>
> In the midst of this hail of steel a human being was no longer a human being. They turned into a creature that was helpless with fear, able to sense their own insignificance in every fibre of their being, one that was waiting for a "merciful blow" to come at any moment, and that prayed for just one thing–that it would happen to them as quickly as possible, as though it was preordained for them. This wave of fire, burying anything in its path, would leave no mound of earth untouched, and had at the start of the artillery barrage already covered a strip a kilometre wide leading back behind the lines. Evacuation of the wounded, especially the seriously wounded, became impossible under those conditions, and furthermore, all communications with logistics had been terminally severed.
>
> The uninterrupted enemy fire had ground our positions for one and a half hours, and only after that did enemy infantry supported by tanks attack several targets, trailing one after another. The artillery barrage continued, but it had been transferred back behind the lines. Somewhere this attacking enemy had been met by fierce fire from our own positions, but this whirlwind of a barrage, which had been beating our positions mercilessly for one and a

half hours, continued to do its thing. The majority of the battalion had already withdrawn from the battle. Our artillery was working effectively and had destroyed several tanks in front of our positions. The fresh baked tank hunters armed with *Panzerschrecks* had also played their part in the destruction of the tanks. They had succeeded in immobilising one tank that was already behind our own lines. This same tank turned out to be fateful for the messenger in our platoon, with whom we had run together to the Company Commander's Command Post at the very height of the battle, when the enemy was approaching us behind the lines from the left flank.

As we were running to report everything to the company commander, we saw beyond the bend in the road the forward part of an enemy tank some 20m from us. A burst of fire from the tank's machine gun rang out at that very moment and went straight into my comrade. He lay there in two halves, as though he had been cut with a penknife. I do not know how I found my way into a culvert myself, at that moment when the machine gun burst had lashed against the heels of my knee high boots. Everything had happened so quickly and instinctively that even up to now I do not understand how I survived that impossible situation.

I continued on my way and reported the situation to our company commander. Some of the company had already abandoned the positions that the enemy had broken through, despite our desperate resistance. The enemy continued their advance behind the lines, and the threat of encirclement was very obvious. In connection with this our company commander took the decision to withdraw from the battle and retreat, whilst offering meanwhile, resistance to the enemy.

All this happened right at the last moment, and, from my perspective, this was the only way out of the situation. If we had stayed there, the company would have been wiped out down to the last man, despite heroic resistance. The enemy's advantage was so overwhelming, that we could not have had any bearing on the course of the battle, and even more so since no help would be forthcoming. The remains of the company, around 30 men, retreated back through the forest in the direction of Kilpeenjoki and Ihantala. On the way we were joined by other surviving soldiers, so our group swelled in number somewhat. Our participation in the battle for Tali ended there, we were redeployed to another sector of the front line.

Kaiyala, Medic, 1st Company, 28th Separate Infantry Battalion

The 3rd Battalion, 48th Infantry Regiment that had been in the second echelon tried to rescue the 28th Separate Battalion near Kalliopelto, after sending the 9th Company under Captain Salokangas. The Captain was killed at the very start of the battle, and his company just scattered. The remaining companies in the Finnish 3rd Battalion tried to slow the advance of the 64th Guards north of the Aniskala and Talinmullu but were not able to beat back the attack and were scattered. According to reports from the battalion they were forced to commence a withdrawal to the north to Ruunakorpi at around 1030 hrs. In the afternoon forward companies of the 64th Guards Rifle Divisions cut off the highway from Vyborg–Imatra and reached the Soppe farmstead after breaking through the Finnish defensive line to a depth of seven kilometres. In view of the open flanks and the severe difficulties with supply along the only highway via Talinmullu the advanced guard of the 64th Guards was forced to withdraw to the south.

The 268th Rifle Division under Colonel Sokolov attacked to the east in the direction of Karisalmi, but they were not able to break through the Finnish defences. Only the 947th Rifle Regiment in this same division achieved any success, advancing to the north in close cooperation with the 64th Guards. By evening on the first day of the offensive the regiment had reached Nurmilampi.

The 45th Guards Rifle Division broke through the defensive line of the 3rd Battalion, 13th Infantry Regiment and by 1700 hrs had reached the crossroads at Portinhojkka. The division had fulfilled and overfulfilled their objective for the day. The 3rd Battalion, 13th Infantry Regiment, which had held their defensive position against Putilov's guards, incurred unprecedentedly high losses. The Battalion, in which there were just two companies, lost over the course of that day 10 company and platoon commanders and 142 soldiers, of which 82 people were killed or were missing without trace. Only five men returned from captivity after the end of the war. The Commander of the 6th Infantry Regiment Lieutenant-Colonel Reino Inkinen ordered the 3rd Battalion in his regiment to close the breach in the defences. The battalion, which were at rest, was alerted and set off apace for the front. On the way to the front line the battalion first came under powerful artillery fire and then were subject to an air attack. The guards in the 64th Division, which had circled round Lake Leitimonjarvi suddenly attacked on the flank, after which they simply scattered. The Finns succeeded in putting together some sort of a defence using the forces of the 5th Jager Battalion under Major Kiviperja, and the front line stopped on the level of the Konkkala–Murokkalio height.

The "thirty-fours" of the 27th Separate Tank Regiment at the start of the offensive did not make an appearance on the battlefield. Major Zuyev, the Regimental Commander, did not find the time to contact the 45th Guards and set up cooperation. This was in spite of a direct order to support the 134th Guards Regiment, which had been issued by the Commander of the 45th Guards Division the day before the offensive! The tank crews did not carry out any engineering reconnaissance either. As a result the new T-34-85s never made it onto the battlefield. Part of the regiment travelled via a forest road, which on the map was shown as a road, but in reality was just a path, which was impassable for tanks. The regiment's principal component, which had advanced in a column along the road from Tali–Portinhojka, stopped ahead of a drainage channel, which was also impassable for tanks. Two tanks immediately became stuck in it. The entire morning was spent building a bridge. A traffic jam had built up behind the 27th Regiment's column, since the "hunters" of the 397th Guards Heavy Self-Propelled Gun Regiment had arrived.

By midday, the channel bridge had been constructed and the mass of Soviet armoured equipment rushed into battle, which was unexpected for everyone including for the Finnish infantry, and for the Finnish self-propelled gun crews, and the 45th Guards, which the tank crews under Zuyev had previously ignored. On approach to the road junction at Portinhojka two self-propelled guns stood in a tank trap. When the column of "thirty-fours" came rushing along the highway the self-propelled gun crews were on their lunch break outside their tank, but they had not left either their guards nearby, nor the duty radio operators in the self-propelled guns on duty. The Soviet tanks went straight past the trap and moved onto the sluice gate at Yustila.

According to other sources the Finnish self-propelled guns still opened fire, but quickly withdrew, since "our shells could not penetrate the armour on the Soviet self-propelled ISU-152 guns."

On passing through Portinhojka crossroads, Soviet tanks headed for the sluice gate at Yustila, after destroying a truck on the way that contained a group of Finnish artillery reconnaissance troops from the 19th Artillery Regiment:

> A grandiose tank column approached us, as if on parade. The artillerymen mistook the tanks for Lagus' tanks and did not pay any attention to the identifying markings. The first tank gave way to the truck "as per all the rules of the road," but the second tank in the column rammed and smashed the truck, and the astonished artillerymen came spilling out into the drainage ditch like peas. Surprisingly, they all got away with their lives, and even the radio survived. The Soviet tank crews were in a hurry and did not fire at the artillerymen, running away into the forest as fast as they could.

During the second half of the day, the Finns began to employ countermeasures. At 1700 hrs the Finnish Heavy Tank Company concentrated on the eastern bank of the canal next to the sluice gates at Yustila and immediately went on the attack. Finnish tank crews met approximately 300 of their infantrymen from different units. The soldiers were demoralised and urged the tank crews to flee and save their own lives. With the help of some strong words and a pistol Major Bjokman succeeded in bringing the infantry round. He announced that from that moment on the infantry would support the tanks. Finnish tanks continued to move towards the crossroads at Portinhojkka. At the head of the column was a KV tank. After another turn on the winding forest road the Finnish KV clashed head to head with a T-34-85 tank. The "thirty-four's" shell hit the armour face on the hull of the tank, leaving a dent the size of a fist, and ricocheted upwards. The hit on the tank was so powerful that the entire crew were left concussed. The Commander of the Finnish KV shouted "Back!" and the tank crawled back beyond the turn in the road in reverse gear. It was there that the crew abandoned the vehicle; each crewmember had a burst eardrum. A Finnish T-34-76 went take the tank's place at the head of the column.

The advent of Finnish tanks caught the 27th Tank Regiment by surprise. Major Zuyev had given an order to retreat. It was at this point that the tank crews also made a blunder. All the "thirty-fours" turned around, turning stern on to the tank crews, and made off as fast as they could. For the Finns this was also completely unexpected. Major Zuyev himself had been injured in this battle.

As a result of this battle, the combat group captured several Soviet tanks almost undamaged. One of those combat vehicles was an ISU-152 self-propelled gun with the tactical number 1212 from the 394th Guards Heavy Self-Propelled Gun Regiment. Major Heikki Mikkola described the battle in his memoirs:

> There were no tanks around the next corner, and the advance continued. The "thirty-fours" and the "Postal vans" (the T-28s), which had greater fire power made short work of the Soviet infantry, and at 1715 hrs the column was already approaching the crossroads at Portinhojkka. The lead patrol that were walking along the side of the road gave a warning sign. The tanks stopped and the reconnaissance troops moved forward from among the tank crews. Beyond the bend on the edge of the drainage channel stood a 43tonne ISU-152 self-propelled gun–the crew of which was similarly taken by surprise. Two more of these self-propelled guns stood a little further down. Tanks could not proceed any further along this road. The ISU had to be destroyed another way. Lieutenant Eilenberg (who was a logistics soldier in the 1st Tank Battalion from the Tank Brigade) and *Fahnrich* Shrey (Major Mikkola's adjutant) along with a group of soldiers managed to outflank the self-propelled gun from behind, but since they did not have any *Panzerfausts* with them they were not able to do anything with it. The crew of this encircled self-propelled gun opened fire from their automatic guns and threw grenades at the Finns. *Fahnrich* Tepo brought a smoke cartridge with him–it was with the help of this cartridge he had managed to smoke the crews out of their tanks before–he threw the cartridge under the self-propelled gun. A second later the hatches opened and the crews jumped out of the self-propelled gun. Not one of them surrendered, they all died with a weapon in their hands–they were an elite unit. Up until that moment we had captured six "thirty-fours," some of which the Russians had succeeded in setting on fire, and a single ISU-152. At that moment we had not incurred any losses among our tanks at all.

A veteran of the battle, the Finnish *Fahnrich* Pentti Hiluten, left a more detailed description of the start of the Finnish counterattack:

The enemy had already passed the fork in the road. There was a danger that the entire Finnish defence would collapse. The armoured division under Major-General Lagus received an order–to launch a counterattack in the direction of the fork in the road using the forces of the heavy tank company under Major Mikkola. The company would receive reinforcements. The company under Lieutenant Eero Vase from the Anti-Tank Defence battalions in the armoured division will be attached to his company.

As before on 25 June. The time on our watches was 1730 hrs. Mikkola ordered Vase to cover the advance of the tanks and the self-propelled guns. Vase leads the first anti-tank platoon into the battle, while the twenty-four year old *Fahnrich* Pentti Hiltunen from Pori leads the second. There is around a kilometre of distance between the crossroads at Portinhoika, Enemy tanks are standing by along the way, which need to be beaten back.

Pentti Hiltunen orders his soldiers in the anti-tank guns that are under-tow to follow the tanks and to be ready to open fire at any moment.

The lead tank reached point 54, that is to say the area around the Kuopelivuori height, west of Portinhoika. A Jager, standing in a culvert, sent a warning of a large ISU-152 self-propelled gun that was around the bend, about 300m away. Finnish tanks mount the edge of the road, Major Mikkola orders Hiltunen to gather a combat group together and encircle the self-propelled gun on the flank via the height itself.

Hiltunen is to order some soldiers from his platoon under the command of the twenty-one year old Junior Sergeant Esko Solonoya to go with him. The group went in a long drawn out column up the slope of the hill to approach the self-propelled gun from the flank. After that the group laid low and prepared to support Hiltunen and Salonoya with covering fire, as they crawled up to the self-propelled gun. The situation was exacerbated by the fact that two Soviet tanks from those that had been abandoned previously by the Finns from their own positions, were within the line of sight of the self-propelled gun. One of the tanks was burning, but in the second the crew were alive and were active. The tank momentarily opened fire, as soon as the crew noticed the Finns.

The Finns who had crawled up to the right hand side of the self-propelled gun threw smoke canisters. At that same time Hiltulen and Salonoya were drawing nearer to the self-propelled gun from the opposite side. The rest were prepared to open fire from the height itself. The wind would not allow a smoke screen to be put up and would have blown the smoke back towards the Finns.

Hiltulen was the first to go forward, Solonoya provided cover. Hiltulen crawled towards the self-propelled gun from behind and to the right and approached the road itself. The smoke screen was laid down, finally, but at that moment the hatch cover clunked open and one of the Russians jumped out onto the road. He fired in all directions and ran to the crossroads. Fire from Hiltulen's pistol and Salonoya from his automatic weapon overlapped as they followed him to the crossroads.

Hand grenades flew out from the self-propelled gun as the crew noticed some movement. A few seconds later two crewmembers jumped out of the rear hatch, firing in all directions. The group on the height opened fire. Hiltulen fired on one of the crew who were running away, with his pistol. He turned around and fired a burst of fire from his automatic weapon. Hiltulen's life hung in the balance, but he made it into the shelter by a few tenths of a second. The enemy was killed either by fire from the height itself, or by Salonoya's automatic weapon.

> Hiltulen jumped onto the side of the self-propelled gun that was facing the height, Salonoya provided covering fire. His leap evidently had been seen from inside the self-propelled gun as a grenade came flying out of the hatch. Salonoya saw this and managed to shout to Hiltulen. After the grenade had exploded he lay for some time where he was, but again managed to climb onto the side of the self-propelled gun on all fours.
>
> The porthole in the side of the self-propelled gun was open, and sounds could be heard coming from the inside. Hiltulen with his pistol at the ready decided to have a very quick glance inside through this porthole. If he noticed any movement inside he would fire. If he heard anything form inside–it meant he had hit his target. He was to learn later that his bullet hit the commander of the self-propelled gun. Sounds were once again heard from inside. Hiltulen thought that it would be safer to take shelter behind the self-propelled gun.
>
> Hiltulen thought about his next move. He turned around and indicated to Salonoya using gestures for him to throw a smoke canister under the conning tower, and he waited for the smoke to grow thicker and heard someone cough from inside the vehicle, and that someone was trying to open the rear hatch.
>
> That someone inside was still alive. With difficulty Hiltulen managed to climb onto the vehicle. No sooner had he got up onto the vehicle than the hatch opened and a hand grenade landed under his feet. Instinctively Hiltulen blocked the hatch from opening with his boot, got rid of his pistol and grabbed the grenade. He opened the hatch just enough for him to throw the grenade back inside. Hiltulen sat on the hatch. The grenade exploded. The effect of the explosion on the hatch cover felt like a blow from a horse's hoof.
>
> At that same moment something else exploded inside the self-propelled gun. Maybe it was a shell, or shells. A short time later Hiltulen opened the hatch and saw a dying man. This twenty-one year old driver-mechanic of a self-propelled gun was Dmitriy Fillipovich Emelyanov. The time was 1905 hrs.

The Finns took the fallen ISU-152 driver-mechanic Lieutenant-Technician Emelyanov from the Voronezh region's *Komsomol* card as a souvenir and published a copy in a unit history. The entire crew of the self-propelled gun were considered missing without trace. In 2016 the relatives of Dmitriy Filippovich, who had been looking for his remains, got in touch. The name of D.F. Emelyanov will be immortalised in a mass grave in Petrovka in 2017.

The Company Commander of the 5th Jager Battalion Captain Lehti added to the description of the battle with the Soviet ISU-152s:

> The fact that an ISU-152 made an unusual stop on the road and in fact partially blocked the road was linked to some of the machine gunners in our battalion that had dug in to the right on the rocks on Kuopelivuori and had opened fire on a tank assault and to throw grenades at the self-propelled guns. This forced the self-propelled guns to stop and one of them got stuck in a culvert. When the self-propelled guns were destroyed these same machine gunners took part in a purge of the western bank of Leytimon-yarvi along with the 2nd Battalion, 6th Infantry Regiment.

That evening on the eastern bank of the Saimaa Canal about Yustila, a Jager Brigade appeared, which were rested and had received reinforcements following fierce tank battles. Finnish self-propelled guns had been drawn up too. At 2030 hrs near the Kuopelinvuori height the officers of the armoured division gathered for what was the final meeting ahead of the counterattack. The task was set out clearly: The 3rd Jager Battalion supported by a second battery from the attack gun battalion is to strike along the road via the Portinhoina crossroads–the target–was to reach Tali station. After that the 2nd Jager Battalion would enter the battle, which were to strike in the direction of Repola. The 4th and 5th Jager Battalions–were to be held in reserve at the crossroads.

At 2100 hrs the Finns went on the attack. They soon succeeded in driving back the 45th Guards Division around two kilometres to the east in the direction of Tali station. Immediately beyond the crossroads the Finns captured another ISU-152 self-propelled gun, supposedly, bearing the registration number 1236.

After covering approximately another kilometre and coming out onto the marshy fields on the Isthmus between the lakes, the Finnish self-propelled guns and Jagers fought a fire-fight with Soviet tanks. The tank crews of the 27th Separate Tank Regiment were taken by surprise and began to retreat. Guards Colonel Shpiller, the Commander of the Armoured Tank Units in the 21st Army leant Major Zuyev's actions a more devastating aspect:

> Instead of organising a circular defence on the boundary they had reached, the tanks and self-propelled guns of the 397th Guards Self-Propelled Artillery Regiment continued to stand in a disorganised fashion along the highway and in doing so were subject to blistering, close-range fire from the enemy's Anti-Tank Defences. After dispelling the panic, the Regimental Commander again gave the order to retreat, which actually made the situation worse.
>
> As a result of this management of the battle the 27th Tank Regiment lost the following within the space of a few hours:
>
> | | |
> |---|---|
> | Burnt-out: | 6 |
> | Destroyed: | 9 |
> | Bogged down: | 2 |
> | TOTAL: | 17 |
>
> Apart from that it is necessary to report the shortcomings in the work of headquarters, which proved incapable of providing reconnaissance and coordinating issues surrounding cooperation with other branches of the armed forces. The headquarters, which lagged behind other combat subdivisions, did not ensure that combat vehicles were supplied regularly with ammunition either, as a result of which one tank company was left without ammunition at the most critical moment.

The Finns encountered difficulties also; the untested reinforcements for the Jagers were nervous and panicked under fire. By midnight, the Finnish advance had stopped and had become a fire fight. The ammunition for the Finnish self-propelled guns had run out. In a duel with Soviet tanks a self-propelled gun from the 2nd Battery under Captain Talvitie sustained a direct hit and since he was in the Commander's position artillery reconnaissance oficer of the 14th Heavy Battalion Lieutenant Siitonen was killed. As a result the Finnish self-propelled guns withdrew to the edge of the forest west of the fields and dug in, having occupied advantageous firing positions in the ridges.

North of Lake Leitimonyarvi, the 2nd Jager Battalion went on the offensive. The battalion succeeded in moving along the edge of the forest west of the Kuusela farmstead, but any further progress was stopped by fierce Soviet fire. The artillery attacks did not help either–a group of artillery reconnaissance personnel were moving among the advancing ranks of the Jagers. The Soviet guards had concentrated a large collection of guns at the farmstead itself and had beaten back all the Finnish attacks.

The result of the offensive's first day was breakthrough of the Finnish defences in both the directions that the 30th Guards Rifle Corps' advance had taken. The left flank of the 97th Rifle Corps east of Vyborg had advanced onto the bank of the Saimaa Canal. On the right flank of the

Corps the 178th Rifle Division had succeeded on their third attempt to occupy the height from marker 23.0.

East of Tali Station, the 265th Rifle Division under Colonel Andreyev, which had attacked Karisalmi, did not move even a metre forward. The division had been weakened after the first Vyborg Offensive Operation and attacked in rocky terrain without the necessary artillery support. The attack by the division on 25 June was only supported by the 1,309th Anti-Tank Artillery Rifle Brigade that were firing at close range. The result was both predictable and sad. By 27 June, all that remained in the division's regiments was the following: the 951st Rifle Regiment–293 men, the 941st Rifle Regiment–261 men; this same situation held sway in the division's 450th Rifle Regiment.

The Finns introduced their reserve into the battle–Lagus' armoured division. For the first and only time elite units met on the battlefield–the 30th Guards Rifle Corps under Hero of the Soviet Union General Simonyak and the armoured division under Cavalier of Mannerheim Cross No. 1 Major-General Ruben Lagus. Both sides were going all out to win. The fact that between 600–700 soldiers per day arrived at the 64th Guard Division's medical and sanitary battalion from 25–30 June alone is testimony to the intensity of the battle.

The armoured division declared that 38 enemy tanks had either been lost or captured in the first day of the battle. This claim exceeds the actual losses of the two Soviet regiments by more than double (the 27th Separate Tank Regiment lost 17 vehicles, while the 397th Self-Propelled Artillery Regiment lost five vehicles).

Two Soviet 27th Separate Tank Regiment T-34-85s captured during the 25 June battle still stand to this day at the gates of the Finnish Defence Force Armoured Brigade headquarters. The ISU-152 self-propelled gun with the number 1212, the crew of which chose to perish rather than surrender, is exhibited to this day in the armoured tank forces museum of the Finnish forces in Parola. A self-propelled gun numbered 1236 was immediately repaired by the Finns and was lost in battle on 28 June south of the Portinhoyka crossroads.

Finnish artillery was still unable to deploy fully. The reinforced artillery group of the 18th Infantry Division under the command of Colonel Georg Lukander, opened fire using the forces of nine divisions and fired 6,680 shells on 25 June.

The weather for 24-25 June was recorded by Finnish and German air forces as inclement. On 25 June Lieutenant-Colonel Klumay issued an order to ensure that there remained a reserve of bombs on the airfield as well as enough fuel for five sorties for each air wing aircraft.

18

26 June

The counter attack by the reinforced Jager Battalion continued on the night of 25-26 June and petered out by 0600 hrs in the morning. The Finns began to attack using individual battalions on the right flank of the corps, but unsuccessfully. A coordinated Finnish attack using the forces of the 2nd Jager Border Battalion, the 2nd Battalion, 13th Infantry Regiment, and the 3rd Battalion, 48th Infantry Regiment did not happen at all owing to the constantly changing environment. Soviet units continued their offensive and were able to push the Finns back to an area around Toyvola farmstead. At the same time, the strategic significance of the crossing over the small stream at Tali station became clear. The entire Soviet attack alignment was supplied across these bridges–the 30th Guards Rifle Corps, the 268th Rifle Division, and the tanks and artillery. The bridges became the target of daily raids by the Finnish Air Force and the German *Kuhlmey* Air Wing.

The next morning, the following aircraft were at combat readiness in the German air wing: 23 Ju 87Ds, 19 Fw 190As, four FW 190Fs, and three Bf 109G reconnaissance aircraft.

The Finnish Air Force carried out a bombing raid on the area around Tali station using 26 bombers. Eleven Blenheims dropped forty-four 100kg bombs on the German positions, forty-four 50kg high-explosive bombs, and forty-four 12.5kg fragmentation bombs, in total 7,150kg. The second wave of 15 Blenheims dropped sixteen 100kg bombs, twenty-two 100kg fragmentation, and fifty-eight 50kg high-explosive bombs–in total 6,700kgs.

Five German dive-bombers carried out two combat sorties on the Tali crossings as well as Soviet positions in the area around Nurmilampi. According to their report, one bridge sustained a direct hit and was destroyed.

Soviet anti-aircraft crews described enemy aviation operations as follows:

> There were rich pickings to be had today! In foreseeing their own defeat evidently the Finns had gathered all their aircraft and directed the main attack on the crossing near Tali.
>
> All the regiments in the division opened fire on the enemy aircraft. This battle could really be called a duel. Despite the bombardment and the artillery and mortar fire not one officer, sergeant or private left their position. They fired accurately, as an expert would, sparing no effort, blood, or loss of life.
>
> The first hit by the dive bombers was taken by the 3rd Battery 1,393rd Anti-Aircraft Artillery Regiment under the command of Senior Lieutenant CHEBOTARYEV, which had got everyone to their feet earlier at Tali crossing, but this was on 23 June 1944, when the gun crews under Senior Sergeant GOLUB and Sergeant NECHVOLODOV shot down five aircraft in a day.
>
> Today the last Platoon Commander and the first Gun Commander of the 1st Battery, 1,893rd Anti-Aircraft Artillery Regiment was killed by shrapnel from a shell. The Battery Commander Captain FOMIN remained alone with three old gun commanders. Despite

> his terrible fatigue FOMIN was able to support the battery's will to fight, and all six guns continued their intensive fire. The first battery in the division was noticed by the group of Ju 87s on the approach to the target and shot down one of them as they entered a dive.
>
> The 4th battery of the 1,393rd Anti-Aircraft Artillery Battery under the command of Senior Lieutenant CHEREDNICHENKO, in fulfilment of a combat order, repaired the bridge under fierce enemy artillery and mortar fire and advanced to the area north of the crossing.
>
> The quartermaster of the 2nd battery, 1,393rd Anti-Aircraft Artillery Regiment Senior Sergeant FOKIN stood in for the injured forward air controller, and then replaced the injured commander and shot down one Ju 87.
>
> The Gun Commander of the 2nd battery, 1387th Anti-Aircraft Artillery Regiment Sergeant BAKHAREV changed a gun cable under enemy fire. Having gone deaf as a result of the explosions of the shells and mortars, he continued to command his crew. This is a truly heroic achievement. For the entire course of these raids only one small calibre bomb landed on the diminutive bridge, which was repaired three hours later. The rest of the bombs fell to the side of the crossing and only because the enemy aircraft, which had incurred losses, were not quite aiming correctly. In the course of a day some 136 sorties by enemy aircraft, and 14 bombing missions were undertaken. The division's units shot down three enemy aircraft.

Aleksandra Fyodorovna Kochneva, 134th Guards Rifle Regiment

> The battles were tough – the terrain there was rugged, craggy. There were enormous cliffs in one of these gorges and the situation for us was such that we only began to take cover once the Finns had started to bomb us. I looked around but there was nowhere for me to take cover, I ran up to one of the crags, and our regimental engineer was taking cover there–the entire left side of his chest had been torn away by shrapnel. Completely. That was it, he had just been cut open. I could see–his heart was still beating! A real life human heart was beating before my very eyes! I was flabbergasted, but he was still able to prop himself up with his hands, his eyes were completely wild, he looked at me and then fell face first onto the ground. What could I do to help though? His chest had been cut away completely. This was what the fierce battles just outside Vyborg were like. We did not know the names of the stations, or the geographical locations. We were just soldiers, we are given a reference point and a direction, and we go there.

In connection with the enemy's stubborn resistance and constant Finnish counterattacks, the 30th Guards Corps was forced to alter its plans. The talk was not of fording the Saimaa Canal and of an advance to Nuijanmaa and Imatra. Now the task for the day was to capture the eastern bank of the Saimaa Canal and the road junction in the village of Ihantala. By beating back the Finnish counterattacks on 26 June the 45th Guards Rifle Division lost 85 men killed, and 773 wounded, that is to say 10 percent of the initial complement of personnel.

On the Finnish side, the losses for the 18th Infantry Division as a result of combat activity on 26 June reached a level of 40 percent. In the Finnish Army these losses would have been considered close to a loss of combat capability. In connection with this the Command of the 4th Army Corps took the decision to pull back the division's depleted battalions to the rear and to introduce the fresh 11th Infantry Division that had arrived from Karelia into the battle. The artillery, signals and sappers of the 18th Infantry Division remained in their positions and again became part of the 11th Division. Unwilling to give up, Finnish command was prepared a second counter-attack.

19

27 June

On the evening of 26 June, units received an order–to purge a section of the highway from Ihantala–Portinhoikka in the area around the junction at Vakkila farmstead of units from the 64th Guards Division. A group of T-26 tanks was allocated to this along with a T-34 tank, which was supported by sappers. The battles for the highway lasted up until 2130 hrs, when a thick fog descended on the terrain and put an end to the combat activity.

At 0445 hrs the fog dissipated and the Finnish tank crews resumed their advance. Suddenly a strange obstruction appeared on the road–a pile of bodies of fallen Finnish soldiers. The tank crews hesitated and at that moment a hail of bullets rained down on their T-26 from a Soviet anti-tank gun. Combat vehicles with tactical numbers 653, 650, 161-1 and 163-7, were damaged. Four tank crews were killed instantly, and three injured. Two tank crewmembers in the course of the offensive were recorded as missing without trace. The Finns had abandoned one tank on the battlefield.

The northern alignment of the 30th Guards Corps, as they were advancing towards Ihantala, represented a worthwhile target for a counterattack and encirclement. The width of the access point for the breakthrough in the area around Talinmylly was no more than four to five kilometres, and the flanks of the guards appeared open. Finnish command could not help but take advantage of this situation and all night from 26–27 June they prepared a large-scale operation against the northern alignment of the 30th Guards Corps. The plan for the counterattack incorporated a simultaneous attack from the west, east and north. The entire first half of the day was spent in organising cooperation.

The objective for the counterattack was not only the encirclement of the Soviet attack alignment, but the restoration of the principal defensive line in Tali:

Bjokman's combat group (the 2nd Battalion Jager Border Guards, the 3rd Battalion of the 48th Infantry Regiment, 2nd Battalion, 13th Infantry Regiment, and the 14th Separate Infantry Battalion) was to attack in the direction of Talinmylly–Aniskala and is to dig in at Tali station between Lakes Leitimojarvi and Repolanjarvi.

Forsberg's combat group (the 1st and 2nd Battalions, 48th Infantry Regiment, the 3rd Battalion 13th Infantry Regiment) is to attack from the north along the highway from Ihantala–Vyborg, and to purge the area around the Mutalahti farmstead and continue the advance towards Nurmilalampi, the objective for the day is to reach the principal defensive line. The assault guns of the German 303rd Brigade are to support the advance.

Puroma's combat group (the 2nd, 3rd, 4th, and 5th Jager Battalions and the Heavy Tank Company) is to attack to the east in the direction of Aniskala farmstead and there is to join up with Bjokman's combat group.

The 2nd Battalion, 6th Infantry Regiment is to attack Tojvola farmstead, covering the left flank of Puroma's combat group.

In total, 12 battalions took part in the Finnish counterattack; some of these however were not at full strength by that time.

Puroma's combat group went on the offensive at 1600 hrs. In the forests and crags east of the highway a fierce battle was raging; both sides fought intelligently, stubbornly, and bravely.

The 2nd Jager Battalion moved forward quickly, but stopped ahead of the *Kolbasa* height, north of the Aniskala farmstead, the battalion did not have the resources to capture it. The 1st Company lost all its officers in this battle, and a powerful Soviet artillery barrage scattered the company.

The 3rd Jager Battalion immediately encountered fierce Soviet resistance. At the very beginning of the attack the Commander of the 3rd Jager Battalion Major Leppjanen was fatally injured in the neck. He was awarded Mannerheim cross No. 135 posthumously.

At what was a critical time for the guards the access point for the breakthrough narrowed down to one or two kilometres; but the Finns just did not have the resources to close the objective fully. Soviet tanks offered a great deal of support in not allowing the Finnish infantry to move around the battlefield freely; the light T-60s held the Finns at a distance using their automatic weapons and combed through the forests, purging them of Finnish infantry.

Finnish units that had been advancing from the east, suffered a complete fiasco. Lieutenant Bruno Tiainen, the Company Commander of the 2nd Jager Border Battalion recalls this event in his memoirs:

> In order to solve the situation and the encirclement of the powerful alignment our battalion was sent into the counterattack from the west with other units from the area around Ruskeavuori via the fields at Nirmulami to height 33, and from there to the south, with the objective of taking the boundary near Kuusela farmstead, which was where the Jager Brigade was advancing to from the west.
>
> The advance of the border guards began at a good pace at 1615 hrs on 27 June 1944 with the support of mortar fire. The promised spotter never materialised. We also crossed open terrain near Nurmilampi successfully. We encountered more serious resistance only we circumvented the forest on the craggy slopes of height 33. The 3rd company and the Jager platoon, in spite of the order, were not able to support the storming of the height by the 1st company as they were supposed to. The 2nd Company, which could also have supported the 3rd Company in a flanking attack remained for the most part passive and laid low in the forest on the left flank. It was only on the third attempt that the 1st Company succeeded in pushing a powerful enemy off the height. The number of trophies that were taken across an area 100x150m are testament to the start of the battle: 11 sub-machine guns, four heavy machine guns, a tank radio and countless semi-automatic and automatic weapons. The battle raged over every metre of ground. The platoons under lieutenants A. Vyayanyanena and E. Yarvinenam who had acted as attack groups proved themselves especially well in these battles, they managed to purge this labyrinth of gun emplacements.
>
> The Battalion Commander Major E. Avepa was injured before the capture of the height 33. He was replaced by the Commander of the 3rd Company Captain U. Petyaya, but he too was injured a short time later. The Command of the 3rd Company was taken up by Lieutenant Lahtinen. After Petlyaya Lieutenant Piitulainen became the Battalion Commander, and the Commander of the 2nd Company was Lieutenant R. Ketonen. It later emerged that Colonel S.K. Bjorkman appointed Major T.O. Erven as the Commander of our battalion (he was the Commander of the 3rd Battalion, 48th Regiment), but he never appeared in the theatre of operations, while the other officers in our battalion were unaware of this appointment. Therefore two soldiers who were senior in rank–Lieutenants B.

Tiiainen and Piitulainen decided the issue of command between them. On the suggestion of Lieutenant Tiiainen a decision was taken to continue the execution of the combat mission, although one third of the battalion had disappeared somewhere. At that time the following events occurred:

- The Company under Lieutenant Himottu from the 3rd Battalion, 48th Regiment replaced the 1st and 2nd Companies on height 33
- Captain U. Petyaya reported to Colonel Bjokman that the 2nd Jager Border Guard Battalion had concentrated in full on the far slope of height 33 and were ready to continue their offensive in the direction of Kuusela. This message bore absolutely no relation to what actually happened. The 3rd Company under Lieutenant Lathinen had left the battlefield and headed off somewhere towards the ridge from Ihantala–Talinmylly, so they had withdrawn from the game. The Jager Platoon as a result of the battle had almost ceased to exist. Our mortar platoon was totally wiped out by an enemy artillery barrage back in the area around Ruskeavuori. The anti-tank platoon was also missing– this platoon remained somewhere behind the battlefield in the area around Ihantala. The platoon under Lieutenant V. Kaskela from the 1st Company was providing cover for someone somewhere and was also absent.

Thus the 2nd Jager Border Guard Battalion could continue their advance only by using the forces of half of the 1st Company's complement. It is worth noting that the latter in the storming of height 33 lost 54 men killed or injured!

Although they understood the gravity of the situation the border guards still left height 33 in their thinned out lines and moved in the direction of Kuusela. The order of battle was as follows: the 2nd company that was at full complement was in front, the weakened 3rd Company–was in the second echelon. During the course of the advance by the battalion's order of battles to the starting positions the enemy rained down rocket fire on us. The enemy also attacked, which was more akin to a foray, against our flank. The 1st Company beat back this foray in a short, but fierce hand-to-hand battle. The 2nd Jager Border Guard Battalion was ready to continue the offensive.

The hand of fate however intervened at this point and intervened cruelly. Himmotu's company from the 48th Regiment pulled back to the north, and our right flank was open. Since the 3rd Company under Lahtinen had by that time already left the battlefield and had left a sector from height 33 to Nurmilampi without provision for cover, a catastrophe was inevitable. The enemy got onto the battalion's flank and rear. A reconnaissance group under Sergeant Lallukka from the 1st Company, which had been sent behind the lines, only confirmed the threat. The situation was impossible. We had to save what remained of our battalion. There was no question of an attack. We had to find some way out of the encirclement before the entire battalion perished. This was how our entire front collapsed at Nurmilampi. Victory was within our reach, but it turned into a crushing defeat. After a short military meeting in which lieutenants Ketonen, Piilumlainen, and Tiiainen participated, a decision was taken to pull the battalion back to the area around Ruskeavuroi. We had no radios, and there was no other way of reporting the sudden change in the situation and what we needed to do immediately to Colonel Bjokman.

The 2nd Company had prepared for the breakthrough, and the remains of the 1st– covered the withdrawal. It took just seven minutes of time to regroup, but in those seven minutes the 2nd Battalion had left the battlefield along with Lieutenant Piitulainen. Only the tracks left in the white moss indicated the direction in which the company had gone.

This was another blow. I had nothing left with which to take a bearing or to head off after the company that had departed ahead of us by following their tracks. Sub-machine guns opened up against us from 150m away, putting out a dense field of fire. I decided that this could have been the border guards, who had lost their heads, from the 2nd Company, and I shouted out: "Don't shoot, we are Finnish!" The gunners answered tersely in Finnish: "Get away, we will not fire!" We had gone some 10–20m and someone opened fire on us again. This sleight of hand drove us crazy and we immediately launched a fierce attack, sending them packing somewhere in the direction of Nurmilampi. As we were approaching the field, from where the attack had begun, we had to turn to the north so we could move forward using the forest as cover. We soon encountered the enemy. We forged a way forward by firing our sub-machine guns, automatic weapons, *Panzerfausts* and *Panzerschrecks*. We reached Kivilampi with difficulty, but the enemy stopped us there. We had gone on the attack three times across the field, and three times we had been forced to pull back under intense enemy fire. On the third attack it was only Sergeant Martikainen who followed me across the field, so the enemy fire was only aimed at us two. Mud and dust began to swirl around us, but under covering fire from our own forces we somehow reached the forest.

It became clear that we had not been able to reach our own lines this way. There was no sense in waiting for any assistance from anywhere; I feverishly looked for a way out of this trap. Then I noticed that Lieutenant R. Kannelkoski and a few of the border guards to the right of Nurmilampi had, further on, managed to tear across the field and break out of the pocket. I gathered all the volunteers and decided I would get through the same way. The enemy had already noticed our movements and had occupied a series of houses beyond the breakthrough point and had opened fierce fire on us from the rear. We rushed across the field like prairie hares and fired in all directions in the intervening moments between speed marches. The first thing to do was to pin down anyone who was firing at us from the front line, and then fire behind the lines, and then do the next dash. This was the scariest race of my life. In the course of the breakthrough I had lost a fabulous Border Guard Corporal E. Yuranen from the directorate section, E. Rikonen and V. Mensonen; the Commander of the directorate section Senior Sergeant A. Ikonen was injured. Border Guard Corporal V. Mensonen literally died in my arms, and I managed in that same field, under fire, to forgive and thank my loyal former comrade and bodyguard. That moment of farewell will remain with me for the rest of my life. Later on I was able to hand over his wallet and his watch to his relatives. Another burst of fire and I ran up to a group under Lieutenant Kannelkoski, which had taken shelter behind the wall of a granary in the middle of the field.

We did a quick head count – there were 17 of us left in the company.

We caught our breath a little and scattered in all directions as fast as we could away from the granary, and I, probably set a record for running the 400m, since I was the first to reach the forest and the small lake in the marsh. The time was not recorded but the record holder in the 400m in the battalion was Sergeant A. Kuljokyas and he was the second man to complete the run. Maybe my excellent result could be explained by the fact that enemy tanks had opened fire on us from their guns on the opposite side of the field.

We survived this time, but where our own troops were, and where on earth we actually were–nobody could say. We carefully set off towards the Ihantala Ridge. As we approached the highway we could see many of our fallen soldiers on it, as well as dead horses, broken vehicles, and Finnish Vickers tanks that had been taken out of action. From these obvious clues we deduced that we were still behind enemy lines.

The battalions of the 48th Infantry Regiment also moved forward, but they came under fierce artillery fire and withdrew. Colonel Forsberg reported that his unit was no longer capable of advancing due to high losses. The 303rd Assault Gun Brigade informed the Finns that their load of ammunition had run out and left the battlefield. In cooperation with the Finns the German self-propelled gun crews had a number of problems, since the brigade had arrived at the front line without a single interpreter.

The Finnish Air Force attacked the bridge at Tali with eight "hounds," dropping eight 100kg, eight 50kg high explosive, and eight 12.5kg fragmentation bombs. In the evening, the Germans attacked the bridge using five Stukas and claimed the bridge had been damaged.

That evening, the Finns continued the counterattack, aiming to encircle the Soviet alignment that was advancing to the north along the only forest road between Tali–Talinmylly–Rauhamjaki–Ihantala. The Commander of the 30th Guards Corps Simonjak introduced his reserve–the 63rd Guards Division–into the battle. It was due to start the advance immediately, but in connection with the activity by Finnish units Brigade Commander Shcheglov delayed the advance by a day. That day and the white night that followed it, was spent beating back the Finnish attacks. The 190th and 192nd Guards Regiments, which had not even gone on the attack, lost 994 men either killed or injured in the space of one day. In sacrificing his elite units, sparing neither the Jagers, nor the ordinary infantry, or the Jager border guards, the Finns tried to win some time, recapture the initiative and hold the boundaries they had captured.

On that day, 268th Rifle Division lost its Commander—Colonel Nikolay Dmitrievich Sokolov. He had been fighting since 1918 and had taken part in the Soviet-Finnish War and had been a participant in the Battle of Hanko, and it was ludicrous how a career officer in the Red Army had perished. The Division's Chief of Staff, Colonel Pyotr Arsentyevich Bolshakov, recalled the death of the brigade commander:

> It happened on a white night, in a short break in the fighting. An enemy shell exploded at the command post and a small piece of shrapnel, which had flown through the canvass skin of the tent, had ricocheted off the steel crossbeams of a bunk, and had pierced his temple. Everyone in the division was in deep mourning after learning of the death of their favourite Commander. Colonel Voytulevich replaced the fallen commander.

A column of Soviet infantry entering Vyborg on the Isthmus Highway, 20 June 1944.

A T-34-76 missing a roadwheel on the move in Vyborg, crossing of Torkkelikatu and Karjalankatu streets. The tank belongs to the 152nd Tank Brigade, 20-21 June 1944.

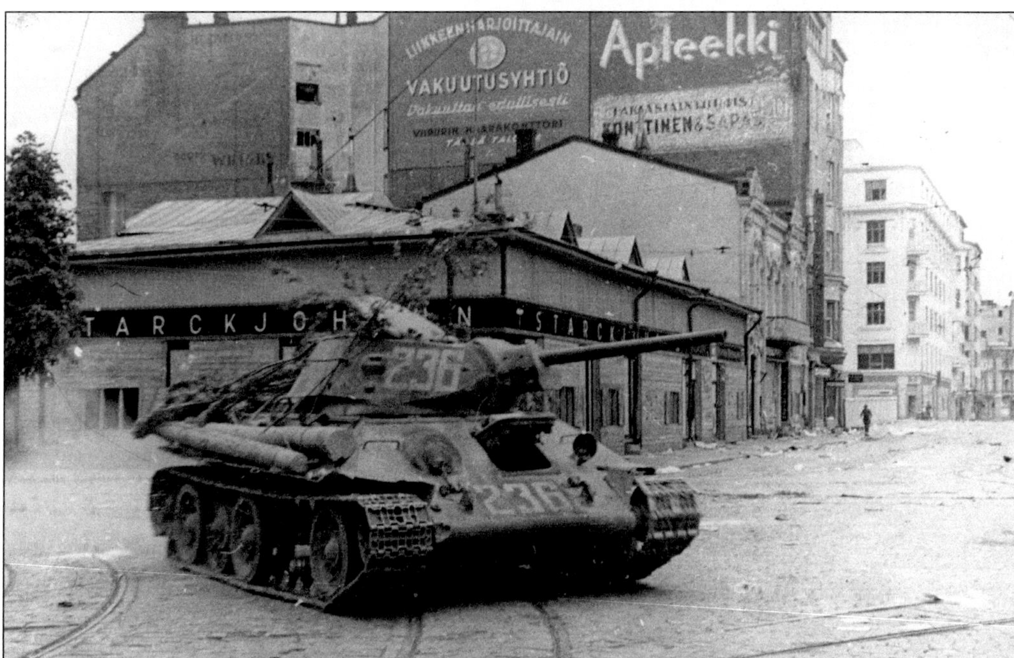

Soviet soldiers inspecting a knocked-out BT-42 Finnish assault gun.

Soviet heavy JS-2 tanks, 26th Guards Heavy Tank Regiment, on Karjalankatu Street in Vyborg. 20-21 June 1944.

Evacuation of goods and commodities via Saimaa Channel, 26 June 1944.

Destroyed JS-2 heavy tank, 26th Guards Heavy Tank Regiment in Tammisuo. The tank presumably belonged to Company Commander Guards Lieutenant Kharlov. The whole crew was killed and posthumously awarded with Golden Stars of Hero of the Soviet Union, 21 June 1944.

Battle for the islands. A crew of Soviet 45 mm gun firing at the Finnish positions. Place and date unknown.

An abandoned Finnish T-26 light tank, place is uncertain (Portinhoikka/Liikola).

A heavy JSU-152 assault gun number 1212 captured by Finns in Portinhoikka, 25 June 1944.

Destroyed T-34-85 tanks from the 27th Tank Regiment, Portinhoikka, 25-26 June 1944.

A destroyed T-34-76 burning on the road inside the Finnish positions. Note two camouflaged German StuG IIIs at the side of the road. The German assault guns belong to the 330th Assault Gun Brigade dispatched to Finland from Estonia, 30 June 1944.

The image that became a symbol of the Battle of Tali-Ihantala. Finnish infantry passing the destroyed T-34-76, turret number 450 from the 30th Guards Tank Brigade, 2 July 1944.

Destroyed Soviet JSU-152 heavy assault gun number 1140, north from Ihantala, 9 September 1944.

Tanks of the 27th Guards Heavy Tank Regiment, 30th Guards Tank Brigade, 394th Guards Heavy Assault Gun Regiment trapped north of a destroyed bridge in Ihantala. Image taken from a Finnish artillery observation post.

JS-2 tanks, 27th Guards Heavy Tank Regiment stuck just north from a destroyed bridge in Ihantala. Image taken from a Finnish artillery observation post.

Soviet T-34-76 tank, tactical number 420, destroyed at Ihantala. The tank belonged to the 30th Guards Tank Brigade, 14 July 1944.

Finnish forward artillery observation post, a Finnish trump card in the Battle of Ihantala, 11 July 1944.

A German Assault Howitzer belonging to the 122nd Infantry Greif Division in Säkkijärvi, northern parts of Karelian Isthmus.

Geschwader Kulhmey Stukas in flight.

German Stukas flying in to support Finnish defences in Ihantala.

A damaged FW 190 from Geschwader Kulhmey that managed to return to its base after suffering damage in a dogfight, 27 June 1944.

Finnish tank busters from the Tali-Ihantala battle. Junior Sergeant Paul Renvall and Senior Sergeant Kurt Engman, 2nd Battalion, 13th Infantry Regiment armed with Panzerfausts and Panzerschrecks. Note tank destruction badges on the right sleeves, 28 July 1944.

Colonel Wahlbäck, commander of the 49th Infantry Regiment, 3 May 1944. He was killed during a Soviet air raid at the beginning of the Battle of Äyräpää – Vuosalmi.

Finnish infantry inspecting a T-34-76 tank, 222nd Tank Regiment, destroyed by Panzerfaust. Vuosalmi, 7 September 1944.

A new T-34-85 tank of 226th Tank Regiment stalled in swamp and destroyed, Vuosalmi, 20 July 1944.

KV-1S, tactical number 660, destroyed by Panzerfausts at Vuosalmi. The tank belonged to the 46th Heavy Guards Breakthrough Tank Regiment.

Finnish reinforcements arrive. Assault Gun Battalion at Vuosalmi. Note a Soviet M39 helmet used by the Finns with insignia of the Lagus Division, 30 July 1944.

Finnish tankers with a captured Soviet T-34-85 turret number 908, 226th Tank Regiment in Räisälä. Presumably, September 1944.

The war is over. A Soviet and a Finnish officer compare their pocket watches near Vyborg, 4 September 1944.

Soviet and Finnish officers share a cigarette together, 4 September 1944.

The symbol of peace. Soviet and Finnish officers saluting each other as the Finnish delegation crosses the frontline to go to Moscow for peace negotiations, 7 September 1944.

The last farewell. A Finnish Army Lotta (auxiliary female volunteer) and her brother march though their home village Räisälä and lay flowers at grave of their brother, 14 August 1944. The area was ceded to the USSR as per truce conditions one month later.

The Soviet officers for the Allied Control Commission arriving at Malmi Airport, Helsinki, 23 September 1944.

20

28 June

By the morning of 28 June, Finnish attacks on the flank of the 30th Guards Corps had narrowed the breakthrough access point down to one kilometre, but the Finns were unable to advance any further. Oesch considered that the closing of the ring of encirclement was still possible and gave an order for a third counterattack on the morning of 28 June. The battle reached its apogee.

Soviet command introduced the fresh 168th Rifle Division to cover the right flank of the Guards Corps. The division advanced in the direction of Karisalmi station.

Finnish units were augmented by two battalions and again went on the attack. The entire day was spent in the fiercest battles. The Finns attacked Soviet positions at 1045 hrs, 0915 hrs, and 0950 hrs. Several times the Finnish units almost closed the breakthrough access point. At critical moments, the distance between the Finnish units attacking from the west and the east was no more than 400–500m. The guards however fought hard and still managed to hold onto the road. In the forest north of Kuusela the Finns circumvented the units of the 63rd Guards Division, recaptured the road, severed the lines of communication again, and surrounded the 68th Guards Separate Anti-Tank Battalion. The anti-tank crews took up a circular defensive position. The battle raged for an entire day, and the anti-tank crews incurred heavy losses in terms of personnel.

Ammunition ran out and had to be assembled on the battlefield. Artillerymen fired buckshot at the advancing Finns. Guards Battery Commander Lieutenant Asmolovskiy distinguished himself especially well in beating off the Finnish attacks, and it was for this operation that he was recommended for the title of Hero of the Soviet Union.

The 260th Guards Tank Regiment lost almost all their combat vehicles, by 29 June all that remained in the formation were just two KVs. A mobile group from the 21st Army–made up of the 30th Guards Tank Brigade, and the 27th Guards Heavy tank Regiment was introduced into the battle. In the afternoon, the "thirty-fours" had passed the sectors that were being raked with fire and had joined the infantry.

Shcheglov remained unhappy with the actions of the tanks and self-propelled guns, which had been entrusted with the objective of supporting the infantry. The tank crews of the 260th Guards Heavy Tank Regiment under Krasnoshtan and the self-propelled gun crews of the 394th Guards Heavy Self-Propelled Gun Regiment under Yudin, who were afraid of the "*faustniks*," positioned themselves some distance back behind the infantry's orders of battle, after engaging the Finnish assault guns as well as the Finnish Anti-Tank Guns in battle at long-range. Shcheglov was critical of their actions:

> Thus the advance by the 30th Separate Heavy Tank Brigade into the 192nd Guards Rifle Regiment's theatre of operations without incurring losses along the very same route along which the 260th Separate Heavy Tank Regiment together with the 394th Self-Propelled Artillery Regiment that was subordinate to it, had taken confirms unequivocally the

> indecisiveness of the actions of the Commander of the 260th Separate Heavy Tank Regiment Krasnoshtan, and the inconsistency of his decision to hang back a long way behind the infantry. In doing without the support of the infantry and fighting a duel like battle, the regiment would incur unjustified losses from the enemy's anti-tank riflemen and from their assault guns.

The tank crews and self-propelled gun crews proved their passivity in the absence of crossing equipment for crossing the ditches and the other difficulties presented by the terrain.

The Finnish Air Force dropped on Tali and on the bridge near Tali 21.5 tons of bombs during two bombing raids. The first of these raids was carried out by three *Dornier* aircraft, and a single DB and one Il-4 that dropped twenty 100kg bombs, thirty 50kg high-explosive bombs, and thirty 50kg fragmentation bombs. The second wave arrived in the evening and was made up of 11 *Junkers* aircraft, which dropped five one tonne bombs, twelve 50kg bombs, and twenty-two 250kg bombs.

The Germans bombed the bridges for the entire day from 0700 hrs in the morning to 1900 hrs in the evening, completing in total four bombing raids and 78 combat sorties. The crossing had been destroyed a second time. From 1900 hrs in the evening until 0700 hrs the following morning the Germans bombed the bridge on another two occasions, completing 41 combat sorties using *Stukas*. FW 190 fighter-bombers attacked the bridge twice, completing eight combat sorties. In connection with the white nights the German dive-bombers transferred onto a twenty-four hour regime of combat sorties; they would appear over the battlefield several times a day.

Within the combat journal of the Supreme High Command's Reserve 32nd Anti-Aircraft Artillery Division the events of the day are reflected as follows:

> The enemy again deployed their aircraft against the crossing near Tali, which we were defending. Since this was managed in different ways the aircraft approached from different directions in order to bomb the crossing; from out of the cloud cover, out of the sun and using a range of other methods. The crossing though remained intact. The bombs drifted off to the side. The majority of them fell in the north-western part of Lake Mulluyen-yarvi, without causing any damage.
>
> The regiments in the division, which were subject to the bombing from the air as well as an artillery barrage from the ground, were constantly firing. According to preliminary information, two Ju 87s were shot down. They were shot down by the 1,393rd and 1,387th Anti-Aircraft Artillery Regiments. They crashed in the area around marker 24.0 and north of the outskirts of Repola. In the course of the air battle with the enemy's fighters a single Finnish La-5, and one Finnish Yak-7 were shot down. The pilots bailed out by parachute. At 1230 hrs an aerostat set an observation balloon on fire. The observer escaped by parachute.
>
> At present we have sustained heavy losses in terms of materiel, for the most part due to muzzle swelling. Twelve 37mm guns have failed. Seven of them have been repaired.

Tali crossing still bears the scars of that battle up to the present day–the bomb craters can be clearly seen right next to the old bridge. In recent years, when the Russian Railways have carried out repairs on all the bridges almost all the bomb craters have been filled in. Academician Inozemtsev, who in 1944 was an Artilleryman-Sergeant-Major, recalled:

> The famous crossing in Tali–the "damned bridges." It is unlikely that anyone who had dared set foot on it in the course of the battle would forget it even 10–15 years later. A bottleneck between two lakes. A railway line and a church, which serve as exceptional landmarks. Our units moved north approximately eight to ten kilometres from the crossing. Both lakes were

under the control of Finnish snipers. These crossings, (there are two of them in a sector covering 800m), are constantly attacked by artillery and mortars. There is nowhere to avoid or take shelter from the explosions, on the sides of the road are marshes studded with mines. Despite this the infantry are moving up (to be more accurate they are running, since any movement here is at the double).

A direct hit on a Studebaker. The vehicle is destroyed. It is quickly dragged into a ditch along with its driver, and the march continues. The soldiers quicken their pace and then everyone, wherever they are, flattens themselves against the ground–some 24 *Focke-Wulfs* are in the air. They are flying at altitude, and then turn headlong into a dive. Fierce barking of the anti-aircraft guns. One of the vultures crashes into the ground. A tractor is destroyed. A tank moving behind it rams it off the road. The injured would soon be bandaged up, nobody would pay any attention to the dead, and the procession would continue on its way.

The pace quickens again–on the tails of the *Wulfs* there would be *Junkers* aircraft, and the Germans of course were punctual in everything. Some 10–12 mins later the air is filled with a steady roar–some 30 aircraft are approaching in a tight formation. They drop 500kg bombs, alternating them with 100kg ordnance. The crossing is destroyed. The infantry scramble over its ruins–since a cessation of movement across this bridge is tantamount to suicide. One and a half hours later movement across the bridge resumes once more.

The signals troops, who had restored communications, captured three Finnish soldiers sitting with a radio in the ruins of a church and adjusting fire. The next mortar barrage ensued. A signals and escort officer, together with one of the Finns are killed, the two others try to escape but come under a hail of bullets aimed at them from both sides. The crossing lives.

21

29 June

On the night of 28-29 June, the 97th Rifle Corps introduced another division into the fray–the 358th Rifle Division under Colonel Zaretskiy. The 108th Rifle Corps was deployed from Vyborg into that area and were ready to send the 46th and 90th Rifle divisions into battle. As a result the Soviet units in the area around Portinhoikka broke through the Finnish defence and created a threatening situation for the units of the 11th Infantry Division.

The commander of the 46th Rifle Division, Colonel Semyon Nikolayevich Borshchev, in his book *From the Neva to the Elbe* described how the Finnish defensive line was broken and the Gulf at Ventelanselka traversed. This is one of the few descriptions of the battle for Tali-Ihantala from the Soviet perspective:

> On 26 June I was ordered to report immediately to the Commander of the 21st Army under Colonel-General D.N. Gusev to a Command Post belonging to the 97th Rifle Corps, which was situated on the north-eastern edge of Vyborg.
>
> Corps commander General M.M. Busarov observed, "The Commander did not wait for you and left," as he greeted us.
>
> I learned from him that our division was to cross the Ventelanselka Gulf as soon as possible, destroy the enemy, that were situated on the eastern bank, and capture a stronghold there. Subsequently we were to advance in the direction of the settlement of Pyrti, get behind the alignment that were preparing a counterattack, and in conjunction with the forces of the 30th Guards Rifle Corps, we were to destroy the alignment. The start of the offensive was to be at 0900 hrs on the morning of 27 June.
>
> It was late evening. I worked out all our options and decided that the timescales for preparing for an offensive that we had been given were unrealistic. Nothing good would come of all this haste: we would just be sending men into battle to die. I voiced my thoughts to Busarov.
>
> He was surprised:
>
> –"Colonel, think about it, what are your thoughts?" At the end of the day this was the Commander's order.
>
> –"That's just it"–I said–"I have thought about it and I want to secure a realistic timescale for the offensive."
>
> General Busarov reported this to the Commander by telephone, that Borshchev has arrived and didn't want to fulfil the order.
>
> D.N. Gusev ordered the Busarov to let me speak to the Commander directly. After he had greeted me the Commander asked:
>
> –"What's the problem, Borshchev?"

At that moment I remembered how Dmitriy Nikolayevich himself, who had given us–students at the M.V. Frunze Academy a course of lectures on tactics, had warned us about rushing preparations for any battle. This gave me greater assurance that I was right. I answered the Commander saying that the Division was 70km from the gulf. The commanders of the various units would reach here any earlier than three hours from now. The entire division would only be able to be concentrated fully by morning. We would not have time to carry out the reconnaissance, set objectives on the ground, work out any issues concerning cooperation, plan artillery support, and occupy forward positions for the offensive by 0900 hrs in the morning. Apart from that we did not have any crossing equipment, and nobody had promised us any.

After listening to my concerns the Commander asked:

–"What then do you suggest?"

–"I would like to request that you allow us one day for preparation and for acquiring crossing equipment to ford the water barrier.

The Commander responded asking if one day would be enough for preparation, and, after securing a positive reply, he immediately agreed.

Not wasting any time I with my operations group that consisted of officers from operations and reconnaissance sections as well as artillery headquarters, departed for the 178th Rifle Division's Command Post in order to get an update on the situation. This division had already tried to cross the Gulf, but without success. The Divisional Commander looked very preoccupied and worried. He told us in detail about the enemy and their defences, as well as the reasons for their unsuccessful crossing of the Gulf. I reached agreement with him on the procedure for rotating the units.

Our regimental commanders had arrived by 0300 hrs in the morning. We carried out reconnaissance. A short time later all our divisions had concentrated not far from the Gulf. Our crossing equipment was delivered (in the shape of pontoons and rafts), as well as rubber inflatable suits for the rifle subdivisions. The commanders updated the objectives on the ground and we reached agreement on cooperation. Up until the beginning of the offensive we had already carried out battalion and company exercises on lakes behind the lines: "To cross the water barrier, capture a stronghold and fight deep behind the enemy's defensive line."

We had learned from experience that if a dingy overturned then the inflatable suit would save us. There were curious incidents in the course of the exercises too. Soldiers, who could not swim, jumped out of the dinghies and began to shout: "Help!" but would then notice that they were not sinking–their inflatable suit was keeping them above water. They would get to the bank themselves and were the butt of laughter and jokes from their comrades.

All this time in the path of the division's offensive we would keep an eye on enemy movements. It seems there were quite a number in the space of one day!

On the night of 28 June the division's units along with our 393rd Artillery Regiment and the 1,237th Self-Propelled Artillery Regiment, the 1,235th Artillery Regiment, and the 594th Mortar Regiments that had been attached to it occupied their starting positions for the offensive. The order of battle was set out in two echelons. In the first echelon of the offensive were the 340th, and 176th Rifle Regiments, while in the second, the 314th Rifle Regiment.

In the evening, when it grew dark, the Commander of the 340th Regiment Lieutenant-Colonel A.I. Zimin sent a reconnaissance detail forward–a section led by Junior Sergeant Mikhaylov–to search for an accessible sector of the Gulf. The reconnaissance personnel found a shallow area with a depth of no more than a metre. Zimin decided under cover of fog to send his first echelon across to the eastern side of the Gulf. I approved this decision. At dawn on 29 June the battalions under Captains M.F. Petrov, and F.S. Mikhaylov waded across the Gulf and camouflaged themselves amongst the rushes.

Our artillerymen had prepared for this battle carefully. The Commander of the 2nd Battalion, 393rd Artillery Regiment Major I.I. Karalishchenko along with the Commander of the Battalion Captain M.F. Petrov identified the firing sectors, and the crossing points, as well as the approaches to them. The Commanders of the batteries Senior Lieutenants Nekrasov, Yermolayev, and Captain Serdyuk agreed the objectives on the ground with the company commanders, and selected the reference points, made adjustments, and prepared the initial data for firing at the targets.

The Commander of the Directorate of the 5th Battery Lieutenant Levchak, as well as two reconnaissance personnel, and two radio-operators, crossed over to the opposite bank. They were located at the 1st Company Commander's Command Post. Up until the start of our artillery barrage the enemy had not yet discovered our infantrymen and artillery personnel on their side of the water. They opened fire on the lakes and on our former observation posts when there was no longer anybody there. They rained fire down on their own battalion in the first trench as well as at targets they had identified.

At 0820 hrs in the morning our powerful general artillery barrage began. The battalions under Petrov and Mikhaleyev were the first to go on the attack. At this time all the subdivisions from the 340th and 176th Regiments crossed the Gulf. The crushing blow delivered by the first two battalions as well as the artillerymen stunned the enemy. This made fording the Gulf easier. The division broke through the defensive line across a three-kilometre sector. The pontoons were immediately deployed across which the 393rd Artillery Regiment and the 1,237th Self-Propelled Artillery Regiment crossed to the other side of Ventelanselka. The enemy's resistance had been broken for good. By 1900 hrs we had captured the highway crossroads and the settlement of Portnihoika.

It was only us who managed to dig in here after news reached us that the enemy was preparing to counterattack using the forces of the dismounted 1st Cavalry Brigade together with tanks. A representative of an aviation unit that had been subordinated to our headquarters to enable cooperation reported this to his Command and indicated the location where enemy forces had concentrated. As soon as the cavalry brigade and tanks had been deployed for the counterattack our aviation, and then our artillery dealt the enemy a powerful blow. All we had to do was to finish what we had started. Here the enemy was completely routed. Battered and twisted guns and tanks was all that remained on the battlefield.

A short time later we called the Commander of the 30th Guards Corps General I.P. Simonyak and informed him that the Finns on his sectors of the division had ceased their counterattack and had begun to retreat. Consequently, I decided, the enemy would now counterattack the subdivisions in our division again, in order to capture the crossroads and push our forces back from the pocket that had been formed to the Saimaa Canal. Whatever happened we would need hold the crossroads. The 340th Regiment coped with this task exceptionally well. The battalions under Captains Petrov and Mikhaleyev also distinguished themselves, they had routed the enemy head on.

After the battle Captain S.F. Mikhalev noticed two medical orderlies, who were carrying an injured soldier on a stretcher. The Battalion Commander recognised on this stretcher Senior Lieutenant N.V. Kostenko, whose company had been the first to capture the crossroads. When the enemy, who had been forced back by General N.P. Simonov's guards, had tried to recapture the crossroads, Kostenko had sent his troops into a counterattack on three occasions. The company had held the crossroads but at the time during the final counterattack Kostenko had sustained four bullet wounds; in the head, chest, back, and leg. The Battalion Commander thanked the Company Commander. He reported his achievement to Regimental Commander Lieutenant-Colonel A.I. Zimin, and in turn Zimin reported it to me. I ordered Aleksandr Ivanovich to put Kostenko forward for the Order of the Red Banner. I remember how Zimin sighed and said: "Evidently this will be awarded posthumously."

A month later on the list of those awarded the Order of the Red Banner I noticed Kostenko's surname but nothing was known of the fate of the courageous Company Commander. Then completely out of the blue I received a letter from N.V. Kostenko. Nikolay Vasilyevich told me of himself: "I am working as the Head of the Rechitsa Regional Information Processing Centre of the Central Statistics Directorate of the Belorussian Soviet Socialist Republic. I would like to visit the locations of the battlefields on the Karelian Isthmus and hear from my comrades in arms how the fighting had been going since I was injured on 30 June."

In the course of 30 June after overcoming the enemy's stubborn resistance the units in the division had continued to advance. By the end of the day we had captured strongholds at Torriko, and Vlahove, crossed the river Kimpenjoki and advanced to a boundary extending from Harakamjaki–Yulevese. Here again we encountered organised resistance. The following day the enemy went on the attack following an artillery and aviation barrage. It was clear that they wanted to restore the previous status quo. We succeeded in beating back even this counterattack though. The enemy incurred heavy losses. There were also losses in our division. Regimental Commanders A.P. Melnikov and I.N. Fadeyev were injured. The Commander of the 393rd Artillery Regiment Lieutenant-Colonel N.D. Solodkov died a hero's death on the battlefield.

The 64th Guards Rifle Division following four days of battle consisted of the following units:

191st Guards Rifle Regiment–160 active soldiers
194th Guards Rifle Regiment–151 active soldiers
197th Guards Rifle Regiment – 157 active soldiers

That afternoon a meeting took place between Corps Commanders Laatikainen and the Commander of the Armed Forces on the Isthmus Oesch. It was clear that the Finnish counterattack had petered out and units on the front line were on the verge of losing their combat capability due to high losses. Finnish Command decided to pull their forces back to a boundary that was more advantageous for defence and to engage the guards in combat on a series of heights between the Saimaa Canal and Lake Ihantaljarvi. The new line of defence ran along a series of peaks from Ventelanselka–Yustila–Vakkila–Ihantalanjarvi–Salojarvi–Kokkoselka and further along the original VKT line.

Ihantala village as well as the height of Pyorakangas became the principal strongholds. There were expansive fields between the Soviet and Finnish positions, which were clearly visible from the heights. The Finnish artillery alignment was growing in strength by the day: by 30 June the Finnish battalions were ready to support up to 12 battalions. The artillery reconnaissance personnel furnished advantageous observation posts, from which Soviet positions could be seen to a depth of approximately up to two to three kilometres.

Simultaneously, Lagus' armoured division was pulled back to the reserves in the area around Kilpeenjoki. The Jager Brigade's losses over the course of five days of fighting were 1,205 men, of which 144 were killed, 856 injured, and 205 were recorded as missing without trace. This was up to 40 percent of the strength of personnel. Losses among the officers on the front line seemed even higher. The jager battalions that had scattered in the course of the battle did not come back together straight away. On the night of 29–30 June Colonel Puroma reported to Lagus that there were 40 men each remaining in the 3rd and 5th Jager Battalions, while in the 4th Jager Battalion there were 25 men remaining.

Other frontline Finnish regiments were not in the best of shape either. The 6th Infantry Regiment lost up to 60 percent of their personnel. In the 48th Infantry Regiment there was no more than a company of men remaining. The testimony of Finnish veterans is also evidence of the state of Finnish units after five days of uninterrupted battles. Bruno Tiiainen of the 2nd Battalion Jager Border Guards: "The tendency of the indigenous guns to jam and to malfunction made waging war harder.

The soldiers who did know how to use the *Panzerfausts* were no longer with us. Eight tanks broke through to Ihantala. They were subsequently destroyed." Tuovi Pasuri of 2nd Battalion of Jager Border Guards observed:

> Where? For God's sake?! Everyone–in a line! There are just a couple of tanks and a few Russian guys there. Get in line!
>
> "Who are you an Unter-Offizier?"–a Major asked Lieutenant Yarvinen. When he was surrounded he had removed his lieutenant's stars but had left the shoulder belt in place.
>
> "I'm a Lieutenant, Major sir."
>
> "And where were you heading?"
>
> "Major sir, we were given permission to withdraw for rest and recuperation. We have been fighting for three whole days.
>
> "And who are you?"
>
> "Jager border guards."
>
> "How many in your company?"
>
> "Six, Major sir,"– answered Yarvinen and gestured towards us.
>
> "And who gave you permission to withdraw?"
>
> "A colonel who was on the front line with us."
>
> "Sure! It's not the colonels who give orders around here, but the motherland and a general, who is in there–the Major pointed to the forest behind the lines with the barrel of his pistol–Everyone! Get in line. Everyone, down to the last man! I will tell you when you can go for rest and recuperation.
>
> During the course of the conversation between the Major and Yarvinen a large number of soldiers had gathered, including border guards. Everyone returned to their foxholes that they had just left. The enemy was not attacking us any more either. Four hours later the Major's signals officer ran along the lines shouting:
>
> "Where are the border guards? You can go on leave!"

> Six worn-out soldiers got up from their foxholes and shuffled off to Kilpeenjoki along the highway towards the rear. Fresh units came towards us. The sun grew warmer. Enemy artillery was beating down on us. Their iron fist was smashing down the door to our country in Ihantala.

In connection with the high losses and the minimal progress near Ihantala Marshal Govorov turned his attention to the other sectors of the front line, which it appeared, promised a swift victory. Preparations had begun for offensive operations in Vyborg Bay and on the River Vuoksi.

22

30 June

By 30 June 1944 the guards, gunners and tank crews had advanced to Lake Ihantalanjarvi and were ready to begin to storm this same village, which was situated on a height the other side of a small stream. The bridge across the stream was mined, and Finnish anti-tank guns stood in ambush on the edge of the road, German assault guns of the 303rd Brigade, which had been hurriedly redeployed from Estonia, as well as Finnish infantry armed with *Panzerfausts*.

In the course of five days of uninterrupted battles the 30th Guards Corps had incurred heavy losses and to a large extent had petered out. The Finnish and German air attacks on the crossings near Tali station followed one after another. Furthermore the Finns succeeded in breaking the radio ciphers used by the 30th Guards Tank Brigade, and they had prior knowledge of all the Soviet side's plans.

Information concerning the battles fought on that day differs significantly in terms of the Soviet and Finnish sources, therefore these are cited with an indication given as to which unit provided the accounts in the first place.

According to the Combat Journal of 394th Guards Heavy Self-Propelled Gun Regiment, an ISU-152 under the command of Lieutenant-Colonel Yudin went on the attack against the village of Ihantala at 0500 hrs in the morning. The self-propelled advanced to the southern edge of Ihantala and at close range at short distances away destroyed all the Finnish gun emplacements inside the houses. The village was destroyed. Despite the repeated demands made by Lieutenant-Colonel Yudin the other Soviet tank units, which were standing further south in the area around the Rauhamjaki height, did not join the attack.

Lieutenant-Colonel Yudin was seriously injured in the head in the attack, which he spent in his self-propelled gun in the regiment's order of battle. According to a report written by the regiment the self-propelled guns approached the village several times and were forced to get back behind their own infantry, which were delayed and were in no hurry to move forward, while the Lieutenant-Colonel conducted himself in battle with courage, which bordered on recklessness.

At 1000 hrs in the morning the 394th Guards Heavy Self-Propelled Artillery Regiment was made operationally subordinate to the 30th Guards Tank Brigade. The entire day was spent organising cooperation between the different branches of the armed forces. The second Soviet attack on Ihantala only began at 1745 hrs. Aside from the "thirty-fours" IS-2 tanks from the 27th Guards' Tank Regiment and ISU-152s from the 394th Guards' Heavy Self-Propelled Gun Regiment also went into battle. The 188th Guards Rifle Regiment incurred heavy losses in their starting positions and were simply not able to escort the armoured equipment. The tanks and self-propelled guns advanced in a column along the highway and moved quickly across the bridge. All the Finnish sappers, who were supposed to blow the bridge, had perished in the course of the Soviet artillery barrage. The tanks entered the ruins of the village and immediately became caught in the crossfire of *Panzerfausts* and anti-tank guns. A "thirty-four" with the tactical number 450 tore past the village and headed along the highway to Kilpeenjoki (now Komsomolskoe), the "thirty-four" turned back however and moved along the highway towards Enso (now Svetogorsk). After it had gone some two kilometres however towards Kilpeenjoki (Komsomolskiy) the "thirty-four" turned back and moved towards Ihantala. At that time two German assault guns were approaching the highway from the 303rd Brigade. On the other side of the road Finnish infantry had dug in armed with *Panzerfausts*. The first shot fired by a German sergeant hit the starboard side of the tank and the "thirty-four" ground to a halt. The second hit from the *Panzerfaust*–which hit the tank's left hand side–destroyed the tank. The ammunition in the tank detonated, and the vehicle was burnt out. Since the "thirty-four" ended up deep behind Finnish defences and it could be approached without representing any threat to life, Finnish military correspondents organised an entire photo session next to the burnt out tank. The photograph showing the "thirty-four" that had been destroyed, with the Finnish infantry marching past with *Panzerfaust* guns on their shoulders has become the most famous photograph of that battle.

Further south in this same village Soviet tank crews continued the battle against the Finnish *faustniks* and anti-tank guns. The Finns announced that three tanks had been burnt out by *Panzerfausts* on the very first day of the battle. Soviet infantry was stopped by artillery and machine gun fire whilst they were still on the approaches to the stream. Indeed the will to attack for the guards was already low. The position of the Soviet tank crews in the village deteriorated after Finnish Artilleryman-Lieutenant Karhunen from his Command Post near the parish cemetery in Ihantala began to adjust the fire on the bridge and succeeded in destroying it. On 1 July, the bridge was blown up and a group of Soviet tanks in the settlement found themselves cut off from the rest of the units. The tiny stream with its marshy banks was impassable for IS-2s and T-34s. The guard's tank crews had not received an order to abandon their combat vehicles, so the tanks assumed a circular defensive position and continued to fight.

Three ISU-152s were burnt out, one of them remained right on the highway in Ihantala itself. The tactical number of this vehicle–1140. A self-propelled gun with the tactical number 113 was destroyed further to the east and remained on the battlefield near the lake. A guard's IS-2 under Senior Lieutenant Vladimir Petrovich Borisov (bearing the number 424) passed very close; to the Finnish positions on a church mound and was immediately hit by a *Panzerfaust* grenade in the starboard side of the turret. The tank caught fire and all of the crew perished. The guards are buried alongside their brothers in arms in Petrovka.

The tanks that remained in the village maintained constant radio contact with Brigade Command. The tank crews collected the bullets and shells, as well as batteries for the radios that remained in the vehicles that had been destroyed. The injured crewmembers remained where they were.

A military doctor in the 30th Guards Tank Brigade observed:

> I remember the brigade's personnel were lined up and the Brigade Commander stood before us. He said that some of our tanks remained in enemy occupied territory, and that we needed to get to them. Anyone who was able to deliver the necessary ammunition to the tanks would be rewarded. Someone from our ranks managed to get to the tanks.

The Soviet tanks stood close to the Finnish positions on open terrain. All the tank crews understood very clearly the danger posed by the *Panzerfausts* and opened fire in response to any movement around where the tanks stood. All the approaches to the tanks were exposed to fire from the Finnish side.

Only on the night of 4-5 July 1944 did two sappers from the 27th Guards Heavy Tank Regiment–Guards Junior Sergeant Viktor Stepanovich Novikov and Guards Red Army soldier Nazar Ali Nadzharov–were able to get to the crews of the IS who were worn out from hunger and thirst, and who had been holding on inside their tanks since 30 June. They were able to deliver food, water, and batteries for the radio sets to the tank crews. They were both recommended for the Order of Lenin. In the statute for the award dated 15 July 1944 the Commander of the Armoured Tank Forces Major-General Shpiller downgraded the award for both soldiers to the Order of The Patriotic War 2nd Class.

Tank crews, who had been cut off from their own lines, had spent more than four days in semi-encirclement. The 15 tank crews from the 30th Guards Tank Brigade were recommended for the title of Hero of the Soviet Union for their actions in this battle. Not one of them was to receive the country's highest award, but they were all awarded the Order of the Red Banner.

How had this day of fighting unfolded for the infantry of the 30th Guards Rifle Corps? The 63rd Guards Rifle Division spent the whole night from 29-30 June beating back a counterattack from the Finnish infantry. By morning only 250 men remained from the 192nd Guards Regiment. The remainder of the regiment were formed into a single battalion that was consisted of three companies: three rifle companies – with 61 men in each, a machine gun company – with 38 men, and a mortar company–with 59 men. That evening, the regiment withdrew back to the reserves.

The 188th Guards Rifle Regiment began to advance to the front line in battalions. After covertly building up in the orders of battle of the 190th Guards Regiment, the 3rd Battalion attacked the Finns, recaptured the Kokkomjaki height and advanced to the southern bank of the stream. The regiment's allied 2nd Battalion, which had been on the edge of the forest north of Rauhamjaki had come under concentrated fire from 24 dive-bombers. They had not been able to commence their attack.

23

1-4 July

In the course of a day's fighting the 63rd Guards Rifle Division lost the Commander of the 188th Guards Regiment Major V.F. Davidenko, the Commander of the 2nd Battalion Guards Captain Luchinskiy E.A., and the Commander of the Guards 3rd Battalion, 190th Regiment Guards Major Polyakov G.F., all of whom had been injured. Guards Major Bannikov replaced the injured Davidenko. All the Soviet attacks in the height near Ihantala were beaten back. Vasiliy Fyodorovich Davidenko recollected this as follows:

> Then on the Karelian Isthmus on 1 July 1944, I was very seriously injured. This happened close to Vyborg, at Tali-Ihantala. The Germans were very persistent in their bombed of us there, and we incurred heavy losses. The entire terrain was strewn with rocks, and huge boulders, and we hid behind them. The first batch of bombs did not hit us. The Germans though had seen us and approached us from the rear. It was then that the heavy losses began. I was injured, I needed to be taken away to safety but the Finns were right next to us! The vehicle could not get through. The tank crews said they would take me in a tank. I told them to reconnoitre the route first that they would be taking, so that they could get past the danger zone quickly. They crawled around there for two hours, looking for a route. I drunk a flask of alcohol and I was put inside a tank and taken to safety. Bannikov stayed behind in my place. After 1 July there was more fierce fighting, and they fiddled around there without me. There was no advance as we had incurred very heavy losses. I can tell you that as I lay there in that hospital, Shcheglov, our Divisional Commander, arrived and awarded me the Order of Suvorov. He said that there were 200–150 active soldiers each remaining in the regiments. We had incurred very, very heavy losses.

German aircraft all but halted their bombardment of the crossings at Tali station and had switched to storming Soviet infantry and tank units on the front line. Ejno Pohjamo observed:

> The field near the road began to fill with tanks… I could see at least 40 combat vehicles. They stopped at a distance that would have been in the range of a gun and began to pick away at the positions of the 12th Infantry Regiment in Ihantala from there. The time was 1220 hrs…since such rich pickings were to be had on the field and on the height, a "turkey shoot" as the Germans called it, the birds of war were ordered to carry out an air strike on the field–the *Stukas*.
>
> The *Stukas* arrived but the enemy was ready for them, they had learned over a number of years how to defend themselves from these eagles that had held sway in the skies in the first few years of the war. The Germans were greeted with a dense wall of anti-aircraft fire. It was at least from the ground impossible to distinguish one explosion from another. The

> whole sky was covered by black puffs of smoke from the explosions. It seemed that their attack had become disorganised. The attack was inflicted without any grouping, at least, that was the way it seemed from down on the ground. One of the bombers, after it had achieved a direct hit would depart, very nearly catching the tops of the trees. In order to level his aircraft out the pilot dropped his last bomb. It exploded behind our lines. It also fell amongst the tanks...

By the beginning of June the scales had begun to tip in favour of the Finnish side. The Soviet guards troops and tank crews had clearly withered, whereas the Finns had only just been augmented by the forward units of the 6th Infantry Division, under Major-General Vihma. Even more importantly in terms of cementing the Finnish defence was the artillery alignment, which had grown to 334 guns per three kilometres of front. A large proportion of the howitzers and guns in this attack force had arrived from Karelia–while the Leningrad Front had paid their own high price for their successes on the Karelian Front. This was how it had been envisaged in the plan developed by Soviet General Headquarters.

Finnish artillery Vakkila–Ihantala Sector, 1 July 1944

Artillery	Quantity	Artillery system	Date of arrival
The 4th Infantry Division			
The 1st Field Artillery Regiment			
1st Battalion	12	76 K 02	
2nd Battalion	12	76 K 02	
3rd Battalion	12	152 N 09-30	
22nd Separate Heavy Battalion	8 4	152 N 38 105 K 29	
6th Infantry Division			From the Maselga isthmus
14th Field Artillery Regiment			28 June 1944
1st Battalion	12	75 K 17	
2nd Battalion	12	122 N 10-30	
3rd Battalion	12	155 N 37	
13th Separate light Battalion	12	105 N 37	
The 11th Infantry Division			

4th Field Artillery Regiment			
1st Battalion	12	155 N 17	
2nd Battalion	8 4	76 K 02 122 N 10-30	
3rd Battalion	8 4	76 K 02 122 N 10-30	
1st Separate Heavy Battalion	12	155 N 17	
23rd Separate Light Battalion	12	105 N 17	Personnel: 15 June, guns 20 June
17th Infantry Division			
8th Field Artillery Regiment			From the Onezh Isthmus on 14 June
1st Battalion	12	84 K 18	
2nd Battalion	12	155 N 17	
3rd Battalion	4 8	122 N 10-30 84 K 18	
18th Infantry Division			
19th Field Artillery Regiment			
1st Battalion	12	76 K 36	
2nd Battalion	12	122 N 10-30	
3rd Battalion	12	76 K 02	
26th Separate Heavy Battalion	8 4	155 N 17 120 K 78-31	
24th Separate Light Battalion	12	105 N 37	
17th Separate Heavy Battalion	12	105 K 29	
OTHER UNITS			
30th Separate Heavy Battalion	12	152 N 10-30	From the Onezh Isthmus on 29 June
33rd Separate Heavy Battalion	12	152 N 38	From Maselga Isthmus on 15 June

40th Separate Heavy Battalion	12	152 N 33	From the Onezh Isthmus on 20 June
20th Separate Light Battalion	12	105 N 33	From the Onezh Isthmus on 20 June
3rd Battery, 4th Super Heavy Battalion	4	203 N 17	
14th Separate Heavy Battalion	12	150 N 40	Armoured division artillery
4th Separate Motorised Heavy Battalion	4	122 K 31	Separate Battalion
8th Separate Motorised Heavy Battalion	2	152 N 37	Separate Battalion X
TOTAL	334		

2 July

On this day 13th Air Army Command decided that finally they would attack their Finnish and German opponents. At 1958 hrs on Immola airfield the scramble was sounded and just a few short minutes later the first bombs were raining down on the airfield. A single group of four German fighters were able to take off: *Leutnant* Thyben (in aircraft black "eight?"), *Oberleutnant* Radtke (in aircraft black "two"), *Leutnant* Arnecke (in black "ten") and *Unter-Offizier* Assman (flying white "nine"). Arnecke and Assman were not able to get airborne. The first was injured by bomb shrapnel that went into his foot, and his aircraft caught fire. Assman had already taken off in his *Fokker* when a bomb exploded right next to him and blew the engine off his aircraft. Heinz Muller recalled:

> The 2 July was a fine day. The *Sovs* made quite a good job of burning us up in a mass raid on Immola airfield. It was a lovely evening, and we were once again getting ready to eat sandwiches in the tent. We were discussing the recent air raid when at 1959 hrs all hell broke loose. Bombs thundered, bursts of fire chattered and we all ran out of the tent to our aircraft. I could see that the duty pairs were already taking off, among them was *Leutnant* Arnecke, whom I had known from back in flight school days. My mechanic was running towards me and gesturing that the aircraft was not yet ready. What was I to do now? All I could do was to get a move on and run into the protection of the forest.
>
> The Ilyushins were chasing us like we were hares. We just had to run, even though we were ready to drop, and make it to safer ground. At a distance of 50m from the edge of the forest I took refuge in a shallow trench and noticed a bomb fall from an Il-2 in a dive. It was coming straight for me. This is it I thought. Thank God that the charge did not go off. The low angle trajectory of the bomb meant that it fell horizontally five metres away from me and then ricocheted and flew over me, exploding some 10–15m behind me.
>
> I made it to the forest, but I was not out of danger there either. The shells would explode in the trees and bushes. I ran as fast as I could before I reached a large boulder, which offered some kind of shelter at least. There were two soldiers standing there, one was

a German the other a Finn. The latter was seriously injured. A shell had taken his leg off, and we bandaged him up. We circled around the rock, guided by the noise of the engines. It seemed like this went on for an eternity. Bursts of shells would explode one after another, bullets would cascade off the rock and fly in all directions. Finally it let up a little and we set off again for the airfield. The Finnish soldier behaved very courageously and in the chaos that was unfolding in the field, we found a medic who offered him first aid.

Little by little everyone returned to the tent. A look of profound shock was written on everyone's faces, which was unavoidable. The first thing we all had to do was to come to our senses again.

As I was running away from the airfield I could see that *Leutnant* Arnecke's aircraft had caught fire in a hail of bombs. Arnekce sustained 1st and 2nd degree burns to his face and his left hand. In addition a piece of shrapnel from a bomb had entered his left leg. Nevertheless he had managed to get out of his aircraft and set off for the hospital. He was lucky in that he stayed alive during the course of the long drawn out raid. He only got back to us when we were already in Finland. I think that a debt of gratitude is owed to the Finnish doctors for this.

A bomb had severed *Unter-Offizier* Assman's aircraft "white nine's" engine right at the point of take-off. The aircraft turned through 90 degrees and crashed into the forest. The pilot survived with only minor injuries. I went to have a look at this miracle landing after the raid. The aircraft had become entangled in the trees. The wings were hanging up in the trees, the fuselage had got stuck amongst the pines, and the cockpit was in one piece. The engine was on the runway.

3 July

In early hours of 3 July, the Soviet units received a new order for an offensive. The objective for the 30th Guards Corps was put as follows: "From the morning of 3 July 1944 launch a decisive offensive to the north and north-western directions, with the following immediate objective–to capture Ihantala, height 52.0 (4,800), 33.0, 36.0, and 28,0 and advance to a boundary leading to Lahdeaho, at height 22.0 (4,999), Usitorpa, and Risari."

On the night of 2–3 July, Finnish signals intelligence intercepted and deciphered an order for an advance, and interpreted it as follows: "The enemy is to launch a general offensive at 0550 hrs in the morning of 3 July 1944."

All the front line Soviet units were brought up to a state of full combat readiness. At 0430 hrs the Finnish preparations to beat back the Soviet offensive were completed. At 0450 hrs Finnish artillery launched a powerful attack on the possible locations in which the Soviet infantry could concentrate. The Finns however had made an error in terms of the start of the Soviet offensive. Only at 0745 hrs did the Soviet Air Force conduct a mass bombing raid on Finnish positions along the Vikkala–Ihantala front and up to three kilometres behind the Finnish lines. The Finns assessed the Soviet force at 200 bombers. An artillery barrage also began.

At 0835 hrs the Soviet bombers departed, and in keeping with tradition ground attack aircraft took their place. The artillery barrage continued, at 0910 hrs the Finns remarked on an especially heavy mortar attack on their own positions. During the course of the aviation and artillery barrage the majority of the Finnish soldiers in the area around the cemetery and the road junction in Ihantala abandoned their positions and escaped back behind their lines. The officers stopped them at their second line of defence in the area around the Korpela farmstead and sent them back.

At 0930 hrs A Finnish private, who had run to the 1st Gun Platoon's position in the 23rd Gun Company close to Vanhatorppa farmstead, reported to Lieutenant Hallavo that a large number of "shirkers" had been forced to get back combat positions on the height. Lieutenant Hallavo also ordered an infantry platoon, which had been covering his guns, to stand to the last man. At that moment Soviet mortar crews launched their second heavy mortar attack on Finnish positions.

At 0945 hrs the advance by Soviet infantry, who had been able to concentrate by night in a trench by the small river, began their offensive. Finnish infantry in the area around Vanhatorppa did open fire at some point, but again abandoned their positions. Hallavo could not stop this platoon, who were running as fast as they could back behind their own lines to the Oyala farmstead. Hallavo ordered all the anti-tank crews to occupy positions on the edge of the forest beyond Vanhatorppa and was able to halt the advance by the guards of the 64th Division some metres from his own positions. After this Soviet infantry directed their principal attack on Pyorakangas height, where by all accounts there were no more Finnish soldiers remaining since the height had been captured in no time.

At 1405 hrs the Finns began their counterattack on Pyorakangas height using the forces of two battalions supported by infantry, and some were sent to fire at close range. In a stubborn battle by 2000 hrs the Finns had succeeded in purging the height. The front line was stabilised at this point.

The Deputy Political Instructor of 188th Guards Regiment Guards Major Aram Arshakovich Silonyan had perished putting the regiment's 1st Battalion into action. The Chief of Staff of the 188th Regiment Guards Major Bondarev was injured, as was the last surviving Battalion Commander in the 188th Regiment – the Commander of the 3rd Battalion Guards Captain Tselykh. Bondarev and Tselykh refused to be evacuated and remained with the regiment. As a result of his heroic act, Guards Major Bondarev lost both his legs.

In the evening of 3 July the 30th Guards Rifle Corps began their withdrawal from the front and set off for the rear for rest and recuperation. This was easier said than done. It turned out that groups of Finnish machine gunners had infiltrated the logistics of the 190th Guards Regiment, and the units that were due to replace the guards of the 109th Rifle Division had to fight their way out to the front line. The fiercest of battles that thundered in the crags and forests north-east of Vyborg, which had lasted for ten days straight however, had already come to an end. The active phase of the battle for Tali-Ihantala was over.

4 July

By 4 July, the Soviet offensive in the direction of Ihantala had finally petered out. Losses in terms of personnel and materiel had been high, while the Finnish defence had become more organised and stronger. Finnish artillery had played an enormous role in the battle. Communications between the Observation Posts manned by the artillery reconnaissance troops and the firing positions, which had been very efficiently laid out, enabled the Finnish artillery to inflict concentrated attacks on agglomerations of Soviet infantry whilst the latter were still in the course of departing to their starting positions. Soviet artillery and aviation were not able to identify and suppress Finnish batteries behind the lines and concentrated on operations directly on the Finnish front line. In the course of the battle Finnish artillery had only incurred insignificant losses in terms of materiel and personnel and operated in minimal impact conditions as far as Soviet aviation was concerned. As the result of the battle showed, this was a serious, if not fateful error by Soviet Command.

Conclusions to the battle for Tali-Ihantala were summarised in the combat journal of the 30th Guards Rifle Corps as follows:

1) Despite the disadvantageous conditions for the deployment of the corps units, when the entry into battle was undertaken consecutively by regiment and on a very narrow sector of the front line, which allowed the advancing units of the enemy's orders of battle not only to fire using artillery and mortars but actually with automatic-machine gun fire–the corps units coped with the combat missions they had been given, which forced the enemy in doing so to hurriedly pull together against the advancing units, the units of seven infantry divisions, of which the corps units rendered the following lifeless: The 18th Infantry Division, four Jager battalions in Lagus' armoured division and the 13th Infantry Regiment, 17th Infantry Division which incurred heavy losses, together with the 30th Infantry Regiment from the 7th Infantry Division, the 50th Infantry Regiment from the 11th Infantry Division, the 2nd Jager Border Battalion from the 15th Infantry Division, the 1-2/35th Infantry Regiments from the 1st Infantry Division, and the 391st Tank Battalion.

2) At the end of eight days of fighting the corps units, which had overcome stubborn resistance from the enemy's defending units, and which to begin with consisted of six infantry battalions and by the end had swelled to 18 infantry battalions and a single tank battalion in Lagus' armoured division, expanded the stronghold north-west of Tali, creating, in so doing, advantageous conditions for the deployment of the forces of the 21st Army in the northern, and western directions.

3) The complexity of the theatre of military operations (the dense forest, stone boulders, the spurs, and the lack of roads), the fact that the flanks are exposed, the engineering fortifications and barriers in the form of forest barriers, barbed wire fences, stone and granite obstacles and a densely equipped firing arrangement–created exceptionally difficult conditions for conducting an offensive operation in terrain such as this.

4) The infantry shouldered the entire burden of the battle, fighting at close quarters and against an enemy stubbornly defending their position, on what were naturally advantageous boundaries that had been prepared in advance, and which enabled the enemy to shelter behind the folds of the terrain, covering the approaches to these boundaries using a system of a protective interdiction barrage made up of artillery and mortar fire, and with an Observation Post located the maximum distance from the front line, and in doing so ensuring that in the event of an infantry withdrawal, the infantry could be moved as planned, without reducing their fire power, around our advancing units.

5) Considering the complexities of the terrain and the enemy's defensive tactics, the corps units were forced to change their offensive tactics as well; from an offensive using continuous lines of infantry they changed to one that made use of attack groups and to manoeuvring tactics with the aim of capturing individual commanding heights and wedges into the enemy's orders of battle that were protected by engineering barriers and a densely equipped system of all manner of fire power, and to allocate reserves drawn from the battalions and regiments for the fight against troops armed with automatic weapons that had infiltrated the enemy's orders of battle, and which could eradicate these troops that were active behind the lines as they were taking out communications and command structures and had attempted to attack headquarters and artillery gun emplacements.

6) The decisive, persistent, and uninterrupted offensive operations by the corps units in the northern and north-western directions threatened a breach of the Finnish overall defensive system on the approaches to the state border, a breach of the latter and of the principal fortified line on this border, which protected the approaches to Finland's southern coastline, and this in turn forced the Finns, without counting the cost in any way, to hurriedly draw up

additional forces from other sectors of the front line, to create the best alignment, so that the advance of our troops could be stopped at any cost at the intermediate boundaries, before they had reached the state border.

7) At the cost of high losses the Finns succeeded in creating what was the best alignment in terms of firepower in the direction in which the corps units, that had lost their fire power up to this point, were active, and which was designed to block their decisive advance forward.

The Tali-Ihantala battle had come to an end. The German *Kuhmey* Air Wing had played an important role in it. Over the period from 22 June–6 July 1944 the German dive-bombers flew 1,028 combat sorties and dropped 47tonnes of bombs on the Soviet advancing units. The Finnish Air Force in this period dropped half the number of bombs–in total just 190tonnes–in the area around Tali-Ihantala. The daily destruction of the bridge at Tali station, on which the supply of the entire Soviet alignment depended, as well as the constant attacks on the supply route made the offensive much more difficult.

The Finns call this the largest battle in the history of Scandinavia.

21st Army Losses

Day of battle	**25 June 1944**	**26 June 1944**	**27 June 1944**	**28 June 1944**	**29 June 1944**	**30 June 1944**	**01–07 June 1944**[1]
Killed	400	508	427	650	711	402	No information
Injured	1,690	2,970	2,298	3,089	2,769	1,733	No information
Vanished without trace	22	28	17	12	28	15	No information
TOTAL	2,112	3,506	2,742	3,751	3,508	2,150	2,988
						TOTAL	20,757

The Finns assessed their losses at 1,100 men killed, 1,100 missing and 6,300 wounded.

1 The losses for the 30th Guards Rifle Corps for 1–3 July 1944 have been included in the Army losses for the first ten days in June.

24

Amphibious Assault, 7-9 July

On the Soviet side, the problems of naval and land forces cooperation continued. A document concerning the 224th Rifle Division's amphibious landing operations on 7, 8 and 9 July 1944 is cited in full below:

> Over the course of 7 July 1944 the division conducted local operations:
>
> The 185th Rifle Regiment–two companies to capture HALENEN-SARI,
>
> The 143rd Rifle Regiment–a single company to capture the KARPPILA peninsula.
>
> The start of the operation for both amphibious assaults was planned for 1200 hrs on 7 July 1944. Due to the absence of BShK KMOR vessels the timescale for the assault was postponed until 1800 hrs. In fact the vessels arrived between 1900–1920 hrs on 7 July 1944 but they were not the full complement. Instead of what should have been there–according to the calculation, the 185th Rifle Regiment–a single tender and six ZIS, while the 143rd Rifle Regiment–one tender and five ZIS, what actually arrived was as follows: the 185th Rifle Regiment–one tender and five ZIS, furthermore one of these was unserviceable, the 143rd Rifle Regiment–a single tender and three ZIS.
>
> The BShK vessels were not brought under the overall leadership of the commander of the amphibious landing. The group of smoke screen generating launches had their own commander, the group of ZIS had their own commander, and the commanders of the tenders did not know which was their flagship vessel.
>
> Due to the late arrival of the KMOR vessels and the delay to the amphibious landing (which was in view of the poor availability of the vessels) the cooperation between the KMOR aircraft was lost, they began to undertake air strikes on the targets of the amphibious assaults at 1930 hrs, while at that time the subdivisions were just being loaded onto the ships.
>
> The vessels departed in a disorganised fashion at 2030 hrs to the area around the bay between the islands: RAVAN-SAARI, HIETA-SAARI, RAHKA-SAARI, ESI-SAARI, KURIN-SAARI. The vessels, which had no overall command, spread out around the bay. The enemy, seeing the confusion, began to rain a fierce fire down on amphibious assault. The element of surprise was lost. Thanks to the intervention of NO-1 under Major Alyonnikh, who had sailed out into the bay in a launch, the vessels adopted their order of battle at 2055 hrs and departed to the amphibious landing points where they were to land the troops.
>
> At 2120 hrs the 185th Rifle Regiment's amphibious assault landed on HALENEN island. As a result of the night battle by 0320 hrs on 8 July 1944 they had captured the southern and central parts of the island. At 0320 hrs the enemy launched a counterattack

with forces of up to a battalion in size from the northern and eastern parts of the island, forcing the assault troops into an encirclement. The assault troops, incurring heavy losses, began to pull back in the direction of the island of HANNUSTIEN-SARI and at 0600 hrs, leaving both islands, they crossed onto the island of PENIN-LUOTO, It subsequently emerged that a group of these same assault troops in a collective of around 15 men had up until this time been on the south-eastern part of HANNUSTIEN-SAARI. A single officer had been sent there to organise a defence.

The assault troops from the 143rd Rifle Regiment, who had incurred losses in the sea (the tender had been taken out of action, and one ZIS had caught fire), did not land on the KARPILLA peninsula. After leaving two ZIS with their commander on his initiative when landing his infantry on the island of HALENEN-SARI in the 185th Rifle Regiment's area of operations. Subsequently a group from the 143rd Rifle Regiment participated in the battles on HALENEN-SARI jointly with the amphibious assault troops of the 185th Rifle Regiment.

THE COURSE OF THE BATTLE TO CAPTURE THE ISLANDS: SYRJASAARI, PUNKISAARI, and the HARJAU-HIEMI HEADLAND (this refers to Harjuniemi) on 9 July 1944.

The execution of the operation fell to the 143rd Rifle Regiment, for which two assault detachments were formed underneath the regiment, each of which was a rifle battalion in size, the rifle companies of which contained between 40–50 men. In order to augment the detachments a single rifle company from the 185th Rifle Regiment was placed at the disposal of the 143rd Rifle Regiment from the evening of 8 July 1944.

The deployment of the detachment across the Gulf was planned as follows:

a) 1st Detachment (2nd Battalion /143rd Rifle Regiment)–on six BShK tenders,

b) 2nd Detachment (3rd Battalion/143rd Rifle Regiment)–on sapper craft and pre-prepared rafts.

By the close of the day on 8 July 1944 both detachments had been taken out to the landing sites:

a) 2nd Battalion/143rd Rifle Regiment–the forested areas of the island of ESI-SAARI.

b) 3rd Battalion /143rd Rifle Regiment– to the bay in the south-eastern part of the island of RAHKA-SAARI.

The start of the 2nd Battalion 143rd Rifle Regiment's amphibious landing in BShK vessels was intended for 0700 hrs on 9 July 1944. In reality the tenders only began to be loaded at 0710 hrs. The excellent organisation of the amphibious landing meant that the vessels could depart for the outer harbour on schedule. At 0900 hrs the battalion departed in the direction of the HARJAU-HIEMI HEADLAND with the objective of landing on its western shore and capturing it.

As they approached the gulf between the islands: HIETA-SAARI and RAHKA-SAARI the amphibious assault was subject to long-range artillery fire. Incurring losses, the assault continued its movement towards the landing site.

At 1000 hrs as the amphibious assault reached the HARJAU-HIEMI headland and as it was turning to make the landing the enemy began to strafe the vessels with concentrated long-range artillery fire, as well as close-range guns, and heavy infantry fire. The amphibious assault incurred heavy losses in terms of personnel and materiel: of the six tenders two of

> them were burnt out, four were taken out of action, of which only two returned successfully at 1230 hrs back to the landing site. The personnel 89 men were either killed or drowned, 29 were injured, and a further 29 men were missing without trace. In total the losses amounted to 147 men.
>
> One of the tenders, which had come close in to the shore, at 1040 hrs did successfully land a group of around 25 men on HARJAU-HIEMI, who were immediately wiped out by the enemy, but some of them were taken prisoner.
>
> The 3rd Battalion, 143rd Rifle Regiment was tasked with landing on SYRYA-SARI island, and subsequently on capturing this island, to cross over to PYNKI-SAARI.
>
> In the course of the landing using sapper craft at 1000 hrs they were subject to massive artillery and mortar fire and were strafed by oblique machine gun fire from the island of PUNKI-SAARI. The landing was completed. The element of surprise however was lost.
>
> Subsequent attempts by the battalion, which were repeated again several times up until 1200 hrs, were also unsuccessful and were beaten back by the huge density of all the enemy's different types of weaponry.
>
> Overall conclusions:
>
> 1) The division did not manage to complete its mission in full, capturing only the principal islands, and not purging the coastal islands.
>
> 2) The success of the operation to capture the islands of Suonion-Saari, Esi-Saari, Uran-Saari and others was decided by artillery fire and aviation and by rapid infantry movements, that is to say by cooperation with all the branches of the armed forces.
>
> 3) The failures of 7 and 9 July can be explained by inadequate organisation in support of cooperation between the branches of the armed forces and the lack of reserves, and also by massive enemy artillery and mortar fire, and the fact that the battery could not be taken out.

According to Finnish records, the situation on Hapenensaari looked as follows. When the Soviet amphibious assault began the next exchange of Finnish and German units was taking place. The battle on the island raged all night long, and by morning on 8 July the Soviet amphibious assault, which, based on Finnish assessments was up to two companies in size, was forced into the sea. The bodies of the fallen Soviet assault troops were laid behind a stone wall on the Hapenensaari estate.

On 9 July, the last attempt by the 59th Army to land amphibious troops on the north-western shore of the Gulf of Finland began. The 224th Division could only send a single battalion to the Haruniemi headland. Only one tender reached the headland: the 25 assault troops that landed on the shore, were either killed or taken prisoner by the Germans within one hour. The battalion's total losses amounted to around 150 men.

The assault detachment, which had set off for the Niemilautta headland from Teikarinsaari island only managed to capture Koivusaari island, in other locations attempts to land amphibious assault troops were beaten back by the Germans. After 9 July active combat operations by the 59th Army in the archipelago came to an end.

Senior Lieutenant Vladimir Mikhaylovich Spindler, Assistant to the Chief of the Intelligence Staff of the 406th Rifle Regiment, 124th Rifle Division:

> On that day on 4 in the morning the Commander of the 59th Army ordered a regiment to be made available to him personally, so that he could command it. Our regiment was allocated, the 406th Rifles. Neither the Divisional Commander nor the divisional headquarters had commanded us, as our Divisional Commander wrote in two pages in his biography. The

Army Commander himself Korovnikov personally came to see us in the afternoon of the 4 July, when the 224th Division's operation had ended unsuccessfully. Approximately two battalions of troops were loaded onto the vessels as well as an intelligence platoon, which I, naturally, headed. On the right flank was the intelligence platoon–we had a launch–and the 1st and 2nd Battalions were in a tender. Furthemore. We were not told anything concrete. We were to land there, where we were taken. We knew nothing of where we were going. We departed Vysotska, and formed into a column, we had not reached Teikarisaari, some 10 kilometres away, when we were stopped. Abeam the islands we began to form into a line and stop. The Army Commander was in personal command of us–when he accepted command of us he was already in an agitated state following a failure that morning, and now how he was going to make the best use of was weighing on his conscience. He used everything that he had–aircraft and artillery. When we pulled up opposite the island a powerful artillery barrage began. This barrage lasted for approximately 20 minutes. We stood there, the sun was beating down on us–it was approximately 1400 hrs in the afternoon and we could see where our shells were landing, and how our aircraft were diving. They destroyed everything that they could. The explosions from the bombs and shells rose up taller than the trees. There the island had forests, and the crags, in the northern part there were lowlands and a settlement was located there. The water and the shoreline were also attacked so as to destroy the mines.

As soon as the barrage stopped we moved forward. On each vessel–the Commander of the Baltic Fleet told us where we were going, where we were to be landed. It turned out that the intelligence troops had been landed on the right flank so as to secure a bridgehead. To the left of the island was a bay—the first attack battalion in the tenders was to land there with us providing covering fire, then they were to cross the island and turn north. The third battalion landed next to them, with the same objective, they were to turn to the south.

I, the Commander of the intelligence troops, had an agreement with the Commander of the launches–as soon as he knew he was not able to approach the landing site he was to let me know, and I would give the command and we would jump into the water. When he gave me that signal I gave the order to jump, several of our men jumped, and immersed themselves in water. I gave him such an angry look, he made a few more turns. Then he stopped, and we all jumped out, including me, the Deputy Regimental Commander Major Taran was also with us in the water. The shore was some 10–15m away. We were met by machine gun and automatic weapon fire, and only four of us made it to the shore–me and three other intelligence troops. There were rocks on the shoreline, and we went from rock to rock and we still had to hold our automatic rifle. The rest were either killed or injured. The launch had landed us there and immediately pulled back. The tenders remained in position, but the launch departed.

Four of us made it onto the shore, and I was lucky, there were four Finns left there who were still alive, they lifted their arms above their heads and surrendered. That meant I already had prisoners, and nobody was firing at me–which meant I could capture the stronghold. Sometime later, maybe half an hour later, a soldier came running up from the Commander of the First Battalion and reported to me that I was the only officer still left, and that I had three intelligence men with me and nobody else. The Deputy Regimental Commander was with us–he had sat on the launch at the last moment. I did not know if he had sat on the craft himself or if he was ordered to join our boat. But at 1600 hrs he was seriously injured. In the Medical Battalion in the area around Johannes he was buried. He had died of his injuries. That's how events turned out for me. I had four Finns, who did not speak Russian, I could not interrogate them. It fell quiet, it was as though the war had ended. That soldier came running up to me again, half hunched over, carrying an automatic rifle: "The Commander of the 1st Battalion, Captain Mashchenko, ordered me to tell you that he has reached the settlement to the north of the island, but the Finns are sending over reinforcements." I responded to him automatically: "Tell the Battalion Commander that he should dig in on the boundary that he has reached and that he should be ready for a possible counterattack by the Finns." In other words, he should gather together all his troops and wait. That silence again. The soldier ran off. I looked around–my Finns were beginning to stir and were taking amongst themselves–that meant they had understood what that soldier had said to me! When I had tried to interrogate them they had not understood Russian at all, but now I could see that they understood. They were worried, and I could understand their concern–if the Finns were to counterattack now and they were released, they would be asked why they had given themselves up and not killed us all and reported back that we had landed. As soon as I understood this I decided to split them up into two groups. They, as far as I understood, were an officer, a sergeant and two young rank and file soldiers. I split them into two groups–I showed them: you and me over there, and you two stay here. I detailed one of my intelligence men to keep watch on each group, armed with an automatic rifle.

Silence again, the sun was shining. Suddenly I looked–from the Trangzund direction the same launch was approaching, the one that had landed us. Moreover it was moving in a zigzag pattern, dodging any possible fire. I got up to my full height and waved at it–over here, man, over here. When he saw me he went straight for the shore, and on board it turned out was the Divisional Commander Colonel Papchenko. When the launch had landed us and departed we did not have any communication, no radio, nothing. The other two battalions did not have any either. Why had that soldier come running up to me: "The Battalion Commander has ordered me that I tell you..?"–because the Battalion Commander had thought that the Deputy Regimental Commander was with me, a higher ranking officer. He however was seriously injured, and what was more, apart from me there were no officers at all.

I could not immediately grasp–why would Papchenko come to see me?? Evidently when the launch had landed us and returned, the Army Commander had said to Papchenko: "They do not have any communications, we do not know anything, so go back in the launch to where you landed the intelligence troops." When Papchenko arrived he brought with him the divisional intelligence troops, and a radio. We had only just set up the radio and he ordered another regiment to be sent here immediately. The arrival of our troops began, and a second battalion approached. In other words, the situation that had unfolded on Igriv was the reason why the Finns had abandoned it. I have an extract from a book written by a Swedish historian who had studied the war on the eastern front, and he had written in this extract, that the Finns had abandoned that location using anything they could find–some on boats, while other swam. When a further regiment arrived, the Finns felt that they would be defeated, and ran away. They did not run away without a fight though, since our division incurred heavy losses for the entire duration of these battles–thousands of men killed and injured, for the most part in our regiment. The Finnish and German navies also began to pull back to their own lines.

We had officially liberated Teikarsaari by 2100 hrs on 5 July. The neighbouring island of Mellansaari (today this is known as Kormovoy) was also liberated. Thus on 4 and 5 we

> liberated these islands, and on the 6 July we occupied all the other islands that were in the Gulf between the southern section and the mainland. The last island remained, which was called Lamasaari. This was quite a small island, circular, with a diameter of 600m, but it was close to the mainland. The 1st Attack Battalion were sent to this island on two tenders with the objective of skirting round Mellansaari and landing on this final island. On the night of 6–7 July we could all see that the Finns had taken these two tenders out of action and they had gone to the bottom. It was then that the head of intelligence in the division, in giving me an order, asked me: "Did you see how they went down?" "I did" "So is it the Finns or our own forces on this island? Here take a radio, and a dinghy, go and see tonight who it is on that island. If it is the Finns then we will land another company there." We got into the dinghy, a group of four of us in a four-oared dinghy–me and three of my intelligence soldiers–and departed. We are on our way, it was night, and suddenly I looked I looked up–a launch was already coming up out of the water, and sitting in it, like hares in the Grandfather Mazai and his hares, were our own soldiers. We could not come any closer since they would not ask me permission but would throw themselves into the dinghy. There were several men there who were form our troops, from tenders that had gone down. "Comrade Senior Lieutenant, take us with you!" I told him: "I am going there, where you didn't go, what do you think, is that our troops there of Finns?" "We can't be sure, take us with you" "I can't take you with me, but if everything is okay there, I will send a boat that will pick you up."
>
> Approximately 150m from the island the Finns somehow noticed and started to fire, evidently, using their mortars. Alongside the dinghy were columns of water but there were no direct hits. I ordered the crew to get onto their oars, and we emerged onto dry land on then move, and once on the land I could see–figures of men! I shouted loudly "Are you Slavs?!"–and they answered me in Russian. It turned out that there were around 10 of our troops on the island from tenders that had gone down. We went over the island with a fine tooth-comb and there were no Finns there at all. I relayed this by radio and sent a boat to the rock. The company had to wait for three days and I took steps to defend the island. The Finns however made no attempt to take back the island, and by 9–10 July an order came through–to cease combat activity. This was Govorov's order. The 59th Army were intending to liberate these islands, and land on the mainland–and from there it's a direct road to Helsinki. Finland pulled out of the war and entered negotiations. We remained there–whoever was alive was alive, and whoever had been killed had been killed. The entire division, along with the artillery regiment, and everyone who had been on these islands. I relayed the figures for 10 July back from the islands to Trangzund, where our medical battalion was located. I appeared there to the surprise of many–"we saw your body, but you're alive." It was a miracle to still be alive there, and not be injured, even more so that I still could not swim very well. I did though remain whole and undamaged. All these islands were occupied by the remains of the 224th Division for garrison duty, we were taken to a location near Vyborg.

The outcome of the battle in the archipelago turned out to be the same as the other battles in the second stage of the Vyborg Offensive Operation. After initial success, incurring losses, the Soviet side purged some of the islands of the Finns, while on the other hand–there was no question of capturing Lappeenranty. The 224th and 124th Rifle Divisions incurred heavy losses, and there was no strength of will left to continue the offensive. On the Finnish side the fresh German 122nd Infantry Division appeared with powerful artillery. The Finns had not even been able to put all their reserves into battle on the shores of the Vyborg Bay. The Front in the bay had stabilised prior to the signing of the armistice on 4 September 1944.

It has to be said that the 59th Army was only an army on paper. During the course of the operation in Vyborg Bay the army had activated all its divisions, with an overall strength of around 10,000 men; the 80th Rifle Division, which had arrived on the front line on 4–5 July did not participate in the battle. The 124th Rifle Division all but failed to activate their 781st Rifle Regiment. The 260th Separate Marine Infantry Brigade, which is often mentioned by Finnish historians as coming under the 59th Army, took part only in the first half of the landing on Teikarinsaari. Thus the fragment in Mannerheim's memoirs in which the Marshal writes about the powerful forces of the 59th Army is a significant exaggeration:

> The enemy still continued to forego their objective of opening the gates to Southern Finland. When the advance on the Ihantala sector came to nought, the enemy began to advance via Vyborg Bay on the Vuoksi front in the area around Vuosalmi, with the obvious objective of a pincer movement to encircle our defensive positions between Vyborg and Vuoksi.
> From these two operations the first, undoubtedly, was the more dangerous, since from the last two weeks of June it became clear that the Russians had also gone on the offensive on the maritime front using the forces of the 59th Army, which had only recently been redeployed to the Karelian Isthmus.

The 224th Rifle Division lost in these battles from 30 June-9 July 2,623 men, of which 1,280 had been killed, 1,167 injured, and 176 were missing without trace. On 25 June there were 5,331 men in the division, that is to say losses amounted to half the personnel. The 124th Rifle Division's losses in this period amounted to 500 men.

25

Right Flank of the Soviet Attack: Battle Between the Lakes, 20-27 June

Following the losses on the VT line in the centre of the Karelian Isthmus the depleted Finnish units began an organised retreat to an advantageous defensive line–the River Vuoksi. The retreat was covered by a rear guard action. The 23rd Army advanced forward slowly, carefully, which was a cause for concern for the Army Commander Lieutenant-General Cherepanov. On 17 June, the army was subordinated: the Directorate of the 6th Rifle Corps, the 13th Rifle Division and other augmenting units. On 18 June the 6th Rifle Corps prepared to storm the Mannerheim Line in the Muolaa fortified district–despite the fact that all the structures on this line had lain in ruins for four years prior to that date! The legendary line was captured surprisingly quickly, which led to an even greater euphoria at army headquarters. In one of the 23rd Army's documents dated 20 June 1944 the following can be read: "The enemy, paralysed in the preceding battles, is in no fit state to offer any serious resistance."

That same day army headquarters decided that the Finns can abandon their positions on the northern bank of the Vuoksi River and withdraw to the north towards Saimaa. In connection with this an order was issued to pursue them. Army Command understood the importance of supporting the fast pace of the advance, which was reflected in a coded telegram sent to corps commanders:

> Coded telegram No. 1075 dated 20 June 1944
> To the Commander of the 98th Rifle Corps
> To the Commander of the 6th Rifle Corps
> Copy: To the Chief of Staff of the Leningrad Front
> Today the neighbour on the left flank is going to attack Vyborg.
> To defend the neighbour's flank, it is especially important not to let the enemy draw up any reserves from the north from the Vuoksi region, so as to prevent the enemy from strengthening their position and gaining a stronghold, I hereby order:
> 1) That today's objective be completed on time
> 2) To report on the course of the combat operations at the appointed times
> 3) To report that this has been completed by 2300 hrs on 20 June 1944.
> Cherepanov, Shamanin

According to an order issued by the Leningrad Front the 23rd Army by the 20 June was to advance to a line from Vyborg–Antrea. By 21 June, the forward 6th Rifle Corps was to have advanced to a line from Kuukauppi–Kuparsaari. By 23 June, the corps units were to have captured crossing points across the Vuoksi in Antrea and north of Yaski. Then the 98th Rifle Corps was to join the battle, which crossed the Vuoksi and took the offensive on to Hiintola along with another rifle corps.

Army command had assigned the right flank in the area around Kyulya–Paakolla–Yajurjalia secondary importance at that point in time. Evidently Cherepanov thought that the units of the 2nd Infantry Division had incurred heavy losses in battles on the VT line, and they were scattered and demoralised. Only the 281st Rifle Division attacked the 2nd Division on 20 June with the objective of "purging the southern bank of the Vuoksi of the scattered Finnish units." This assessment of the enemy's forces and of their options was completely incorrect.

The principal blow was inflicted by the 6th Rifle Corps using the forces of the 13th and 382nd Rifle divisions along with augmenting units–the 46th Guards Heavy Tank Regiment, the 226th Separate Tank Regiment, and the self-propelled guns of the 938th and 952nd Regiments and the artillery units–the 47th Gun Artillery Brigade and the 96th Heavy Howitzer Artillery Brigade.

On 20 June Soviet regiments moved forward. The 13th Rifle Division captured the settlement of Lyykyla and continued the advance to Naatala, having encountered fierce resistance from the enemy in the evening. The division's losses for the day were 19 men killed and 134 injured.

The 382nd Novgorod Division captured Kaantuma and carried the offensive forward along the only road to Kuukauppi. At 2030 hrs on 20 June the 226th Tank Regiment received an order from the Commander of the 6th Corps to pursue the retreating enemy with a tank borne assault along the Heinjoki–Kaaanjuma road, and to advance to a boundary from Kuukauppi and capture the crossing over the Vuoksi. At that moment there were nine combat capable T-34s remaining in the regiment, and five tanks in for running repairs, while another three tanks required a medium repair.

According to the information provided by the tank crews nine "thirty-fours" with infantry from the 1,269th Rifle Regiment, along with a sapper platoon and the self-propelled guns of the 938th Self-Propelled Artillery Regiment were able to capture Kaaantjuma by 0200 hrs on 21 June. The terrain for tanks was all but impassable outside the confines of the roads due to the large boulders. One tank was blown up by a mine. Further on the advance was stopped, after it had encountered an organised Finnish defence.

The objective for the day–was to advance to a boundary from Kavantsaari–Kuukauppi– but this turned out to be impossible. Soviet attacks throughout 23 June were also beaten back. "Waging stubborn battles for every boulder, the division's subdivisions moved approximately 150–200m." This was how the outcome of the day was recorded in the Combat Journal of the 1,267th Regiment, 382nd Rifle Division. In the evening and that night the regiment fought off eight Finnish counterattacks. The Commander of the 3rd Rifle Battalion Major Miroshnikov was killed in the battle.

Units of the 6th Rifle Corps spent the 24 June preparing for the new offensive. The 177th Rifle Division had moved up to the front line and were a fresh division, with whom the tank crews were due to capture height 39.6 and Repola, subsequently taking the offensive forward to Kuukauppi.

At 0620 hrs on 26 June the 502nd Regiment and the tank crews of the 226th Regiment began their offensive. Five tanks crossed the crossing point at Esi-Lampi at high speed and rushed up to the height. In front of the height the "thirty-fours" encountered a minefield, and a tank trap, as well as the Finnish anti-tank guns that had not been suppressed. As a result of all this all five tanks were taken out of action or were blown up by mines. The crossing was again destroyed by Finnish fire. The tank crews and intelligence crews had been trying to find ways around the crossings all this time but had not found any alternative–on all sides there was nothing but marsh and boulders.

Despite the superhuman efforts of the sappers, who had worked on the crossing under a hail of shells, the remaining tanks stood idle before it up until 1300 hrs. Only at that time did two tanks pass over the crossing and proceed onwards towards height 39.6. The 502nd Rifle Regiment's infantry had incurred losses close to the channel, and had dug in under fierce Finnish fire, and were in no position to capture the height. The highway had still not been cleared of mines and the tanks could not move any further along it. The tank crews fired intensively from their location on their own, without infantry. The Combat Journal of the 177th Rifle Division described all the difficulties of the battle close to the lakes:

> The sector, which had been selected by the 502nd Rifle Regiment for their combat operations was a defile between lakes, on the right was Lake Kaltovesi, and on the left were lakes Oisin-Lampi, and Vel-Lampi, and to the left of those were the lakes Yannerpun-Yarvi and Lake Noskuon-Selka that were linked together as were the majority of the lakes of Finland, by channels and ditches.
>
> The terrain between the lakes–is very undulating, is covered by forest and huge boulders, in fact the very landscape itself was designed for undertaking defensive operations, where every boulder represented a shelter, which would not concede at all to any artificial barriers.
>
> It has to be said that the enemy, aside from making use of fire from a large number of artillery batteries and mortars, made widespread use of sniper fire, the effectiveness of which was very significant and the units incurred very high losses as a result of this. At that same time the snipers, despite the fierce artillery fire were almost invulnerable, as they were hiding in crevices under the boulders.

On three occasions the German *Kuhlmey* Air Wing attacked the crossing and the tank crew's orders of battle using between 10-15 Ju 87 dive-bombers.

In the course of one day on 26 June the tank crews lost four tanks that were burnt out, two "thirty-fours" were blown up by mines. Six tanks were taken out of action, and a single tank crewman went missing without trace. In the 226th Regiment following this battle there were three combat capable T-34s.

In total in the battles for the crossing from Kaantuma–Repola the irrevocable losses for the armoured tank forces as far as tanks that were burnt out were concerned, amounted to: four T-34s, four KVs, and a single SU-76. Two further "thirty-fours" required heavy repairs. In the area around Naatala two SU-76 self-propelled guns were taken out of action.

Regiments of 382nd Rifle Division were able to advance forward by a kilometre or so. The battles among the boulders were more akin to combat activity in a built up area and were constantly transferring to hand to hand fighting using hand grenades and anything that was to hand. The Commanders of the 23rd Army remained unhappy with such modest success, and on 27 June Colonel Yefimenko was relieved of his command of the 382nd Division. He was replaced by Colonel Zolotarev.

Following the failure of the offensive of 26–27 June the Command of the 23rd Army refused to undertake an offensive in this direction and drew their gaze away onto the army's right flank where, as fierce fighting was raging on the southern bank of the Vuoksi River. The army's depleted tank units withdrew from the battle near Kaantumaa and set off for the south-east. Both sides prepared for the next round. By 4 July, the battle on the Vuokse was ready to flare up with renewed fighting.

26

21-25 June

Part of the 23rd Army had advanced out to the dunes on the southern bank of the Vuoksi by 20 June 1944. As with the neighbouring 21st Army's units the mood in the headquarters was upbeat. It appeared that the Finns were beaten and would run away. In connection with this the 98th Rifle Corps received an order to take the height on the southern bank of the Vuoksi on the move, ford the river and continue the offensive against Raisala, Sairala and Antrea. In Soviet military documents the tone is more of "purging the heights," rather than "storming them". The commander of 98th Corps, General Shvetsov, only allocated the 281st Rifle Division to this, which furthermore had been depleted in the Siiranmyaki fighting. On 21 June 1944, the division's regiments went on the offensive attacking the height without tanks. The sappers still built a bridge for tanks across the River Salmenkaita, and another five kilometres south of Vuoksi. The 317th Rifle Regiment from the 142nd Rifle Division were located on the approaches to the front line.

In the very first attack the Commander of the 281st Division noted a significant augmentation of the intensity of the artillery and mortar fire from the Finns. The Combat Journal of the 317th Rifle Regiment described this as follows: "As the regiment approached the heights the 281st Rifle Division stormed the heights. The enemy opened up with frenzied artillery fire, which continued for about an hour."

After the first unsuccessful attack on the heights, on the evening of 21 June the Commander of the 23rd Army Cherepanov wrote in an irritated manner to Shvetsov and Panichkin:

> Up until today you have failed to fulfill my order to liquidate the enemy on the right bank of the River Vuoksi, specifically in the Ayrappa–Niemila sector.
>
> I order you to: by 2400 00 minutes on 21 June 1944 to liquidate the enemy in this sector, comb the forests between the River Vuoksi, Lait-salmi Bay, Heinioki, and the River Salmenkaita.

The Finns consecutively beat back attacks from the 281st Division as well as the 317th Rifle Regiment that was attached to it on 21, 22, and 23 June 1944. On 22 June the Commander of the 1,066th Rifle Regiment Major Kalachev was killed. The Commander of the 3rd Rifle Battalion of the same regiment Srup Moiseyevich Mogutskiy was seriously injured and died of his wounds.

The attacks, which resumed on 25 June, did not lead to success either. On at 0930 hrs on 26 June did the 317th Regiment and the KV tanks of the 46th Guards Regiment manage to climb onto height 44.5 but they only spent one and a half hours on the height itself. By the end of the day on 25 June only 20–25 men were left in each of the battalions of the 1,066th and 317th Rifle Regiments.

Three decades later Major A. Makarov, the Head of Artillery in the 317th Rifle Regiment in a letter to the lads from the Zhitkov Secondary School recalled this battle as follows:

> The battles for the heights on the right bank of the Vuoksi were initially fought by our 317th Rifle Regiment [from the 92nd Rifle Division–author's note], which at that time was subordinate to another division (I don't remember their number).
>
> It has to be said that by that time our regiment in the course of the battles on the Karelian Isthmus had already incurred heavy losses.
>
> The approaches to the heights at that time were open, there was a meadow and a field in front of them. Only in one spot did a small forest of low-level trees lead to the heights along a wide path. The enemy would very often launch artillery attacks along this path. It was for good reason that this forest was nicknamed the "Death glade" back in those days.
>
> Our regiment attempted to attack these heights on a number of occasions, but they could not achieve success since our forces were woefully insufficient, and the terrain was exceptionally well suited to defence: a mass of large boulders provided the opportunity for personnel to be well hidden and protected them from our fire. At that time though it was very easy to open fire because of these natural shelters. The steep cliffs that are angled towards the river were almost never hit by artillery fire and the conditions for observation for the artillery, which were supporting our infantry, were poor and the visibility was very limited. The heights provided complete cover for the river and the enemy crossing points. The terrain prohibited any possibility of using tanks.
>
> Then our regiment, which had by that time incurred heavy losses, was pulled back to the second echelon and returned to our own division..

Soviet forces also attempted to cross the Vuoksi further west. A reconnaissance group from the 203rd Regiment, 92nd Rifle Division, the 5th Company, 22nd Rifle Regiment under Senior Lieutenant Dmitriy Yermolayevich Kolin (20 soldiers) crossed to the northern part of the island of Vitsaari and dug in there. It proved impossible however to redeploy any reinforcements to this small group of daredevils. After the beginning of the Finnish counterattack a dry entry appeared in the regiment's Combat Journal: "Radio-communications with the reconnaissance group have been lost." All further attempts by the 92nd Rifle Division to cross at Vitsaari were beaten back by Finnish artillery, mortar, and machine gun fire.

The reconnaissance group were recorded as missing without trace while in the documents held by the Ministry of Defence of the Russian Federation they are still listed as such today. The island of Vitsaari nowadays is known as a "Hero" island (it is thought it was given this name in honour of Hero of the Soviet Union Klimov, and the soldiers who perished here in 1940). In the Soviet period this island became a popular place for canoeists to spend the night. The author of this book also spent a night on the island at the beginning of the 1980s when he was ten. The Russian name for the island–the "Hero" island–is apt, if one recalls what happened here in 1944:

And in this whole world,
Until the end of its days,
There are neither buttonholes, nor badges of rank,
Left of my tunic

The men of 22nd Regiment should remember these lines as they pass the island in canoes or in launches, when they see the scars of war on the island–the solid Finnish trenches, overgrown with moss and bilberry. The burial site of the Soviet reconnaissance group to this day has never been found....Did they even have a burial site? The Finns could just have cast bodies of the fallen into the river. All of these skirmishes were just a prelude to the bloodiest battle on the Isthmus in the summer of 1944.

In the days that followed (24-25 June), no serious attacks on the heights by Soviet units were undertaken. Both sides regrouped and drew up their reserves. During the course of the hiatus that had arisen the Finns conducted a rotation of the units on the stronghold. In the sector under combat group "V" the 12th Separate Battalion and the 3rd Battalion "the tribal brothers" handed over their sector to the 2nd Battalion, 49th Regiment. This exchange of units took place on the night of 22–23 June. In the defensive sector under combat group "E" on 26 June the remaining subdivisions of the 1st Battalion, 7th Regiment arrived at the stronghold. Some of the subdivisions of the 2nd Battalion, 7th Regiment withdrew from the stronghold. The 6th and 7th Companies remained in the reserve in this defence sector.

In the daytime on 26 June an order arrived at the headquarters of the Commander of the 23rd Army:

> To the Commander of the 98th Rifle Corps
>
> Copy to the Chief of Staff Lenfront
>
> The actions by the units of the 281st Rifle Division and the 92nd Rifle Division are very half-hearted. At that sort of pace your execution of the order to liquidate the enemy stronghold on the western bank of the Vuoksi is under threat.
>
> The Army Commander has issued strict orders as follows:
>
> 1) Objective 1. The liquidation the stronghold is to be completed by the end of the day on 26 June 1944 whatever happens.
>
> 2) Bring all available units from the 281st Rifle Division and the 92nd Rifle Division into the battle as well as all the artillery and tanks.
>
> 3. 3) Demand of the commanders of the formations and units that they increase the pace of the advance and throw the enemy into the river by the end of the day.
>
> Bolshakov Goldzberg

The Soviet assault on the heights in the first few hours of 27 June did not happen either. Fierce resistance from the Finns in the area around Tali station led to the units of the 21st Army not being able to achieve a rapid breakthrough or an advance to Laapeenrantu. As a result on 29 June 1944 Marshal Govorov decided to repeat the approach that had already been deployed in the course of the breakthrough of the "VT line." The Commander of the Leningrad Front issued an order to inflict crushing blows east and west of Ihantala. The 23rd Army was supposed to break through the Finnish defence at Vuoksi and continue the advance to Raisala (Melnikovo) and Antrea (Kamennogorsk).

The prevarication on 98th Corps in front of the height over the course of the 12 days led to reshuffles in Soviet Command. On 3 July Govorov removed the Commander of the 23rd Army General Cherepanov from his post and replaced him with Major-General Shvetsov, who up until that time had commanded the 98th Corps.

Preparations for an overall storming of the heights began. Two divisions were to capture the height and ford the Vuoksi–the 281st attacked Rommyaki height, while the 381st Rifle Division attacked the area around the ferry crossing and Mansikkamyaki height and were supported by tanks and self-propelled artillery. By evening on 3 July the 281st and 381st Rifle Divisions had completed their concentration and were ready for the attack.

That same day the Commander of the 29th Separate Punishment Company Captain Pyotr Afanasyevich Kryuchkov was shot for failing to execute a military order. The Company was attached to the 281st Rifle Division and from 29 June had been attacking the height unsuccessfully. The reason for the shooting is unclear to this day; the author suggests however that the Captain refused to carry out the order to attack the heights on 4 July or expressed his personal opinion, for which he paid with his life. We note that in some documents Captain Kryuchkov is listed as having been killed, whilst others as shot.

The 281st Rifle Division with the support of the 29th Separate Punishment Battalions, from the 938th Self-Propelled Artillery Regiment as well as engineering units were supposed to capture the Romjakki height and then cross the Vuoksi as a third echelon regiment, advancing up to marker 26.3 and digging in there.

The 381st Rifle Division, supported the 46th Guards Tank Regiment, the 396th Guards Heavy Self-Propelled Artillery and the 952nd Self-Propelled Artillery Regiment, and the 226th Separate Tank Regiment, as well as the engineers units were to crush the Finnish defence in the area around the ferry crossing, and cross the Vouksa as one unit and then in a decisive speed march capture the stronghold on the northern bank, after advancing up to the natural boundaries of Hansuon – Nitut.

Following on the capture of the stronghold, 92nd Rifle Division was introduced into the battle and built upon the success of capturing the stronghold in the direction of Salokula. At 2100 hrs on the 1,261st Rifle Regiment delivered the crossing equipment to the area where the forces were concentrated. In the lull the Soviet side drew up their artillery, accepted their reinforcements, and conducted reconnaissance. All the pieces had been put in place on the chessboard to continue the great game.

27

4-5 July

Opening of General Assault on the Southern Bank

The Soviet artillery barrage commenced at 0455 hrs. The 23rd Army's artillery fired for 55 minutes. In total Soviet artillerymen in the units of the 6th, 98th, and 115th Rifle corps in the course of the day on 4 July fired around 63,000 shells and mortars.

During the period 0540 hrs to 0710 hrs aircraft serving with the 13th Army attacked enemy positions as well as attacking deep behind Finnish lines. Some 126 bombers and 108 ground attack aircraft took part in the raid. During the course of the artillery and air barrage Soviet pilots bombed the headquarters of the 49th Infantry Regiment in Talala, where the Regimental and Group Commander Colonel Valbek was fatally injured. The Finnish battalions on the southern bank had incurred heavy losses in their officer corps even during the artillery barrage. One defence sector commander was seriously wounded, while another was killed.

Immediately after the end of the artillery barrage the regiments in the 381st Division supported by tanks went on the attack. By 0800 hrs units of the 1,259th Rifle Regiment along with tanks broke through the defences of the 1st Battalion, 7th Infantry Regiment and captured height 44.5 known as the "Southern" height. Colonel Yakushov reported to the Corps Commander that at the start of the attack the Finns did not offer any significant resistance. One regimental battalion, which was not paying attention to the threat from the flank, passed the Finnish stronghold completely and advanced up to the bank of the Vuoksi. On the bank Soviet machine gunners opened fire on the move using three heavy machine guns on the Finnish crossing. The Commander of the Finnish reserve detachment Captain Tikkanen was killed right at the start of the battle. A critical situation developed. Signals Officer of the 1st Battalion 87th Regiment Lieutenant Teijonmaa assumed command and put the reserves into a counterattack. He succeeded in pushing the 1,259th Regiment back from the bank.

At 0615 hrs Ehrnrooth ordered all the reserves that were at hand to be deployed onto the southern bank. Under constant fire from Soviet artillery, mortars and from aircraft companies from the 7th Infantry Regiment had succeeded in crossing the river by 0800 hrs. The author has not been able to find any information concerning losses incurred during the crossing of the river. At 1115 hrs the fresh reserve attacked the right flank of the 1st Rifle Battalion, 1,259th Rifle Regiment. In the most arduous battle the Finns recaptured height 44.5 "Southern." Two self-propelled artillery guns of the 396th Guards Regiment, (the Commanders of which were Dmitrenko, and Baklan), were blown up by mines.

The Chief of Staff of the 381st Rifle Division had to write an explanatory letter about the loss of height 44.5 "Southern." This document is cited in full below:

To the Chief of Staff of the 98th Rifle Corps

Height 44.5 /Southern/ was conceded to the enemy under the following circumstances:

1) I have a signed written combat report signed by the Commander of the 1,259th Rifle Regiment and the Chief of Staff, as well as information received over the telephone that the 1,259th Rifle Regiment of the 1st and 2nd Rifle Brigade had captured height 44.5 /southern/ and advanced north of its slope. This information was confirmed by the Commander of the 226th Separate Tank Regiment, Lieutenant-Colonel KOROBEYNIKOV.

The enemy's 1st Battalion 7th Infantry Regiment, which had been defending a position around height 44.5 /southern/, had been partially destroyed, and some of the men had been taken prisoner, while another proportion had withdrawn in the direction of ALATALO and some had withdrawn to a nameless height north of Lake KAUKISEN-LAMPI while others to the headland some 150–200m north of height 44.5 /southern/.

2) As the 3rd Battalion, 1,259th Rifle Regiment was going into battle with the task of advancing up to the church at HIVIMYAKI at 1000–1030 hrs the battalion on the edge of the road at ALATALO was subject on several occasions to enemy artillery and mortar fire and to counterattacks from infantry from an unnamed height 0.3 east of ALATALO.

The strength of the enemy group conducting the counterattack was two companies.

The 3rd Company from the 1,259th Rifle Regiment, which had lost the majority of its officer corps, withdrew to the forest west of ALATALO, where it was also subject to fierce artillery and mortar fire, as well as strafing and subsequent attacks from aircraft. As a result the enemy began to attack the flank and to the rear of the 1st Battalion from the 1,259th Rifle Regiment, which was located in the area around HARYULA, and the forest to the north-west.

At the same time, the 2nd and 1st Battalions of the 1,259th Rifle Regiment began to beat back enemy counterattacks from HARYULA and the headland to the north of height 44.5/southern/.

By 1230–1300 hrs the enemy, which had managed to replace part of the Observation Post in the area around VUOLSAMI and further north/up to six mortar and three artillery batteries/, began to fall victim to a powerful attack on height 44.5 /southern/ with simultaneous counterattacks from both sides.

Since they were incurring heavy losses, the regiment left height 44.5 /southern/ and by 1700 hrs, whilst beating back the many attacks from the enemy, which up until that time had maintained an advantage, withdrew to their original starting position.

The Chief of Staff of the 381st Rifle Division Colonel RUBAN.

In the course of a day on 4 July the 1,259th Rifle Regiment lost 684 men, of whom 134–had been killed and 550–wounded. In view of the heavy losses the 1,263rd and 1,259th Regiments in the Division changed to a format consisting of two battalions. The Finns succeeded in taking four "thirty-fours" out of action from the 226th Separate Tank Regiment as well as three KV tanks from the 46th Guards Tank Regiment. The 381st Division claimed 18 men captured. Total losses for the 98th Rifle Corps in the first day of the overall offensive were 931 men, of whom 187–had been killed and 744–injured.

A fierce storm raged on the height for the entire day. Soviet and Finnish artillery was firing and was not sparing any shells. The total number expended from the Finnish batteries was around 15,000 shells.

Keilo Luukanen, 7th Infantry Regiment:

From morning on 4 July the enemy had begun a powerful artillery barrage as well as an air raid on our positions on Ayrapaa. We received an order to capture height number two. We climbed up the slope. I found a good dugout and stationed myself there.

Our troops pulled back down the slope but the enemy was all but at their heels. We fired at them using a sub-machine gun. Then I saw a tank in front of me and off to the right. A very large number of infantry were coming up behind it. I transferred my fire down onto them. Naturally, the tank crews noticed my machine gun. First they had to get rid of me. The first shell overshot and exploded. The second injured my comrade Vilho Tuovinen, but I still continued to fire. The third shell exploded so close to me that the shrapnel hit me in the face and damaged the corner of my eye. When I had cleaned the mud out of my eye and began to breathe again, blood was coming out of my mouth and nose.

I went to the dressing station at the stronghold. There were a large number of seriously injured men lying in front of it so I had to walk along the shore. On the way I came across our Company Commander, who advised me to go to the headland where the evacuation of the wounded was taking place. I set off for there. A great number of injured had gathered there, there was an oarsman but not one complete boat.

The oarsman asked us to wait here and left for the other bank to look for boats, he got undressed and swan across the Vuoksi. While we waited we decided amongst ourselves that he was not coming back. He did though come back to us and brought four boats that were tied together. He got dressed and ordered anyone who could row to get hold of a boat and evacuate the wounded. I sat down at the oars. Aside from myself a further four men sat in the boat. As we were rowing, a man sitting on the middle plank was hit in the hand by a bullet, so a tourniquet had to be put on him.

On our bank of the river the oarsman had gathered all the boats, tied them together and had set off again for the wounded. I would like to add that he did this out of conscience.

The situation for the Soviet side was more complex in the area around Rommyaki height, where the 281st Rifle Division had attacked the 49th Infantry Regiment's position. In the first attack Colonel Isakov deployed the first three regiments in his division, gathering them into three echelons. Formation of a small wedge was achieved in the area around the 3rd Battalion, 49th Infantry Regiment's positions but the Finns immediately restored the situation with a counterattack. By 1200 hrs this Finnish battalion's Command Post had been destroyed by Soviet bombers. As a result of a direct hit by a bomb the battalion had lost 10 officers in a single strike. The Battalion Commander Heikki Sankari had been killed and the Head of Artillery Major Matti Koponen. Captain Mauno Puolakka replaced the fallen Battalion Commander.

By the close of the day the 29th Punishment Battalion, which had been attached to Isakov's division, had all but ceased to exist, having lost a large proportion of their personnel either killed or wounded. Losses in Valbek's group for 4 July were at 33 killed and 133 wounded.

Five decades later the commander of 7th Infantry Regiment Ehrnrooth acknowledged in one interview that on the night of 4–5 July he had to leave the stronghold and pull back to the northern bank. The Finns had already won back time, while the battalion, who were awash with blood on the southern bank were needed on the northern bank. In 1944 however everything was different. Late in the evening of 4 July the Commander of the 2nd Division Martola received a report of the losses at the stronghold and he was appalled. The losses among Valbek's and Ehrnrooth's combat groups were around 520 men either killed or wounded. Losses in the officer corps were especially high. He had already signed the order to retreat when Ehrnrooth received a report of the interrogation of a

Soviet prisoner of war who had been captured on the height. According to his evidence out of the six regiments that had attacked the stronghold five had incurred heavy losses and only the 1,261st Regiment, which had been in the second echelon, were still at around half strength.

Ehrnrooth immediately changed his mind and announced that he was ready to hold the stronghold, if he were to receive a fresh battalion. As a result the 25th Separate Battalion under Major Yakko Kuusinen was redeployed across the Vuoksi. The crossing using rowing boats took place under a constant hail of Soviet shells.

5 July

During the second half of the day, Soviet regiments again stormed the height. The attack in the area around the ferry crossing began at 1800 hrs following a heavy artillery barrage.

In order to storm height 44.5 "Northern" a tank group was formed under the Command of Lieutenant-Colonel Korobeynikov, the Commander of the 226th Separate Tank Regiment. Three KVs came under this group, as well as three "thirty-fours" and four SU-76s. By 2330 hrs the riflemen of the 1,261st Regiment had captured the height with the help of tanks. Finnish artillery had taken two "thirty-fours" out of action in the battle, one of which was later towed off the battlefield. Senior Lieutenant Timofey Petrovich Avdeyev, Tank Company Commander from the 226th Regiment and holder of a decoration had been killed, he had been fighting since 22 June 1941. As he had got out of his tank he had planted a red banner on the height and was fatally wounded. He was awarded the title of Hero of the Soviet Union posthumously. The tanks opened fire from the height on the Finnish crossings and on the northern bank, suppressing the enemy's firing positions.

After seizing the height the 226th Tank Regiment withdrew from the battle and set off behind the lines to receive a reinforcement of materiel. By evening on 7 July the regiment was already down to just 19 combat capable T-34 tanks.

Despite superhuman efforts and enormous sacrifices, the Finns were not able to hold their position. The reinforcements proved to be the weak link in their chain. After a Soviet artillery barrage the 25th Separate Infantry Battalion, which had just arrived from the stronghold, abandoned their positions on the height in a panic. Captain Raasina immediately sent in barrier detachments, but they were unable to halt the exodus of these young soldiers. The soldiers who had gone crazy with fear tore off their clothes and set off across the Vuoksi either swimming or using boats. Soviet machine gunners as well as tank guns fired on them from the height. Officers fished the survivors out of the reed beds on the northern bank.

Automatic rifleman Otto Hakkarainen of 3rd Company, 7th Regiment who was injured in the battle recalled: "On that bank Soviet ground attack aircraft attacked anything that moved. Somehow we survived. In the forest we came across a soldier who was completely naked. He had swum across the river. Colonel Ehrnrooth rebuked him severely and ordered him to return to the southern bank as soon as he had received a new uniform."

A fierce firefight raged on the height for the whole night of 6–7 July. By midnight Soviet artillery had carried out an artillery attack on the stronghold and had begun a new attack on the heights. Communications with the 2nd Battalion, 7th Infantry Regiment were cut almost immediately. By 0230 hrs a report arrived at Ehrnrooth's headquarters stating that Captain Raasina was surrounded along with his headquarters on the bank. In reality the 2nd Battalion had been split into two parts and was pushed back to the river. Raasina succeeded in capturing the headquarters and anyone who was still capable of holding a weapon fought off several Soviet attacks and broke through along the bank towards Harjule and the ruins of the church. Captain Savolainen's detachment, which was closer to the ferry crossing, was much less fortunate. By 0300 hrs there were only around 40 Finns left alive on a patch of ground 300m wide, which they continued desperately to defend. The result of the battle was a predictable one–after the ammunition had run out anyone who was able to swim set off for the far side, looking for salvation on the northern bank. Those who could not swim were either killed or surrendered as prisoners of war.

Martova again made an announcement concerning the need to preserve soldier's lives and to withdraw to the northern bank. The Corps Commander General Siilasuvo, a hero of the battle for Suomossalmi, rejected this proposal and ordered the stronghold to be held to the last man. The fresh 4th Battalion from the 19th Brigade under Lieutenant-Colonel Alfons Sundublad was deployed to the northern part of the stronghold. The objective of this battalion was to strike along the river bank and to establish communications with the southern part of the stronghold. Finnish counterattacks only led to one thing–to enormous losses. Twice on the night of 5-6 July the fresh battalion went on the attack supported by artillery, and mortar fire, as well as attacks from Finnish and German bombers. Twice they were pulled back under a hail of Soviet fire. Following the third attack, which was carried out a day later, only half of Sundblad's battalion remained.

28

6-8 July

On 6 July Soviet Command deployed several battalions from the 92nd Rifle Division into the battle. They supported the severely depleted 381st Rifle Division's offensive against height 44.5 "Northern".

The 22nd Rifle Regiment lost 197 men that day, of whom 56 were killed and 141 were injured. The regiment claimed that it had captured 150 men, of whom 53 were taken to the headquarters of the 92nd and 381st Rifle divisions, while the rest "were killed for trying to put up resistance whilst in convoy."

By 2000 hrs on 6 July the 381st Rifle Division reported that they had captured height 44.5 "Southern" and "Northern." The Finns, who had tried to save themselves using boats or by swimming, were killed by machine gun, and automatic rifle fire – according to Yakushov's report, "120 men drowned in the Vuoksi." The division claimed it had captured 90 men in the course of the day on 6 July. As Johanness Parkkali of the 7th Infantry Regiment recalled:

> We swam into the middle of the Vuoksi, and then an appalling number of shells rained down on us. There were a great number of direct hits on our boat, and all that remained of them were red blotches in the water. A shell exploded right next to our boat, killing the oarsman. Shrapnel entered his forehead above the eyes and took half his head off. Two injured soldiers continued to row–one of them had one good right hand, while the other one good left hand. I felt a blow to my stomach, and I understood that I had been wounded again, and I thought to myself: "This is the end for me."
>
> Two medics lifted the injured rower out of the boat, and those injured soldiers who were able to move by themselves ran away as fast as they could. This lightened the boat so much that it actually drifted away from the shore. There were three of us wounded lying in the boat. We were drifting towards Vasikkasaari. My right hand was functioning okay as was my left leg, I climbed over the side and splashed into the water. I had enough strength to keep my nose above water and breathe, and I paddled to our own bank with all my strength. The hail of shellfire continued.

The division paid a high price for success. In the course of three days of fierce battles the division had incurred heavy losses, and at 200 hrs in the evening of 6 July 1944 the following remained in the regiments: in the 1,259th Regiment: 474 men, in the 1,261st Regiment: 601 men, and in the 1,263rd Regiment: 653 men.

In view of such high losses the Divisional Commander Colonel Yakushev reported a loss of combat capability and requested command pull the corps back from the front line for rest and recuperation as well as for reinforcements. The division only withdrew to the rear the following day. They still had one more battle left to fight, the last battle on the southern bank of the Vuoksi.

On the night of 6–7 July the 2nd Battalion, 7th Regiment was withdrawn from the stronghold, or to be more precise, the handful of soldiers that were still alive–in total around 20 men. By way of a replacement around 100 soldiers were sent to join them from the 25th Separate Infantry Battalion–among their number were soldiers who had previously swum across the Vouksi and were revived by the officers on the northern bank. From the ranks of the 7th Regiment only the anti-tank crews of the 14th Company remained at the stronghold.

7 July: End of the Southern Stronghold

At 1345 hrs the lines of the 381st Rifle Division went on the attack again against the southern stronghold. An air raid, as well as an artillery barrage that lasted for half an hour preceded the attack. At the very start of the battle some of the soldiers from the 25th Battalion abandoned their positions again in a panic and ran towards the bank.

According to Finnish records Major Kuusinen at the very start of the attack considered it a hopeless situation and ordered everyone to abandon the stronghold and swim. The Major did have grounds for this decision. All the boats it turned out had been destroyed, the injured had not been evacuated, and it had been impossible to deliver ammunition to the stronghold. The survivors pulled back across the cemetery to the shore, they were able to cross the Vuoksi and reach the island of Vasikkasaari. The seriously injured were left to the mercy of the victor. Approximately 30 Finns remained at the cemetery near the church to cover the withdrawal of their comrades but were soon forced to concede–they had run out of ammunition.

By 1430 hrs the soldiers of the 381st Division had almost completely purged the area around the church of Finns. Around 340 bodies of fallen enemy soldiers and officers remained on the battlefield, according to a report from Colonel Yakushov. The division had taken 112 men prisoner.

Corporal Vilo Salo of the 7th Infantry Regiment:

> After we had abandoned the stronghold we went via a dressing station. There were so many soldiers who had been so badly wounded there that they were unable to move. The military doctors as well as the medics had already left for the northern bank. The injured soldiers told us to leave, since they were on their last legs themselves. It was very difficult–we had nothing to help our brothers in arms. There was not one boat that was left in one piece on the entire Vuoksi.
>
> The crossing of the River Vuoksi just degenerated into a complete pandemonium. The enemy was on our heels. We swam, clinging onto driftwood and logs, and they fired at us with all their guns. The strong current together with enemy fire sent many to the bottom.

From artillery Observation Post "*Valo*" ("Light") on the western extremity of the island of Vasikkasaari the course of the last battle and of the purges on the southern bank were clearly visible. The distance from the Observation Post to the cemetery was no more than 300m.

When Colonel Ehrnrooth was told about this he issued an order to open fire on the area around the church using artillery. The Battalion Commander, who received the order, refused to carry it out. Ehrnrooth repeated the order and the Deputy Battalion Commander opened fire.

According to another version of events, which is more acceptable to the Finns, the artillery only opened fire on the southern bank after the Finns had noticed that the soldiers of the 381st Division were killing injured Finnish soldiers on the bank of the river. One way or another the tragic end to the Finnish stronghold on 7 July near the ruins of the church at Ayrapaa became the only well-known episode in the history of an independent Finland, when a Finnish officer issued an order to open fire on his own forces.

The reader may register surprised by the impulsiveness and the severity of Colonel Ehrnrooth's decisions. Was this linked to his recalcitrant disposition? Were there other reasons? One of the versions holds that Ehrnrooth was constantly using "Pervitin" for the whole of that fateful week and this affected his emotional stability.

The battle on the southern bank lasted five days. The number of Finnish soldiers who fought on the southern bank, according to Lieutenant-Colonel Ari Raunio's assessment, some 6,000–7,000 men. Of whom every second man either perished, was taken prisoner, was injured, or drowned in the Vuoksi–according to a report by the 2nd Infantry Division, in the period from 20 June–8 July the total losses for the division were at 3,727 men.

The Soviets also paid a huge price for taking the heights. According to an assessment by the headquarters of the 98th Rifle Corps, the capture of the ridges on the southern bank cost the divisions in the corps the lives of 3,500 men. Of those more than a thousand died. Losses among the 22nd Rifle Regiment's men, who had supported the offensive by the 381st Division, were at 103 men killed or injured in the course of 7 July alone. In total over the period in which the battles took place on the Vuoksi the 381st Division lost 477 men killed and 1,813 injured.

The 281st Rifle Division's losses in the battles against the northern part of the stronghold reached a level that meant out of the surviving soldiers from 1,064th, and 1,062nd Rifle Regiments a single battalion consisting of just one company was formed. The 1,066th Regiment changed to a format consisting of two battalions. The 281st and the 381st Rifle Divisions dug in on the southern bank, waiting to be sent back behind the lines.

8 July

The primary outcome of the battle on the southern bank was that the Finns managed to gain time, deploy their artillery, and to draw up fresh forces as well as drawing up ammunition and organising a defence on the northern Vuoksi. All this cost the 49th and 7th Infantry Regiments a great deal of blood. It is worth remembering that the battle on the southern bank was thundering away at the very same time that the 21st Army was storming the crags and heights in the area around Ihantala. The active advancing forces of the 21st Army ended on 4 July, when the Finns nevertheless managed to hold the heights on the Vuokse. This enabled the Finns to manoeuvre Lagus' armoured division and to redeploy them from Ihantala to the northern bank of the Vuoksi. The forward units of the armoured division arrived at the stronghold late in the evening of 10 July.

On 7 July when the northern part of the Finnish stronghold was still being held, the Commander of the Leningrad Front Marshal Govorov's patience ran out. He sent a scathing letter to the headquarters of the 23rd Army and the 98th Corps, and issued strict orders:

> The Commander of the 23rd Army Lieutenant-General Shvetsov
>
> The abominable organisation of the battle and the absence of responsibility for the execution of the objective that characterise of the actions of the 98th Rifle Corps, remain as they were before.
>
> The Corps continues to mark time, incurring unacceptably high losses and wasting a huge amount of ammunition. The Corps' principal mistakes were and remain as follows:
>
> 1) A complete lack of battle reconnaissance.
> 2) The inability to organise a combined arms operation.
> 3) A lack of management of the battle as a Corps.
>
> As a result of all these errors the advance of the Corps has degenerated into a series of separate partial attacks occurring at different times and made by regiments and battalions.

Even though they have a clear advantage in terms of forces and materiel over the enemy and as an excuse for their own inability to wage war, command is in the process of undermining inexorably both itself as well as its forces by consciously telling lies about the enemy having the upper hand.

I HEREBY ORDER:
1) To stop separate attacks and to only conduct an overall offensive as a Corps,
2) I categorically forbid going into battle blind, when the attack is not proceeded by artillery fire, or the other way round when artillery fire is ordered after the attack has petered out, this characterises all the 98th Rifle Corps' combat activity.
3) To organise a combined arms attack and first and foremost an artillery offensive, which would establish superiority in terms of firepower on the battlefield.
4) To immediately box in the enemy's strongholds using artillery fire and to obstruct the flow from the eastern bank of the River Vuoksi.
Report back once the measures have been taken to finally defeat the enemy on the western bank of the River Vuoksi.

I am sending a warning to the Commander of the 98th Rifle Corps, that no more of this marking time will be tolerated.
Solovyov Popov Govorov

It has to be acknowledged however that this situation could not be rectified. The 281st and 381st Rifle Divisions in the 98th Corps had wasted nearly two weeks on the storming of the heights–the battles took place from 21 June to 7 July. The Corps had almost no strength left, and there could be no question of the 281st and 381st Divisions crossing the Vuoksi. The 23rd Army Command had brought the fresh 115th Rifle Corps up to the river

29

9 July, The Crossing

Following the purge of the southern part of the stronghold the 23rd Army set about crossing the Vuoksi. The fresh 142nd Rifle Division, 115th Corps were to cross the river in the first echelon. For an entire week from 1-8 July the division was located behind the lines and was preparing hard to overcome this significant water barrier. On 7 July officers in the division–the divisional commander, regimental commanders, and the battalion commanders advanced to the area around the forthcoming crossing to reconnoitre the area. The soldiers in the division meanwhile began to equip their starting positions; they dug trenches and Observation Post and drew up boats to these positions. On the night of 8–9 July preparations for the crossing were for the most part complete. In total more than 500 boats had been delivered the area around the crossing point. The sappers in the 20th Engineering Brigade spent the whole night preparing boats and rafts and trained themselves up in how to assemble ferry boats and pontoons.

On 8 July General Odintsov, the Artillery Commander of the Leningrad Front, arrived at the location of the 115th Corps on an inspection visit. During the course of an inspection he made a few comments to the artillerymen. As a result of which the Artillery Commander of the 115th Rifle Corps deployed 127 45mm, 76mm, and 122mm guns onto the height to fire at close range to provide cover for the area around the crossing. The density of large calibre artillery was around 40 guns per kilometre of front.

The "hunters" of 396th Guards Regiment with their ISU-152s along with the KVs of the 46th Guards Regiment advanced onto the heights. Heavy machine gun crews as well as Anti-Tank Gun crews took up positions on the actual river bank itself. The anti-aircraft cover on the river bank was provided by these same Anti-Tank Crews with guns, which were equipped for firing at airborne targets, as well as a regiment of Small Calibre Anti-Aircraft Artillery.

The Finns on the northern bank were also preparing for battle–Soviet observers noticed mine laying work taking place on the river bank, as well as work to clear the field of fire, and equip the firing positions.

In the early hours of 9 July from 0100–0300 hrs the regiments of the 124th Rifle Divisions advanced out to the crossing point. In the first echelon the 946th and 461st Regiments, as well as the 588th Regiment (without a single battalion) were in the divisional commander's reserve.

The Finns asserted that they were able to get a fix on the concentration of rifle regiments from the 142nd Division and the crossing equipment near the ferry crossing: documents record that at approximately 0200 hrs in the morning a Soviet reconnaissance group crossed onto their bank under cover of fog, and that this group were killed. According to other sources Soviet reconnaissance troops were able to get a foothold on the bank and dig in.

Soviet documents do not directly confirm that a reconnaissance group was sent forward on the night of 8–9 July, but the Commander of the 142nd Rifle Division Colonel Sonnikov writes about them in his memoirs.

The crossing sequence of events, planned 23rd Army headquarters, was as follows:

1) Ranging and destructive fire–05 hrs 00 mins–06 hrs 000 mins.
2) Artillery barrage on the crossing point–6 hrs 00 mins–6 hrs 55 mins.
3) "Ch"–the first crossing breaks away–6 hrs 40 mins.
4) Attack on the opposite bank–6 hrs 55 mins.

Chief of Staff Major-General Bolshakov
Chief of the Operation's Section Colonel Goldzberg

When this plan was released to 142nd Division, the divisional commander was aggrieved. According to the memoirs of the Divisional Commander, the disagreements concerning the fording of the river led to a direct conflict between the Corps and the Army:

> Having carefully developed the plan for crossing the River Vuoksi, which was put together by the 23rd Army and the 115th Rifle Corps, 142nd Divisional Command concluded that the crossing could not commence at the exact time stipulated in the plan. This was because at that time the crossing of the units would be supported and covered by a single ground attack and bombing air squadron, since all the artillery, mortars and machine guns at that time would stop firing as a precaution, to avoid possibly hitting their own aircraft.
>
> Such a weak level of cover for a river crossing with a width of around 800m, and using whatever can be found to hand moreover, was woefully insufficient. It would take no less than twenty minutes to cross a barrier of that size, and in that time the enemy's gun emplacements could be activated and they could put a stop to the since aviation alone is never going to guarantee that they can destroy an enemy's entire firing system.
>
> All the requests raised by Divisional Command with the leadership of the Army and the Corps that the crossing of the first echelon could be achieved 20 minutes earlier than time stipulated in the army's plan were rejected. Therefore divisional command took a decision off their own backs: the first echelon consisting of four augmented rifle battalions would begin 20 minutes ahead of the stipulated time. This decision afforded the possibility for the battalions as they were crossing to get across the Vuoksi under reliable covering fire form our massed artillery, as well as mortar and machine gun fire and the echelons would not then be subjected to enemy gun and machine gun fire as well as artillery and mortar fire as they crossed.
>
> It was true that as they landed on the other side, which was occupied by the enemy, our echelons would be subject to bombing from our own aircraft, but recognition and cooperation signals have been agreed with our aviation for this, in order to avoid friendly fire. We felt it would be better to incur small losses from possible shrapnel from the bombs dropped by our own aircraft then have our forces shot in the water by enemy fire, without having achieved their objective. This was the only choice we had, and it proved itself 100 percent and the subsequent events are a great illustration of this.
>
> Ahead of the start of the overall offensive a reconnaissance group crossed over to the bank that was in enemy hands, this group consisted of reconnaissance personnel and sappers and demolition experts to reconnoitre the enemy's engineering obstacles, how they could be destroyed, and how small strongholds could be captured for landing the first regimental echelons.

Some of the 142nd Rifle Division were to cross the Vuoksi across a wide front–from the Gulf of Lauttalahti up to the ferry crossing. Sappers from the 20th Engineering Brigade prepared the boats and ferry boats for five crossings. On the right flank of the corps, the 62nd Regiment, 10th Rifle Division were on the night of 8–9 June to attack the Finns, who as before had been holding the island of Vasikkasaari. After this their fraternal 98th Rifle Regiment was to capture Vasikkasaari in a decisive speed march, after crossing via the channel leading away from the church on the southern bank.

Sunrise. At 0500 hrs Soviet artillery started to fire at targets on the Finnish side. At 0600 hrs the artillery barrage began, which lasted for 55 mins. At the same time 150 aircraft conducted a bombing raid on Finnish positions. At 0635 hrs the *Katyushas* opened up. By all accounts anything that showed any sign of life on the Finnish side was pounded by the "forty-fives' at close range as well as by field guns, SU-76s, KVs, "hunters," Anti-Tank Guns, and machine guns …

The crossing got underway under cover of artillery fire. The pontoons were towed up to the crossing point by SU-76 self-propelled guns from the 952nd Self-Propelled Artillery Regiment. The chemical protection subdivisions put up smoke screens. Simultaneously to the start of artillery fire the 1st Rifle Battalion, 461st Regiment under Captain Grigoriy Filippovich Simankin dragged the boats into the shore, launched them onto the water, and rowed them forward. Captain Simankin had only assumed command of the battalion on 17 June 1944, up until this point he had commanded a machine gun company in this same regiment. Sinamkin had fought in the 142nd Division since 22 June 1941. The boats in the lead company in the battalion under the command of Lieutenant Skvortsov were launched onto the water at 0615 hrs.

Finnish artillery and mortars opened fire. The first losses began, holes appeared in the boats and they went to the bottom. Captain Aleksandr Konstantinovich Mantrov an intelligence officer in the 461st Regiment was killed. Without losing their heads the soldiers plugged the holes in the boats using their service caps. The machine gunners opened fire on the Finnish bank while they were still on board the boats. Battalion Commander Simankin stood on the first boat at his full height, commanding the oarsmen and cheering on his men. Inspired by their commander's example the battalion soon got a foothold on the bank and launched into the Finnish trenches, purging them in the course of a short hand-to-hand battle. The Finns fought desperately, but they were not able to hold their positions by the river. In the battle on the Finnish side of the river the Commander of the 461st Regiment Colonel Petukhov was wounded very early on, Major Belyayev took his place.

Otto Huiskonen of 1st Company, 7th Infantry Regiment, left a poignant testimony to the fighting:

> On 9 July my Platoon Commander Junior Sergeant Yakko Salo sent me to report to the company commander. I threw a rucksack onto my back and ran along the communications trench, which had been dug out in the fields near the Vuoksi.
>
> Our company had a very wide sector. We only had two depleted platoons left, so the line was very thin. I reached our Company Commander Antero Sipinen, gave my report and set off back for my platoon. I almost ended up in the belly of the beast–our defence on the banks of the Vuoksi had been breached. The enemy already knew where our trenches were. I quickly turned back towards Lieutenant Sipinen. A machine gunner ran up to his Command Post and said that the enemy had occupied our positions. Sipinen ordered me to report to the battalion commander that the 1st Company were occupying new positions on the edge of the forest.

> I ran to report my message like I was running the 100m. I reached the location and reported to the battalion commander. He heard me out, shook my hand and said that we would take up defensive positions together in this location.
>
> I remember this gesture by the battalion commander and his ingenuous order like it was yesterday. I moved 15m away from him to the left. I hid behind a knoll. A short time later a soldier I didn't recognise ran up to me and said that Sipinen and his soldiers had only just been killed on the battlefield.
>
> Just at that moment a shell exploded. A fragment broke through my helmet and lodged itself in my skull. A second piece of shrapnel pierced my leg. That was how I got away. I spent more than five months in hospital. I read in the paper that our Battalion Commander Arvo Kuparinen was killed in Vuosalmi on 9 July 1944.

As soon as Sinamkin's battalion had got a foothold on the Finnish side Major Aleksey Petrovich Kurnosov's 3rd Rifle Battalion began to cross under fire from the enemy. After they had got out onto the left bank of the river the battalion immediately turned towards the west and began to purge the trenches along the River Vuoksi, covering Simankin's battalion's flank.

Kurnosov was also a veteran of the division that had fought since 1941. In three years of war he had grown from Platoon Commander to Battalion Commander. He had commanded the division's ski battalion, as well as the junior commander's courses. He had been decorated with the Order of the Great Patriotic War II class for his actions in the battle for the Sinyavino Heights in the summer of 1943. For his actions in the battles on the Karelian Isthmus in the summer of 1944 Major Kurnosov was twice awarded the Order of the Red Banner of Combat. After that he had commanded the 1st Rifle Battalion. On 14 January 1945 Kurnosov's battalion broke through the German defences in the area around Pshemyarovo–Zakrent in Poland and had captured three trenches. The following day the Germans launched a counterattack supported by heavy tanks. Beating back the attacks Kurnosov was injured in the stomach and he later died of his wounds. He was posthumously awarded the Order of the Great Patriotic War First Class.

The Commander of the 142nd Division Colonel Sonnikov observed:

> When the first echelons began to cross in line with the plan that had been developed by divisional command, the Commander of the 115th Rifle Corps Major-General Kozachek ordered me to return them back to their starting position and warned me that I would be subject to a court martial for disrupting the crossing and for failing to fulfil his order. I was not able to return to my own echelons since they had reached the enemy's side of the river without incurring significant losses and had begun to storm their dugouts. In the space of three of four hours of fighting from the moment of the crossing the entire 142nd Division had crossed over to a stronghold that had been captured by the division's first echelon. By the end of the day on 9 July the division had captured a stronghold some five or six kilometres along the front line and to a depth of two to four kilometres.

From 0800 hrs in the morning sappers from the 20th Engineering Brigade had begun to send the rifle units across on ferry boats. Finnish artillery opened lethal fire on the Soviet side and on the river. The western part of the island of Vasikkasaari was again in the hands of the Finns, and from Observation Post "*Valo*" the Finnish artillery spotters could see all the crossings as clearly as they could the palms of their hands. Crossing No. 2 in the gulf of Lauttalahti was destroyed–all the ferry boats were destroyed while they were still on the southern bank. Soviet sappers describe this event as follows: "Crossings No. 2 and No. 4 were only in operation over the course of 9

July, subsequently crossing No. 4 was merged with crossing No. 3, as the 2nd crossing had ceased operations completely."

German and Finnish strike aircraft appeared overhead. Crossing No. 5 worked but with significant delays. Under a hail of bombs and shells the sappers repaired the broken pontoons, and brought replacement pontoons to the water's edge, oversaw the loading, and dragged the damaged vehicles out of the way… Over the course of the whole day on 9 July 1944 Finnish artillery fired more than 13,000 shells at the crossings. Up to 75 percent of the crossing equipment as a whole was taken out of action.

On the right flank of the 115th Corps, the offensive began at 0200 hrs in the night. Soldiers from the 62nd Regiment, 10th Rifle Division had crawled unnoticed up to the severely overgrown reed beds in the south-eastern part of the island of Vasikkasaari by swimming, wading, or using rubber rafts and they then suddenly attacked the Finnish positions on the island. The Finns were taken completely by surprise but they soon came to their senses and held the central and north-western extremities of the island. The fierce battle on the island thundered for the entire day on 9 July. The south-eastern part of the island, which is not covered in forest, had been intensively mined by the Finns, which gave rise to losses among the Soviet riflemen, but also made counterattacks more difficult for the Finns. Soviet artillery rained fire down on the island the whole day; Finnish losses were 80 men killed and wounded. Ehrnrooth redeployed all that remained of the 3rd Battalion, 7th Regiment to the island.

The morning turned out much worse for 98th Rifle Regiment. For some reason the crossing equipment was delivered to the bank of the Vuoksi late. At 0730 hrs the regiment's gunners began to board their boats and a lethal hail of fire was opened up on them using all manner of weapons from the island of Vasikkasaari. The regiment incurred "completely unjustified losses" on the shore and withdrew some 300m back from the bank. The regiment's losses were 16 men killed and 139 wounded. Finnish artillerymen destroyed five pontoons on the shore. At 1050 hrs the regiment received a verbal order from divisional headquarters to cross the Vuoksi in a column behind the 142nd Division in the area around height 44.5. The regiment had arrived at this location by 1500 hrs after coming under fire from enemy aircraft twice along the way.

For the entire first half of the day the 115th Corps Command were unaware of the situation on the right flank. Despite all the preliminary agreements reached ahead of the battle 10th Rifle Division Command "as a result of their own negligence" had failed to contact the corps not by radio, or with the help of messengers. As a result of which the corps was in no position to aid the division, without knowing the situation. The 98th Rifle Regiment only began to cross to the stronghold on 10 July in the second echelon of the corps.

On 9 July two incomplete Finnish platoons still managed to hold the island of Mustasaari.

By midday, two battalions of the 588th Rifle Regiment were sent across to the stronghold. During the day on 9 July the light self-propelled artillery guns in the 952nd Self-Propelled Artillery Regiment were due to cross to the stronghold, but by 1600 hrs crossing No. 5, which had been prepared for them, was destroyed by German and Finnish aircraft. It took all evening to repair this crossing.

By the close of the day regiments of 142nd Division expanded the stronghold by up to five kilometres along the front line and to a depth of two kilometres. The Finns reclaimed all the fields next to the Vuoksi, and Soviet gunners stormed into the forest to the north of the fields. They forced the battalion commander to move the location of the Command Post and were already approaching the 7th Infantry Regiment's Command Post in the area around Lampela. Ehrnrooth categorically banned his forces from abandoning their positions, across all the regiment's subdivisions he issued a strict ban on retreating, ordering his men to fight to the last, even if they were surrounded. Ehrnrooth ordered all the headquarters soldiers to grab a weapon and to lead the counterattack. As a result the Finns still succeeded in stabilising the situation and in stopping the attacks by Soviet infantry.

There was no Soviet armoured equipment on the northern bank of the Vuoksi on 9 July. The regimental and anti-tank artillery was not able to cross either. All the responsibility of the battle lay on the shoulders of the Soviet infantry, which could not fail to have an impact on losses. On that day, or to be more accurate, within the same 24 hrs, in the 48 and then 72 hrs of uninterrupted fighting, the soldiers and commanders of the division lost none of their courage and demonstrated widespread heroism.

In many cases communications with the southern bank were lost in the first few minutes after the landings. The last radio-operator in the 461st Regiment, Private Aleksandr Mikhaylovich Ivanov, was seriously injured in both legs and could not get around independently. When it turned out that there was nobody to replace him, Ivanov refused to be evacuated and requested that he be carried along with his radio set so that he could still provide radio communications for the regiment.

By evening of the first day of the battle on the stronghold Battalion Commander Simankin was also injured, but he too refused to leave the battlefield. For his courage and heroism that he had shown in the river crossing Captain Grigoriy Filippovich Simankin, who had come through all the battles the division had fought since 1941, was awarded the country's highest honour–the Gold Star of the Hero of the Soviet Union. This same award was also given to the radio-operator of the 461st Regiment Aleksandr Mikhaylovich Ivanov.

Over the course of 9 July, Soviet artillery fired, according to an assessment by Finnish artillerymen, up to 30,000 shells of all calibres. Finnish artillery fired 13,500 shells and 5,300 mortars across all calibres. This became a record number of shells fired by Finnish artillery for the summer of 1944 in a single division's defensive belt. The Finnish Air Force and the *Luftwaffe* did not sit still either. The 4th Finnish Aviation Regiment carried out a bombing raid using 32 aircraft on the Soviet side of the river between the ferry crossing and the church mound. The Germans twice flew missions to bomb the crossings using 32 Ju-87s and 15 FW-190s.

Despite the deluge of artillery fire and bombs the crossings continued to operate. At 2300 hrs the second echelon crossed the river–the 92nd Rifle Division under Major-General Panichkin. The first to cross was the 3rd Battalion, 204th Rifle Regiment under Lieutenant-Colonel Novozhilov, who had lost 19 men killed and wounded on the river. By 0900 hrs on 10 July the regiment with all its subdivisions was on the bank of the river. The 317th and 22nd Regiments in this division crossed after them.

Colonel Ehrnrooth relates what were the most critical moments in the battle for his combat group on 9 July 1944:

> Luckily, the division still had some reserves left, which they allocated to me. I formed Ahola's Combat Group from the reserves that I had received from the 12th Separate Battalion and the 2nd Battalion, 15th Infantry Regiment. At my Command Post in Lampela, or to be more accurate, at the Paavilainen farmstead, I had a Jager Platoon, a sapper platoon, and the headquarters itself with strong messenger and signals subdivisions. The combat group that was created from them represented a powerful shield in the path of the enemy as they drew closer to the Paavilainen residence.
>
> I had to hold on with my shield until such time as the counterattack by Ahola's Combat Group in a north-westerly direction from marker 26, began to have an effect on the enemy's flank.

> Let us not forget that artillery played a decisive role in the closing stages of the battle for Vuosalmi. The head of artillery at my Command Post was Major Olavi Arimo. When necessary he would support my regiment with fire from up to 10 batteries.

The Finnish participants remember the battles for the stronghold as being the fiercest and the most bloody. Armas Varionen, the signals officer for the Platoon Commander, 2nd Company, 12th Separate Infantry Battalion:

> The 12th Separate Infantry Battalion, which was attached to the 7th Infantry Regiment carried out numerous counterattacks on 9 July 1944 near Vousalmi in the defensive band of Ehrnrooth's group. The Russians crossed the Vuoksi and captured a stronghold stretching four kilometres along the front line and to a depth of up to two to three kilometres.
>
> The day before these events the battalion received reinforcements–conscripts born in 1925. They arrived with a number of older front line soldiers. My first combat mission was to reconnoitre the path of our offensive along with Matti Kallioniemi. We did not find any Russians or any of our own troops there. We returned to the platoon.
>
> Our attack began at approximately 1100 hrs. We forged northwards away from the Mantyla farmstead, engaging the enemy in combat as we went. We proceeded forward in a line and there were only a few dozen metres between us and the Russians. Major Arvo Ahola commanded the attack directly behind me, with a pistol in his hand. He was cheering on his men and shouting: "Forward, forward!" the Russians threw a grenade at me but it fell short. Our troops supported the attack with fire from a number of directions, so we moved forward. After half a day we reached the coppice north of the Mantyla farmstead.
>
> Both companies of Ahola's Battalion went on the defensive on the edge of the forest, from where the area around the ferry crossing could be seen as well as the opposite bank of the Vuoksi. In the afternoon we continued the attack in the direction of the Mantyla farmstead. The Russians waited for us in the trench, which was in a field some 30m from the alder thicket, which was where we were to start our attack from.
>
> As soon as the first soldiers had gone on the attack, the Russians opened a hail of fire from their automatic guns. From all sides in the battle lines of our company cries of: "Medics, over here!" could be heard. Our attack lasted no more than 10 minutes. After that an order came through to withdraw back to our starting positions on the edge of the forest and to drag our wounded back to that point. It seemed to me that not one of the soldiers who had gone on the attack from the alder thicket ever returned to the edge of the forest. After this counterattack no more than 150 men remained from the two companies of ours in Ahola's Battalion.
>
> We returned to the edge of the forest. It was at this location that former front line soldiers had gathered in numbers equal approximately to sections. They said out loud that Major Ahola should be shot on the spot. He had already sent so many of his own soldiers to their deaths. Ahola had been the last to withdraw and had leapt out of the frying pan into the fire. A Russian prisoner of war and his signals officer were all that accompanied him. Ahola asked the soldiers calmly not to leave him alone, and that they do not abandon their positions in such as difficult situation. Maybe it was after this that all the "wimps" understood the how utterly stupid their suggestion had been.
>
> On the night of 9–10 July the Russians deployed reinforcements across the Vuoksi. They went on the attack against our positions. Luckily, the artillery stopped them with their fire.

> In the morning of 10 July passed quietly, but the well-known General Lagus was to come and assist us with his division and purge this bank of the Vuoksi of Russians. We were certain that it would happen this way, as the guys had a reputation for being tough in Lagus Division. Neither we, nor they however could push the Russians into the Vuoksi.
>
> The Russians continued their attack in large groups. Our lines were growing thinner and thinner. I headed a number of times towards our left flank–to check that we were still fighting shoulder to shoulder with our neighbour to the left. I saw how one of our guys was sitting in a dug out, while sticking out of his back was an unexploded mortar round–ours were falling short. On that very same day a shell from a Russian gun firing at close range fell right in front of us, killing our Company Commander Tanuo Hannuksela. His body remained on the battlefield.
>
> In the first few hours of 11 July more than 10 German dive-bombers appeared in the skies. They bore down on the enemy so we thought that it would be just a little bit easier for us. It did not happen that way, since the enemy's artillery rained down fierce fire on us, which lasted for around two hours. At that same moment our artillery also opened fire.
>
> When the enemy artillery had at last gone quiet enemy tanks appeared on the battlefield. Jagers from the 5th Jager Battalion to the left of us withdrew, and our flank was up in the air. I ran to the Jager positions, through which the enemy had already passed, and pulled out an abandoned *Panzerschreck*. This could never be left to the enemy under any circumstances.
>
> On 11 July we fought desperately and waited to be relieved. We were only relieved in the early hours of 12 July. By that time only 19 soldiers remained around Major Ahola. Among those were *Fahnrich* Antero Alho and the battalion's pastor. All the other officers had been killed or were wounded. *Fahnrich* Alho was killed during the retreat–he had been plastered by artillery; his body remained on the battlefield.

At 2200 hrs on 9 July, the equipment crossing was repaired and the 952nd Self-Propelled Artillery Regiment departed for the stronghold. The first to be loaded onto the pontoons was the 1st Battery under Lieutenant Sushinskiy at 0145 hrs. In the course of the short summer night some 13 SU-76s were sent across. Each self-propelled gun carried one and a half loads of ammunition. They succeeded in not incurring losses in terms of vehicles or personnel. The actual presence of these self-propelled guns was of assistance to the substantially depleted regiments of the 142nd Rifle Division in holding the stronghold and expanding it. The battles for 10 July were so fierce that the self-propelled guns used all their shells in an hour or so of fighting. The ferry boats on the crossing were destroyed by a hail of fire from Finnish artillery. Ten soldiers from the logistics subdivisions of the 952nd Self-Propelled Artillery Regiment using rowing boats and ferry boats succeeded in delivering around a thousand shells to the stronghold, and in doing so they saved the situation.

By 2200 hrs in the evening on 9 July, 2nd Division command received the information concerning losses and availability of personnel from the front line. In 10 of the division's infantry battalions (seven of our own, three that were attached to the division) less than 2,200 men remained. According to the standard there should be around 10,000 men in 10 Finnish battalions.

The 124th Rifle Division claimed they had taken 60 Finns prisoner, 12 of whom were delivered to the headquarters of the 115th Corps on the southern bank, the rest "perished during the evacuation."

For their success the Soviets paid a high price. The 142nd Division lost 164 men killed, and 1,180 injured in single day. In total the 115th Rifle Corps lost 2,388 men on 9 July–478 of whom had been killed, 1,897 injured and 13 were listed as missing without trace. These are the highest losses in one day that the 115th Corps incurred in the entire month of fighting in the battle for Vuosalmi.

30

10-13 July

Vuosalmi is a mass grave. For us, the Finns as well.

(General Heinkris to General Erfurth)

All night from 9–10 July Soviet sappers and supply troops worked feverishly, sending combat equipment across to the stronghold, as well as ammunition, and provisions. The short twilight hours of the white night, had to be used in full.

In the course of a night and a day on 10 July the following was successfully sent across to the stronghold:

- Eight 76mm divisional artillery guns
- Six "forty-fives"
- Eight 76mm regimental artillery guns
- Twenty-five 82mm mortars
- Five 120mm mortars

By 0200 hrs the battalions in the 98th Regiment completed the crossing across the Vuoksi. As they were landing on the northern bank the Regimental Chief of Staff Major Chernyshev succumbed to a mine and was killed. The regiment's artillerymen and the mortar-gunners began to cross immediately after the rifle battalions. The regiment went on the attack without delay from the highway along the river bank to the east, purging the Finnish trenches, and by 1200 hrs they had reached a line running from Notkola–Pasuri. The field guns and the "forty-fives" crossed over to the northern side, and in short order they opened fire at short range. By 1500 hrs the ammunition for the artillerymen had almost run out and the anti-tank gunners had 50 shells remaining per gun, while field artillery had 25 shells per gun.

At 0600 hrs in the morning of 10 July the principal forces of the 92nd Rifle Division began to make their crossing.

On the right, the 204th Rifle Regiment had by 0900 hrs dug into the first Finnish trench and spent three hours inside it doing nothing. Only after midday and the personal intervention of the Regimental Commander did they go into active combat. The regiment's losses for the day were 198 men killed and wounded.

From morning on 10 July the Command Post of the 317th Regiment was blanketed with artillery and mortar fire. The Regiment's Deputy Political Instructor Major Kondratenko and the Party Organiser Senior Lieutenant Melnikov were seriously injured, and the Deputy Regimental Front Line Commander Lieutenant Klimishin was killed. By evening, in connection with the large deficiencies in personnel the Regiment's 3rd Rifle Battalion was disbanded, and its remaining forces transferred to the 1st and 2nd Battalions.

The battery of self-propelled guns under Senior Lieutenant Bolshakov as well as the severely depleted 588th Rifle Regiment beat back three counterattacks, and moreover in one incident the self-propelled gun crews had to beat back the Finnish infantry that were pressing down on them by using hand grenades.

11 July

During the first few hours of 11 July both the Finnish and the Soviet units were planning to advance. The 115th Corps was to have expanded the stronghold and continue the advance to Raisala–Antrea. All three divisions of the 115th Rifle Corps went on the attack, only the 203rd Rifle Regiment remained in the commander's reserve. The corps was given the task of breaking the stubborn Finnish resistance and advancing to the stream at Myull-uya and to begin to pursue the enemy.

The Finnish spearhead was undertaken by Lagus' Armoured Division which in turn planned to deploy units from the 115th Corps in Vuoksi. The division's two combat groups attacked the Soviet positions. Okerman's combat group (which consisted of a self-propelled battalion without a single gun, the 5th Jager Battalion, the 6th Anti-Tank Rifle Company as well as a group of artillery reconnaissance personnel) was to attack the Soviet positions in the area around Vuosalmi and advance to the northern bank of the Vuoksi. Puroma's combat group (which consisted of the 2nd, 3rd, and 4th Jager Battalions) were to go on the offensive from the area around the Suursuo marsh and send the Soviet units into the river.

By 0230 hrs, the Finnish artillery barrage began. Six batteries participated in this barrage, and it lasted 29 mins. Both combat groups were planning to start their attack at 0300 hrs. Up until that moment only a small proportion of the Jagers were ready to advance. From Okerman's combat group it was only the self-propelled gunners and the reconnaissance platoon that went into battle along with the 2nd Company of the 5th Jager Battalion. Dense Soviet fire forced the Jagers to immediately lie low. The self-propelled gun crews were able to advance onto the fields at Vuosalmi but owing to a lack of infantry support they were forced to withdraw to the north, to the edge of the forest, where they took up defensive positions. This night-time Finnish attack took the Soviet units by surprise. Since they had not had a chance to dig in, the battalions of the 98th Rifle Regiment were forced back some 200–250m. The self-propelled guns of the 938th Self-Propelled Artillery Regiment stood side on to the direction of the Finnish attack. They did not have time to turn their "little boxes" round. As a result, according to a report by the 98th Rifle Regiment, five SU-76s were burnt out. The Finns claimed that they had destroyed six Soviet T-34-85 tanks, and self-propelled guns (we note that Soviet tanks only appeared at the stronghold late in the evening of 11 July). The "forty-fives" along with the Anti-Tank Guns of the 98th Regiment opened intensive fire on Finnish "StuGs." After that, as one Finnish self-propelled gun caught fire, the Finns turned back. The self-propelled gun crews of the 938th Regiment acknowledged the loss of four SU-76s and claimed two victories over the "Ferdinands."

By 0550 hrs in the morning the Finnish attack had petered out. The 98th Rifle Regiment had themselves launched a counterattack and had regained their lost positions, where they had also dug in.

Further to the west in Puroma's combat group, of the six Jager companies by 0300 hrs only one was ready to attack. The remainder of the companies only arrived at 1600 hrs. As a result the Jager company that did nevertheless go on the attack immediately came under a squall of gunfire. The

Commander of 2nd Jager Battalion Major Olsoni was seriously injured. He died of his injuries on 7 August 1944.

The battles for the stronghold on that day reached their apogee. Finnish infantry, the Jagers, Soviet gunners, and the self-propelled artillery fought to the death. They went on the attack, bat back counterattacks, and again came up out of their shelters, not sparing anyone their life. On 11 July, the Deputy Divisional Commander of 142nd Division's Political Section, Lieutenant-Colonel Dzhatiev, was killed by a direct hit from a Finnish self-propelled gun shell). The Deputy Head of the Operations Section, Major Razhikh, Head of Signals of 461st Regiment, Captain Chugunov, Field Engineer of 461st Regiment and Captain Belov were also killed.

That evening, all that remained of 142nd Division was as follows: in the 461st Regiment–64 active soldiers, in the 946th Regiment–33 active soldiers, and in the 588th Regiment–160 active soldiers. Nevertheless Soviet gunners and self-propelled gun crews held on and took the offensive forward. The battery crews under Lieutenant Sushinskiy, who were supporting the rest of the 461st Rifle Regiment, pushed the Finns back 100m and only then did they open fire. The self-propelled guns not only fired with their guns but also using their own weapons from inside their thinly armoured SU-76s. The nineteen year old loader Private Aleksey Sergeyevich Kalkunov shot 10 Finnish infantrymen at point blank range using his automatic gun. Junior Sergeant Zhuravlev worked as gun commander, loader and aimer, since all the other crewmembers were injured.

Only at 2330 hrs on 11 July a company from the 226th Separate Tank Regiment was deployed onto the stronghold and consisted of eight T-34-85 tanks. At that same time, the remains of the 938th Self-Propelled Artillery Regiment (seven self-propelled guns) were transferred to the 952nd Self-Propelled Artillery Regiment, and the remainder of the self-propelled gun crews that had survived were sent to the southern bank for rest and to reform.

Tyurin's 7th Infantry Regiment, which by 11 July had incurred losses of more than 70 percent of their personnel, were due to receive replacements that day. The advance by the armoured division however had collapsed, and there were incidents of panic among the rank and file Jagers and the constant Soviet attacks forced the Finnish officers to put the replacement on ice for a short time. Only on the night of 11–12 July were the dugouts filled with fresh Finnish units–from the 57th and 11th Infantry Regiments.

12 July

By the morning of this day the exchange of units for the Finns had been completed. All that remained in the Finnish echelon were a bunch of exhausted soldiers. At 0800 hrs Major Ahola the Commander of the Separate Infantry Battalion, appeared at the 57th Regiment's Command Post. In total just 40 men had come with him from the front line. Ahola reported that he had lost all communications with neighbouring forces the previous day, and the "situation on the front line was very confusing, the Russians had appeared ahead of us, as well as behind the lines."

That morning at the stronghold, a new offensive by Soviet forces had begun, which was supported by "thirty-fours" from 222nd and 226th Separate Tank Regiments. The battles near Siiranmyaki and on the ridges on the southern bank cost the tank crews of the 226th Regiment dear. Only a few veterans remained, but the level of the reinforcements that did arrive was low. In a report on the results of the battle the Regimental Commander Lieutenant-Colonel Korobeynikov characterised it as follows:

> The crews in the marching companies, which had joined the regiment by way of reinforcements and which consisted of 15 crews, turned out to be completely unprepared for

> conducting an offensive operation in conditions of forested and marshy, as well as forested and rocky terrain.
>
> The officer corps in these companies were completely incapable of orientating around the terrain from a tank, and they could not manage their crew in battle, or their platoon.
>
> The driver-mechanics had between five to ten engine hours of practical driving experience, they were not able to drive tanks around a forested and marshy, and rocky terrain whilst overcoming anti-tank obstacles and natural barriers.
>
> Not only did the gun commanders not know how to fire on the move, but they were not able to sustain sufficient concentrated fire whilst standing still.
>
> Overall, the marching companies that had arrived were not efficient and were not ready to conduct an offensive operation.

Nevertheless, the 10th Strategic Division and the tank units that were attached to it planned an attack at 0700 hrs. The tank crews advanced to their starting boundary. At that moment it emerged that the 10th Rifle Division was not ready to start an offensive, and the Divisional Commander postponed the attack for two hours. The tanks in the 226th Regiment stood idle in full view of the Finns for two hours. In that time the Finns succeeded in drawing up and arranging their anti-tank guns. The Finns cut-off the small numbers of infantry from their tanks immediately, using massive artillery and mortar fire. Lieutenant-Colonel Korobeynikov wrote with sadness about the fate of his inexperienced tank crews:

> The tank crews had not been sufficiently well trained, neither did they have any experience of conducting a tank battle, as a result of which they were distracted by the speed of the tank, drew away from their infantry, and did not conduct mass fire on the move. The tanks encountered fierce enemy fire from a gun at Mululya and incurred heavy losses. The infantry, which were comprised of some 30–40 men in total, were cut-off by powerful enemy artillery fire and after incurring heavy losses themselves, they no longer went forward into battle.

Thus during the first and last battle for the stronghold, 226th Regiment incurred the following losses: three tanks burnt out (they carried the tactical numbers 911, 914, and 922), one tank taken out of action and one that became caught in a ditch (with the tactical number 917), another three tanks were recorded as missing without trace (bearing tactical numbers 908, 912, and 928). Out of the entire 226th Separate Tank Regiment a single "thirty-four" remained at the stronghold.

Based on Finnish battlefield photographs taken afterwards, the stronghold had concluded, it becomes clear that a "thirty-four" with the tactical number 908 was captured and subsequently served in Lagus' armoured division.

All that can be found in the 57th Infantry Regiment combat journal is the entry: "Six enemy tanks have been destroyed in front of our positions, and to some depth behind the lines. After this the enemy transferred their attack to the neighbouring forces on our right."

The commander of 222nd Separate Tank Regiment Lieutenant-Colonel Viktor Grigoyevich Makarov lost at least eight tanks (six were burnt out and 2 taken out of action).

The Finns also incurred heavy losses. Captain Lauri Yantti from the 14th Separate Heavy Tank Battalion:

> The counterattack by the armoured division at Vuosalmi turned into a bloody defensive battle that lasted a number of days. The offensive against the enemy on 11 July began at the same time as ours and continued with equal force. The annoyingly accurate enemy artillery fire from the Ayrapaa hills on the far side of the kept our entire front line under fire. This

made the battle a hopeless one for us and required an all out effort. Enemy tanks moved freely around the battlefield, crushing one gun emplacement after another. For the desperate tank hunters this was the only chance they were going to get in life to augment their combat tally, since the individual enemy tanks would return back from their forays along precisely the same route, retracing their tracks. The best tank hunters lay on the battlefields at Kuuterselka and Tali. The reinforcements that arrived were not up to it. The completely "wasted" the *Panzerfausts,* and the same were true of the anti-tank grenades.

Battles that last for days on end lead to nervous breakdowns and inspire the strong in spirit. At the dressing station we met an officer, who had "left for a while to collect some berries," but he told us frankly that he was very afraid. You can't overcome fear permanently in a battle as it tries to become every soldier's trusted companion. Look! He is climbing out of the dugout alone during an enemy attack, he gets rid of his weapon and runs back behind the lines. Another one goes after him. What happens then? Major Hunninen shouts out to the soldiers. It's no use. "Stop! Stop!" cries the battalion commander, making himself angry. With a pistol in his hand he tears off after the soldiers who have been blinded and deafened by the fighting. No, they are not injured. It is just that their nerves have given out. Panic on the front line should be stopped by any means possible as soon as it spreads it inevitably leads to a disaster. The battalion commander soon catches up with the Jagers, who have only one thought on their minds –"Get away, GET AWAY!"

Fugitive faces became hardened from this horror. They were indifferent already. They would squirm around on the ground covering their faces with their hands, awaiting the most extreme form of punishment as deserters. The battalion commander however has already come to his senses; these two unfortunates are still needed behind the lines. Major Hunninen claps them on the shoulder and reassures them: "Listen, we will let you off this time." A few hours later they are back on the front line. "The privates 1st class will sort them out" Hunninen would tell me, after he got back to the Command Post.

Night turned into day at Vuosalmi. The very same battalions are holding the defensive line. They were taking one officer after another that we knew. Even the small groups of reinforcements were greeted with open arms, even if it was written on their exhausted faces, that there was no sense in expecting any miracles from these Jagers.

Major A. Makarov, 317th Rifle Regiment chief of artillery, observed:

The enemy went to desperate lengths to stop us from expanding the stronghold. They even deployed Lagus' armoured division here, the only armoured division in the Finnish Army. The most stubborn of battles unfolded for the stronghold, and the enemy would often launch counterattacks. Our entire regiment succeeded in advancing further than anyone else, we ended up on the tip of a wedge.

The 317 h Rifle Regiment's artillery–both the 45mm and 76mm guns–were, as always, firing at short range. Over the entire course of the battles the whole officer corps at these batteries were only changed once. The mortar companies (using 82mm mortars) were merged into one, while some of the mortar gunners departed to augment rifle subdivisions.

Lauri Yantti recalled:

The fear gets a bigger and bigger hold over you. Then you hide in the furthest corner of your foxhole. The world becomes very small. The sandy walls of the foxhole and the tiny bit of sky above you. Yes, sky. The sky, it seems, is very close, when any moment could be your

> last. Just one of the "large calibre artillery shells" whistling above our heads would be enough for our foxhole. You sit there recalling your sins, crossing your hands over your chest, and you promise yourself that you are going to live differently if you get out of this ordeal alive.

13 July

At 0230 hrs the Jager Battalion commenced the assault following the artillery raid. By morning they had succeeded in purging a single glade of Soviet infantry. By 0830 hrs Soviet units launched a counterattack. The offensive was beaten back by an artillery attack:

> The fire from the Jagers and the artillery strike that I ordered stopped their counterattack. The artillery attack was effective: the Head of Artillery Major Nuolimaa increased the number of shells several times, and it was me that had ordered this. Clods of black earth flew up into my face, the shrapnel whistled past my ears, but it was worse for the Russians on the battlefield. The Jagers just fired at them out of in exaltation. The next day was calm. The ammunition however had run out for the advancing companies, while the flank remained bare. We had to pull back. In a company that had advanced further than any of the others, there were only 22 out of the 50 soldiers left to run on to the target: eight had been killed and 20 were injured. This is taken from the Combat Journal of the armoured division. According to another source in the 3rd company, 5th Jager Battalion one officer was left, as well as four *unter-offiziers* and one *Jager*..

Only at 2230 hrs on 13 July did the 46th Guards Heavy Tank Regiment begin to cross over to the stronghold. By 0400 hrs on 14 July all 19 combat capable KVs in the regiment were on the northern side of the river. The tank crews began to work out how they were to collaborate with the 327th Rifle Division.

15 July: Leningrad Front Command forwarded Directive No. 81/1 to the headquarters of the 23rd Army with an order to stubbornly defend the boundaries that had been attained. The large-scale offensive activities on the Karelian Isthmus were stopped.

By 18 July, the withdrawal of the remains of the 2nd Infantry Division from the front line had been completed. The 49th Infantry Regiment was in the battle without any breaks at all for 40 days. The regiment lost its Commander, 404 men were killed, 2,089 injured, and 56 were missing without trace. Of those 2,900 soldiers and officers in the regiment who had begun the withdrawal from the boundaries near Beloostrov, only one in ten of them would come out of the battles unharmed. The losses for the 7th Infantry Regiment were more or less the same. In total in the course of the battles from 10-18 July the 2nd Infantry Division lost 1,188 men killed, 4,582 injured, and 994 were missing without trace.

Despite the drop in active combat operations the Soviet units on the stronghold continued their attacks with even more force, enhancing their positions and testing the strength of the Finnish defences. Both sides as before attacked one another, although it was true that they were becoming smaller in scale. On 16 July, in a battle near marker 28.0, the Finns managed to take a heavy KV-1 tank with the tactical number "660" from the 46th Guards Separate Tank Regiment out of action using a *Panzerfaust*. The crew survived but the vehicle burned on Finnish territory. Today, as per Yuriy Pasholok, its turret is on display at the Central Museum of the Great Patriotic War, Moscow.

The small-scale skirmishes and battles to enhance their positions on the stronghold cost the Soviets a great deal of lives. On 13 July, some 494 men were killed and wounded on the stronghold, on 14 July the figure was 864 men. In combat on 17 July 1944 the Commander of the 222nd

Separate Tank Regiment Yermakov was fatally wounded. He was in the command turret of his tank when he sustained a serious head wound and died in a field hospital two days later.

The stronghold fighting having died down, Govorov compiled a report in which the actions of the 98th and 115th Rifle Corps Command came under severe criticism. This letter was introduced into scientific discourse a long time ago and has done the rounds in cyberspace. In the light of published documents belonging to the Central Archive of the Ministry of Defence of the Russian Federation, some of the criticism that was levelled at Govorov is unfounded, though the majority of it–is highly justified.

The battle on the southern and northern bank of the Vuoksi became one of the fiercest in the series of battles in the summer of 1944. In total around 60,000 men fought in the battle on both sides. Of those, every third Finnish or Soviet soldier was either killed, wounded, missing or taken prisoner.

Today only two half ruined Soviet monuments stand as reminders of the battle. These are situated on height 44.5 "Northern." To begin with there were cast iron plates on the numbers of all the divisions that fought on the stronghold. In the 1990s every one of them, except the one for the 327th Rifle Division, was stolen by tourists, and by fishermen as anchors, or weights for their nets. The second monument is located on the stronghold itself. It stands on the site of the 142nd Division's former Command Post. The paint on the five stelae (for the five divisions that fought on the stronghold), has peeled off and cracked. Of the five marble plaques on the ends of the bayonets only one remains. Rain, snow and wind have long since stripped the golden paint off the marble. Next to the monument is Dzhatiev's apple tree–it was planted by the daughter of the Head of 142nd Division's Political Section in memory of her late father. Even in a year, which marks the 70th anniversary of the Great Patriotic War the monuments to the fallen in this battle remain forgotten.

The Finns erected a small memorial sign in the forest in the place where the 70th Infantry Regiment's Command Post was located. The stronghold itself became known among the populace as the "minefield," so densely was it strewn with shrapnel from mortars, shells and bombs.

Other rank losses for 92nd Rifle Division were 410 men. Losses for the armoured tank divisions of the 23rd Army in the battle for Vuoksi are set out below in the table. The table below was compiled by Colonel-Engineer Sibirenkov, aide to the Commander of the Armoured Tank and Motorised Troops of 23rd Army on 4 August 1944.

No.	Type of vehicle	No of the vchicle	Which Unit	Nature of damage	Where located	Notes
1	SU-76	660	46th Guards Heavy Tank Regiment	Burnt out	Above marker 28.0 one kilometre east of Koivola	
2	T-34	1708	938th Self-Propelled Artillery Regiment	Burnt out	To right of Koivola Road	

3	T-34	516	222nd Separate Light Tank Regiment	Burnt out	Settlement of Kaliola	
4	T-34	509	-‖-	-‖-		
5	T-34	507	-‖-	-‖-	The Rasuon-nitut tract	
6	T-34	501	-‖-	-‖-	Settlement of Lampela	
7	T-34	505	-‖-	-‖-	In the settlement of Makela	
8	T-34	504	-‖-	-‖-		
9	T-34	524	-‖-	Destroyed by artillery fire	Settlement of Kaukola	Required a heavy repair
10	T-34	934	-‖-	Burnt out	Settlement of Mantula	
11	T-34	911	226th Separate Light Tank Regiment	Burnt out	Settlement of Karpioho	
12	T-34	914	226th Separate Light Tank Regiment	Burnt out		
13	T-34	922	226th Separate Light Tank Regiment	Burnt out	Settlement of Yuvola	
14	T-34	923	226th Separate Light Tank Regiment	Burnt out		
15	T-34	917	222nd Separate Light Tank Regiment	Taken out of action and became stranded	One kilometre west of Mikkola	Required a heavy repair on the front line

<table>
<tr><td>16</td><td>SU-76</td><td>1643</td><td>938th Self-Propelled Artillery Regiment</td><td>Burnt out</td><td>School in the settlement of Pasuri</td><td></td></tr>
<tr><td>17</td><td>SU-76</td><td>1620</td><td>938th Self-Propelled Artillery Regiment</td><td>Burnt out</td><td>Settlement of Mikkola</td><td></td></tr>
<tr><td>18</td><td>SU-76</td><td>1630</td><td>-||-</td><td>Burnt out</td><td></td><td></td></tr>
<tr><td>19</td><td>SU-76</td><td>1633</td><td>-||-</td><td>Burnt out</td><td>Settlement of Mikkola</td><td></td></tr>
<tr><td>20</td><td>SU-76</td><td>1634</td><td>-||-</td><td>Burnt out</td><td>-||-</td><td></td></tr>
<tr><td>21</td><td>SU-76</td><td>1641</td><td>-||-</td><td>Burnt out</td><td>Ayrapaa Station</td><td rowspan="2">On right bank of the Vuoksi</td></tr>
<tr><td>22</td><td>SU-76</td><td>1705</td><td>952nd Self-Propelled Artillery Regiment</td><td>Burnt out</td><td>-||-</td></tr>
</table>

All of the first 20 vehicles are on the left bank of the Vuoksi near Vuosalmi.

Epilogue

By mid-July1944 the battles on the Karelian Isthmus had died down. A positioning war began that only rarely broke out into fierce clashes. Thereafter, the Soviet Union's gaze turned towards the Baltic region.

On 26 July 1944, the Red Army liberated Narva. In September, the entire Estonian coastline of the Gulf of Finland was cleared of German forces. It became clear to the Finnish leadership that they would not get any further assistance from Germany. On 4 August 1944, the new President of the Republic of Finland – Marshal Mannerheim – was sworn in. At the end of August the envoy Paasikivi had again contacted the Soviet ambassador in Stockholm for discussions around an armistice.

On 4 September 1944, the ceasefire agreement officially came into force. The order for the ceasefire still had not reached Soviet forces. In connection with this there were several incidents on the front line of Soviet troops opening fire on the Finns, who had come out of their shelters. The Academician Inozemtsev recalled this as follows:

> At 1100 hrs our "upper leadership" arrived: Zhdanov and Korochkin. Korochkin reported to the Corps Commander: the Finns ceased their fire at 0800 hrs, white flags were raised in many areas. Zhdanov was very surprised. At 1300 hrs an urgent telegram arrived: "Be ready to march at 1500 hrs." Kalish arrived in the evening from the front line and told us the details. Tsvelenev also corroborated his information. Everything was ready to move. The battalions went out onto the road in a line.

Soviet forces received an order to cease firing from 0800 hrs on 5 September 1944. Combat operations on the Karelian Isthmus had come to an end.

The armistice between the USSR and Great Britain and the Republic of Finland came into being on 19 September 1944. Three days later, Marshal Mannerheim issued the order of the day, which drew a line under the conflicts between the USSR and Finland:

> Supreme Command Headquarters
> 22 September 1944
> Order of the day from the Commander-in-Chief No. 132
> Soldiers of the Finnish Army!
> The war, which our people have found themselves in and which has required us to make the ultimate sacrifices, came to an end on 19 September 1944 by way of an armistice. Our bitter experience has taught us that trustworthy relations with all our neighbouring peoples should form the cornerstone of our lives in the future.

This war has come at a great cost to the people of Finland. Their love for their homeland, independence and freedom however has known no bounds.

I thank you, brave soldiers. You have seen and endured much. You were prepared unconditionally to sacrifice what you hold most dear for the Fatherland, as well as submitting yourself to the toughest of tests. True to the cause of the Fatherland, you have come through fierce fighting with courage and a willingness to make sacrifices, and submissively endured all the privations of a war that lasted for years. You fought a strong and courageous enemy with poor armament and modest equipment.

Commanders, officers, *unter-offiziers*, and soldiers of the Finnish Army! The gratitude of the Fatherland will remain with you forever, as will the unconditional recognition of your achievements from an old soldier, your Commander-in-Chief.

I would extend my grateful thanks to the women of Finland, who have carried out their duties faithfully, without thinking of themselves.

The work behind the lines has required an unparalleled all-out effort from everyone whatever the nature of the task. Those who worked behind the lines fulfilled their duties tirelessly. It is with a sincere reverence and also with gratitude that I think of our wounded, and especially of those invalided as a result of the war, who are destined to carry this heavy burden for the rest of their lives.

It is with veneration that I think of our fallen heroes. The white crosses on their graves on our church mounds remind us of those who have made the ultimate sacrifice.

May the respect and gratitude of the Fatherland lighten the burden for the widows and orphans of war.

Soldiers! Hard times lie ahead. The armistice has been agreed, and the terms are enforceable. The situation in Lapland is still unclear at present, and our armed forces still require the same sense of duty and decisiveness that you demonstrated over the entire course of the war.

In the knowledge that you have fulfilled your duty, return home quietly back to your peacetime work. I am sure that you will set to work with the same dedication, enthusiasm and self-discipline that I saw in you on the path of war. I will always admire these qualities of yours.

May peaceful labour across our nation enable our people as a whole to prosper in sincere and friendly relations with our neighbouring countries.

May God protect Finland!

The Commander-in-Chief of the Finnish Defensive Forces
Marshal of Finland
Mannerheim

Peace! The reader may have a number of questions concerning the diplomatic component to the events of summer 1944. Would it have been possible to avoid this conflict and peacefully resolve the issue back in April? To what extent were the Soviet terms, which had been made available to the Finnish side on 29 March 1944, unworkable? In the interest of clarity, the Soviet requirements, which were also incorporated into the armistice agreement, have been set out in the table below.

Soviet Proposal, 29 March 1944	Armistice Conditions, 4 September 1944
A severing of diplomatic relations with Germany and the internment of the German forces and the ships in Finland, or the severing of diplomatic relations with Germany and the expulsion of German forces and ships from the borders of Finland no later than the end of the month of April [30 days are given for this–author's note]. In either scenario the Soviet Government is able to offer assistance from her own armed forces.	Finland is obliged to disarm the German land, naval and air forces remaining in Finland after 15 September 1944 and hand over their personnel to the Allied (Soviet) Command as prisoners of war, for which the Soviet Government will render assistance to the Finnish Army. The Government of Finland is also obliged to intern the German and Hungarian forces that remain on her territory.
The restoration of the Soviet-Finnish Agreement of 1940 and the withdrawal of Finnish forces back to the border, which is to be achieved in stages over the course of the month of April.	In connection with the cessation of combat activities the Finnish side is obliged by 4 September 1944, and the German side by 5 September 1944, to pull her forces back beyond the line of the 1940 Soviet-Finnish border using the procedure set out in the Appendix to this agreement.
The immediate return of Soviet and allied prisoners of war, as well as Soviet allied individuals from the civilian population, who are interned in concentration camps or are used by the Finns for labour, and moreover should an armistice agreement not be signed but a peace treaty the return of the prisoners of war should be reciprocal.	Finland is obliged to immediately return all Soviet and allied prisoners of war in her jurisdiction, as well as those interned in Finland and those Soviet and allied citizens who were forcibly marched into Finland, to the Allied (Soviet) High Command for their repatriation back to their homeland. From the moment the armistice this agreement is signed and right up to the repatriation, Finland is obliged to provide all the Soviet and allied prisoners of war, as well as those forcibly marched into Finland, and those citizens interned in Finland, sufficient food, clothing and medical services in accordance with all the sanitary requirements, as well as providing transport for the return back to their homeland at its own cost. Simultaneously Finnish prisoners of war and those individuals interned within the territory of the Soviet states will be handed back to Finland.

Demobilisation of 50 percent of the Finnish Army, which is to be achieved over the course of the month of May, and the transfer of the entire Army of Finland to a peaceful footing, which is to be achieved over the month of June and July. (This point should form part of the agreement, or it should be drawn up as a separate Soviet-Finnish agreement, which would be signed at the same time as a peace treaty or an armistice).	Finland is obliged to place her Army onto a peaceful footing over the course of two and a half months from the date on which this agreement is signed.
Reparations for losses inflicted by Finland to the Soviet Union as a result of combat activity amounting to six hundred million American dollars, which is to be paid over the course of five years in kind (paper, cellulose, sea going and fishing vessels, as well as a variety of industrial equipment).	Finland is obliged to pay to the Soviet Union reparations for losses inflicted by Finland on the Soviet Union as a result of combat activity and of the occupation of Soviet territory, amounting to three hundred million dollars with disbursal over the course of six years in kind (forest products, paper, cellulose, sea going and fishing vessels, as well as a variety of industrial equipment). The payment of future reparations for losses inflicted by Finland on the property of other Soviet states and on their nationals in Finland during the course of the war, is to be considered, and furthermore the scale of this compensation is to be set separately.
The return of Petsamo and the Petsamo Region to the Soviet Union, which was voluntarily conceded to the Soviet Union by Finland in accordance with peaceful agreements drawn up in 1920 and 1940.	Finland is to return the Petsamo (Pechanga) region to the Soviet Union, which was voluntarily conceded to Finland by the Soviet State in accordance with the Peace Treaties dated 14 October 1920 and 12 March 1940
On the acceptance by the Finnish side of the six conditions set out above, the Soviet Government considers it possible to relinquish its rights to the leasehold over Hanko and the Hanko region– without any compensation	The Soviet Union relinquishes its rights in respect of the leasehold on the Hanko Isthmus, which were provided to the Soviet Union by the peaceful Soviet-Finnish Agreement dated 12 March 1940, and Finland is obliged from her side to provide to the Soviet Union leasehold rights over the territory and expanses of water for the creation of a Naval base in the area around Porkkala-Udd.

This was not discussed	Finland is obliged to provide on demand from the Allied (Soviet) High Command airfields on the southern and south-western coast of Finland with all the equipment of basing Soviet aircraft for a period of time necessary for air combat operations against German forces in Estonia and against the German Naval fleet in the northern part of the Baltic Sea.
This was not discussed	Finland, having broken off all relations with Germany is also obliged to break off all relations with Germany's satellite states
This was not discussed	The validity of the agreement concerning the Aland Islands that was concluded with the Soviet Union and Finland on 11 October 1940 is to be restored in full
This was not discussed	Finland is obliged to restore all the legal rights and interests of the United Nations and its citizens on Finnish territory, to what they were before the war, with full retention of their property
This was not discussed	Finland is obliged to cooperate with the Allied Nations in respect of the arrest of individuals accused of war crimes, and of their trial
This was not discussed	Finland is obliged, in the timescales stipulated by the Allied (Soviet) High Command, to return in good condition, all the valuables and materials that were taken into Finland from Soviet territory during the war, and which belonged to state, public, and cooperative organisations, as well as enterprises, and institutions or to individuals, as follows: equipment from factories and workshops, steam ships, railway wagons, vessels, tractors, cars, historical monuments, museum relics, and any other equipment
This was not discussed	Finland is obliged to hand over as trophies, for the disposal of the Allied (Soviet) High Command, all the military equipment in Finnish territory belonging to Germany and her satellites, including military and other vessels belonging to these countries, and which are located in Finnish waters

This was not discussed	Finland is obliged to prevent any removal, or expropriation, of any kind of equipment (including valuables and currency) that belonged to Germany, or Hungary, or to their citizens living in their territories, or in the territories occupied by them, without the permission of the Allied (Soviet) High Command
This was not discussed	Control from Allied (Soviet) High Command should be imposed over Finnish commercial vessels, with the exception of those vessels that are already under allied control, so that they can be used to serve the overall interests of the Allies
This was not discussed	Finland is obliged to hand over to the Allied (Soviet) High Command all vessels that belong to the United Nations, independent of the purpose to which these vessels are being put, for the duration of the war with Germany, to serve the overall interests of the Allies, these vessels will subsequently be returned to their owners
This was not discussed	Finland is to provide materials and production that may be required by the United Nations for objectives linked to the war
This was not discussed	Finland is obliged to immediately release, independent of nationality and national identity, all individuals that have been imprisoned in connection with their activities conducted in the interests of the United Nations, or for their sympathy for the United Nations, or in view of their race, as well as taking any discriminatory legislation off the books, as well as any limitations arising thereof
This was not discussed	Finland is obliged to immediately disband any pro-Hitler (fascist type) political, military, and militarised organisations, as well as any other organisations engaged in propaganda hostile to the United Nations, and to the Soviet Union in particular, and to prevent the formation of organisations of this nature going forward

This was not discussed	An Allied Monitoring Commission will be set up, which until such time as a peace agreement has been reached with Finland, will take responsibility for the monitoring and control of the execution of these conditions, under the overall leadership, and on the instructions of the Allied (Soviet) High Command, acting on behalf of the Allied Nations

As to whether Soviet requirements set out in March were unworkable or not–that is for the reader to decide. The Finnish upper leadership thought them impossible. The result of this decision was the battle in the late summer of 1944 and the armistice that was agreed on comparable terms. The USSR gave Finland a discount on the reparations and increased the payment period from five to six years. From among the conditions, which for Finland represented a significant deterioration, it is worth noting the leasing of the Porkkala-Udd Cape for a naval base. The distance from the Porkkala-Udd naval base to the centre of Helsinki is no more than 40km, and it is this same base that Rudolf Enkel called "A pistol pointing at the heart of Finland."

In any case, the armistice was settled. A new period had begun in relations between Finland and the USSR. This period was characterised by neighbourly and mutually beneficial years. It was decided that the conflicts, reciprocal claims and wars, which had done so much to poison relations between the two countries, would be forgotten–in the interests of the future.

This "code of silence" on both sides came to an end in 1991. It was then that talk of a "defensive victory" on the Karelian Isthmus began to resonate more loudly in Finland. Today the concept of a "defensive victory" is the official line in Finland, and serves as the general accepted explanation for the events of summer 1944. According to this version in 1944 the Soviet Union wanted to capture and occupy the whole of Finland. This false assertion is not even questioned. Thus, the battle for Tali-ihantala, and for Ayrappa-Vuosalmi and in Vyborg Bay saved the country from losing her independence. The assertion is sometimes made that the USSR incurred such heavy losses in the battles on the Karelian Isthmus in summer 1944 that it all but begged Finland for peace. Specifically Max Jakobson, the well-known Finnish diplomat and historian announced in the 2000s that the "Defensive victory opened the path to peace."

Within the confines of this version the agreements reached at the Tehran Conference between the great powers are suppressed. The Soviet response to the Finnish request for peace after the fall of the Finnish Vyborg in June 1944 is explained simply as a demand for an unconditional surrender. Nobody wants to compare publicly the conditions of the ceasefire that were proposed in March and those to which Finland agreed in September 1944. This false version of events removes what are uncomfortable issues for Finland. Was it necessary to go to war in 1941, and lose 48,000 men who perished, and for the country to make an all-out effort for five years–only to return to Moscow's peace agreement on what were less favourable terms? Was it necessary to reject the Soviet requirements at the end of March 1944 and accept what were almost the same conditions, only worse?

It must be said that glorification and the cult of the second stage of the Vyborg Offensive Operation, in the course of which the Finnish Army succeeded in halting the offensive by the Leningrad Front, also had a positive effect. Finnish war veterans received a great deal more recognition in the post-Soviet years than they had in the Soviet period.

In Soviet historiography, the role of the battles after 20 June 1944 are often suppressed and played down. The capture of Vyborg is represented as the final objective of the offensive operation. The author hopes that he has succeeded in creating an overall, complete picture of the battles in the summer of 1944 and that he has paid tribute to those who perished in our corner of the world in that long hot summer. Let us hope that the peace on the Karelian Isthmus will never be disturbed again.

Bibliography

Primary Sources

Central Archive of the Ministry of Defence of the Russian Federation
National Archives of Finland

Printed Sources

Russian

Anon., *The History of the Order of Lenin Leningrad Military District. Third Ed.* (Moscow: Voyenizdat, 1988).

Anon., *The Soviet Union at International Conferences in the Period of the Great Patriotic War 1941–1945. Vol. II. The Tehran Conference of the Leaders of the Three Allied Powers–the USSR, USA and Great Britain (28 November–1 December 1943)* (Moscow: Political Literature Publishing House. 1984).

Borshchev, S.N., *From the Neva to the Elba* (Leningrad: Lenizdat, 1973).

Bychevskiy, B.B., *Front Line City* (Leningrad: Lenizdat, 1967).

Frolov, M.I., *Artillerymen in the Battles for the City of Lenin.* (Leningrad: Lenizdat 1978).

Mikhalkin, M.S. & Riskin, A.I. (eds.), *Leningrad's Sword of Fire* (Leningrad: Lenizdat, 1977).

Moshchanksy, I., *The Storming of the Karelian Barrage: The Vyborg-Petrograd Offensive Operation* (Moscow: The Military Chronicle, 2005).

Odintsov, G.F., *Masters of Fire* (Leningrad: Lenizdat, 1980).

Shtemenko, S.M., *General Headquarters in the War Years* (Moscow, Military Publishing House of the USSR Ministry of Defence, 1973).

Talanov, M.M., "Kulagin's Red Banner", *Questions of History*, No. 1, 1979.

Various, *Codeword Victory: The Memoirs of Participants in the Battle for Leningrad* (Leningrad: Lenizdat, 1980).

Voronov, A.P. (ed.), *Cabin Boys of the Red Banner Baltic Fleet: A Collection of Memoirs* (Leningrad: Lenizdat. 1981).

Finnish

Efvelgren, E. & Tammi, E., *Viipuri 1944* (Helsinki-Porvoo: WSOY, 2007).

Hämäläinen, V. & Hämäläinen, T., *Siiranmäen päiväkirja Etulinjassa 1941-44* (Helsinki: Koala-Kustannus, 2009).

Käkelä, E. & Lärkä, A., *Suomalaisten Rynnäkkötykkien kohtalot* (Helsinki-Porvoo: WSOY, 2006).

Kantakoski, P., *Suomalaiset Panssarivaunujoukot, 1919-1969* (Hämeenlinna: Karisto Oy, 1969).

Karjalainen, M., *Jatkosodan Taistelut Mikko Karjalainen* (Jyväskylä: Gummerus, 2005).

Kivimäki, V., *Murtuneet Mielet. Taistelu Suomalaissotilaiden Hermoista, 1939-1945* (Helsinki-

Porvoo: WSOY, 2013).
Koskimaa, M., *Tyrjän Rykmentti* (Helsinki-Porvoo: WSOY 2004).
Kuusela, K., *Wehrmachtin Panssarit Suomessa* (Jyväskylä: Gummerus, 2000).
Leskinen, Y. & Yultilainen, A., *Jatkosodan Pikkujättiläinen* (Helsinki–Porvoo: WSOY, 2005).
Mäkitalo, J. & Vainio, J., *Valkeasaaressa läpimurto Jalkaväkirykmentti 1 Jatkosodassa* (Helsinki: Docendo, 2013).
Muistelmat C.G.E, *Mannerheim* (Helsinki: Otava, 1952).
Oesch, L., *Suomen Kohtalon Ratkaisu Kannaksella v.* (Helsinki: Docendo 2014).
Pohjanpää, H. & Kilkki, P., *Suomen Ratsuväen Historia Osa II* (Vammala: Sotatieteen Laitoksen Juljaisuja, 1991).
Porvali, Seppo, *Ristin Ritarit: 191 Suomalaista Sotasankaria* (Helsinki: Valitut Palat, 2003).
Rumpunen, K.I., 'Kohtalon päivät: Uutta tietoa talvi- ja jatkosodan ratkaisun hetkistä', Valitut Palat, *Reader's Digest,* Ab. 2011.
Valtonen, H., *Lento-osasto Kuhlmey:* Saksan *Luftwaffe Suomen Tukena kesällä 1944* (Jyväskylä: Gummerus, 1991).
Various, *Kansa Taistela Journal*, 1957-86.

Swedish

Käkelä, Erkki, *Lagus en i strid, 1943-1944* (Esbo: Schildt, 2005).

English

Churchill, Winston, *Closing the Ring: The Second World War* (Cambridge: Riverside Press, 1951).
---------- *Triumph and Tragedy: The Second World War* (Cambridge: Riverside Press, 1953).
Franklin, William M. & Gerber, William (eds.), *United States Department of State. Foreign Relations of the United States Diplomatic Papers: The Conferences at Cairo and Tehran, 1943* (Washington, DC: United States Government Printing Office, 1961).

Index

T

V

W

Y

Z